"RACE" PANIC AND THE MEMORY OF MIGRATION

Other titles in series:

Specters of the West and the Politics of Translation

edited by Naoki Sakai and Yukiko Hanawa
(2000)

TRACES
A MULTILINGUAL SERIES OF CULTURAL THEORY AND TRANSLATION

"Race" Panic and the Memory of Migration

Edited by
Meaghan Morris and Brett de Bary

香港大學出版社
HONG KONG UNIVERSITY PRESS

Hong Kong University Press
14/F, Hing Wai Centre
7 Tin Wan Praya Road
Aberdeen
Hong Kong

ISBN 962 209 562 3 (Hardback)
ISBN 962 209 561 5 (Paperback)

The name *Traces: A multilingual journal of cultural theory and translation* has been changed to *Traces: A multilingual series of cultural theory and translation.*

British Library Cataloguing-in-Publication Data
A catalogue record for this book is available from the British Library.

Secure On-line Ordering
http://www.hkupress.org

Cover Design: Judy Geib & Sabu Kohso (Border Corp)

Printed and bound by King's Time Printing Press Ltd. in Hong Kong, China

Statement of Purpose

Traces, a multilingual series of cultural theory and translation, calls for comparative cultural theory that is attentive to global traces in the theoretical knowledge produced in specific locations and that explores how theories are themselves constituted in, and transformed by, practical social relations at diverse sites. We eagerly seek theory produced in disparate sites, including that critical work that has often emerged in a hybrid relation to North American or West European "theory" as a result of the colonialism and quasi-colonialism of the past few centuries. We will publish research, exchanges, and commentaries that address a multilingual audience concerned with all the established disciplines of the social sciences and humanities, in addition to such cross-disciplinary fields as cultural studies, feminist and queer studies, critical race theory, or post-colonial studies. At the same time, *Traces* aims to initiate a different circulation of intellectual conversation and debate in the world, a different geopolitical economy of theory and empirical data, and a different idea of theory itself.

Every essay in *Traces* is available in all the languages of this series. Each contributor is expected to be fully aware that she or he is writing for and addressing a heterogeneous and multilingual audience: in the manner of a local intellectual under a colonial regime, every contributor is expected to speak with a forked tongue. *Traces* is an international series. Yet the international space that it generates and sustains, and to which contributors as well as readers are invited, is fundamentally different from that of an internationalism based on one major language's subjugation of other minor languages. Indeed, it is hoped that the social space in which we argue and converse will challenge the space of the nation and national language. Constituted in processes of translation, among multiple languages and registers, this social space is actualized in our exchanges and debates, and in debates among authors, commentators, translators and readers.

Contents

Part 2: Logics of Labor

Part 3: Memories of State

Part 4: Displacement and National Ground

Contributors

Ien ANG is Professor of Cultural Studies and Director of the Institute for Cultural Research at the University of Western Sydney, Australia. With a background in communication studies, she is currently doing research on culture and globalization. She has published *Living Room Wars* (Routledge, 1996) and *On Not Speaking Chinese: Living Between Asia and the West* (Routledge, 2001).

Jacqueline ARMIJO teaches Religious Studies at Stanford University, USA. A scholar of the history of Islam in China, her current research projects include Islamic education in China and the impact of Chinese Muslims studying in Islamic universities overseas. She has recently published "The Customs of Various Barbarians" in *Under Confucian Eyes: Texts on Gender in Chinese History,* edited by Susan L. Mann and Yu-yin Cheng (University of California Press, 2001).

Brett de BARY teaches Asian Studies and Comparative Literature at Cornell University, USA. Recently, she edited *Gender and Imperialism,* a special issue of the *US-Japan Women's Journal,* Spring, 1997 (Japanese edition, 1998). She is currently doing a study of late twentieth century Japanese and American fiction and film, entitled *Orientalism in the Inter-Cultural Imaginary.*

Yann Moulier BOUTANG is Professor of Economics at the University of Brittany in Vannes, and at the Institut d'Études Politique de Paris. His *De l'esclavage au salariat, Économie historique du salariat bridé* was published by Presses Universitaires de France in Paris in 1998.

Erica BRINDLEY is a Visiting Assistant Professor in Chinese history at the University of Oregon, USA. She is finishing a dissertation on the issue of authority and human agency during "Warring States" China.

Rey CHOW is Andrew W. Mellon Professor of the Humanities at Brown University, USA. Among her numerous publications in English is, most recently, *Ethics after Idealism: Theory—Culture—Ethnicity—Reading* (Indiana University Press, 1998). Her new book, *The Protestant Ethnic and the Spirit of Capitalism,* is forthcoming from Columbia University Press in 2002–2003.

Luke GIBBONS teaches English and Film, Theatre and Television in the University of Notre Dame in both the USA and in Dublin, Ireland. His most recent book is *Transformations in Irish Culture* (University of Notre Dame Press, 1996) and his current project is a study of *Edmund Burke and Ireland: Aesthetics, Politics and the Colonial Sublime,* forthcoming from Cambridge University Press.

Joshua GOLDSTEIN is a historian of China teaching at Franklin and Marshall University in Lancaster, Pennsylvania, USA. He has recently published "Mei Lanfang and the Nationalization of Peking Opera," in *positions east asia cultures critiques,* Winter, 1999.

Ghassan HAGE teaches in Anthropology at the University of Sydney, Australia. His research focuses on migration, settlement, and viability, and his most recent book is *White Nation: Fantasies of White Supremacy in a Multicultural Society* (Pluto Press, 1999). He has also edited *Arab-Australians: Citizenship and Belonging* (Melbourne University Press, 2002).

HUANG Ping is a member of the Institute of Sociology at the Chinese Academy of Social Sciences. Currently he is doing research on young rural laborers in urban China. *Seeking for Survival: A Sociological Study of Non-Agricultural Activities in Contemporary China* (Kunming: Yunnan Press, 1996) is among his many publications.

JUNG Yeong-hae teaches at Otsuma Women's University in Tama City, Japan. She is currently studying the issue of cultural/ethnic diversity and mental health care. With Lisa Go, she has written *Watashi to iu tabi: jenda to neishizumu o koete* [*The Journey Within: Beyond Racism and Gender*], published by Seidosha, in Tokyo, in 1999.

KIM Seong-nae teaches in the Department of Religious Studies at Sogang University in Seoul, Korea. She is currently researching modernity and popular religiosity in Korea. In addition to her publications in Korean, she has published the English-language article "Lamentations of the Dead: The Historical Imaginary of Violence on Cheju Island, South Korea" in the *Journal of Ritual Studies*, Summer, 1989, Vol. 3, No. 2.

KOMAGOME Takeshi is on the Faculty of Education at Kyoto University, Japan. His research and publications investigate aspects of Japanese colonial rule in Taiwan and Korea. His book *Cultural Unification under the Japanese Colonial Empire* (*Shokuminchi teikoku nihon no bunka tôgô*) was published by Iwanami Shoten in 1996.

Victor KOSCHMANN teaches in the History Department at Cornell University, USA. He is doing research on the philosophy of technology in 1930s Japan. His *Revolution and Subjectivity in Postwar Japan* was published by the University of Chicago Press in 1996.

MÔRI Yoshitaka teaches in the Graduate School of Social and Cultural Studies of Kyushu University in Fukuoka, Japan. He is the co-author, with Ueno Toshiya, of *Introduction to Cultural Studies* [*Karutyuraru stadeizu nyûmon*] (Tokyo, Chikuma Shobô, 2000) and has published the English-language article with Hiroki Ogasawara, "Cultural Studies and Its Discontents: The Pacific Asia Cultural Studies Forum in Britain" in *Japanese Studies* (Japanese Studies Association of Australia, 1998).

Meaghan MORRIS is Chair Professor of Cultural Studies at Lingnan University in Hong Kong. Her research is on popular historiographies in cinema, mass media and journalism, and her most recent book is *Too Soon, Too Late: History in Popular Culture* (Indiana University Press, 1998).

Tessa MORRIS-SUZUKI is Professor of Japanese History at Australian National University. She is well-known for her work on the economic and technological history of Japan. Recently she has published *Re-inventing Japan: Time Space Nation* (M.E. Sharpe, 1998).

Bernard G. PRUSAK is a Ph.D. candidate in philosophy at Boston University and an adjunct professor in the Institute for Liberal Arts and Interdisciplinary Studies at Emerson College. He works in philosophical anthropology. His translation of Dominique Janicaud's critical essay *The Theological Turn of French Phenomenology* appeared recently from Fordham University Press.

OKA Mari teaches in Osaka Women's University in Osaka, Japan. She is now writing about the Palestinian refugee issue from a philosophical perspective. She has translated the writings of Edward Said and has recently published *Kanojo no "tadashii" namae to wa nanika: Daisan sekai feminizumu no shiso [What Is Her "Proper" Name: Third World Feminist Thought]* (Tokyo: Seidosha, 2000).

SAKIYAMA Masaki teaches in the Department of International Relations at Ritsumeikan University in Kyoto, Japan. He does teaching, research, and publication in the area of Latin American Cultural Studies, including work on the Chiapas rebellion. He has also translated the writings of Gayatri Spivak.

Jiwon SHIN is a Ph.D candidate in Korean Literature at Harvard University. She is writing a dissertation on the spatio-temporal imaginary in nineteenth-century Seoul, focusing on urban poetry clubs.

TOMOTARI Mikako is a sculptor who teaches at the Kyushu Institute of Design in Fukuoka, Japan. Her sculpture memorializing Ainu lifeways stands near the recently completed Nibutani Dam in Hokkaido. She is now working with disabled persons on a new project, *Able Art.*

INTRODUCTION

MEAGHAN MORRIS

This is the second volume of *Traces*, an international series of cultural theory and translation established to challenge the ways in which "theory" and "culture" are distributed and "translation" is imagined and structured in the long aftermath of old colonial and Cold War regimes. *Traces* is not alone in issuing this challenge. Many scholars today lament the assumption continuing in practice that a universalizing "West" produces and exports theory to a "Rest" that is brimming with cultural data but bereft of intellectual means to evaluate its rich particularities and render them intelligible to "Western readers." Debate is everywhere increasing about the legacy of the division between the "humanities" (defining the universal) and "area studies" (redeeming the particular), the value-laden distinction between theoretical and pragmatic or everyday knowledge, and the role played by other divisions (East and West, South and North, ex-colonial periphery and metropolis) in a so-called "new global economy" of knowledge. At the same time, however, the power to widely *distribute* such debate is increasingly concentrated in the hands of a few transnational English-language publishers based around the North Atlantic. An "old colonial" division of labor sustains a new hierarchy of languages even more narrow than that inscribed by imperial maps on which Spanish, French, and German were privileged, as were Japanese and Chinese. We may lament and have local debates in many tongues; to produce "international" theory today we must write or *be read* in English.

As a multidisciplinary translation series, *Traces* seeks a different circulation of academic conversation and debate. This series is published in multiple language versions; in principle, each essay is made available simultaneously in Chinese, Japanese, Korean, and English editions. (Other languages may be added as resources and labor permit.) Each author contributing to *Traces* uses a language and scholarly frame of reference of his or her choice, but on the understanding that writing for *Traces* entails a "heterolingual" address:[1] each essay is written to be read not only in multiple languages but by mixed readerships that are neither enclosed in a common culture nor neatly divided into separate "communities." Translation is understood here not as a form of diplomacy between rival national-linguistic states but as a means to form a new international space of theoretical exchange, in which questioning and counter-questioning about "the same" issue — and "the same" text — can occur between people who might otherwise never converse. In the practice of forming this multilingual space, *Traces* seeks a new conception of cultural theory.[2]

The inaugural volume, "Specters of the West and the Politics of Translation," outlined the series project for a genuinely comparative cultural theory that would not (as the introduction puts it) "neglect the form of the act which gives rise out of differences to that which is commensurate and thereby brings heterogeneous items onto the plane of comparison."[3] The difficulties as well as the urgency of that project are foregrounded in this second volume, which focuses on the mobilization of virulent racism and xenophobia in response to escalating migration, severe economic displacement, and geopolitical upheaval across the world in recent decades.

The value of a multilingual response to such a global problem seems obvious. In all of the languages of *Traces,* there is discussion of this frightening development and there exists a supply of sociological, economic, and political analysis on which to draw. An immediate aim of this collection, then, is to bring some of these discussions and analyses into a shared intellectual space. Translation works as a means to link diverse readerships as well as authors who might not otherwise converse; in encountering critical responses being developed in languages other than those we speak, often addressing situations that differ greatly from those we think we know, we gain new ways of understanding contexts that directly concern us.

This is a traditional benefit of international academic exchange, and it is a vital one in conditions where the catch-phrases of transnational capital's *political* legitimation — "the new economy," "global restructuring," "information revolution," "level playing field" and so on — circulate globally to create a policy continuum that not only generates real social conflicts and economic distress but offers utopian promises of remedy: racist outbreaks (one version of the story goes) may occur in the transition to a new economy amongst the "losers" of globalization, but these are merely "irrational" surges or atavistic "returns" of a primitive fear of the Other that can be dispelled by technological progress and further economic "reform." In recent years, "ethnic cleansing" in Bosnia, the re-emergence of unashamed anti-Semitism across Europe from France to Russia, attacks on ethnic Chinese in Indonesia, attacks on migrant workers from Africa and the Middle East in France, Germany and Sweden, and the "white panic" of Pauline Hanson's One Nation Party in Australia (to name but a few) have all been seen in these wishfully reductive terms. By bringing together scholars who work in different zones of the globalizing policy continuum (discussed here for its impact on Ireland by Luke Gibbons, in China by Huang Ping, more obliquely on Japan by Jung Yeong-Hae, and in Japan and Australia by Tessa Morris-Suzuki), this volume of *Traces* establishes a "plane of comparison" on which the promises of market utopianism can be questioned at the same time as racist reactions to its practical effects are contested.

Between these two broad activities, our more specific aim is to examine the historical and affective complexity of particular migratory and racializing movements. The lived burden of colonialism and patriarchal nationalism is a primary focus here, along with emigrant and immigrant experience. In many of the violently racializing clashes of recent years, new forces of economic and social dispossession have been impacting on people still struggling with the legacy of earlier or other imperialisms and nation-building campaigns. The essays collected here explore the work of cultural memory as it responds to and *participates in* densely layered situations of conflict and displacement; they ask how memories and stories of conflict in the past inform the tensions of the present, as well as analyzing the contemporary contexts in which memories of displacement are mobilized.

In the process, a different tracing of the global is written on to the world-historical map still implicitly assumed by a great deal of "theory" that circulates in English. This is a map of the distribution of Eurocentrism, European imperialism, and White supremacism over the past few centuries. It emphasizes the global spread of their impact, and yet does so in a way that dramatically foregrounds key areas of Western Europe and the United States; the eye is continually drawn back to the intensively micro-mapped "centers" of this theoretical world, while the rest remains shadowy and vague: a broadly-brushed background indispensable for framing a critique yet never the focus of critical attention. This map tells us little about the responses to Eurocentrism and White supremacism shaping thought and politics in other places that took themselves to be central, still less about how such movements in thought and politics impacted in turn on "the West"; it does not feature events in which "Whites" and "Europeans" were minor players, third parties, or unimportant.

This map is not up to the job of helping us think globally today. The problem lies not with what it shows us or even with what it leaves out of account but with the obstacles posed to thought by the *form* of a theoretical geography that repetitively channels critical desire towards the familiar bits of "the West" even as it limits our capacity for thinking through histories other than those that it gives us to inherit (wherever we are) as our own.[4] The difficulties that ensue are practical and mundane: vast new works of scholarship add detail to the vague parts of the map, but few are widely read for their theoretical import and methodological innovations beyond the boundaries of an allocated discipline or field (in an English-language context, usually "area" or "postcolonial" studies).[5] Anyway, what is to be done? Life is short, time is limited: even if it were feasible and desirable to produce such a thing, a panoramic map of the theoretically world-historical would be impossible to use in academic working conditions today.

The multilingual tracing of the global that emerges from this volume of *Traces* is neither an exhaustive nor a "more representative" picture of, say, the world distribution of racisms and migrations today. The contributors were not expected to set aside "parochial" interests or to abandon projects that matter in their usual working lives, and they were not brought together on the basis of achieving a judicious spread of national, ethnic, or disciplinary belongings; *Traces* is not a United Nations of theory. Vast areas of the world, many racisms, and many modes of migration forced and voluntary are not considered here; this volume does not deal with slavery nor directly with refugees. Rather, it came together "in translation" as an international discussion of a *problem* urgently felt but loosely defined; the contributors were asked only to think simultaneously about a context of crisis (or a "panic") of immediate concern to them, and about its lived historical dimensions — to work through what Komagome Takeshi calls "successive layers of violence."

The global is traced, then, *between* the essays by the emergence of unplanned lines of connection, surprising points of convergence, and unexpected passages of overlapping research and reflection. For example, Komagome's study of the racializing role of religion under Japanese colonial rule requires an "intertwined history" of Britain, China/Taiwan and Japan that links directly to Luke Gibbons's account of the colonial force of the Scottish Enlightenment, and his critique of its invocation in the work of Richard Rorty. Gibbons's reflection on rising racism against immigrants in Ireland presents material for thought along the lines suggested by Yann Moulier Boutang's critique of schemas or "protocols of rationality" predominant in histories of immigration, on the one hand, and powerfully shaping anti-immigrant traditions of action and feeling in the international labor movement on the other. Along another "diagonal" of the collection, Gibbons's essay also touches (in a different mood) on some of the "secrets of ethnic abjection" that preoccupy Rey Chow in her essay on the politics of *writing* about ethnicity in a North American context of "euphoria" for a multiculturalism fraught with "unresolved tensions" of racism and class discrimination.

Chow's exploration in her context of an "*affective* dissonance" between theoretical writing about cultural hybridity and fictional or autobiographical writing echoes the efforts of Ien Ang and Ghassan Hage to find a mode of discourse capable of articulating, respectively, the sense of "victimhood" lived by Chinese Indonesians, ambivalent between violently shifting historical registers of ethnic, national, and economic belonging, and (for Hage) the dilemmas of responsibility and participation facing non-British/Irish migrants in an Australia torn by conflicts not simply between "black" and "white" but between "indigenous people" and "settlers" — conflicts arising from a colonialism for which those migrants, targets of racism themselves, are not ancestrally responsible but which they more or less inherit. And in their attention to the autobiographical all three essays participate in the sense of "responsibility" that Kim Seong-nae defines, in her essay on the April Third Massacre that took place on Cheju Island off the Korean peninsula in 1948, as beginning with an act of "*listening attentively* to the individual stories of each victim."

The emphasis on Kim's words here is mine, but the listening-based mode of learning and solidarity that she sees in Korea as both a "task" and a "debt owed to the body in pain" is variously practised by Jacqueline Armijo in her study of how commemorative narratives "engender" survival among descendants of the state-sponsored massacre of Muslims in Southwest China in 1873; by Tomotari Mikako's meditation on the making of her sculpture in response to the Nibutani Dam that submerged former homelands of the Ainu people of Hokkaido; and by Môri Yoshitaka's commentary on Tomotari's artwork. An art as well as a politics of listening is also fundamental to Huang Ping's sociologically inflected study of the "subsistence rationality" practised by peasants out-migrating on a vast scale across contemporary China, and of the ways in which its positive significance as well as its unintended consequences may conflict with a logic of "economic rationality." Such listening is also, of course, a basic enabling condition of the texts written closely in response to others by Victor Koschmann, Tessa Morris-Suzuki, Sakiyama Masaki, Oka Mari, and my co-editor Brett de Bary.

There would be many other ways to trace connections between the essays in this volume. My point is simply that the "value" of a multilingual response to a global problem is methodological as well as informative; as we encounter new ways of approaching apparently familiar questions, their "familiarity" is transformed and the frameworks in which we pose them are opened up and multiplied. Repeatedly reading through the essays for this project, Brett and I both learned a great deal about situations differing greatly from those we thought we knew; perhaps we each learned even more about our own. Reflecting on this process and the everyday labor it entails, Brett's essay "Editing Journal" concludes the volume with (in my view) the most lucid, subtle, and suggestive argument I have read during the years of *Traces*'s development for a conception of cultural theory grounded in the *work* of translation and comparison involved in shaping a multilingual space of intellectual exchange.

However, let me draw attention to a difficulty; let me not neglect "the form of the act" (of editing, as well as of translation and of writing *for* translation) that has enabled the commensurating claims I have just made to frame as a "volume" the essays assembled here. The essays were first written in five languages (English, French, Chinese, Japanese, and Korean), from academic locations in Australia, the United States, Ireland, France, the Chinese mainland, Japan, and South Korea, and they deal with conflicts and historical burdens not only in those nations, in Indonesia, and in Taiwan under Japanese colonialism, but also in places and for people whose difference has been sanctioned — with great violence in some cases — in the process of its *definition* by diverse national or imperial norms: *peranakan* and *totok* Chinese, Asian-Americans, Cheju Islanders, the Hui of Yunnan, the Ainu people, the *yamabushi*, Aboriginal Australians, Arab-Australian youth, Kyushu. I write this list a little carelessly, emphasizing its almost random nature as a grouping of "heterogeneous items." A few of these names are familiar to me, but some I had never heard of before beginning work on this project for *Traces* in 1999. Yet, here I am presuming to introduce studies organized by these names and written in some cases by scholars whose academic lives and languages are largely or entirely unknown to me.

I am writing in English, from an institutional location in Hong Kong but with a sense of "agenda" and a set of protocols in my mind that are shaped both by my involvement as a white Australian with the highly charged and entangled politics of "race" and migration in that country, and by my more sporadic participation in an Anglo-American academy that spans the Pacific. From each of these sources (which are not the same) of my academic and personal experience, habitual questions arise as I write. For example: have I used the phrase "heterogeneous items" with sufficient care? Cited out of its context in the first volume of *Traces* (a technical discussion of the act of translation), is it likely in this new context of discussion about racism and migration to create the impression of an "ethnic collection" in the zoological sense?[6] Will it make *Traces* appear to be a liberal pluralist exercise in marveling at how much diversity we can pack between two covers? And if it will have this appearance for some, no matter what I say — in this context, do I care? On the other hand, should I justify or regret more explicitly the limitations — or the "omissions" (as one usage influential today terms any act of selection or product of chance) — structuring this list? These questions I can do my best to deal with as I go. Much more difficult, however, is a problem to which I cannot even begin to imagine a response: what will be the significance of these same questions — and of my posing of them as "*habitual*" — when this text is read in Korean, Japanese, or Chinese as the Introduction to a volume of essays in those languages? Indeed, what *kind* of sense will be made of my outline of the themes of this volume and my claims about the global when this outline and those claims are read in languages and academic cultures other than those in which I make them?

The fact is that I have no idea. I do know that "heterogeneity" does not necessarily carry in all the languages of *Traces* the same reified, glamorized force that it can have in academic English today. I know that not every academic culture in the world ("the West" included) is given to affirming "diversity" as an intrinsically good thing and "difference" as a positive value — at least, not in the same ways as those that have come to prominence in societies founded, like my own, on settler colonialism and state-sponsored mass immigration. I know that deep misunderstandings easily arise when discussions of migration make simultaneous reference to situations where a "guest worker" model of temporary residence is entrenched as a norm (as in Hong Kong), those in which immigration has long been debated in terms of the conditions of real or potential national citizenship (as in Australia), and those in which economic changes have recently rendered immigration a sensitive and in some ways new topic of debate (as in Ireland and Japan, for example). To these shreds of knowledge, I can add my certain ignorance of the possible agendas and protocols that might have shaped this Introduction if I were conversant with theoretical debates occurring today not in "Korea," "China," and "Japan," but in Korean, Chinese, and Japanese *languages*.

This difficulty is at the heart of the *Traces* project. You simply don't know what the significance of your words and assumptions might become when translated into unfamiliar languages and unknown contexts of reading. This is no doubt true of all writing that circulates beyond the author's vicinity, but most writing also depends on ignoring or rendering insignificant both the form of the act of translation and the *uncertainties of address* (and therefore of reference) that are multiplied by this act. Of course, scholars who must routinely change languages to secure an "international" hearing are familiar with these uncertainties and their unsettling effect in thought. In standard "academic English," however, translation is a secondary event; we write for imagined readers with whom we share not only a language but a set of intellectual priorities, an etiquette, and a political as well as professional frame of reference. Under this regime of translation, any wider circulation of a text is taken to be subsequent and more or less accidental; a pleasant but unexpected sign of success. Writing for *Traces*, that familiar simulacrum of audience loses definition; for everyone, "other readers" are there from the beginning and actively shaping the text. To put translation first involves a loss of control, even as it weakens the force of the defensive strategies that can consume so much time and space in routine critical work. Misunderstanding is inevitable in this project and it must be accepted as a factor intrinsic to our effort to converse with each other. The emphasis of labor, therefore, shifts away from preemptive avoidance and towards the effort to converse itself. To write and to theorize together multilingually is not a declaration of linguistic particularism. Rather, it involves taking the risk of sometimes *making generalizations* mundanely across linguistic as well as national and cultural borders. I do stress "making"; the process involved is practical and collective. It is erratic and it can fail.

The stakes of making such an effort are clear in conditions of intensifying confusion about the relations between biological and cultural racism, nationalism, colonialism, and economic exploitation active *at present* across the world. Some scholars work on these issues surrounded by confident debates about the decline of the nation-state, and/or the kind of elite consensus I mentioned earlier that racism of any kind is a vicious but historically outdated phenomenon. Others inhabit contexts where a different version of the transnational moment prevails: "new" or resurgent nationalisms, chauvinisms, and/or racially exclusive paradigms of belonging are mobilizing feelings and memories, if not always at the level of a "nation"-state, then variously also around a neighborhood, a town, a city or city-state, a sub- or supranational region, or even a "civilization."[7] This contrast is overdrawn, and it obscures a variety of situations in which it would indicate only two ends of a spectrum, or two poles of an antagonism which might itself be one of many. However, my point is simply that by engaging in a multilingual discussion of these issues we complicate but do not abandon the effort to make sense transnationally of a globally complex present.

Under what conditions may any worldly issue be considered "the same" issue debated in different languages? What happens as it circulates between distinct academic cultures that may or may not overlap? When I agreed to edit this volume for *Traces*, these questions had bothered me vaguely over the years. Trained to think academically in French, I puzzled in the 1970s and 1980s over those strange outcomes of English translation called "post-structuralism" or just plain "Theory" in Britain and the United States; I stopped when those outcomes had so transformed intellectual agendas in the Australian contexts I worked in that French became a distant memory. Yet around the same time, it seemed to become more difficult to pursue those agendas beyond Australia *in English*.[8] I began to see enough awkwardly international debates about "multiculturalism" to be convinced that diverse Americans, Australians, Canadians, and New Zealanders (for example) do not easily understand each other on "this issue," because of differing historical experiences and forms of affect about the state — and because not all parties to a given discussion will equally accord value and significance to the ways in which they differ.

Moving from Sydney in Australia to Hong Kong during the editing of this volume greatly sharpened my sense of urgency about the need to question "the same" in contexts of translation. I do not speak Cantonese, and on leaving a life in which I used an overwhelmingly dominant language that had happily been for me (as for my Irish family before me) a medium of upward class mobility, I expected difficulty in adjusting to the limitations of an English powerfully marked in Hong Kong as the minority language of former colonial elites, now of local or "expatriate" (like me) post-repatriation elites — yet also devalued by other measures of race and class in Hong Kong when used by migrant workers, especially women from the Philippines, India, and countries in South-East Asia. Having taken pleasure in *thinking* through Australian popular idioms in my theoretical work on national culture, I was prepared for a sense of displacement (more strongly, *dépaysement* in French) to inhabit my efforts to work in a place where I have no access to popular cultural life beyond badly subtitled movies, and insufficient knowledge both of China and the complex politics of the Hong Kong Special Administrative Region (HKSAR) even to join discussions in English of matters "national" here. In short, I was prepared for difference. However, coming to Hong Kong from a country racked by the entry of open racism into "respectable" public discourse for the first time since my schooldays, I was not at all prepared for a disconcerting sameness in Hong Kong media stories screaming *in English* about "illegal immigrants" and "snakeheads" ("people smugglers" in Australia) and about mainlanders "pushing down salaries" (as legal migrants in Australia are also held to do). Nor was I prepared for the terrible familiarity of the controversies that followed an inquest into the death in a Hong Kong hospital of Harinder Veriah, an Indian Malaysian solicitor, about whether Han Chinese racism against darker-skinned people is a problem in Hong Kong or not ("is Australia the most racist country in the world or one of the best multicultural societies?").[9]

I do not read Chinese and hear only reports in translation of how these controversies are dealt with by the more extensive and, I'm told, diverse Chinese media. The English stories that startle me with their familiarity are signed, like the responses they elicit, by predominantly Chinese and Anglo-something names;

most seem to arise from a fairly narrow spectrum of more or less liberal opinion on issues of race and migration. I share the values expressed and the politics at work in many of the articles and letters attacking racism and class exploitation in Hong Kong. Yet their uncanny impact for me (as I wonder if I've really left home) derives from the way they carry another kind of divisive force: these are media stories and controversies framed by a syndicated continuum of "global news" that delivers *similarly to each market* an atomizing image of its own distinct, uniquely awful, social conflicts.[10] Along this continuum comparisons are rare and often polemically twisted — reading a Hong Kong story about how much more dynamic young people are on the mainland, I remember learning the same thing in Australia about young people in Hong Kong and Taiwan — and the *genres* of narration are fixed and standardized: reportage, human interest, op-ed, think piece, scare story, lifestyle, profile. Trying not to panic over reports in the *South China Morning Post* of a "resurgence" of the One Nation party in Australian state elections in early 2001 (at which its vote in fact declined), I find a light-hearted "fluff piece" about Pauline Hanson's plans to launch a fashion label.[11]

This is a fluent English for watchful elites, in which every place is much the same yet disconnected from all the others. In contrast, the stammering English of the classroom strains continually for comparison and "cross-cultural communication" without always being able to produce much of either. Teaching debates about racism and multiculturalism in my first semester is a strain all around. My examples, diverse and pressing in an Australian or U.S. context, are suddenly remote and monotonously "Western"; the parochial limits of my reading are painfully on display, and the students' patience with this is remarkable to me. So is their capacity to make me read these "Western" materials in a different way: one group insists that an American essay about how hierarchies of race, color, class, and language are internalized and relayed socially is really just about status relations between bosses and employees; I can't agree (nor do others in the class) but I think I see what they mean.[12] Sometimes I am jolted by a positive use of the English word "racism" to describe a natural outlook on the world, and by the categories of a blood-and-motherland raciology affirmed as common sense; I feel I'm listening to Pauline Hanson, or my grandparents. I'm not, so I learn more about this by reading.[13] But at these times, I have no idea what these students think I have been saying, or what I would think of what they might say if I understood Cantonese. Frequently my denseness in response to their comments is the major classroom problem; too often, I simply do not know what to say.

At all times, my students' fluency in my first language is far greater than mine in theirs and we do the best we can. It takes an enormous effort each week to create a working sense of security that we are *trying* to talk about "the same thing," and if this effort to construct a referent often fails in its objective, it transforms the conditions of our effort in a way that brings the objective closer. No "standardized" genres of class discussion really work to help us: my "read this and we'll talk about it" approach fails dismally when they can't manage enough English reading; their way of talking loudly in Cantonese throughout a lecture (often, it turns out, discussing the translation of things said five minutes ago) drives me crazy. Eventually, we improvise a genre that works for the topic at hand: something like a translation *relay* where students help each other in Cantonese to gloss what I'm saying in English, and students tell me in English what they've been saying in Cantonese. It takes a lot of trust and I'm not always sure why they're laughing. But in the process, it is from them that I learn enough about Hong Kong's Chinese debates about "race" and migration to become a more critical consumer of the English language media.

The question of genre in translation should be central to the theoretical projects of *Traces*, and it is formidably difficult. For this particular collection it arose from the outset as a practical problem: in what conditions might it be possible not only for widely dispersed contributors to write on highly sensitive matters in the language that suited each best, but also for each to participate in defining the topic? Two levels of editorial self-interest were at work: first, the desire for a volume to hang together well enough to be readable as cohesive; second, the need for that "same" topic to be of useful interest in every language edition of the series. Reconciling these two pressures is not an easy task. However, I believe that publishing in multiple languages is not enough to challenge the prevailing distribution of theory unless academic genres and protocols, too, are opened up for critical scrutiny and reworking. The English language academy now has globally powerful ways of talking, and of criticizing others talking, about racism on the one hand, and migration on the other. To translate the intellectual strength and political force of work in English on how these concerns intersect and interact with others to do with class, gender, and sexuality, it is vital for scholars working in other languages *also* to be able to make available for translation their own "ways of talking," their ways of doing criticism, their ways of formulating what counts as an "issue."

For this reason I am grateful, in retrospect, that we were not in a position to hold one big international conference and publish the proceedings. A productive genre for many kinds of academic work, magically exciting at times, it can too soon close off the process of *establishing* a shared concern. The American practice of reading aloud a written paper followed by discussion followed by tightening revisions (good for generating books in English, but also widely used in East Asia as a comprehension aid when English is the *lingua franca*), has a way of rendering discussion ritually agonistic: I give a finished paper, you find the flaws, I defend the paper and go home to fix the flaws. This approach was all the more unsuitable for this particular volume of *Traces* in that for a long time we could not decide what the *title* of our project should be. While we were happy to leave it to authors to interpret "panic" in connection with "memory" and "migration," how to name that *site* of panic where a mobilized violence erupts became a framing problem of producing the volume not only across languages but between several cultural contexts of usage.

As an outcome of both necessity and chance, this collection was shaped slowly by its contributors under four working titles in English and across a series of events including a great many emails and three separate workshops attended by different people. Naoki Sakai invited me in 1998 to edit a volume of *Traces* to be called "White Panic" after an essay I'd written on how the White Australia policy (1901–1973) created a racially phobic imaginary of "Asian invasion" that drew on myths of the terrifying loss of home experienced not by the Aboriginal owners of the land but by the white settlers who violently displaced them. For *Traces*, I was unhappy with that title: the kind of panic I had in mind is by no means the province only of white *people*, but this is not obvious from the English phrase alone. Nevertheless, a meeting in Tokyo pragmatically used this title to sketch a huge list of potential themes and contributors; when I shared my doubts a suggestion of "Yellow Panic" created amusement and, since the emphasis of that meeting was largely on East Asian-based conflicts, some support. But what sense might that make in other contexts of discussion? In English, such a title could well be scandalous, with its overtones of the lurid color typologies and "perils" of late nineteenth century racism.

Making a generalization, I wrote a formal proposal under the title "Race Panic and the Memory of Migration" and began corresponding with contributors. Serious collective discussion began with a workshop in English held, with the support of the Society for the Humanities and with a great deal of help from Yukiko Hanawa, at Cornell University in October 1999; Luke Gibbons and Ghassan Hage presented work-in-progress papers, and a moving response to Gibbons was given by the Korean scholar of Irish literature, Kim Young-min. Along with participants from *Traces* a group of about twenty people came along to share ideas throughout the day. This workshop had yet another title, "Ethnic Panic and the Memory of Migration," which some organizers felt worked better for a U.S. context where the word "race" and the propriety of using it are much contested, and where "ethnicity" is a term widely used to cover a broad range of issues to do with heritage and cultural belonging.

I found it a little too diffuse for the broader international context of the project, or perhaps too easily dissociated from the critical study of racism and racialization that we wished in that context to foster. Two months later a workshop on "Race Panic and the Memory of Migration" was held in Japanese, English, and a little French at the Asian Art Museum in Fukuoka on the island of Kyushu, Japan. A heavy burden of translation, impromptu and unpaid, fell over two days on a few participants: Brett de Bary, Victor Koschmann, Môri Yoshitaka, Tessa Morris-Suzuki, and Naoki Sakai. The essays published here by Ien Ang, Jacqueline Armijo, Yann Moulier Boutang, Jung Yeong-hae, Komagome Takeshi, and Tomotari Mikako had a first hearing at this workshop along with the responses published by Koschmann, Morris-Suzuki, Sakiyama Masaki, and Oka Mari; so did Môri's collaboration with Tomotari. Among other interventions that could not be published here (including a paper by Hage), an eloquent closing response by Lee Chonghwa questioned the modes as well as the "rationality" of our discourse in terms of its impact, and lack of impact, in displaced women's lives. These responses were informal and intended to assist authors preparing to write for a more varied readership than monolingual publication assures. However, so great was their contribution to the conceptualization of the project (as it was now beginning to emerge) that I asked those discussants not already burdened with an essay to send us their texts in writing. I am deeply grateful to everyone who accepted this unexpected and unprogrammed task, which in some cases generated substantial new essays, and I very much regret that circumstances prevented Lee Chonghwa from writing her contribution. The memory of her words, however, has had a lasting effect.

At the end of this workshop, I again raised the question of the title — white? yellow? ethnic? "race"? — but no obvious solution arose. (Nor did anyone but me seem to mind, perhaps the first indication that a conversation was actually forming). We put the problem into suspension as the huge labor of collecting, refereeing, revising, translating, and correcting texts in five languages began. During this period three authors who had been unable to attend any workshops — Rey Chow, Huang Ping, and Kim Seong-nae — generously added their thoughts and advice by correspondence to a project of which they had only a sketchy description. Soon into this process it became obvious that Brett de Bary was doing from Cornell (and later the Reischauer Institute at Harvard University) quite as much conceptual and certainly more practical work than I was in Australia, and she agreed formally to co-edit the volume with me; had she refused, the project would have collapsed. Brett also did more than her share of translation into English of texts in Japanese, and she liaised with all those "translators to English" whose unstinting, meticulous scholarship made this volume possible in no routine way. For without the work of Victor Koschmann, Jiwon Shin (who acknowledges the helpful editorial suggestions of David McCann), Erica Brindley, Joshua Goldstein, and Bernard Prusak along with Brett in producing an English version, and without the manifold forms of assistance provided throughout by Kojima Kiyoshi in Tokyo, I would not have been able to read most of this volume that I am now introducing.

These acknowledgments belong in the middle of things, not at the end where they usually go. Translation is not only an enabling condition and a theoretical object for *Traces*; it also composes the very substance of our intellectual project. It is a salutary experience to chair a workshop mostly held in a language that you don't understand and then to edit a publication you cannot read until the very last minute. Only after the labor of translation was finished did the long-distance editors have the pleasure and relief of finding that the collection does hang together, its cohesiveness a product not of editorial fiat but a multilingual collaboration developed through several layers of discussion and translation and extending across various networks of activity. We grouped the essays loosely into Parts that were not planned in advance but arose in our reading of and across the essays. The section headings are interpretations that we have imposed, combining essays posing intimately difficult questions of conduct and feeling, self-regard and self-composition in migrant experience ("Migratory Questions of Ethics"); essays examining the relations between labor mobility, nation or population building, and policy frameworks and stories rationalizing the management of these ("Logics of Labor"); essays exploring deep histories of state violence — in two cases, violence especially against women — and the questions of commemoration and testimony that arise for survivors and for witnesses ("Memories of State"); and essays that push the boundaries of form to articulate what Ghassan Hage calls a "sea of subjectivity" that tosses around struggles for identity in contact with others as migrants, displaced people and indigenous peoples are caught up and "settled" by nationalizing narratives of land ("Displacement and National Ground").

These are the lines of connection we chose to emphasize, but among others that we might have taken up the themes of family, education, and religion are perhaps equally strong. Having made our choice, however, the matter of the title was easily settled; across a spectrum that runs from Huang Ping's essay, wholly about migration, to Kim Seong-Nae's on the racialization as "Red" of the bodies of the inhabitants of Cheju Island, most of the essays deal with the fabrication of an *idea* of "race" — with "the arbitrariness of racial divisions, the absurdity and pettiness of racial typologies, and the mortal dangers that have always attended their institutionalization" — and they grapple with "raciology," that "lore," as Paul Gilroy defines it in a powerful new book, "that brings the virtual realities of 'race' to life."[14] In *Against Race*, Gilroy calls in a utopian spirit for a "fundamental change of mood" away from the ambivalent relationship to the idea of "race" that he finds historically installed in black political culture and towards "a heterocultural, postanthropological, and cosmopolitan yet-to-come." Invoking the future of the planet as the temporal horizon that should orient political tasks in the present, Gilroy draws on Franz Fanon's memorable refusal, in *Black Skin, White Masks,* to be a "prisoner of history." If this volume participates (as I would wish it to do) in the urgent project that Gilroy describes as "making raciology appear anachronistic," then it will be because the "*planetary* humanism" that he calls for cannot develop — in time for the planet — only in English and for intellectuals based in the West. Utopian it may be, but it is indeed on a planetary scale that "careful judgments" need to be made about what "histories of our heterocultural present and our cosmopolitan future" should entail for a "new" agenda.[15]

I am less sure how to name the genre that we improvised in order to produce this heterocultural volume; insofar as it included some passages of fumbling but none the less productive partial communication, it had something of the translation relay about it. However, I think I prefer the simple and unheroic term, "workshop."

A workshop held as a meeting is a singular event of convergence, as Oka Mari points out in her essay; for her, the Fukuoka workshop left its participants facing questions at the end. A finished publication has a different temporality, slow-release and expansive: the authors' work on these texts is over for now, and the singularity and eventfulness of whatever "plane of comparison" it has established (for no such plane was given at the beginning) pass over to the contexts of reading. However, Oka's questions also pass on and prolong or reiterate a creative moment of doubt: "we were left to ask," she writes, "what it really means to 'speak different languages' or even to 'speak the same language.' And what it could mean to share the experiences of the Other."[16] For other questions arising for the future rather than from the past of this publication, I pass over to Brett de Bary's essay at the end of the volume.

ENDNOTES

1 On "Writing for Multiple Audiences and the Heterolingual Address," see Naoki Sakai, *Translation and Subjectivity: On "Japan" and Cultural Nationalism* (Minneapolis and London: Minnesota University Press, 1997), 1–17.

2 This account is based on a prospectus for *Traces* co-authored by Naoki Sakai, Thomas Lamarre, and Peng Cheah.

3 "Introduction," Naoki Sakai, *Traces* 1, "Specters of the West and the Politics of Translation" ed. Naoki Sakai and Yukiko Hanawa, 1 (March 2001).

4 This line of thought was suggested by Pred's remarks in a different context on the mechanisms of denial involved in "a certain popular geographical imagination" that projects racism elsewhere by regarding it as "typical of a limited number of places associated with hideous events"; Alan Pred, "Memory and the cultural reworking of crisis: racisms and the current moment of danger in Sweden, or wanting it like before," *Environment and Planning D: Society and Space* 16 (6, 1998), 635.

5 I have in mind such innovative works as Heather Goodall's *Invasion to Embassy: Land in Aboriginal Politics in New South Wales, 1770–1972* (St. Leonards, NSW, Australia: Allen & Unwin, 1996); Gail Hershatter's *Dangerous Pleasures: Prostitution and Modernity in Twentieth-Century Shanghai* (Berkeley, Los Angeles, and London: University of California Press, 1997) ; Anne McClintock's *Imperial Leather: Race, Gender and Sexuality in the Colonial Context* (New York and London: Routledge, 1995).

6 Ghassan Hage, *White Nation: Fantasies of White Supremacy in a Multicultural Society* (Sydney: Pluto, 1999).

7 See Kuan-Hsing Chen, "Not Yet the Postcolonial Era: the (Super) Nation-State and Trans*nationalism* of Cultural Studies," *Cultural Studies* 10 (1, 1996), 37–70.

8 I discuss this in "Afterthoughts on Australianism," *Cultural Studies* 6 (3, 1992), 468–475.

[9] Veriah, 33, died in Ruttonjee Hospital on January 2, 2000, after suffering an epileptic fit. Before her death, she told her husband, Martin Jacques, "I am at the bottom of the pile... I am the only Indian here, everyone else is Chinese." A campaign subsequently developed to press for antiracist legislation in Hong Kong, deemed unnecessary by the SAR government. See "More could have been done for lawyer," *South China Morning Post,* November 22, 2000.

[10] In an example of this, Veriah's death was taken up (to the outrage of Martin Jacques) by some of the English press as a "scare story" about Chinese nurses in British hospitals. For his own account see Jacques, "Life and death of the bottom of the race pile," *South China Morning Post,* March 6, 2001.

[11] "Hanson fashions career change," *South China Morning Post,* February 15, 2001.

[12] The reading in question was Patricia Williams's wonderful essay on "The Ethnic Scarring of American Whiteness" in *The House That Race Built,* ed. Wahneema Lubiano (New York: Vintage, 1998), 253–263.

[13] Frank Dikötter, *The Discourse of Race in Modern China* (Stanford, CA; Stanford University Press, 1992).

[14] Both quotations in this sentence are from Paul Gilroy, *Against Race: Imagining Political Culture Beyond the Color Line* (Cambridge, MA: Harvard University Press, 2000), 305, and 11. This book is published in Britain under the title *Between Camps: Race, Identity and Nationalism at the End of the Colour Line* (London: Allen Lane, 2000).

[15] This paragraph draws on Gilroy, 324–326.

[16] Oka Mari, "Words of the Other," p. 383 below.

Part 1

Migratory Questions of Ethics

Trapped in Ambivalence: Chinese Indonesians, Victimhood, and the Debris of History

Ien Ang

The unraveling of Western modernity as the master narrative for universal human progress has prompted many peoples to put themselves forward as victims of/in history — as having been wronged in the violent processes of European colonialism and capitalist modernization. Such claims to victimhood generally rely on the representation of previously untold historical narratives which can make sense of a particular people's real and imagined suffering, past and present. Often, the narrativization of victimization and victimhood on the public stage marks an important moment of self-empowerment for previously subordinated or oppressed peoples, paving the way for efforts to redress past injustice and present disadvantage: the case of indigenous peoples in settler colonial societies such as Australia is exemplary here. But, in their very proliferation, discourses and narratives of victimhood can also have less desirable effects; not just in fact, or in moral or political terms, but because they fail to provide subjects in history with a complex and evenhanded sense of their own past, one that is appropriate for the conditions of the present.

One could argue, for example, that the obsessive Japanese collective memory of victimization as a result of the nuclear destruction of Hiroshima and Nagasaki is problematic not just because it represses Japan's own history as perpetrators of violence, oppression, and injustice to other nations and peoples, especially in Asia; but also, in more practical political terms, because it inhibits an open and honest reconciliation with old victims, who on their part have not forgotten their suffering at the hands of Japanese colonizers and refuse to forgive without a proper sign of regret and remorse.[1] As Lisa Yoneyama has remarked, "The act of remembering is always mediated by and inseparable from the positions that one establishes in relation to social and political arrangements, in both the present and the future."[2] In a time when self-positionings as victims of history have proliferated throughout the world, accompanied by claims for apology and reparation to be paid by those who are accused of having committed the crimes against the victimized, it is not surprising that the accused often have great difficulty in dealing with their own past as "baddies": they prefer not to be reminded of it, resorting to the commemoration of their own, real or imagined, victimhood instead.[3] Victims, after all, have clean hands, are subjects of virtue, and cannot be held responsible for any immoral acts. Discourses of victimhood, in other words, afford the luxury of the moral high ground.

My starting point in this essay is not a critique of discourses of victimhood as such, nor a doubting of the real difference between "right" and "wrong." Human history is full of distinguishable oppressors and oppressed, known killers and killed, recognized malefactors and their casualties — and there is no doubt that they all have to be recognized as such, in the context of the prevailing relations of domination and submission in which they operated. The problem with an unchecked cultivation of victim status, however, is practical: in their binary simplification of the world between good and bad, and in their historical positioning of the victim subject as a true "goodie," they generally fail to grasp the moral, as well as factual, *complexity* of history. Identifying ourselves exclusively as historical victims not only inhibits critical self-reflexivity (preventing us from recognizing the multiple and often tricky articulations of our historical subjectivities, and not always under morally immaculate circumstances), but also constrains the creation of the conditions of possibility for reaching out, reconciliation, and coexistence, especially with those we feel rightly or wrongly victimized by. In this sense, the cultivation of positions of self-victimization could be said to work against the establishment of social and political arrangements which can help negotiate, if not overcome, the violent divisions inherited from the past, often to the detriment of the self-declared "victims" themselves as they struggle to construct a livable present and future.

Such is the case, I will argue in this essay, with the group of people generally referred to as Chinese Indonesians or Indonesian Chinese (the conflation of these two combinatory terms is itself, as we shall see, an indication of the problem I am setting out to explore here). I should say at the outset that my purpose here is not to declare, from a god-like judgmental vantage point, that Chinese Indonesians are or are not victims of/in history. My argument will be that we have to go *beyond* the discourse of victimhood and victimization to come to a proper and properly sensitive understanding of the Chinese Indonesian predicament — past, present, and future. Writing this essay in 2000, I am afraid that Chinese Indonesians are condemned to live with their predicament indefinitely, both in Indonesia and in diaspora — a predicament that can be characterized as being "trapped in ambivalence."[4] It is a predicament which has been the unintended, unwilled, and unwanted outcome of the "debris of contemporary history"[5] for which there is, experts seem to agree, no imaginable "real" solution.[6] This historical debris, as I will elaborate below, arises out of the entangled confluence of the overlapping histories of European colonialism, competing nationalisms, and the process of decolonization, in which Chinese Indonesians (or Indonesian Chinese) are neither unambiguous victims nor indisputable perpetrators. If anything, they are both, although it is necessary, as I have suggested, to avoid compromising terms, such as "victims" and "perpetrators," to fully grasp the intricacies and the agony, moral and otherwise, of the Chinese Indonesian predicament.

In his book *Indonesian Chinese in Crisis*, published in 1983, historian Charles Coppel has observed that "the Indonesian Chinese have been ...captives of their own situation and of their own history."[7] Coppel made this observation in light of the perilous minority status in which Indonesians of Chinese descent, currently estimated as about 3–4% of the population, or six or seven million people, find themselves in the modern nation-state of Indonesia. Their crisis, to refer to the title of Coppel's book, is an enduring feature of Indonesian postcolonial history: people of Chinese descent have systematically been treated as second-class citizens, and they are constantly referred to as "foreigners" or "aliens," despite the fact that most Chinese Indonesian families have lived in the country for generations. They have regularly been the target of mass violence, and anti-Chinese racism and prejudice are a pervasive part of everyday culture.[8] As Wang Gungwu has observed, referring to the first few decades after 1945, "For whatever understandable reasons, nowhere have more Overseas Chinese been killed or wounded, run away or been chased away, and been so insecure during the past twenty years than in Indonesia."[9] How has it come to all this? How can Chinese Indonesians explain their own wretched predicament to themselves? Most scholarly and political treatments of the position of the Chinese in Indonesia define the problem in narrow state-related terms such citizenship rights, formal political loyalties, assimilation policies, and economic relations. However, as important as these issues are, they do not provide a thorough *subjective* understanding of what it means to be Chinese Indonesian (or Indonesian Chinese) today. If Chinese Indonesians are to have a more culturally meaningful understanding of their "crisis," they would need a narrative identity that goes beyond the disempowering story of "the Chinese problem," as their situation has officially been called by the Indonesian government. It is here, I suggest, that it is important to understand the Chinese Indonesian situation as being trapped in ambivalence. There is a long and complex history to be told, which can be traced back to the role the Chinese played in the complexly oppressive divide-and-rule policies of the Dutch during their more than 300-year colonial rule,[10] but the Indonesian Chinese have hardly come to terms with this fateful historical legacy when it comes to defining who they are and where they are now. I suggest that it is this lack of historical understanding which has left them, as Coppel perceptively observed, in captivity of their own situation and their own history — a captivity which is easily experienced in terms of victimhood. Or to put it differently, precisely because there does not seem to be an effective story through which Chinese Indonesians can make sense of themselves as a people with a particular, complex history, a clearheaded and honest story about why and how it is that they are deemed such a persistent "problem," a paralyzing sense of being eternally victimized can emerge.

I hasten to add that my own interest here is not that of the scholarly historian or the political activist. The history I am trying to recapture and re-present here is to a significant extent a personal one: I was born into a Chinese Indonesian family in the 1950s and lived in Indonesia until 1966. My parents decided to get out of Indonesia precisely to escape the bad situation they were in: the harassment, the insecurity, the appalling social discrimination — something I experienced myself as a young child there. My personal family history has long been a source of bewilderment and anguish, deepened by a total inability to comprehend why it was that we, an ordinary family living an ordinary life, were the object of such hostility. A profound sense of unjust victimization was thus a common emotion among people of my family background — a victimization for which there was apparently no clear, livable explanation, no story to tell except through the discourse of victimhood itself. The result is an intensely confused sense of identity, a crippling sense of living in a perpetual impasse without knowing why. One reason for me to write this essay, then, is to contribute to a softening of this quite debilitating feeling of stalemate confusion.

I would think that the suasion of this discourse of victimhood would be particularly strong amongst diasporic Indonesian Chinese (such as my family), for whom Indonesia is no longer a real place to live in but an abstract symbolic space associated with a traumatic past. Under such conditions, memories of hurt, frustration, and discrimination could easily become decontextualized and objectified in terms of overall and eternal victimization. Holding on to a singular victim identity would be much more difficult for those Chinese Indonesians who continue to live in Indonesia to this day, as they are faced with the challenge to negotiate the full complexity of social life within Indonesia, in which they would not survive if they were to see themselves merely as ultimately passive "victims." Still, that feelings of disempowerment are quite widespread among many Chinese in Indonesia in the 1990s is amply suggested by research on their lived identities, for example by Mely Tan, who has reported on the general frustration and confusion among many about "feeling Indonesian, *but* being of Chinese origin" (the "but" connotes the strongly felt incommensurability here), of never feeling entirely accepted, of always having to be on the alert.[11]

Recent developments in Indonesia suggest clearly that by the late 1990s, the basic paradigm of antagonism between "Chinese" and "Indonesian" has not changed much since Wang's observations about the period after 1945 and the publication of Coppel's book in 1983. When the Asian economic crisis hit Indonesia in 1997, news reports abounded about angry mobs who scapegoated the ethnic Chinese for the hardship of the populace in the wake of the crisis. In early 1998, the world was informed about riots that broke out in many towns and villages across the country, always targeting Chinese-owned shops and businesses. This culminated in a major, three-day rampage in the streets of Jakarta in May, during which, reportedly, about 1,200 people were killed.[12] Many Chinese-owned shops and businesses were looted and burned and, as became evident later, dozens of Chinese women were gang raped.[13]

It is not surprising that these traumatic events have rekindled memories and discourses of victimhood amongst people of Chinese descent inside and outside of Indonesia. I remember the chaos and distress sweeping across Indonesia after the violent failed coup of October 1965, when at least half a million people were killed in riots and mass attacks on communists and people who were otherwise targeted as culprits, many of whom were Chinese.[14] I was still living in Indonesia then, experiencing the event as a young girl, and I remember vividly how anxious and fearful my parents were. During the 1998 eruption of mass violence, memories of the earlier event circulated frantically. In diaspora in the Netherlands now, where my parents had decided to seek refuge after 1965, there was a bitter sense of being victimized yet again as a people, if not personally (for we were "lucky" not to live in Indonesia anymore).[15] Indeed, as I have already remarked, the diasporic condition seems actually to intensify the feeling of victimhood, and with it the hatred of the Indonesians who were inflicting it on "us." Being away from the scene of violence, fear, and trauma allows diasporans to absolutize their abstract (if very heartfelt) sense of victimhood.

In 1998, such long-distance diasporic concern was massively amplified by the expansive workings of the Internet.[16] Here, however, the common denominator for the diasporic community is no longer a nationally specific "Chinese-Indonesianness," but a presumably borderless, transnational "Chineseness." Chinese diaspora websites such as Huaren (*www.huaren.org*),[17] for example, which has its base in California and was established in direct response to the crisis in Indonesia, quickly produced a dramatic outpouring of global Chinese solidarity with the brethren in Indonesia.[18] During the days of most furious rioting in May the Huaren bulletin board functioned as a virtual space for calls for help, rumors about new riots, eyewitness accounts, stories of pain and suffering, tips on how to defend oneself, encouragements to fight back or advice on how and where to flee, calls for all *huaren* (ethnic Chinese) in the world to protest and express solidarity, and rising anger about the *pribumi* (indigenous Indonesians). In the midst of the fear, despair, and anger, imaginary strategies to deal with the whole situation were thrown up which signaled a desire to solve the problem once and for all. Some suggested organizing the exodus of all ethnic Chinese out of Indonesia to whatever country would be prepared to take them in. Others proposed the creation of a separate state for Indonesian Chinese, to create another "Singapore." Some cast their hope on China to become the strongest nation in the world. Still others wanted to see Indonesia completely bankrupt. In such imagined futures, any connection with "Indonesia," and the possibility of living together with non-Chinese Indonesians, was given up. Even more moderate voices, those who still allowed some discursive space for the prospect of coexistence, tended to reproduce and feed on the dichotomy:

> To those responsible pribumi and Indonesian politicians and pribumi business people, you can not afford to sit and wait for the current atrocities against Chinese to blow over and expect Chinese will forget about it. This time you are wrong. ...The lack of positive and responsible actions in Indonesia despite continual urging and cry for help from the victims will only make the global Chinese communities more angry and united to intensify the campaign.[19]

In the consternation and confusion expressed within the electronic diasporic community, a history of the present was being written that relegated Indonesia and the so-called *pribumi* irrevocably to the realm of the Bad Other against which the Good Chinese Self has to defend itself — a Chinese Self defined in absolutist terms of innocent victimhood, at the passive receiving end of aggression and violence.

But what does such a discourse of self-victimization achieve, apart from providing some therapeutic comfort to desperate, hurting souls? It is clear that retreating into such a pure and untainted victim identity will not clarify or solve anything. On the contrary, for most Chinese Indonesians there is no other future than in Indonesia itself! In this essay I wish to take a step back and develop a story that moves beyond the mutually exclusive binary of good and bad, and beyond the fantasmatic recourse into "final solutions." Instead, I think it is important to come to terms with the notion that we are, in a fundamentally irrevocable way, trapped in ambivalence. In this, I am guided by Zygmunt Bauman's "postmodern wisdom" that "there are problems in human and social life with no good solutions, twisted trajectories that cannot be straightened up, ... moral agonies which no reason-dictated recipes can soothe, let alone cure."[20] It is this more sobering, if ultimately saner, perspective on history that I wish to mobilize in the rest of this essay. My aim, to emphasize once more, is thus not to provide a more "objective" or "accurate" understanding of Chinese Indonesian history (I will borrow mainly from existing scholarly knowledge produced by specialist professional historians), but to revisit and re-present that history so as to help us to *work through* its complexities and ironies, its ambivalences, in more (self-)critical and self-reflexive, and therefore more empowering ways.[21]

Postcolonial Nationalism and Its Discontents

The Chinese Indonesian sense of victimhood is generally rooted in their precarious experience of political and cultural marginalization within the Indonesian nation. Indeed, modern Indonesian nationalism has never managed to accommodate successfully the presence of a Chinese minority in its construction of a national imagined community.[22] While the Indonesian nation was from its inception imagined as a multiethnic entity — something which was necessary to unify the hundreds of ethnic and linguistic groupings making up the archipelago whose spatial boundaries were determined by the imposition of Dutch colonialism — the place of those marked as "Chinese" in this "unity-in-diversity" has always been resolutely ambiguous and uncertain. In most recent decades, the Suharto regime (1966–1998) demanded that ethnic Chinese assimilate into mainstream Indonesian society through name-changing policies, bans on the public display of Chinese cultural expression such as the use of Chinese language and Chinese New Year celebrations, and so on. At the same time, however, those of Chinese descent were always reminded of their categorical difference as the government insisted on differentiating between indigenous and nonindigenous groups; for example, by using special identity cards for ethnic Chinese. Here then a very contrary, if not cynical, politics of ambivalence is deployed by the Indonesian state: on the one hand, the Chinese were forced to delete all memories of their migratory past and the traces of their cultural heritage, but on the other hand, they were prevented precisely from ever forgetting their nominal Chineseness. As a result, no matter how much they would comply and Indonesianize themselves, they would never be able to become "true" or "real" Indonesians.

In this context, the recourse to identification with Chineseness rather than Indonesianness amongst some Indonesians of Chinese background is a very understandable response: it is a symbolic attempt to claim a vicarious "home" where a secure sense of belonging to Indonesia has been thwarted. But staking a claim to a belonging to the "Chinese diaspora" poses its own problems, given that most Indonesian Chinese do not speak, read, or write any Chinese, no longer have any connections with China (the imputed ancestral motherland), and have very little active knowledge of Chinese cultural traditions, rituals, and practices.[23] Thus, for those who identify themselves as "Chinese Indonesian" or "Indonesian Chinese" — the very interchangeable use of the two reveals the uncertainty and ambivalence many have in locating themselves — the imaginary belonging to a vast and powerful "Chinese diaspora" can never provide a satisfactory solution to the question of "home." Imagining oneself to be a member of the Chinese diaspora aligns one with a dispersed, deterritorialized community notionally bound together by an abstract sense of "racial" sameness and an equally abstract sense of civilizational pride, but it does not relieve one from the difficulties involved in the very concrete, historically specific condition of occupying a diasporic minority status in the social and political context of the Indonesian nation-state. Indeed, it is the very objectification and hardening of the category "Chinese" that is part of the problem rather than the solution to "the Chinese problem" in Indonesia. Through the absolutization of "Chineseness" as a separate and monolithic identity, the "problem" itself is symbolically constructed and reproduced.

It should be pointed out that who "the Chinese" are in Indonesia is not a question with a straightforward, objective answer. Those of Chinese ancestry who live in the country are a very diverse group. An important distinction stemming from colonial times is often made between the more locally rooted *peranakan* Chinese (who migrated many, many generations ago, intermarried with local women, and have adopted many local customs including the local language) and the more recently arrived *totok* Chinese (who have generally maintained their links with their ancestral village in China and are more generally still steeped in Chinese language and culture). A more recent, postcolonial distinction is that between those ethnic Chinese who are Indonesian citizens and those who are not. While the latter distinction has been crucial for both government policy and for Indonesian Chinese leaders, society at large generally does not use passport identities as markers of difference. Coppel therefore includes in his definition of Indonesian Chinese those "who are regarded as Chinese by indigenous Indonesians (at least in some circumstances) and given special treatment as a consequence."[24] This definition thus includes people who regard themselves as Indonesians and have refused to identify themselves in any sense with "Chineseness," but whose notional Chinese characteristics (mostly physical appearance) still allow them to be labeled and treated as "Chinese." Thus, the borderline between "Chinese" and "non-Chinese" is not always clear; "the Indonesian Chinese" are neither an internally homogeneous nor a securely bounded category of people. As I will argue later, understanding adequately how "the Chinese" came to be historically solidified as a persistently problematic category in postcolonial Indonesia — that is, to come to terms with its complicated and conflictive historical construction — is crucial in any engagement with "race relations" in contemporary Indonesia. These relations have been severely damaged by the May 1998 riots, but have had a much longer history going back to colonial times, a history which has left behind multiple traumatic memories but has now often been forgotten or disowned.

Contemporary media accounts of "the Chinese problem" do not generally look very deeply into the historical context of its emergence. Instead, simplistic, quasisociological accounts abound. In the wake of the 1998 crisis, for example, international, mostly Western, newspaper reports repeated a narrative that is monotonous in its constant reiteration of the following refrain: "The six million Chinese make up only 3% of the total population of 200 million in Indonesia, but they account for 70% of the country's wealth." The apparent obviousness of the "fact" provides the illusion of a simple, parsimonious "explanation" for the whole crisis, a sense of immediate understanding that does not warrant any further questioning. This does not mean that the "fact" is not "true" in some superficial empirical sense, but we all know that any "truth" is not only constructed, but also produces a sense of reality that compresses and represses the intersecting power relations and complex historical contradictions that have worked to generate it. What is particularly disturbing about the constant reiteration of this "fact" is that its seductive simplicity will only serve to reinforce the way in which "the Chinese" are permanently locked into an antagonistic relationship with the *pribumi* (indigenous Indonesians), and with "Indonesia" more generally.

To be sure, the "fact" reflects a common-sense truth shared and accepted throughout all layers of Indonesian society: that the Chinese are richer and more well off than the *pribumi*. As a Chinese Indonesian myself, I have always known this truth for a fact: it was the taken-for-granted experiential reality within which my family lived when we were still in Indonesia, and a statement I heard repeated countless times after we left. Chinese-Indonesian common sense would have it that anti-Chinese sentiment amongst the majority Indonesians is to be blamed on jealousy, whereas many non-Chinese Indonesians routinely accuse the Chinese of arrogance and exclusiveness. The depth of feeling that keeps the two categories apart cannot be overestimated: it pervades daily life and colors everyday social interaction and experience to this day.

Yenni Kwok, for example, an *Asiaweek* journalist in her mid-twenties and born and bred in Jakarta, told her readers how she grew up without getting to know any Indonesians of non-Chinese background. "For most Chinese," she says, "the only *pribumi* they ever get to know is their household maid, their *pembantu*. Once they reach adulthood, there is almost no further social contact. Even in professional life, the two groups rarely mingle." She also testifies to the tacit sense of superiority that many ethnic Chinese have in relation to their non-Chinese fellow Indonesians:

> I remember, when I was a youngster, asking my father why they [*pribumis*] were referred to as *fangui* (literally "rice devils," but meaning inferior). "We eat rice too," I said. "So we're also *fangui*, right?" My father just smiled. It was too difficult — and probably too embarrassing — to explain.[25]

Kwok's experience illustrates only too clearly what is more or less common knowledge: the Chinese are (stereotyped as) the "haves" by most in Indonesia, and they often behave as such.

According to Leo Suryadinata, a Singapore-based expert on the situation of the Chinese in Southeast Asia, "some of Indonesia's wealthiest citizens are Chinese, but most Chinese are not rich."[26] However, as an urban-based minority, they are a major component of the Indonesian middle class. Throughout the country they always have dominated commercial life and the retail trade. It misses the point here to suggest, as more Marxist-inclined analysts would do, that the "Chinese problem" in Indonesia is not one of "race," but one of "class." The problem is that in this context, "class" is lived in the modality of "race": Indonesia is an intensely racialized social formation, in which the Chinese/*pribumi* distinction is generally read in terms of economic advantage/disadvantage. In other words, "Chineseness" in contemporary Indonesia does not connote primarily cultural identities, but *economic* identities. It is this real and perceived economic divide that determines, in the first instance, the manner in which real and perceived cultural differences are transformed into social incompatibilities and antagonisms, both ideologically and in practice.[27]

A detour through history is necessary here to avoid simplistic, prejudicial explanations for how this came to be so. From reading through the historical literature, it is clear that the current ethnic Chinese capacity to accumulate wealth is inextricably linked to a long history of early regional commerce, European colonialism, and twentieth century capitalist modernization. Chinese merchants and traders have been active throughout Southeast Asia long before the arrival of the Europeans, but during the period of European colonialism their role as an "entrepreneurial minority" strengthened and became structural to the economic life of the region. Just like Jews in Central Europe, Chinese in Southeast Asia played a crucial role in trade, money management, and capital accumulation — commercial practices that instigated the slow but irrevocable reconfiguration of these disparate societies under the weight of the globalizing forces of capitalist modernity.[28] Chinese merchants were indispensable buyers and sellers to the large European companies during the mercantile colonial period (which ranged from the mid-1500s up to the mid-1700s and was dominated first by Portuguese and Spanish traders, and later Dutch and British monopoly trading companies). When the European colonial state expanded in the nineteenth century, ethnic Chinese became brokers mediating between the colonial powers and the natives, particularly in the system of tax farming for the collection of state revenues. As Anthony Reid notes, "the Chinese tax farmer and his agents were the economic arms of government in rural areas" in colonial Java.[29] As such, Chinese gained access to and mingled with the "natives," but also, as a group, aroused resentment, especially as their demands on peasants for revenue increased. During this period, ethnic Chinese communities grew in wealth and mobility, enjoying a significant autonomy while being essentially loyal to and working with the European colonial order. As Reid puts it: "Colonial policies encouraged a division of function, a dual economy, between the 'native' majority of peasants, under their own, often anti-commercial, aristocratic-bureaucratic hierarchy, and the commercial sector of Europeans, Chinese, and other minorities."[30] Later, the legacy of this dual economy resulted in a relative lack of capitalist know-how, experience, and contacts among the "natives," and as indigenous merchants had to fight unequal battles with much stronger Chinese competitors, appeals to anti-Chinese sentiment received a popular hearing, and it was a major aspect of an emergent Indonesian nationalism in the early twentieth century. Thus, the anti-Chinese populism that still fuels today's assaults on Chinese-owned shops and businesses has a long and deep-seated history.

History's Bitter Ironies

A dispassionate understanding of this history is important here in order not to recede into an unproductive politics of blame, which is all too easy to do when one feels victimized. It is quite a common attitude among ethnic Chinese to commemorate this history as a means of blaming the divide-and-rule policies of the Dutch colonizers for the current situation. And indeed, one of the mainstays of the colonial order was the legal classification of the Chinese as Foreign Orientals (*vreemde oosterlingen*), who were placed in between Europeans, on the one hand, and the "natives," on the other. Benedict Anderson makes this point very clear by emphasizing how it was the Dutch who created the "Chinese minority" in the first place — a minority on whose support and loyalty the colonizers could rely.[31] The very category "Chinese" was an imposed one to begin with, not one of self-identification. As Anderson cynically remarks: "it was not until the 1890s that some Southeast Asian Chinese realized what the Europeans had insisted upon since the seventeenth century — that they were, *après tout*, Chinese."[32] By developing a separate jurisprudence for the "Chinese," who "were clearly unaware of being such, being unable to read Chinese characters and speaking mutually unintelligible mainland languages if they spoke any non-indigenous language at all,"[33] the Dutch colonizers instituted an increasing segregation of the Chinese in terms of legal status, required costuming and barbering, residence, possibility of travel, and so on. This apartheid strategy had a "fateful" effect, in Anderson's words: "By the nineteenth century these policies had produced in Java a non-Chinese-speaking ethnic Chinese minority that increasingly was detached from any native coalition and hitched to Batavia's wagon."[34]

The implication here is that without colonial intervention, there would not have been a "Chinese problem" in latter-day Indonesia: that the problem itself is a legacy of European colonialism. Such an interpretation does have some credibility. One can, for example, as Anderson does, point to the smooth assimilation of Chinese traders into the ruling class in Thailand or to the intimate ties between Chinese and Malays in precolonial Malaya as indications that the separatism imposed by colonial ethnic politics was "unnatural." Again, regarding ourselves as victims is tempting here: it wasn't our fault, we were *forced* to distance ourselves from the "natives." Indeed, in my own experience blaming the Dutch colonizer is a routine politics of memory among many Indonesian Chinese, especially those who are old enough to have known colonial times. But while accusatory gestures in the direction of the powerful Western Other may produce short-term therapeutic effects or induce reassurances of one's own innocence, they tend to explain away any sense of agency in the making of history. To put it differently, what I think is important to acknowledge is that Chinese in the Dutch East Indies did actively contribute to the making of their own history, even though they didn't have much control over the conditions in which that history was being made. We have to recognize that many Chinese subjects, faced with the constraints and limitations imposed on them by Dutch colonial rule, negotiated a role and a livelihood for themselves which *structurally* positioned them in a relation of power and tension vis-à-vis the "natives." They took up the entrepreneurial challenges of early colonial modernity both because they were constrained from other economic activities (e.g., agriculture) and because of their entrenched cultural orientation toward trading and commercialism. In the process they further developed the necessary capital, not only financial but also cultural, to place themselves favorably in relation to the changing requirements of modernizing society (terms such as "adaptability" and "flexibility" are often used in this context).[35] In the early twentieth century, when Dutch colonial governance was modernized and developed the preoccupations of a modern bureaucratic state, including mass education for its subjects, the Chinese responded most vigorously to the new opportunities. They were in an advantageous position to do this, so Reid suggests, because they were "the most urban, commercial, and uprooted,"[36] that is, positively predisposed towards the transformative requirements of modernity, in which formal education was increasingly becoming an indispensable asset for future success.[37] This also meant, incidentally, that the cultural conditions were established early on in which ethnic Chinese could be most successful in the quest for upward mobility that is the name of the game in life in the modern capitalist society of the post-World War Two period, both through business and through entry into the ranks of the professions. To this day, as is well known, ethnic Chinese throughout Southeast Asia have been able to seize on this advantage, an advantage that has been historically inscribed in their very habitus, cultural orientation, and mode of subjectivity.[38]

The point of recounting this history here is to foreground how in colonial times, the Chinese were not simply at the passive receiving end of oppressive and exploitative colonial "divide-and-rule" policies; those policies — and their own active, if not opportunistic responses to them — also placed the Chinese in a position of advantage and superiority vis-à-vis the "natives," who were relegated to the bottom of the colonial hierarchy. After decolonization, this position of advantage and superiority did not simply go away, at least economically. Indeed, most Chinese businessmen became even better off economically after the end of the colonial era, at the expense both of the retreating Dutch (who until then had monopolized the most lucrative and powerful areas of economic activity) and the indigenous Indonesians, who were far behind on the ladder of commercial advancement.[39] Postcolonial national government policies to change this situation often had unintended contrary consequences, as testified in President Sukarno's 1959 decision to ban Chinese small business from rural areas to give *pribumi* Indonesians control over trade in the villages. As a result, however, as Indonesian historian Ong Hok Ham has remarked, Chinese became even more urban and, consequently, even more economically dominant.[40] Furthermore, it is common knowledge that Suharto depended disproportionately on Chinese entrepreneurs to develop the national economy during his rule, and that ethnic Chinese on the whole benefited most handsomely from the increasing affluence and wealth during the New Order period. A large number of the crony capitalists around Suharto were, in fact, ethnic Chinese[41] — one of the most visible reasons for indigenous Indonesian resentment against the Chinese as a group.

But if an unintended legacy of colonial rule has been a Chinese economic advantage throughout Southeast Asia, including Indonesia, the rise of anticolonial nationalism and the postcolonial nation-state has left them more or less politically powerless. Indeed, it is hard to avoid the conclusion that it was the end of colonialism and the arrival of Indonesian independence that dealt a decisive blow to the not fully satisfactory but relatively secure position of the Chinese during colonial times: they were caught in the rapids of world-historical change without knowing adequately how to respond. Wang Gungwu, for example, remarks about the *peranakan* Chinese in Indonesia, who were a large and active community before independence, that "they failed to adapt as a group" to Indonesian nationalism since 1945, without giving reasons for that failure.[42] Anderson similarly alludes to how the Chinese "attempted frantically to adjust themselves to nationalist regimes" in post-independence Southeast Asia without, however, giving up on maintaining powerful international connections (particularly with China, Taiwan, or the West).[43] In Indonesia, many Chinese did not know whether to choose for the side of the Dutch colonizers or for the Indonesian nationalists during the struggle for independence. As Coppel puts it: "In the turmoil and uncertainty of the revolutionary period, a common reaction of the Chinese was a studied neutrality."[44] But this "studied neutrality" was, understandably, considered tantamount to collaboration with the colonizers by the Indonesians, who were fighting to liberate themselves from their oppressors. Coppel cites a Chinese leader of that time who claimed that the Chinese inability to take sides was beyond their control (blaming it on the Dutch who didn't allow them to enter into full political life), not because of opportunism or fence sitting. But how could such doublemindedness be acceptable in the revolutionary language of anticolonial nationalism that gained such momentum in a rapidly decolonizing world?

The historical experience of the Indonesian Chinese points to a lacuna in much contemporary postcolonial theory, which is generally preoccupied with the binary relationship between the European colonizer and the indigenous "native," without a serious eye on the distinct role and fate of those who were caught in between.[45] Coppel remarks in his historiographical study of the Chinese in Indonesia that "the dominant theme of Chinese political activity in the late colonial period was to press for equality of status for the Chinese with the Europeans."[46] Very few Chinese in this period saw any benefit in forging alliances with the "natives," who were at the bottom of the oppressive colonial hierarchy. This element of complicity may be difficult to acknowledge, but it may be one reason why the Chinese "failed to adapt" when decolonization became inevitable.

The fact is that it was the very ascendancy of liberatory, anticolonial nationalism which made it harder and harder for middleman minorities such as the Indonesian Chinese to find an effective political voice. As Daniel Chirot puts it:

> the rise of modern nationalism hardened attitudes toward those newly viewed as outsiders. Entrepreneurial minorities, previously seen as just one more among many specialized ethnic and religious groups that existed in most complex, premodern agrarian societies, now became, in the eyes of the new nationalists, something considerably more threatening.[47]

Thus, while during the colonial period the emergent Indonesian nationalism was not in general directed against the Chinese but against foreign European rule, after independence, when the postcolonial nation-state was established, the presence of Chinese increasingly posed a problem in the process of new nation building. As a result, in Wang Gungwu's observation, the Chinese in Indonesia, as elsewhere in Southeast Asia (except Singapore) were condemned to the ambivalent role of "being an instrument of economic growth without either political ambition or social respectability."[48]

But there is a further, crucial historical irony, which prefigures a later tragedy. In colonial Indonesia, nationalist awakening occurred earlier among the Chinese than among the "natives." But most Chinese rallied behind a *Chinese* nationalism, one oriented towards China, not Indonesia.[49] The Chinese revolution of 1911 strongly emboldened Chinese pride and faith in China's power to challenge European hegemony. Many local Chinese who had "lost" their Chineseness (i.e., the *peranakans*) began to resinicize themselves, at least partially (e.g., by learning the language, sending their children to Chinese schools, and so on), encouraged by nationalist Chinese scholars and professionals and some local community leaders, as well as the Chinese government. In the 1920s and 30s, pan-Chinese nationalism (which is a striking early manifestation of organized Chinese diasporic activity) was booming, and political activism in colonial Indonesia became increasingly polarized along racial lines.[50] Is it surprising, then, that at a later stage, when the "natives" mobilized themselves, they didn't rush to invite the Chinese into their ranks?[51] Postindependence efforts by Indonesia-oriented Chinese leaders to be fully accepted into the syncretic national community of "Indonesia" have always had to struggle against the legacy of separateness reinforced by the competing force of Chinese nationalism. As Suryadinata puts it, "the Indonesian nationalist movement, having emerged after overseas Chinese nationalism in Java, understandably tended to exclude the Chinese from the movement."[52]

How then can we make sense of this disturbing history? How is this past still relevant, if at all, to the present? Again, it is not a matter of guilt and blame here. Rather, what is important is to recognize the convolution of historical entanglements, not in order to point fingers at goodies and baddies, but to understand how subjects in history leave legacies that become the conditions within which future generations must make their own histories. In a structural sense, it needs to be underlined that the emergence of modern nationalism in colonial Indonesia has solidified the distinction between the "indigenous" and the "nonindigenous" — a distinction that continues to frame ethnic relations in Indonesia today. As Takashi Shiraishi has remarked, "the rise of modern politics...signified the 'awakening' of the Chinese as Chinese and of 'natives' as natives."[53] Postcolonial Indonesia inherited this state of affairs, and is living with its legacy to this day.

As modern nationalism involves in principle a practice of constructing a unified peoplehood, the question of who does and who does not belong to the Indonesian people is central to the operation of the Indonesian nation-state. Thus, while ethnic Chinese people during colonial rule were not in general concerned about the formality of their national belonging — such a concern being a feature of full-fledged political modernity which simply didn't apply on colonial territory[54] — after decolonization those who chose or were forced to stay in Indonesia were faced with the necessity to declare formal loyalty to the new nation-state, now under control of "the natives." In other words, ethnic Chinese subjects were placed in the quandary of having to take on, formally, a singular, bounded, and exclusive national identity: in terms of nationality, they had to become *either* Indonesian *or* Chinese. Being both was a blemish in the hegemonic logic of competing, mutually exclusive nationalisms, which both the Chinese and Indonesian governments took years to resolve.[55] This very logic still informs the fundamental felt incommensurability of "Chinese" and "Indonesian" in the cultural imaginary of the new nation. As a result, even those ethnic Chinese who are Indonesian citizens always remain under suspicion that their loyalty might not be undivided — the trace of their Chineseness (mostly read off their faces) always read as a sign of imperfect national belonging, as *not quite* Indonesian.

Diaspora: The Transnational Solution?

By the late 1990s, the uncomfortable position of Chinese Indonesians on the inside/outside borderline of the nation had become an entrenched and virtually taken for granted aspect of Indonesian life. In this light, the eruption of anti-Chinese riots in May 1998 was only the most visible and explicit confirmation of a long-term and deep-seated antagonism, which, as I have tried to show above, goes back much further than the socially discriminatory policies of the Suharto years. Perhaps it is precisely because the riots were so devastating, on the one hand, and so fitting into an historically familiar pattern, on the other, that the sense of victimization has been so intense. As prominent ethnic Chinese businessman Sofjan Wanandi said, "Never before have the Chinese felt so totally hopeless and unprotected."[56] This is the feeling of a people who see no way out of their abject predicament — trapped in ambivalence.

My interrogation of history above will not relieve anyone from the acute sense of despair, on the contrary. But it may provide us with a greater insight into how the impasse of the present came to be. This history is replete with what Dipesh Chakrabarty wishes to highlight in the representation of the postcolonial history of modernity: "the ambivalences, contradictions, the uses of force, and the tragedies and the ironies that attend it."[57] Most poignantly, we must come to terms with the messy fact that the very construct of the "Chinese in Indonesia" is intimately entangled with the historical emergence of "Indonesia" itself, which in turn cannot be separated from the global history of modernity.

What has become the "Chinese problem" in modern Indonesia is intrinsically bound up with the relentless, uncompromising, and ever more all-embracing forces of capitalist modernization, on the one hand, in which ethnic Chinese play a dominant role, and the antagonisms and dependencies emanating from the creation of the modern postcolonial nation-state, on the other, in which ethnic Chinese find themselves politically and culturally disempowered. It is one of the contradictions of modernity that no one really knows how to solve this "problem." The dominant ideology, embraced both by the national government and by important representatives of Chinese-Indonesian community leaders,[58] has advocated complete assimilation, but it is clear that the planned absorption of the Chinese minority into the Indonesian majority and the eventual disappearance of the distinctive presence of Chineseness in the fabric of Indonesian society — which is the abiding desire behind the modern idea of nationalist assimilation — is an impossible strategy, one that is bound to fail. Indeed, as Ariel Heryanto has argued, the very emphasis on the need to assimilate the Chinese — a need which was proclaimed loudly by Suharto's New Order regime but is also insisted upon by many Chinese Indonesians themselves — tends to reinforce "the active and conscious othering of the Chinese" in "the reproduction of the native Self."[59] In other words, the very process of assimilation ensures that Chinese Indonesians remain trapped in the ambivalence of (non)belonging that the rhetoric of assimilation purports to resolve.[60]

The irony remains, however, that Indonesia to a large extent *depends* on its ethnic Chinese population if it is to continue on its road of economic development — a goal "third-world" nation-states simply cannot renounce in the name of anticapitalist, antineocolonial resistance.[61] Indeed, it is not surprising that one of the first things the newly elected President Abdurrahman Wahid did in October 1999 was to call on his Chinese Indonesian fellow citizens who left the country a year before to come "home" and bring back the capital that they had taken with them in their flight after the May 1998 riots.[62]

In this context, it is unnerving to note that prospects for a softening of "the Chinese problem" have generally remained cast firmly *within* the evolutionary framework of modern capitalist "progress." Thus, in the mid-1990s Ariel Heryanto saw a positive step in the growth of a broad-based middle class: "a multi-ethnic capitalist class is...in active formation, economically and politically. Although this class remains far from anything near hegemony over Indonesian life, its very formation has helped soften old racial antagonisms."[63] And writing one year before the 1998 crisis, Linda Lim and Peter Gosling fastened their hope partly on "the continued trickle-down effect from Indonesia's rapid economic growth, to which the Chinese business community and the Suharto regime have positively contributed."[64] What such projections do not account for, however, is that capitalism is a deeply contradictory and unpredictable economic system, underscored by the Asia-wide economic crisis which was the trigger for the renewed flaring up of anti-Chinese mob violence. Indeed, the symbolism of the May 1998 violence suggests that the anger of the urban poor, from whose ranks the rioters were recruited, was to a large extent aimed at the cultural icons of affluent middle-class lifestyles. As one commentator observes, these young urban poor are not only anti-Chinese, but are alienated by the entire modern economy from which they have been increasingly excluded: "They take it out on the inaccessible symbols of the new rich — banks, automatic teller machines, supermarkets, car showrooms, hotels, the cars of the Chinese. The retail revolution that is sweeping Indonesia has repeatedly angered those whose livelihoods remain dependent on more traditional markets, which were not nearly as badly affected [during the riots]."[65] In other words, modern capitalist "progress" has profoundly contradictory effects: on the one hand, the creation of a multi-ethnic middle class and the trickle-down effect serves to ease ethnic tensions, but on the other hand, capitalism's inevitable production of a marginalized underclass only serves to strengthen the traditional equation of "the Chinese" with economic privilege.

To this we should add another, troublingly complicating factor. As the twentieth century has drawn to an end, capitalist modernity has become such a globalizing force that it poses the single most formidable threat to developing nation-states and to national control over economic life.[66] It is well known that in the Asia Pacific it is precisely ethnic Chinese family conglomerates such as the Salim group, headed by Indonesian-Chinese businessman Liem Sioe Liong,[67] who have been at the forefront of transnational capitalist development and of the spectacular success of the "dragons" and "tigers" in the past few decades, drawing on Chinese business networks and contacts throughout the region. This development has led to the rise of what Aihwa Ong and Donald Nonini call "modern Chinese transnationalism,"[68] a highly fluid, mobile and flexible economic, social, and cultural formation that explicitly evades, transcends, and subverts the territorialized fixities of the nation-state. It is not surprising, however, that the rising power of this hypercapitalist and ultraprofitable Chinese transnationalism has only raised lingering accusations of Chinese greed and lack of "loyalty."[69]

The recent emergence of an invigorated, increasingly assertive, global Chinese diaspora — as expressed by the Huaren website I mentioned earlier — only adds to the ambivalent situation of Indonesian Chinese. On the one hand the diaspora promotes "Chinese" as a sign of strength and power, on the other hand this very assertion fuels resonances with an earlier, Chinese nationalist tendency to bind all scattered Chinese to a single notion of "China" and away from their land of residence.[70] For some Chinese Indonesians redefining themselves as cosmopolitan transnationals may be an imaginary solution to their predicament, but this will come at the cost of a further real and perceived disengagement from the Indonesian nation. For example, an increasing number of well-to-do Chinese Indonesian families decide to have their children learn Mandarin as an investment in their economic future. This is read as a sign of resinicization by many indigenous Indonesians which is regarded as detrimental to the objective of full assimilation.[71]

The trouble is that the high profile of the transnational Chinese business elite, stirred up by Western media and commentators,[72] and the more general diasporic emphasis on transnational Chineseness, tend to lead to an overemphasis on the mobility of ethnic Chinese, on the alleged looseness of their connection to the nation-states in which they reside. The majority of ethnic Chinese in Indonesia, however, are profoundly anchored in the locales where they live and work, and their existence is deeply territorialized, determined by and dependent on economic, political, and ideological forces (many of them transnational, to be sure) which shape social relations *within* the nation. It is for this reason that, as a group, Indonesian Chinese cannot yet give up the struggle for their full inclusion in the national-imagined community of "Indonesia." Indeed, in the wake of the May 1998 riots, political consciousness among Chinese Indonesians is said to be growing, and the realization that something needs to be done to overcome the "problem" is becoming widespread across the nation.[73] As Yenni Kwok, the *Asiaweek* journalist, reports: "It may take years to change [antidiscrimination] laws and longer to alter deep-seated prejudices. Nevertheless, something is stirring among younger Chinese, who want people to know that they are just as Indonesian as anybody else."[74] Formulated this way, however, it is clear that the specter of assimilation still haunts ethnic Chinese in Indonesia: their desire to be "just like anybody else" is induced precisely by the persistent perception — reinforced in myriad ways by actual practices of (self)distinction within and beyond the nation — that they are not. How can they deal with the fact that as they cease defining themselves through the discourse of victimhood, they will not cease being trapped in ambivalence? How can they come to terms with the fact that the very sign of that ambivalence is "Chineseness"?

ENDNOTES

1 See, e.g., Lisa Yoneyama, *Hiroshima Traces: Time, Space and the Dialectics of Memory* (Berkeley: University of California Press, 1999).

2 Lisa Yoneyama, "Critical Warps: Facticity, Transformative Knowledge, and Postnationalist Criticism in the Smithsonian Controversy," *positions east asia cultures critique*, 5, no. 3 (1997): 780.

3 Examples are the Afrikaners of South Africa, who as "the white tribe of Africa" strive to commemorate their own suffering at the hands of British colonizers, or white Australians whose own narratives of victimization on the harsh Australian land complicate their acknowledgement of Aboriginal oppression. Jenny de Reuck, "A Politics of Blood: The 'White Tribe' of Africa and the Recombinant Nationalism of a Colonising Indigene," *Critical Arts. A Journal of Cultural Studies*, 10, no. 2 (1996):139–157; Ann Curthoys, "Expulsion, Exodus and Exile in White Australian Historical Mythology," *Journal of Australian Studies*, 61, December 1999.

4 I derive this notion of "trapped in ambivalence" from Zygmunt Bauman, *Modernity and Ambivalence* (Cambridge: Polity Press, 1991).

5 Aihwa Ong and Donald Nonini, *Ungrounded Empires: The Cultural Politics of Modern Chinese Transnationalism* (London: Routledge, 1997), 330.

6 See, e.g., Mely G. Tan, "The Ethnic Chinese in Indonesia: Issues of Identity," in *Ethnic*

Chinese as Southeast Asians, ed. Leo Suryadinata (Singapore: Institute of Southeast Asian Studies, 1997), 33–65.

[7] Charles Coppel, *Indonesian Chinese in Crisis* (Kuala Lumpur: Oxford University Press, 1983), 171.

[8] For a detailed and thorough analysis of anti-Chinese violence in postwar Indonesia, see J. A. C. Mackie, "Anti-Chinese Outbreaks in Indonesia, 1959–1968," in *The Chinese in Indonesia*, ed. J. A. C. Mackie (Honolulu: The University Press of Hawaii in association with The Australian Institute of International Affairs, 1976), 77–138.

[9] Wang Gungwu, "Are Indonesian Chinese Unique? Some Observations" in *The Chinese in Indonesia*, ed. J. A. C. Mackie, 204.

[10] The Dutch colonization of what came to be called the Dutch East Indies began in the seventeenth century (when Dutch mercantile capitalists established Batavia, today's Jakarta, as their trade center in 1619) and ended in 1945, when the Indonesian nationalists declared the new postcolonial nation's independence. The Dutch only accepted the loss of their colony in 1949, after a four-year-long, bloody war of independence.

[11] Mely G. Tan, "The Ethnic Chinese in Indonesia: Issues of Identity."

[12] It is important to stress that not all of those killed were Chinese. Many non-Chinese looters were killed as well during the violence. While this eruption of collective violence has been widely designated as "anti-Chinese riots," it is important to note that there is clear evidence that sections of the Indonesian military had a hand in fuelling the "riots." In this respect, one commentator has described the May 1998 violence as "racialized state terrorism." Ariel Heryanto, "Flaws of riot media coverage," *The Jakarta Post*, 15 July 1998.

[13] For an analysis of the complex politics of these, what the author calls, political rapes, see Ariel Heryanto, "Race, Rape and Reporting," in *Reformasi. Crisis and Change in Indonesia*, ed. Arief Budiman, Barbara Hatley, and Damien Kingsbury (Melbourne: Monash Asia Institute, 1999), 299–334.

[14] According to official history, the coup was masterminded by the then very large Indonesian Communist Party (PKI) and supported by the communist regime in Beijing. The mass killings were mostly targeted at communists, not Chinese, although the association of communism with the People's Republic of China did create an atmosphere of suspicion against Chinese. According to Coppel (*Indonesian Chinese in Crisis*, 58), however, "killings of the Chinese because they were Chinese were more sporadic and less systematic." Around the time of the 1998 riots and attacks, diasporic Chinese memory often blurred the distinction between communists and Chinese, (mis)remembering the 1965/1966 killings as mostly anti-Chinese.

[15] There is a small Chinese Indonesian diasporic community in the Netherlands, mostly comprised of people of my parents' generation (and their offspring) who left Indonesia around the 1965 coup.

[16] The resonance here is with what Benedict Anderson has dubbed "long-distance nationalism." Anderson points to the fact that many destructive, extremist causes in third and second world nation-states (e.g., India, Sri Lanka, Croatia) have been supported

by diasporan migrants in Europe, North America, and Australasia (e.g., through the financing of weapons, the spread of extreme nationalist ideologies, the running of websites, and so on). Benedict Anderson, "Long-distance nationalism," in his *The Spectre of Comparisons. Nationalism, Southeast Asia and the World* (London: Verso, 1998).

17 "*Huaren*" is the generic pinyin transliteration for the word "Chinese."

18 I provide a more detailed analysis of the politics of Huaren in "Indonesia on my mind," chapter 3 in my book *On Not Speaking Chinese: Living Between Asia and the West* (London: Routledge, 2001).

19 "Decent pribumi should control those mobs before they drive Indonesia deeper into ground," Bulletin Board, 27 May 1998, <www.huaren.org>.

20 Zygmunt Bauman, *Postmodern Ethics* (Oxford: Blackwell, 1993), 245.

21 See Yoneyama, "Critical Warps," 786. Yoneyama relies on the work of Dominick LaCapra to discuss the ritual role of the historian in the working through of historical trauma.

22 For historical accounts of the position of the Chinese minority in the Indonesian nation-state, see, e.g., Leo Suryadinata, *Pribumi Indonesians, the Chinese Minority and China* (Kuala Lumpur: Heinemann, 1975); J. A. C. Mackie, ed., *The Chinese in Indonesia* (see note 8 above); Charles Coppel, *Indonesian Chinese in Crisis* (see note 7 above).

23 I have critiqued essentialist and organicist notions of "Chineseness" elsewhere. See Ien Ang, "On Not Speaking Chinese," *New Formations* 24 (1994), 1–18; "Can One Say No to Chineseness?," *boundary 2*, 25 no. 3 (1988): 223–242. Both essays are reprinted in my book *On Not Speaking Chinese.*

24 Coppel, *Indonesian Chinese in Crisis*, 5.

25 Yenni Kwok, "How Indonesian Am I?" *Asiaweek*, 25 May 1998.

26 Leo Suryadinata, "Quo Vadis, Indonesian Chinese?" *The Straits Times*, 25 February 1998 (reproduced in Current Focus, <www.huaren.org>).

27 For the theoretical formulation of the economic as determinant in the first, not last, instance, see Stuart Hall, "The problem of ideology: marxism without guarantees," in *Stuart Hall: Critical Dialogues*, ed. David Morley and Kuan-Hsing Chen. (London: Routledge, 1996), 25–46.

28 For a comparison between Jews and Chinese as entrepreneurial minorities, see Daniel Chirot and Anthony Reid, ed. *Essential Outsiders. Chinese and Jews in the Modern Transformation of Southeast Asia and Central Europe* (Seattle and London: University of Washington Press, 1997).

29 Reid, "Entrepreneurial Minorities, Nationalism and the State," in *Essential Outsiders*, ed. Chirot and Reid, 45.

30 Reid, 54.

31 Benedict Anderson, "Majorities and Minorities," in his *The Spectre of Comparisons*, 318–330.

32 Ibid., 323.

33 Ibid., 321.

34 Ibid., 321.

35 E.g., Daniel Chirot, "Conflicting Identities and the Dangers of Communalism," in *Essential Outsiders*, ed. Chirot and Reid, 25.

[36] Reid, 50.

[37] The issue of education was one of the focal points of Chinese political activism in colonial Indonesia from the first decade of the twentieth century onwards.

[38] The literature on whether or not there is a peculiarly "Chinese capitalism" based on reified Confucian values is huge. For a critique, see, e.g., Arif Dirlik, "Critical Reflections on 'Chinese capitalism' as paradigm," in *South China: State Culture and Social Change During the 20th Century*, ed. Leo Douw and Peter Post (Amsterdam: Royal Netherlands Academy of Arts and Sciences, 1996).

[39] J. A. C. Mackie and Charles Coppel, "A Preliminary Survey," in *The Chinese in Indonesia*, ed. Mackie, 13.

[40] Quoted in John Colmey, "The Eternally Blamed," in *Time Magazine* (Asia), 151, no. 7, 23 February 1998 (reproduced in Current Focus, <www.huaren.org>).

[41] Anderson, "Sauve Qui Peut," in his *The Spectre of Comparisons*, 304. Anderson (315) adds that Suharto deployed his own *divide and impera* system by encouraging the Chinese minority to concentrate exclusively on business, while the indigenous Indonesian elite would concentrate on political power.

[42] Wang, "'Are Indonesian Chinese Unique?," 207.

[43] Anderson, "Majorities and Minorities," 323.

[44] Charles Coppel, "Patterns of Chinese Political Activity in Indonesia," in *The Chinese in Indonesia*, ed. Mackie, 41.

[45] For a discussion on these issues, see, e.g., Gyan Prakash, ed. *After Colonialism. Imperial Histories and Postcolonial Displacements* (Princeton: Princeton University Press, 1995).

[46] Coppel, *Indonesian Chinese in Crisis*, 15. The Chinese demand to be granted the formal status of Europeans was inspired by the fact that the Japanese had managed to acquire such a privileged status in 1899.

[47] Chirot, "Conflicting Identities," 8.

[48] Wang Gungwu, "Are the Indonesian Chinese Unique?," 209.

[49] Lea Williams, *Overseas Chinese Nationalism* (Glencoe, Ill.: the Free Press, 1960); Stephen Fitzgerald, *China and the Overseas Chinese* (Cambridge: Cambridge University Press, 1975).

[50] For the complex patterns of political activity among Indonesian Chinese before and after Indonesian independence, see Coppel, "Patterns of Chinese Political Activity in Indonesia."

[51] The inclusionary/exclusionary limits of Indonesian nationalism are also of relevance here. According to Coppel ("Patterns," 36) most Indonesian nationalists in the pre-independence period were ambivalent about their acceptance of nonindigenous people in their movement.

[52] Leo Suryadinata, "Introduction," in *Political Thinking of the Indonesian Chinese 1900–1977. A Sourcebook*, ed. Leo Suryadinata (Singapore: Singapore University Press, 1979), xv.

[53] Takashi Shiraishi. "Anti-Sinicism in Java's New Order," in *Essential Outsiders*, ed. Chirot and Reid, 205.

[54] In colonial times all inhabitants of the colony were "Dutch subjects," with no citizenship

rights in the modern, nationalist sense of that word. Some Chinese political organizations did campaign against their secondary status as Dutch subjects (Nederlandsch Onderdaanschap); see Leo Suryadinata, *Peranakan Chinese Politics in Java 1917–1942* (Singapore: Singapore University Press, 1981), chapter 2.

55 The Chinese government, through the principle of *jus sanguinis*, in 1909 claimed all people of Chinese descent as citizens of China, regardless of birthplace and country or residence. In response, the Dutch colonial government introduced a nationality law on the principle of *jus soli*, according to which all persons born in the colony would be Dutch subjects. The Indonesian government inherited the resulting "dual nationality" problem, which was not resolved through negotiations with the Chinese government until 1962, when all Chinese with dual nationality had to make a choice for either Indonesian or Chinese citizenship. See Mackie and Coppel, "A Preliminary Survey," 9–12, for a brief overview of this complex episode of legal wrangling, which did nothing to assuage Indonesian distrust of their Chinese co-inhabitants.

56 Quoted in David Jenkins, "The Business of Hatred," *Sydney Morning Herald*, 28 October 1998.

57 Dipesh Chakrabarty, "Provincializing Europe: Postcoloniality and the Critique of History," *Cultural Studies*, 6, no. 3 (1992): 337–357.

58 For a detailed account of the adoption of assimilationist policies by Suharto's New Order, see Coppel, *Indonesian Chinese in Crisis*.

59 Ariel Heryanto, "Ethnic Identities and Erasure: Chinese Indonesians in Public Culture," in *Southeast Asian Identities: Culture and Politics of Representations in Indonesia, Malaysia, Singapore and Thailand*, ed. Joel S. Kahn (Singapore: Institute of Southeast Asian Studies, 1998), 101.

60 Zygmunt Bauman, *Modernity and Ambivalence* (Cambridge: Polity Press, 1991), has given an astute analysis of the contradictions of the assimilation process in relation to Jews in modernizing Europe: "The fact that their cultural similarity had been *achieved* [rather than inherited] made the acculturated aliens different from the rest, 'not really like us', guilty of duplicity and probably also of ill intentions. In this sense, cultural assimilation in the framework of the national state was self-defeating." (142).

61 A comparison with Uganda is salutary here. In the early 1970s, Idi Amin expelled all South Asians, who occupied a similar position as an entrepreneurial minority, to the disastrous detriment of the economic development of the country. By the mid-1990s, the Ugandan government had developed policies to woo these people back into the country.

62 "Bring funds home, ethnic Chinese told," *The Straits Times*, 28 October 1999.

63 Quoted in Reid, 62.

64 Linda Y. C. Lim and L. A. Peter Gosling, "Strengths and Weaknesses of Minority Status for Southeast Asian Chinese at a Time of Economic Growth and Liberalization," in *Essential Outsiders*, ed. Chirot and Reid , 300 (285–317).

65 Gerry van Klinken, "The May Riots," Digest 63, *Inside Indonesia*, 29 May 1998 (<http://www.insideindonesia.org>). There has been considerable discussion about whether the riots were spontaneous or in fact orchestrated by forces within the Indonesian

military. The latter would imply, according to some, that anti-Chinese racism itself was deliberately promoted by powerful interests. Whether or not this is the case, it should be pointed out that any mass orchestration of anti-Chinese attacks could not have been successful had it not resonated with already existing sentiments against Chinese.

66 One important issue in this respect is the controversial role of the International Monetary Fund in imposing economic measures on developing countries receiving IMF assistance (such as the abolition of subsidies on basic commodities such as fuel) without recognizing the adverse social consequences of such economic rationalism.

67 Liem Sioe Liong was one of the business magnates whose house in Jakarta was attacked during the May 1998 riots. He reportedly fled to Singapore soon after, taking his billions with him, but announced he would return and reinvest in Indonesia after the election of the new President, Abdurrahman Wahid. "I'll take my money back to Jakarta: Liem," *The Straits Times*, 8 November 1999.

68 Aiwah Ong and Donald Nonini, ed. *Ungrounded Empires. The Cultural Politics of Modern Chinese Transnationalism* (New York: Routledge, 1997).

69 Lim and Gosling, 299.

70 Professor Wang Gungwu has expressed similar reservations on the basis of his thorough historical analysis of the now discarded ideology of the Chinese sojourner (*huaqiao*) in his "A Single Chinese Diaspora? Some Historical Reflections," in *Imagining the Chinese Diaspora: Two Australian Perspectives* (Canberra: Centre for the Study of the Chinese Southern Diaspora, Australian National University, 1999).

71 A. Dahana, Comment on Mely G. Tan, in *Ethnic Chinese as Southeast Asians*, ed. Suryadinata, 68.

72 See, for example, Jeremy Seagrave, *Lords of the Rim. The Invisible Empire of the Overseas Chinese* (London: Bantam Press, 1995).

73 For example, President Suharto's successor, B. J. Habibie, ordered the abolition of the distinction between *pribumi* and non-*pribumi* in all official circumstances.

74 Yenni Kwok, "A Daring Leap of Faith," *Asiaweek*, 16 July 1999.

Response to Ien Ang: "Trapped in Ambivalence ..."

Victor Koschmann

As a relative stranger to the Indonesian milieu I am unavoidably trapped as well — not in ambivalence, for ambivalence implies a keen awareness of the complexities and ambiguities that attend any real-life situation, but rather in ignorance, that blissful state in which problems look deceptively simple. As a naive observer, I can only make a tentative suggestion or two in the hope that it can be constructively adapted by more knowledgeable interlocutors. At best, therefore, uninformed commentary such as this can be productive only in dialogue.

In her intensely personal as well as scholarly reflections on the predicament of Chinese Indonesians, Ien Ang eloquently outlines the "convolution of historical entanglements" that has defined "Chinese" in opposition to "Indonesian" on the archipelago and reinforced the entrapment of the former. At the same time, she expresses the hope that by working through that history, it might be possible to construct a "narrative identity that goes beyond the disempowering story of the 'Chinese problem'." The essay invites us to imagine how such a narrative identity might be spun, and where it might lead, but because its scope precludes elaborate prescriptions, the essay can only offer a hint or two to help us along. Such hints as it offers are premised upon certain promising factors in the socioeconomic realm. We are told that "Indonesia to a large extent depends on its ethnic Chinese population if it is to continue on its road of economic development..." and that, indeed, one can detect in Indonesia the nascent formation of a "broad-based middle class" that includes *pribumi* as well as Chinese. At the same time, whatever hopefulness such factors might occasion regarding new forms of national economic engagement between *pribumi* and Chinese is moderated by a recognition that globalization seems to be propelling ethnic Chinese businesses toward increasingly transnational rather than national enterprise, thus reinforcing their diasporic "Chineseness" at the expense of deeper Indonesian identity.

The socioeconomic understanding of the Chinese Indonesian predicament that Ien Ang's essay provides is, of course, sine qua non, but a practical grasp of that predicament can begin to emerge only when socioeconomic factors are grasped subjectively as the elements of a political program. If, indeed, "political consciousness among Chinese Indonesians is...growing," where is it headed, and what will it seek to accomplish? What new political identities are in the process of formation? And is it possible that the socioeconomic factors that Ien Ang so lucidly presents might take on new meaning if framed according to a political rather than an exclusively socioeconomic logic? By "political," I refer a logic of choice that can never be determined conclusively by socioeconomic factors.

Socioeconomic logic usually conceives of identities as linked to more or less fixed dimensions of class, ethnicity, locality, occupation, and so forth. On the other hand, in political logic, identities are viewed as contingently formed and reformed in accord with discursively constructed articulations among different subject positions. Such articulations need not imply full agreement among occupants of those subject positions; more often, a crucial role in the formation of a new political alliance is played by antagonism toward a common enemy. One might ask, therefore, what subject positions with respect to history, nationalism, national and global economies, and various other ethnicities are practically available to Chinese-Indonesians? Does transnationalism always subvert the nation-state, so that their expanding involvement in transnational economic ventures is bound to be at the expense of their stake in national economic life? If not — and if it is true that they are "profoundly anchored in the locales where they live and work" and "cannot yet give up the struggle for their full inclusion in the national imagined community of 'Indonesia'" — might it not be advantageous for them to link up with Indonesian nationalists in opposition to certain foreign economic interests? Especially in the wake of the so-called Asian economic crisis, why couldn't Chinese Indonesian conglomerates align themselves with nationalist forces opposed to meddling by foreign investors, the World Bank, and other outside interests? In other words, by joining forces against a common enemy, Chinese-Indonesian actors might be able to strengthen their political stance as Indonesian.

No doubt, such political options are deeply sensitive to context and must constantly be reevaluated in response to changing environments; an outside observer can only speculate on what choices might realistically be available at a given time. My point here is not to recommend that Chinese-Indonesians adopt one or another political direction, but rather to suggest that as an appropriate next stage in her extremely fruitful analysis Ien Ang might reexamine the issue of Chinese-Indonesian identity in light of the specifically political choices perceived to be available. Perhaps if this were done, the Chinese-Indonesians could begin to seem less "trapped" — whether by history, society, or the logic of victimhood.

The Secrets of Ethnic Abjection

Rey Chow

> [W]e were mongrels, confused children whose parents came from different worlds, which in our cases meant Asia and Europe. We were what was left after the collision; we were the things they had dropped on the floor.
>
> We live on the poison we secrete, and spend our nights characterizing ourselves in derogatory terms. It is the only defense we know.
>
> ("A Little Memento from the Boys," John Yau)

The Difference-Revolution

An indispensable and indisputable accomplishment of poststructuralist theory in the past several decades has been the permanent unsettling of the stability of referential meaning, what had been presumed to be anchored in the perfect fit between the signifier and signified. We might say that what poststructuralist theory ushered in was the era of "difference" — to be further amplified as both the acts of differing and deferring — which would take the place of sameness as the condition for signification. As Ferdinand de Saussure's summary statements indicate: "[I]n language there are only differences. Even more important: a difference generally implies positive terms between which the difference is set up; but in language there are only differences *without positive terms . . . [L]anguage is a form and not a substance."*[1] With this difference-revolution, it is no longer possible to speak casually about an anchorage for meaning: if the very ground of intelligibility itself is now understood as the temporal movement of differencing, a permanent process of delay and differentiation, then the old-fashioned presumption about epistemological groundedness cannot hold. In its stead, the conception of linguistic identity becomes structurally defined, with linguistic elements mutually dependent on one another for the generation of meaning.

Such a revision of the fundamental assumptions about signification (or what some would still prefer to call human communication) has major ramifications for many fields of study in the humanities and the social sciences, including those that seem at first to have only the most distant relation with semiotics. It is not difficult to see that the most basic tenets of structuralist linguistics and semiotics — difference, identity, value, arbitrariness, convention, systematicity — carry within them connotations that have resonances well beyond the terrain of a narrow sense of language. Not surprisingly, therefore, one of the most productive uses of what I am calling the difference-revolution is to be found in an area where existential identity itself is most at stake — the area of multiculturalism, postcoloniality, and ethnicity.

A theorist and critic such as Stuart Hall, for instance, astutely makes use of the poststructuralist dislocation of the sign to articulate a radically different manner of conceptualizing identity in the postimperialist, postcolonial age. In his well known essay, "Cultural Identity and Diaspora," Hall argues that there are at least two different ways of thinking about cultural identity. The first way, we might say, reminds us of the pre-poststructuralist sign, dedicated as it is to the production of a unified oneness anchored in specific locations and histories; the second way takes as its point of departure the ineluctable presence of difference:

> The first position defines "cultural identity" in terms of one, shared culture, a sort of collective "one true self", hiding inside the many other, more superficial or artificially imposed "selves", which people with a shared history and ancestry hold in common . . . [the] second position recognizes that, as well as the many points of similarity, there are also critical points of deep and significant *difference* which constitute "what we really are" . . . Cultural identity, in this second sense, is a matter of "becoming" as well as of "being". It belongs to the future as much as to the past.[2]

Hall's use of poststructuralism for an antiessentialist identity politics is especially germane for the histories of diasporic populations, who are, as a rule, caught among their original native homelands, the lands of their colonizers, and (possibly also) the lands of their eventual settlement. Referring to the case of Caribbean identity, he points out that its construction moves through Africa and Europe to finally arrive in the "Third, 'New World' presence" — "the juncture-point where the many cultural tributaries meet . . . where strangers from every other part of the globe collided."[3] Hall goes on to describe the "'New World' presence" as "itself the beginning of diaspora, of diversity, of hybridity and difference."[4] What defines diasporic realities, paradoxically, is what cannot be unified — "precisely the mixes of colour, pigmentation, physiognomic type; . . . 'blends' of tastes. . . the aesthetics of the 'cross-overs', of 'cut-and-mix'. . ."[5] For Hall, this new, hybrid space, which was derived from former cultural spaces but which can no longer be reduced to them, is the paradigmatic space of diasporic identity — a type of identity that is, much like the poststructural sign, permanently in flux.

For an undoing of entrenched ways of approaching identity and cultural tradition, as Hall demonstrates, the relevance of the difference-revolution cannot be emphasized enough. In retrospect, it is precisely the broad-minded work of theorists such as him that has made it possible for others working in similar areas to reconceptualize the existential issues accompanying cultural dislocation in the aftermath of Western imperialism and colonialism.[6] At the same time, it is important to remember that the flip side of the difference-revolution is its refusal of reference, a refusal whose consequences are no less problematic for those engaged in postcolonial cultural studies. In a fairly recent essay, for instance, Pheng Cheah challenges this notable encounter between poststructuralist theory and identity politics, which I just outlined by referring to the work of Hall, by questioning the philosophical bases that inform it. Rather than using the term "difference," Cheah focuses on a special variety of difference — hybridity and hybridity theory — as his primary concern. The drift of his critique, however, is commensurable with what I have been discussing as the legacy of poststructuralist theory, which Cheah examines in close relation to the concept of culture.

Cheah argues that, in their tendency to place an eminently positive value on tropes having to do with flux, activity, mobility, displacement, contingency, and the indeterminacy of the sign, etc.,[7] contemporary hybridity theorists — his primary examples being Homi Bhabha and James Clifford — are working largely within the framework, characteristic of philosophical modernity, in which culture —

and with it the human acts of signification and symbolization — is assigned the status of *freedom from the given* ("given" in the sense of a predetermined condition, such as nature, for instance). "Contemporary postcolonial studies," Cheah writes, "has modulated from antiuniversalist/anticosmopolitan discourses of cultural diversity to discourses of cultural hybridity that criticize the neo-organicist presuppositions of the former."[8] What is significant in this modulation is that culture itself has taken on an emancipatory function as opposed to various forms of oppression. In terms of topography, then, what is given (that is, what is oppressive) tends to be imagined in terms of the stagnant, immobile, firmly-in-place, and unchanging, whereas the opposite tends to be viewed (by hybridity theorists) as inherently liberating. In the "translational understanding of transnationalism" often proposed these days, Cheah continues, "globalization . . . is reduced to cultural hybridization in transnational mobility."[9] As a result, "hybridity theorists are especially attracted to historical cases of migration and diasporic mobility because they see such cases as empirical instances of the flux they regard as the ontological essence of culture",[10] while "those postcolonials for whom postnationalism through mobility is not an alternative"[11] more or less fall outside the purview of such emancipationist, hybridist thinking. Because of this, hybridity theory is, Cheah concludes, a kind of "closet idealism."[12] What makes it idealist, we may add, is precisely the euphoric valorization of difference or, to be more accurate still, the hasty, optimistic replication of the difference-revolution, as found in poststructuralist linguistics in the sociocultural and geopolitical realms.

Just how is the insufficiency of hybridity and the difference-revolution to be grasped? In what kinds of situations does it become clear that a simple affirmation of hybridity and difference, and a refusal of reference, fall short of being viable formulations? I believe Cheah's critique can also be understood in a somewhat less philosophical light. There is a way in which, in North America at least, the current euphoria about hybridity must be recognized as part of a politically progressivist climate that celebrates cultural diversity in the name of multiculturalism. In this context, the criticism voiced is often not so much directed against multicultural hybridity itself as it is an attempt to call attention to what is effaced by its ostensible celebration.[13] Speaking of Canada's Multiculturalism Act, for instance, Smaro Kamboureli refers to such a state of affairs as a "sedative politics":

> When the Canadian government introduced multiculturalism as an official policy in 1971, entrenched it in the Charter of Rights in 1982, and tabled the Canadian Multiculturalism Act in 1988, it made substantial proclamations of responsibility concerning ethnic diversity. The Multiculturalism Act (also known as Bill C-93) recognizes the cultural diversity that constitutes Canada, but it does so by practising a sedative politics, a politics that attempts to recognize ethnic differences, but only in a contained fashion, in order to manage them. It pays tribute to diversity and suggests ways of celebrating it, thus responding to the clarion call of ethnic communities for recognition. Yet it does so without disturbing the conventional articulation of the Canadian dominant society. The Act sets out to perform the impossible act of balancing differences, in the process allowing the state to become self-congratulatory, if not complacent, about its handling of ethnicity.[14]

What Kamboureli's passage clarifies is that the difference-revolution, far from being simply the accomplishment of high theory, has in fact also taken place at the level of the official articulation of the political state — that it is none other than ethnic "difference" and "diversity" that the policy makers of Canada try rhetorically to encompass within the nation's *raison d'être*. Yet this awareness of difference, an awareness that at the level of government policy becomes an attempt to be inclusive and celebratory, in the end serves to mask and perpetuate the persistent problems of social inequality.[15]

M. Nourbese Philip, in a piece entitled "Why Multiculturalism Can't End Racism," puts it in a similar and more succinct manner: "The mechanism of multiculturalism is . . . based on a presumption of equality, a presumption which is not necessarily borne out in reality."[16] If, as Cheah writes, culture is imagined in an a priori manner as a kind of freedom from the given, then the presumption of equality to which Philip alludes can be translated as: multiculturalism = freedom X multiple cultural times. For Philip, however, it is precisely this *positive* endorsement of culturalism (rather than a negative use of it as a way to point up the differences that have been suppressed from normative reality) that is symptomatic of a certain blindness toward those inequalities that remain in the midst of multicultural enlightenment.[17] Chief of such inequalities is racism. Also addressing the situation of Canada, Philip writes:

> In short, multiculturalism, as we know it, has no answers for the problems of racism, or white supremacy — unless it is combined with a clearly

> articulated policy of anti-racism, directed at rooting out the effects of racist and white supremacist thinking.[18]
>
> However, unless it is steeped in a clearly articulated policy of anti-racism, multiculturalism will, at best, merely continue as a mechanism whereby immigrants indulge their nostalgic love for their mother countries.
>
> At worst, it will, as it sometimes does, unwittingly perpetuate racism by muddying waters between anti-racism and multiculturalism. It is not uncommon to read material from various government departments that use these words interchangeably so as to suggest that multiculturalism is synonymous with anti-racism. It is not. It never will be.[19]

In a different but comparable argument to Kamboureli's and Philip's, Philip Deloria has proposed, through his work on Native American culture, that multiculturalism, by assuming that identity is by choice and consent, is simply fraudulent.[20] As ethnic identities become part of a commodified global culture — a phenomenon Deloria demonstrates with the many forms of "playing Indian" in American and world history — there also remains an entrenched hostility toward those ethnics — often dispossessed, dislocated migrants — who are poverty-stricken.[21]

Let me sum up the points I have made so far in this brief discussion. First, poststructuralist theory has made a crucial contribution toward undoing the deadlock in signification by loosening the presumed fixed correspondence between signifier and signified. In terms of signification, difference rather than sameness now becomes the key to a radicalized way of thinking about identity. Second, one of the consequences of theory defined this way is the replication of the dislocated sign in the sociocultural frame of identity formation, so that (the experience of) dislocation per se often becomes valorized or even idealized — as what is different, mobile, contingent, indeterminable, etc. Third, as Pheng Cheah points out, these poststructuralist arguments about identity are, philosophically speaking, traceable to the same tradition in which culture itself is considered definitively as a form of emancipation from the tyranny of the given. Culture, in other words, occupies something of the status of "difference," which is associated with fluidity and movement, and thus with freedom. Obviously, this is not an entirely accurate view of culture, since, far from being essentially emancipatory, culture often also partakes of the constraints, oppressions, and inequalities of the given. Fourth, from this we may understand why culture in the plural — as multiple forms of differences, as cultural diversity, as multiculturalism — is fraught with unresolved tensions such as those of racism (inequality between different racial and/or ethnic groups) and class discrimination (inequality between groups of the same racial/ethnic background as well as between groups of different racial/ethnic backgrounds). In other words, once transposed into sociocultural and/or geopolitical terrains, the poststructuralist specialization in difference, a revolution on its own terms, appears quite inadequate in accounting for how the purportedly liberating movements of difference and hybridity can and do become hierarchically organized as signs of minoritization and inferiority in various contemporary world situations.

Ethnicity, Temporality, and Writing

What the foregoing indicates is that there is a certain rift between the laudable theorizations of difference, on the one hand, and the numerous sociocultural and/or geopolitical situations in which difference has led not so much to emancipation as it has to oppression. This rift — this incommensurability between what are, to my mind, equally compelling arguments about difference — is the key problem for any ethically responsible discussion of the politics of ethnicity today, and one ought not to think that a solution can be had simply by choosing one over the other. It would be more instructive to let the rift stand as a reminder of the ineluctable, overdetermined complexities which are at hand.

While I do agree with Cheah, Kamboureli, Philip, and Deloria in their persuasive critiques of the contemporary theoretical and/or institutional espousals of liberated culturalisms, I would also propose that something more must be at stake because of the strong sense of discomfort they express toward such espousals. This something more needs, ultimately, to be grasped in terms of the politics of *writing* — and in particular the politics of writing about ethnic and multicultural identities in our post-civil-rights age. To put it in a different manner, one of the things that has surfaced prominently in the relevant debates is not cultural difference or ethnic diversity per se but rather a distinctive *affective* dissonance between theoretical writing, on the one hand, and fictional and autobiographical writing, on the other. It is, I believe, to this affective dissonance, which marks many plaintive responses to the euphoria about hybridity and multiculturalism theory, that we should be devoting more attention. For this reason, it is not sufficient simply to criticize theorists for ignoring the realities of cultural difference; it is more important perhaps to recognize that theoretical discourse itself, however attuned it may be to such realities, is always subject to its own discursive limit of rationalism and abstraction — a limit which translates into a necessary distance from the experiences being alluded to — in such a manner as to neutralize precisely the very emotional effects of injustice that persist as the remnants of lived experience. When critics protest against (poststructuralist) theory's inadequacy, they are implicitly alluding to these remnants of lived experience; consequently, it is also to the rift, the incommensurability, between theoretical and nontheoretical writing as such that they are unwittingly pointing.

Such dissonance may be further defined in terms of the difference between a conceptual, declarative mode of speech, and an experiential, suggestive one. While the former, by its very operation, tends to be forward looking — since the declarative enunciates by projecting ahead — the latter tends instead to double back on experiences that are felt to be not quite finished, whose effects are still with us, haunting us, and waiting for some kind of articulation, however incomplete. The difference between these two modes of speaking, expressed in this manner, is also a *temporal* disjunction, but this is not so much a disjunction simply among the future, the present, and the past, as it is a matter of producing different — perhaps irreconcilable — *values* through relations to time, so that time may be in the form of anticipation, of looking ahead, or in the form of memory, of revisiting in yet another way what has become past. With the foregrounding of time and value in writing, Cheah's point that hybridity theorists tend to associate hybridity with *freedom* can now be restated in this manner: freedom, as implied in the difference-revolution and in hybridity theories, is the futurist, anticipatory mode of speech. Creative writers, on the other hand, tend to go in a different temporal direction because their mode of speech is derived from looking backward even as they are propelled forward in time: it is life remembered but explored in language as though it were lived and grasped for the first time that constitutes the libidinal force of such writing. When the subject matter involved is of the nature of injustice — such as the very controversial issues of ethnicity, cultural diversity, and racism — these fundamental discursive incommensurabilities in time (and its value production) simply become critical.

Such incommensurabilities at the level of writing regarding a similar set of social situations cannot exactly be characterized as a new problem. The closest parallel to our current concern is the well-known discussion in Marxist theory about literary writing and aesthetic representation — indeed, about the entire issue of reflection itself.[22] Albeit theoretically forward-looking, Marx and Engels, we remember, were careful to advise writers who solicited their opinions not to turn literature into socialist propaganda in which fictional characters simply become mouthpieces for revolutionary doctrines. "[T]he solution of the problem," writes Engels, "must become manifest from the situation and the action themselves without being expressly pointed out and . . . the author is not obliged to serve the reader on a platter the future historical resolution of the social conflicts which he describes."[23] Embedded in these discussions is an astute sense that theoretical and literary discourses are distinguished by an essential articulatory difference, and that literary discourse, which specializes in indirection, can only become dull and mediocre should one turn it into a platform for direct proletarian pronouncements. Even where the subject matter cries out for justice to be done, literary writing tends to accomplish its task more effectively when it does not explicitly solicit the reader's sympathy as such. In literature, the modus operandi is not to speak about something expressly even when one feels one must — in a way quite opposite the clarity and forthrightness of theoretical argumentation. "The more the opinions of the author remain hidden, the better for the work of art"[24]: a very different kind of power for producing change, in other words, is in play. As David Craig puts it in a nutshell:

> Surely, if literature affects action or changes someone's life, it is not by handing out a recipe for the applying but rather by disturbing us emotionally, mentally, because it *finds* us . . ., so that, after a series of such experiences and along with others that work in with it, we feel an urge to "do something" or at least to ask ourselves the question (the great question put by Chernyshevsky, Lenin, and Silone): "What is to be done?"[25]

These are, of course, old and well-debated issues having to do with the politics of representation. My point in introducing them is not really to repeat arguments that many others have made before about the literary and nonliterary as such, but rather to bring the gist of such arguments to bear on the politics of writing about ethnicity. For the problem of ethnicity is precisely the kind of issue of social liminality — much like that of the working class in nineteenth-century Europe — that finds itself both in the forefront of highly politicized and theorized debates, and in the forefront of new ideas about literary writing. Yet because of the limits set by each type of writing, this encounter — and collision — between theory and literature is always a difficult one. Today, with theory occupying a more or less hegemonic, managerial position in the humanities, it is not surprising that discourses about ethnicity constitute one of the places at which criticisms of theory's *oversight* are the strongest and most vociferous.

The incommensurabilities occasioned by hybridity are perhaps best seen in actual cases of authors who have been writing as cultural hybrids. I will turn next to a collection of personal essays edited by Garrett Hongo, *Under Western Eyes*, which offers excellent instances for furthering the discussion of our issues.[26]

Ethnicity, Autobiography, and Narcissism

If hybridity is, as Hall argues, the core of immigrant experience in the New World, and if immigrant writing, as Azade Seyhan points out, is almost exclusively autobiographical in nature,[27] what is the relation between hybridity and autobiography? How is it that a mode of experience which allows theorists an occasion to speak generally and abstractly about difference, hybridity, and freedom, is by contrast always handled by nontheoretical writers in the autobiographical mode, in what seems to be a retreat into the personal; a withdrawal that is, in terms of temporality, a retrospective search, a looking-back through the fragments of history? This discrepancy may be best addressed by turning to what is perhaps the most banal, yet unshakable, issue of writing about ethnicity — the problematic of self-formation, around which hybridity produces important consequences. Hongo's collection interestingly features a variety of autobiographical, personal voices, all of which acknowledge — indeed take as their points of departure — the hybridized historical contexts in which they are speaking. However, instead of a valorization of hybridity itself, what we encounter is rather ambivalence, anger, pain, melancholy, shame, and abjection. How might we elaborate this very different way of inscribing difference and hybridity?

When I taught Hongo's book, at least once I taught it in the context of an undergraduate course on narcissism. My point was to ask my students to see ethnicity and its representation in relation to a set of theoretical issues that were relevant to, but seldom juxtaposed with, them in this pedagogical manner. The vicissitudes of sexuality defined in the broad sense provided a theoretical framework in which my students became able to read the personal essays in terms of the symptoms of a kind of narcissism that was, arguably, central to the cultural self-formation in much of North American ethnic and immigrant writing. Again, it is important to emphasize that my intended focus, in that course as much as in the present essay, is on writing: what kind of writing is possible under the conditions of cultural migration, of ethnicity refracted narcissistically through verbal language?

Contrary to the conventional associations of narcissism as an excessive selfishness, Freud, we recall, defines narcissism as an essential concomitant of life. Rather than a misplaced perversion, narcissism is, he argues, simply the basic instinctual mechanism of self-sustenance — "the libidinal complement to the egoism of the instinct of self-preservation, a measure of which may justifiably be attributed to every living creature."[28] And yet, as in the case of human sexuality in general, things are never as simple as that. Among Freud's extended comments, the most thought provoking is that narcissism is something we have to give up at an early point in our lives. He thus sets up a scenario for the unfolding of an inevitable psychological disorder: albeit essential to the human organism, narcissism is nevertheless something that tends to be blocked — and out of reach. Narcissism, in other words, is constructed by Freud as a lost object, a part of the self that is, somehow, destined to becoming missing. This is the reason, he writes, we tend to be attracted to those who appear narcissistic — who appear somehow not to have been obliged to surrender that precious, intimate relation with the self that we ourselves have been obliged to surrender. As we look with adoration upon such still-narcissistic people, we are unconsciously reliving the part of ourselves that has been sacrificed. Freud's passage goes as follows:

> It seems very evident that one person's narcissism has a great attraction for those others who have renounced part of their own narcissism and are seeking after object-love; the charm of a child lies to a great extent in his narcissism, his self-sufficiency and inaccessibility, just as does the charm of certain animals which seem not to concern themselves about us, such as cats and the large beasts of prey. In literature, indeed, even the great criminal and the humorist compel our interest by the narcissistic self-importance with which they manage to keep at arm's length everything which would diminish the importance of their ego. It is as if we envied them their power of retaining a blissful state of mind — an unassailable libido-position which we ourselves have since abandoned. [29]

If narcissism is, libidinally speaking, about self-preservation, why is it also something we have to give up? What are the factors that extirpate it and what is the cost of this to those who can no longer be healthily narcissistic? Approached in these terms, Freud's conceptualization of narcissism does not simply teach it as a love of the self but rather paves the way for a cultural theory to be formulated as to how even something as fundamental as "self-preservation" is, nonetheless, always mediated and *assailed* by social forces. Because of the likelihood of a conflictual encounter between self and society, narcissism is capable of becoming a disorder. The rest of his essay goes on to argue how *self-regard* — in the visual as well as social senses of the term — is the complicated result of the self's negotiations with the observing collective conscience ("The institution of conscience was at bottom an embodiment, first of parental criticism, and subsequently of that of society"[30]): how we look at ourselves and how much we value ourselves, that is, depends a great deal on our sense of being watched, approved of, and loved by others.

Contemporary ethnic and immigrant writings provide wonderful illuminations for these psychoanalytic questions while at the same time showing up their limitations. An *affective* complaint that surfaces time and again among Asian American writers, for instance, is that there is no corresponding image or reflection — what may be redefined as "regard" — in the culture at large of the truth of Asian American experience: Asian Americans, it is often pointed out, are simply omitted from mainstream representations. To this extent, the phrase "under Western eyes" in the title of Hongo's collection is meant to underscore the preemptive indifference to and vigilant assailing of the ethnic subject by mainstream society at large. Whereas a legalistic response to such a complaint might involve increasing the number of Asian American representations in the media and providing larger quotas for various ethnic groups in major professions, the affective implications of the complaint can only be grasped by way of another type of question: what does this complaint mean *in terms of narcissism*? What is known as marginalization — the lack of proper societal representation, the absence of societal approval — can now be redefined in terms of a narcissistic relation that cannot be developed or, as Freud puts it, has to be forsworn early on. Because of this need (imposed by mainstream society) to abandon one's narcissism, because the love of oneself, a love which is vital, is thus thwarted, every encounter with the social order at large by necessity turns into a painful reminder of this process of suppression and wounding.

At the same time, the Asian American instance goes significantly beyond the parameters set by Freud. As in the case of many of his other works, Freud's analysis here remains confined to a binary opposition between self and society, an opposition which does not apply without problems in the case of the "Asian American" because the narcissism that is thwarted is not necessarily individualistic in nature. Indeed, precisely because "Asian American" (and its equivalents in American society, such as "African American" and "Native American") is construed as a minority culture or minority community which mediates between the single individual and society at large, its status is that of an extra category — one that is neither strictly a private, personal self nor strictly a public society out there which includes everybody. The "self versus society" opposition is no longer sufficient for the purpose of analysis.

If and when the notion of a lost or wounded narcissism — a narcissism that is not allowed to take its course, that has become inaccessible — is felt by an entire group of people, narcissism becomes, arguably, a transindividual issue of attachment and belonging. Would it be possible, therefore, to say that in the complaints about marginalization from Asian American writers, what we witness is the symptom of a perceived narcissistic damage, an aggression that is felt to be directed by American society at large against the "self" that is the "Asian American"? But what is the "Asian American"? Would it not be necessary to locate the loss and wounding of narcissism more specifically at the transindividual level of ethnicity, so as to clarify that what the "Asian American" feels she cannot love is not just any part of her but precisely her "Asian American-ness" — a mark that is not reducible to a single individualized self (because the identity it designates is collective by definition) yet that meanwhile is a fluid, historical sign of difference, something that cannot be positivistically pinned down and categorized once and for all (as a statistical reality) without turning into a cultural stereotype?[31]

At this juncture, representation such as writing becomes an intricate matter. How is the experience of an inaccessible narcissism to be "represented"? How can something that has not, as it were, been allowed to develop, and is therefore not empirically available, be written about? It is at this limit of what is representable — of the need to write "about" something whose existence has nonetheless been placed out of reach — that the tendency to be autobiographical among immigrant writers takes on special significance. For, seen in this light, autobiographical writing is perhaps not simply a straightforward account about oneself but more a symptomatic attempt to (re)gain access to a transindividual narcissism — to grope for a "self-regard" that has not yet existed. If this is indeed the case, then to be autobiographical could be seen as the narcissistic act *par excellence* because it is the act through which it becomes possible, perhaps for the first time, to connect and *compose* oneself, and thus to gain the "self-regard" that seems to be absent all along. Moreover, it is access to such self-regard that might serve to vindicate the group's identity — the elusive yet undeniable something called "Asian Americanness." Pursued along these lines, autobiographical writing returns us to the question of freedom: does ethnic writing, autobiographical in the sense of a cultivation of that self that is ethnically defined, finally make narcissism available, albeit in a belated fashion? Does such belated narcissism lead to freedom, and for whom? What is the relation among ethnic writing, narcissism, and freedom?

Hongo's "Introduction: Culture Wars in Asian America" cogently articulates the ambivalence toward these questions. From the premise of the injustice faced by Asian Americans, Hongo focuses on the issue of what it means to attempt to speak about/against such injustice. It is immediately clear that speaking and writing are not simply and straightforwardly therapeutic or liberating activities. Instead, the writer faces a dilemma. On the one hand,

> it is nearly impossible to ignore issues of representation, white privilege, and freedom of expression when we examine the images of peoples of color authorized by our culture. African Americans, Native Americans, Hispanics, and Asian Americans have long been subject to the power of the stereotype regarding their portrayals in the cultural mainstream.[32]

On the other hand, "To speak *about* a trauma or social prohibition, to speak against silencing, can initiate further acts of trauma, silencing, and prohibition of the speaker."[33] What this means, in the terms of our discussion, is that the pattern of a thwarted narcissism may in fact be perpetrated further precisely through the act of writing, in such a manner as to turn one's relation to the self into self-hatred — or an internalization of the exclusion it experiences from society at large. Hongo uses the traumatic example of the internment of Japanese Americans in the United States during the Second World War to make his point about the vicious circle of entrapment involved in the attempt to be autobiographical:

> When you have to be silent about something as cataclysmic and monumental as the relocation camps were, it tends to govern your

> willingness to live in *any* emotion at all. You feel your exclusion quite acutely. You feel your *difference*, your perception as an outcast *Other* in your society that is hostile to you. And you begin to internalize this hostility as self-hate — the inability to cherish your own inner life, your own social history, your own status as an individual and member of a community. At the level of the unconscious, you begin to perform an internalized silencing of your own perceptions and to rewrite your story according to patterns other than those of your own life. You uphold what is *not you* and live as if your own experiences were of little value. It's kind of a censorship or handicap — an illness.[34]

This "illness" can then become contagious within the ethnic community, turning one member against another through the repeated acts of mutual silencing, internalized oppression, discrediting of others' authenticity, and so forth.

Paradoxically, however, it is in this fraught context of the difficulties of speaking about trauma and injustice under Western eyes — what in the terms of our discussion is already an autobiographical act, an effort to regain access to the self and to ethnic narcissism — that Hongo locates the relevance of the autobiographical *personal essay* as the appropriate genre for what he calls "internal questing".[35] Should not the autobiographical, personal essay thus be thought of as a second-order autobiography, an autobiography that writes about the failure of a narcissism (itself a kind of autobiography) that was, culturally speaking, always already blocked and silenced?

Because the narcissism in question is, as I have been arguing, one that exceeds the boundaries of the individual self, the autobiographical tendency in immigrant writing more often than not takes as its point of reflection the history of the entire group rather than any single individual's life. Indeed, one of the prominent features that link the diverse collection of essays — by men and women authors of Indian, Philipino, Chinese, Japanese, Okinawan, and Vietnamese descent — is the question of heritage, of what is being handed from one generation to the next among immigrants. In his own essay on his grandfather, "Kubota," for instance, Hongo recalls how the old man, having lived through the injustice of the Japanese internment during the Second World War, would, unlike other people, insist on not forgetting that experience but passing it on to his grandson:

> Japanese Americans were busy trying to forget it ever happened and were having a hard enough time building their new lives after "camp." It was as

> if we had no history for four years and the relocation was something unspeakable.
>
> But Kubota would not let it go. In session after session, for months it seemed, he pounded away at his story. . . I was not made yet and he was determined that his stories be part of my making. . . He gave his testimony to me and I held it at first cautiously in my conscience like it was an heirloom too delicate to expose to strangers and anyone outside of the world Kubota made with his words.[36]

While other Japanese Americans choose to silence themselves, for Hongo, ethnicity is a kind of defiled history that demands articulation:

> It was out of this sense of shame and a fear of stigma, I was only beginning to understand, that the Nisei had silenced themselves. And for their children, among whom I grew up, they wanted no heritage, no culture, no contact with a defiled history. I recall the silence very well. The Japanese American children around me were burdened in a way I was not. Their injunction was silence. Mine was to speak.[37]

Other essays in Hongo's collection are similarly written from a sense of ethnic tenacity, an attempt to hold on to something from the transindividual past that is not quite finished. In almost all of them, hence, the point of representation lies in the act of remembering. The loose or casual structure of each piece notwithstanding, these essays typically begin with a memorable incident or series of incidents, which then leads on to the larger question of family, ancestry, and heritage, a question that is often introduced through some object (Lillian Ho Wan), practice (Peter Bacho, Jeanne Wakatsuki Houston, David Low), use of language (Amy Tan, Chang-rae Lee), or personal figures from the past (Chitra Banerjee Divakaruni, Geraldine Kudaka, Li-Young Lee). In those pieces in which there is a visit to the native home, real or imaginary, the idea of home usually becomes the occasion for irresolvable ambivalence (Debra Kang Dean, Geeta Kothari, Nguyen Qúi-Duc). The authors, long displaced from and often never having set foot in these homelands, are self-conscious of their uses of language, appearances, attitudes, and habits; all of which mark them as neither of the "original" place nor of their current "home," North America. Permeating their writings is a strong sense of ontological liminality, of living between cultures, and of being stigmatized themselves or being witnesses to others' stigmatization for precisely that reason.

In the more extreme case depicted by David Mura in his piece "The Internment of Desire," the sense of alienation from mainstream society since childhood becomes a determinant in his sexual formation. Looking at the pornographic images from *Playboy* and fantasizing about white girls dominate his fantasy life. In this way, he becomes obsessed with masturbation, an ultimate narcissistic act, here situated in a context in which it is part of a confused adolescence in a "foreign" land where he feels powerless, and ashamed of being who he is. Interestingly, Mura compares the shame he feels about being trapped in his pornographic desires — a private and individualistic affair — to the collective experience of internment undergone by the Japanese Americans during the Second World War.[38] Shame, he writes, is like the racism that has been internalized by the victimized groups.[39] The fluidity and mutuality perceived between the self and the minority group, across history, makes this intense personal essay especially fascinating to read.

Yet despite the permeability of boundaries between the current self and the distant collective past, that past is not always readily available. Mura compares the fragmented nature of ethnic writing to briocolage: "Like a bricoleur, I must make do with the tools at hand — a few anecdotes from my aunts, some stray remarks from my parents, history books, a few works of literature by Japanese Americans, and my own guesses and intuitions . . .".[40] He also puts this in a different way:

> A Japanese American writer I know says that those of us who come from marginalized cultures are often bequeathed fragments, brief bits of the past, and nothing more. There are no unbroken threads, no fully developed tales or histories. There are too many secrets and occlusions, there are too many reasons to forget the past. And there are forces which do not want us to remember, do not want us to take those fragments and complete them, to restore them to some fuller life.[41]

Contrary to the theorists of hybridity, the writers of these personal essays, all of which are about the experience of actually living as cultural hybrids, offer pictures that are anything but freedom from the given. Instead, hybridity itself, as the cultural given, becomes for these ethnically marked writers a form of existential entrapment; some, as in the case of Mura, would go as far as comparing it to internment, an oppressive condition which does not simply improve with its representation in writing. The act of writing autobiographically in these pieces is much more than being "selfish"; it is simultaneously writing collectively about the inherited, *shared* condition of social stigmatization and abjection.

The Secrets of Ethnic Abjection

In the final piece to the volume, entitled "A Little Memento from the Boys,"[42] John Yau brings this sense of stigmatization and abjection to the crux by narrating the "secret" three ethnically hybrid men deposit on the walls of a woman, Lila, who has hired them to renovate her apartment. From the beginning, the essay is marked by a plenitude of references to bodily elimination — decay, discharge, things being dropped. John and his friends first meet in a crummy, dilapidated bar — suggestively named Mike's Last Dive — and their friendship literally develops, in an ambience filled with smells of urine and disinfectant, when they are on their way to the bathroom:

> Mike's Last Dive was a decaying, turn-of-the-century bar with sawdust on the floor. It had one pool table in the center of its square, high-ceilinged room, like a brightly lit, grass-covered traffic island at night, meandering lines of cars rushing by. There was a long, narrow bathroom that smelled as if grizzled whalers used to line up and piss there. A sweet, sickly smell of disinfectant, urine, cigarettes, and stale beer had soaked into the bathroom's tile walls, tin ceiling, and wooden floor. I always felt like I was pissing in a cold cave or a decrepit refrigerator. . .
>
> Late one night, Johnny, Virgo, and I kept crossing each other's paths on the way to the toilet or, while standing and watching some of the regulars playing pool, we'd look up and see a face looking back, curious. We began checking each other out, circling each other, slowly, like animals in heat.
>
> Why did we begin talking? Well, the obvious reason is that we immediately recognized that we were mongrels, confused children whose parents came from different worlds, which in our cases meant Asia and Europe. *We were what was left after the collision; we were the things they had dropped on the floor.*[43]

It is possible to think of the psychological landscape constructed by Yau in terms of what Julia Kristeva calls the abject — the often culturally tabooed condition of an excessive, rejected being that nonetheless remains a challenge to the body that expels it. Kristeva writes:

> [W]hat is *abject*, . . . the jettisoned object, is radically excluded and draws me toward the place where meaning collapses. . . And yet, from its place of banishment, the abject does not cease challenging its master.
>
> Abject. It is something rejected from which one does not part, from which one does not protect oneself as from an object. Imaginary uncanniness and real threat, it beckons to us and ends up engulfing us.
>
> It is thus not lack of cleanliness or health that causes abjection but what disturbs identity, system, order. What does not respect borders, positions, rules. The in-between, the ambiguous, the composite.[44]

Examples of the abject, as Elizabeth Grosz comments, would be substances such as "tears, saliva, faeces, urine, vomit, mucus," which are "neither simply part of the body nor separate from it." Although "[t]he subject must expel these abjects to establish the 'clean and proper' body of oedipalization," they can "never be expelled, for they remain the preconditions of corporeal, material existence."[45]

In Yau's essay, there is a strong suggestion that ethnic hybridity itself is a form of abjection. The essay's conscious comparison of the lives of these men to things people "had dropped on the floor" is resonant with the feelings of neglect, dismissal, and humiliation that we often encounter in autobiographical accounts of peoples of color living in North American society. Though the perfect embodiments of hybridity — the three men are Japanese, German, English, Chinese, Dutch, and Spanish by heritage — they certainly do not feel their mongrelized status is an advantage. Quite the contrary. The question that arises with their very first descriptions is: what kind of self-representation is being produced? If these men are what was "dropped on the floor" by their parents after their collision, they are neither objects nor subjects of their environment; rather, they exist as abjects, along the fluid line of demarcation, undecidedly both inside and outside, precariously inerasable yet vulnerable. What kind of an autobiography is possible, with abjects?

As the men spend their days and nights telling one another their life stories, the narrator comments, "We live on the poison we secrete, and spend our nights characterizing ourselves in derogatory terms. It is the only defense we know."[46] How is self-deprecation a defense? To defend something is to set up a safe boundary around it, so that it is less likely to be attacked by others. Here, however, the boundary is set up paradoxically through *self*-attack. In this conscious play on the notions of defense and boundary, the slippage of meaning Yau introduces between "secret" and "secrete" is highly evocative.

As we all know, there is nothing intrinsically enigmatic or valuable about secrets. Although a secret may occupy the status of a precious hidden treasure, it may also simply exist as something about which no one knows or cares. In this sense a secret is not unlike what we have been describing as narcissism, a condition whose reality lies both inside and outside in that it is liminally between the need for self-preservation and the need for others' attention, recognition, and respect. Insofar as the details about these men's existences are unknown and ignored by most people, they are secrets; at the same time, because no one cares, their secrets take on the status of precisely that thwarted narcissism which is deprived of self-regard. It is in this manner that narcissism, the secret of the self, turns poisonous: the only defense (self-preservation) of which the men are capable is "characterizing [themselves] in derogatory terms." The inaccessibility of narcissism stands here both as a secret, a hidden inner wound — and as a kind of secretion or discharge outward. In this secretive/secreting state, the hybrid ethnic men become abjection in human form.

So what do the three men do in Lila's apartment? Out of sheer mischief, these men have been searching for the woman's belongings while moving furniture around during their work, and have found a gigantic vibrator under her pillow. They also turn up her diary, which is filled with fantasy confessions of fantasy sex experiences with various men. Stimulated by the exposure of their employer's privacy, John and his friends decide to play a practical joke on her. First, they use the remaining film in her camera to take pictures of each of them posing with the vibrator and ejaculating into the remaining can of paint (the camera with the film in it is afterwards left behind in the apartment); then they use the paint, now mixed with their semen, to finish their job on her walls.

Understandably, some readers will find the ejaculators violent and exploitative of the space belonging to a woman. Indeed, leaving their semen on her walls in the manner they do can be seen as a metaphor for gang rape, as if the woman whose own sexual secret has been exposed must also be subjected to the collective mockery, defilement, and defacement by a group of men. This, of course, is another reason the story is disturbing: the victims of social marginalization, the very recipients of social dismissal, we are made to realize, tend to become themselves perpetrators of violence against a more or less innocent person. The crux, though, lies in the fact that, when the victimized insist willfully on being recognized, such insistence is often perceived as a violent *act.* It is as if the very bodies that are normally rejected — whose secrets are considered mere shit — must implode from within a society's boundary between what it wants and what it does not want, with a secretive secretion that is, literally, "in your face" (walls being, after all, faces).

By playing on the affinities between the secret (as what is unknown and unrecognized, and therefore confined within), and secretion (as what is discharged outside into the public realm), Yau has crafted a thought-provoking essay on the ineluctable nature of the violence involved in ethnic Americans' negotiations with their historical situations. Ostensibly, this violence is the violence of boundaries-breaking, as evidenced in the three men's transgressive ejaculation and writing on the wall; but it is, upon closer reflection, also the violence of *boundaries-making* — the violence that is built into the division, categorization, and classification of peoples by way of race and ethnic differences; the violence that is responsible for these men's exclusion in the first place. It is the latter, that is, the enforcement of a certain kind of secret inside as society proper (a space unreachable for those without permission), that simultaneously requires the exclusion and discharge of those "improper" others who then become society's secret-ion, that is the focus of Yau's implied critique.

In the woman's apartment, then, these men stumble upon an opportunity to make their secrets/secretions part of a permanent display, part of the new (sur)face of her walls. Much as this collective act itself once again turns into another secret — the secretion permanently frozen on the wall, staring at the woman in a way unbeknownst to her until, perhaps, she develops the film they leave behind — it has also acquired the status of writing, both in the sense of the semen being a kind of writing on the wall and in the sense of the personal account that will eventually be read by Yau's readers. In this manner, Yau brings together the multiple forms of violence which constitute the narcissistic negotiations of identity in a society not yet capable of understanding racial and/or ethnic otherness except by rendering such otherness in terms of class. And class is reinforced precisely through the images of waste matter, of secret-ions to which no one cares to pay attention. Contrary to the fashionable sentimentalism attached to racial and ethnic otherness as some kind of exotic difference, Yau gives us instead a stark portrayal of such otherness as something lethal — and the first one to become poisoned, his tale tells us, is the bearer himself.

Does the writing on the wall, the permanent inscription of the secrets of ethnic abjection in someone else's space, accomplish anything for the men apart from being a wicked joke at someone else's expense? Does the expression with semen amount to any kind of freedom through representation? Yau's ending does not so much give an affirmative answer as it repeats the plaint of ethnic voices wanting to be heard. The wish for recognition, that social response that makes narcissism available to the self, persists because it is not yet fulfilled:

> Hey, Lila, there's three mongrels out there, somewhere in America, who have drifted into different orbits. But they still have one thing in common, their sperm mixed in the paint covering your walls.
>
> Hey, Lila, it's okay if you went out and hired someone to paint them over. It's even okay if your walls are now blue or pink or gray, because the sperm is still there, beneath whatever you have done. . .
>
> [W]ishing a person or a thing was never born, that's why Johnny, Virgo, and I did what we did. We wanted a different kind of diary, one that was written permanently on a wall where everybody could read it. It's why we took the pictures. We wanted someone to know who and what we had been.[47]

In this desperate cry for a self-regard that seems forever out of reach, the autobiographical act remains haunted by and trapped within the given of abject hybridity — of hybridity as abjection. "We wanted someone to know who and what we had been": despite being full-bodied personifications of difference, global migranthood, multiculturalism, and nomadism, these ethnic figures have yet to succeed in setting themselves free.

ENDNOTES

1 Ferdinand de Saussure, *Course in General Linguistics,* intro. Jonathan Culler, ed. Charles Bally and Albert Sechehaye in collaboration with Albert Reidlinger, trans. Wade Baskin (Glasgow: Collins, 1974),120, 122. Emphases in the original.

2 Stuart Hall, "Cultural Identity and Diaspora," in *Colonial Discourse and Post-Colonial Theory: A Reader,* ed. and intro. Patrick Williams and Laura Chrisman (New York: Columbia University Press, 1994), 393–394. This essay was originally published in *Identity: Community, Culture, Difference,* ed. J. Rutherford (London: Lawrence and Wishart, 1990), 222–237. For other examples of poststructuralist discussions of identity, see *The Identity in Question,* ed. and with an intro. by John Rajchman (New York: Routledge, 1995) and *Displacements: Cultural Identities in Question,* ed. Angelika Bammer (Bloomington: Indiana University Press, 1994).

[3] Hall, "Identity and Diaspora," 400.
[4] Ibid., 401.
[5] Ibid., 402.
[6] See, for instance, the essays on Hall's work in *Stuart Hall: Critical Dialogues in Cultural Studies*, ed. David Morley and Kuan-hsing Chen (New York: Routledge, 1996).
[7] A typical example of this tendency is found in this statement from the call for papers for the *Publications of the Modern Language Association of America* (*PMLA*) special issue "Mobile Citizens, Media States": "As national borders become increasingly problematic in an era of global media culture, categories of citizenship and local forms of identity are becoming more mobile, nomadic, and hybrid." *PMLA* 114, no. 5 (October 1999), "Special Topic" page.
[8] Pheng Cheah, "Given Culture: Rethinking Cosmopolitical Freedom in Transnationalism," *boundary 2* 24, no. 2 (Summer 1997): 160. Cheah's essay can also be found in *Cosmopolitics: Thinking and Feeling beyond the Nation*, ed. Pheng Cheah and Bruce Robbins (Minneapolis: University of Minnesota Press, 1998).
[9] Cheah, "Given Culture," 167.
[10] Ibid., 168.
[11] Ibid., 172.
[12] Ibid., 172.
[13] For this reason, David Palumbo-Liu argues (in an essay about the politics of canonizing ethnic literature in American literary studies) that it is necessary to pursue a "critical multiculturalism" — one that is alert to the social problems masked by the liberalist celebration of diversity. See his "Introduction," in *The Ethnic Canon: Histories, Institutions, and Interventions*, ed. David Palumbo-Liu (Minneapolis and London: University of Minnesota Press, 1995), 1–27.
[14] Smaro Kamboureli, *Scandalous Bodies: Diasporic Literature in English Canada* (Oxford University Press, 1999), 82.
[15] For a comparable argument, see Lisa Lowe's critique of how the North American university itself perpetuates the contradiction of protecting Western cultural study "as a largely autonomous domain" while "'democratizing' the institution only to the extent that it addresses the needs of an increasingly heterogeneous student population through the development of business, engineering, technical, and other professionalizing programs." Lowe's point is that multiculturalism institutionalized in this manner is simply serving the interests of the capitalist market economy. "Canon, Institutionalization, Identity: Contradictions for Asian American Studies," *The Ethnic Canon*, 50.
[16] M. Nourbese Philip, *Frontiers: Essays and Writings on Racism and Culture* (Stratford: The Mercury Press, 1992), 181.
[17] See Kamboureli for a similar critique of the work of Linda Hutcheon, pp. 162–174. "[M]aking room for [other] voices [to be heard]," she writes, "does nothing to change their minority positions" (171).
[18] Phillip, *Frontiers*, 185.
[19] Ibid., 186.
[20] Philip Deloria, *Playing Indian* (New Haven: Yale University Press, 1998), 173.

[21] The case of illegal immigrants from mainland China in western Canada is a good case in point. Among those who speak up most loudly against these immigrants in Vancouver, according to a report in the *New York Times* (29 August 1999, Y6), are wealthy Chinese immigrants who are well established and leading a comfortably settled life in the city.

[22] For useful discussions of the problematic of (aesthetic) reflection in Marxist theory, see, for instance, Pierre Macherey, *A Theory of Literary Production*, trans. Geoffrey Wall (London: Routledge and Kegan Paul, 1978); Terry Eagleton, *Criticism and Ideology* (London: Verso, 1978). For related discussions, see Henri Arvon, *Marxist Esthetics*, trans. Helen R. Lane, intro. Fredric Jameson (Ithaca and London: Cornell University Press, 1973); *Marxism and Art: Essays Classic and Contemporary*, selected and with historical and critical commentary by Maynard Solomon (New York: Knopf, 1973); and Theodor Adorno, Walter Benjamin, Ernst Bloch, Bertolt Brecht, and Georg Lukács, *Aesthetics and Politics*, afterword by Fredric Jameson, translation ed. Ronald Taylor (London: Verso, 1980); as well as the essays collected in *Marxists on Literature: An Anthology*, ed. David Craig (Penguin 1975).

[23] Friedrich Engels, "Letter to Minna Kautsky," in *Marxists on Literature*, 268. See also chapters 8, 9 (Marx's and Engels' letters to Lasalle), and 13 (Engels' letter to Margaret Harkness), all reprinted from Marx and Engels, *Selected Correspondence* (Moscow, n.d.).

[24] Engels, "Letter to Margaret Harkness," in *Marxists on Literature*, 270.

[25] David Craig, "Introduction," *Marxists on Literature*, 22. Emphasis in the original.

[26] *Under Western Eyes: Personal Essays from Asian America*, ed. and with an intro. by Garrett Hongo (New York: Doubleday Anchor, 1995).

[27] "Modern immigrant writing is almost exclusively autobiographical in nature. It defies and redefines the boundaries of the genre." Azade Seyhan, "Ethnic Selves/Ethnic Signs: Invention of Self, Space, and Genealogy in Immigrant Writing," in *Culture/Contexture: Explorations in Anthropology and Literary Studies*, ed. E. Valentine Daniel and Jeffrey M. Peck (Berkeley: University of California Press, 1996), 180.

[28] Sigmund Freud, "On Narcissism: An Introduction," in *A General Selection from the Works of Sigmund Freud*, ed. John Rickman, M.D., appendix by Charles Brenner, M.D. (New York: Doubleday Anchor, 1957), 105.

[29] Ibid., 113.

[30] Ibid., 118.

[31] "The term [Asian American] is inherently elastic and of fairly recent currency . . . It carries within it layers of historical sedimentation. Not merely a denotative label with a fixed, extralinguistic referent, it is a sign, a site of contestation for a multitude of political and cultural forces." Sau-ling Cynthia Wong, *Reading Asian American Literature: From Necessity to Extravagance* (Princeton: Princeton University Press, 1993), 5. Wong offers a useful summary account of the legalist definitions and ramifications of the term in recent United States history. Similarly, David Palumbo-Liu writes that "as it at once implies *both* exclusion and inclusion, 'Asian/American' marks both the distinction installed between 'Asian' and 'American' *and* a dynamic, unsettled, and inclusive movement" (*Asian/American: Historical Crossings of A Racial Frontier*

[Stanford: Stanford University Press, 1999], 1; emphases in the original). For related discussions, see also Elaine H. Kim, *Asian American Literature: An Introduction to the Writings and Their Social Context* (Philadelphia: Temple University Press, 1982); Sucheng Chan, *Asian Americans: An Interpretive History* (Boston: Twayne, 1991); *Reading the Literatures of Asian America*, ed. Shirley Geok-lin Lim and Amy Ling (Philadelphia: Temple University Press, 1992); Sheng-mei Ma, *Immigrant Subjectivities in Asian American and Asian Diaspora Literatures* (Albany: State University of New York Press, 1998).

32 Hongo, *Under Western Eyes*, 5.

33 Ibid., 8. Emphasis in the original.

34 Ibid., 10. Emphases in the original.

35 Ibid., 25.

36 Ibid., 118.

37 Ibid., 120.

38 David Mura, "The Internment of Desire," in Hongo, *Under Western Eyes*, 289–291.

39 Ibid., 281.

40 Ibid., 292–293.

41 Ibid., 193

42 John Yau, "A Little Memento From the Boys," in Hongo, *Under Western Eyes*, 321–332.

43 Ibid., 323–324; my emphasis.

44 Julia Kristeva, *Powers of Horror: An Essay on Abjection*, trans. Leon S. Roudiez (New York: Columbia University Press, 1982), 2 (emphasis in the original), 4.

45 Elizabeth Grosz, "Julia Kristeva," *Feminism and Psychoanalysis: A Critical Dictionary*, ed. Elizabeth Wright (Oxford: Blackwell, 1992), 198.

46 Yau, "A Little Memento," 325.

47 Ibid., 332.

Guests of the Nation: Ireland, Immigration, and Post-Colonial Solidarity

Luke Gibbons

> One can only reach out into the universe with a gloved hand, and that glove is one's nation, the only thing one knows even a little of . . .
>
> — W. B. Yeats, *Letters to a New Island*

> Just as friendship...need not be the only reason of someone who goes to the aid of a friend, so a commitment to compatriots, fellow citizens or other locally specific communities does not have to exclude more general humanitarian concern.
>
> — Norman Geras, *Solidarity in the Conversation of Mankind.*

The recent (1999) controversy surrounding the suspension of a prominent Gaelic footballer from the Irish "compromise rules" football team in Australia for a racist slur directed at a young Australian player raises important questions about perceptions of racism and cultural diversity in Irish culture. The obscene remark was followed by an apology after the game which was accepted by the aggrieved player. Though the incident did make the Australian press — a six paragraph story in the Melbourne *The Age* — this paled by comparison with the blanket coverage in the Irish media, leading to a trenchant editorial in *The Sunday Tribune,* denouncing the original incident but reserving even more scathing criticism for the handling of the episode by the team management.

The *Tribune* editorial placed the incident against the wider backdrop of the emergence of a new racism in Ireland as the Irish economy, straddling the "Celtic Tiger," has begun to attract migrants, refugees, and asylum seekers to a society noted more for its chronic emigration than immigration in the past:

> Racism is not regarded as a major problem in Ireland. An empty cliché, that has often been boasted, is that the Irish are the least racist people in the world, especially as they have been on the receiving end of it themselves and realize the danger and unfairness of being targeted on account of ethnic origin. But such complacency is misplaced.[1]

In support of its warning, the editorial cites the record of the Irish overseas: "Despite suffering from racial prejudice themselves, some of the Irish who emigrated have developed a reputation for racism and intolerance of other colours."[2] Similar arguments have surfaced in the expanding literature on the need for greater vigilance against the growing threat of racial and cultural intolerance in Ireland. In a statement issued by the Irish National Teachers Organization, the whole myth of "Ireland of the Welcomes," so cherished by the tourist board, is thrown into question by the new stirrings of racism:

> Racism. An invisible scourge. Can we adapt at home to what we did abroad for centuries? On a pro rata basis more Irish people have settled abroad in other countries than almost any other race of people.... They were resented, except by their own, and struggled to find work and achieve an acceptable standard of living. Even today we still feel angry when we hear of the "No Irish need apply" type of attitude they faced all those years ago, alone and afraid in a foreign country.... Ireland today has a small influx of immigrants and refugees each year. Many of them are from countries to which we sent missionaries and aid workers over the years. We are proud of that. We were also proud when Irish people were the highest per capita contributors to "Live Aid"...
>
> [The new wave of immigrants] will be from another culture, they may speak with a strange accent or their English may be poor. They may have a different skin colour.... Remember these were our great great grandparents arriving in North America from Irish Gaeltachts and Galltachts more than a century ago. [3]

These statements are made in the context of a recent increase in the number of immigrants from Eastern Europe and Africa seeking asylum in Ireland, rising from 39 in 1992 to a total of almost 17,000 by 1999.[4] What is of interest for the present discussion is the particular historical inflection given to the arguments against racism or intolerance, and the way relations drawn between attitudes to immigrants at home stress both the treatment of the Irish diaspora and the sympathetic responses to the plight of developing countries overseas shown by Irish people in the past. Though embracing conceptions of human rights, as in UN charters or declarations of the rights of man, expressions of solidarity with other cultures are not couched in abstract, ahistorical terms. Instead, the recourse to universality draws on Ireland's colonial past, attempting to establish cross-cultural sympathies through a shared history of discrimination or oppression. It is my contention that universality is not compromised, but may even be enhanced by such a politics of location, speaking from one's particular position in place and time. As Clifford Geertz has expressed it: "Men's most importune claims to humanity are cast in the accents of group pride."[5]

That this "cultural cosmopolitanism,"[6] deriving from the specificities of one's local or national identity, is not simply a matter of empty gestures or pious aspirations towards an ideal of solidarity that remains unworkable in practice is clear from its formative role in Irish foreign policy, particularly during the brief phase of the Cold War in which Ireland, as a nonaligned nation, exerted an influence at the United Nations out of all proportion to its size. This was during a major period of decolonization in the late 1950s and early 1960s when Western powers, and many of the principles of the Enlightenment which were considered to have legitimized Western expansion were all but discredited in the eyes of those breaking free from colonial rule. Ireland's pursuit of an independent, activist stance, outside both the Anglo-American and Soviet axis, ensured that it was one of the few Western countries to gain credibility with the newly emergent nations. To this end, it took the lead among Western opponents of apartheid in South Africa, and was also to the forefront in defending small nations invaded by more powerful neighbours (such as Egypt, Hungary, Tibet, and Tunisia); in attacking the disastrous recourse to partition in Cyprus, Korea, Vietnam, Germany, West New Guinea, and Algeria; and in mediating disputes in Kashmir, Somaliland, South Tyrol and the Belgian Congo.

Ireland's most controversial stance — at least where American interests were concerned — took place in 1957 when it endorsed an Afro-Asian motion, proposed by India, to lift the embargo on discussing the admittance of China to the UN. This led to a vehement backlash by Cabot Lodge, John Foster Dulles, and other cold warriors at the UN, which extended to their urging the Vatican, and Cardinal Cushing of New York, to twist the arm of the Irish delegation. Had they been more aware of the contingencies of Irish history, they would have realized that Frank Aiken, the Irish Foreign Minister, had been excommunicated by the Catholic church for IRA activities during the Civil War, and was singularly immune to such blackmail. Moreover, it was precisely such an historical awareness which informed the concept of human rights invoked by Aiken to justify Ireland's stance at the General Assembly. Referring to its "historical memory" of domination by a foreign power, he explained that this was:

> a memory which gives us a sense of brotherhood with the newly emerging peoples of today, a memory which makes it impossible for any representative of Ireland to withhold support for racial, religious, national or economic rights in any part of the world, in South Africa or Tibet, in Algeria or Korea, in [Egypt] or Hungary. We stand unequivocally for the swift and orderly ending of colonial rule and other forms of foreign domination.[7]

As I shall attempt to show, though this localized, historical approach offers a viable way of negotiating human rights from a postcolonial or even a wider cultural perspective, it was not considered a valid basis for international or global solidarity by the dominant Western strands in Enlightenment thought. Notwithstanding their political differences, the French, American, and German Enlightenments were agreed in divesting "rights" of their specific cultural or historical settings, recasting them in terms of abstract conceptions of the presocial "individual," or a common "human nature." This was the basis for the new model of the cosmopolitan citizen, freed from the encumbrances of time and place, and subscribing instead to the higher ideals of progress and universal reason required to make the transition to modernity. By contrast, historical grievances and the experience of oppression were relegated to the backward look of romanticism or cultural nationalism, becoming manifest in the "romantic agony" of the losers of history. "Nobody can suppose," wrote the great apostle of liberalism, John Stuart Mill, "that it is not more beneficial to a Breton, or a Basque" to be assimilated into advanced French forms of civilization:

> than to sulk on his own rocks, the half savage relic of past times, revolving in his own little mental orbit, without participation or interest in the general

> movement of the world. The same remark applies to the Welshman or Scottish Highlander as members of the British nation.[8]

For Mill, the injustices of the past have no claim upon the present, being part of the cost of progress, the collateral damage of the civilizing process. Hence the pathos of the dying Gaul, the last of the Mohicans, or the melancholia of the insular Celts, cut adrift from the onward course of history. These nostalgic narratives are perhaps tinged with a grudging respect and even pity for "the last of the race,"[9] but what is not always recognized is how much the discourse of universal human rights, with its attempt to transform the native into a citizen of the world, is often responsible for legitimizing "ethnocide" in the name of progress, and bestowing on "primitive" or undeveloped societies the benefits of modernity. This, perhaps more than any other factor, was responsible for discrediting the civilizing mission of the Enlightenment in the eyes of those on the receiving end of colonialism. Thus, for example, as early as the French Revolution, the association of traditional peasant cultures and regional diversity with counter-revolution led to the outlawing and extermination of the culture of half the population in France: Bretons, Basques, Alsatians, Flemings, and other local cultures. As Patrice Higonnet describes the Jacobins' policy towards cultural minorities:

> By 1793, however, when they set as their goal the enforcement of their universalist point of view, they rejected dialects. On June 4, 1794, Gregoire spoke of the 'needs and means to wipe [dialects] out '... and by 1794, Saint Just had come to entertain visions of linguistic if not ethnic cleansing. German speakers from Alsace would be resettled in central France, while Alsace would be Frenchified. Alsatian villages would be renamed for soldiers who had died at the front.[10]

Mill's recipe for the Bretons is simply a more sophisticated version of this, and its contemporary intellectual equivalent may be found in the myth of the "counter-Enlightenment" fostered by Isaiah Berlin, Eric Hobsbawm, Ernest Gellner, Michael Ignatieff, and others, who discern in romanticism, and its political cognate, cultural nationalism, the pathologies of atavism and savagery which the eighteenth century projected onto "primitive" societies. The possibility that genocide and ethnic cleansing may have as much to do with modernity and progress, with what Zygmunt Bauman has described as "the mass industrialization of death" refined in the twentieth century,[11] eludes this comforting version of the civilizing process, of a benign Enlightenment without tears.

"Supporting One's Local Sheriff": Rorty and Postmodern Patriotism

> To advocate cosmopolitanism is not to deprive a culture of its right to be understood on its own terms and its need to resist other cultures from which it distinguishes itself.
>
> — Anindita Niyogi Balslev to Richard Rorty, *Cultural Otherness*

Partly in response to such antinomies of Western liberalism, attempts have been made in recent decades to challenge the inflexible universal sweep of Enlightenment ethics, and to work out new conceptions of rights and justice more sensitive to the contingencies of culture and society. Among the most prominent challenges to the grand narratives of human emancipation espoused by the classic Enlightenment is Richard Rorty's critique of Kantian ethics (and, by extension, its Rawlsian or left-wing Habermasian versions), based on a postmodern variant of American pragmatism. Rorty's suave civility draws on a neglected current in liberal thought that escapes many of the strictures of the postmodern avantgarde such as Foucault and Lyotard,[12] that adumbrated by the Scottish Enlightenment which grounds ethics in the somatic self, and the social relations of sympathy and solidarity. According to Rorty, the desire to ground a universal morality in a shared human attribute such as "rationality," which distinguishes humanity from animals, is fundamentally misguided, all the more so as it derives part of its popularity from "Kant's astonishing claim that sentiment has nothing to do with morality, that there is something distinctively and transculturally human called 'the sense of moral obligation' which has nothing to do with love, friendship, trust or social solidarity." The basis of morality for Rorty lies in what might be properly termed "sentimental education," in which notions of rights:

> are not a matter of sharing a deep true self which instantiates true humanity, but are such little, superficial, similarities as cherishing our parents and our children — similarities that do not interestingly distinguish us from many nonhuman animals.[13]

Or as he puts it elsewhere: "The difference between an appeal to end suffering and an appeal to rights is the difference between an appeal to fraternity, to fellow-feeling, to sympathetic concern, and an appeal that exists independently from anybody's feelings about anything — something that issues unconditional commands."[14]

In arguing thus, Rorty is developing a powerful strand of the eighteenth century Scottish Enlightenment, with its influential dictum, promulgated by David Hume, that "reason is slave of the passions." Setting out to replace the sovereignty of reason by the "man of feeling," Hume, Adam Smith, and others helped to promote the cult of sensibility, and its attendant ethics of sympathy and "fellow-feeling," which swept the Anglo-American world and Europe in the eighteenth century. Sentiments and moral sentiments became the new connective tissue in a civil society characterized by commerce and possessive individualism rather than traditional customary or communal bonds. In this sense, the epithet "imagined community" which Benedict Anderson uses to describe the sense of nationhood generated by print culture might more accurately be seen as a "sentimental community," extending from sympathetic ties and shared identifications with characters and events in novels, newspapers, and other popular forms to wider national narratives promulgated by public culture.[15] However, the main difficulty with this alternative to the cerebral ethics of universalism, as Rorty's enthusiastic embrace of American patriotism and loyalty to "Old Glory" shows, is that it ends up as a case of supporting your local sheriff.[16] In its classic formulations, sympathy turns on resemblance and similarity, on what we have in common with each other, and thus implicitly presupposes a shared culture, region or nationality. As John Stuart Mill saw it, the remit of "fellow-feeling" only extends to a homogeneous national culture, and is in fact corrupted by any expression of cultural difference:

> Free institutions are next to impossible in a country made up of different nationalities. Among a people without fellow feeling, especially if they read and speak different languages, the united public opinion, necessary to the working of representative government, cannot exist.[17]

For Rorty, these sentiments are evinced by the concern we show for family and kin, extending to local allegiances and, particularly in times of adversity, to patriotism and national solidarity. It is clear that by patriotism here, Rorty has in mind the kind of civic nationalism developed in American political culture, or what he euphemistically refers to as the "lucky" nations of the West. But this leaves cultural nationalism — the sense of belonging acquired through race, ethnicity, or history itself — out of the equation. While Rorty is willing to ascribe ethical aspirations to its urbane civic counterpart, as exemplified by the assimilating ethic of American identity, he is less willing to grant them to the cultures that *are to be* assimilated — the ethnic ingredients of the melting pot — whether they be American first peoples, African-Americans, Asian-Americans, Mexicans, Hispanic cultures, Jews, Irish, Italians, or other minorities. These are the kind of embedded identities that have to be sifted through the "ironic solidarity" or "transcendental" narrative of American-ness before they emerge on the other side as capable of participating in civic culture, or in the everyday transactions of the public sphere.[18] Solidarity on ethnic lines in diasporic cultures, considered from this point of view, might be seen as having a temporal or ancestral dimension, involving a problematic long-distance affiliation with the homeland which militates against successful integration into the modernity of the host culture. The persistence of refractory cultural difference along similar lines on a world scale may also be seen as obstructing the spread of ironic solidarity in its American mode — the highest stage of civilization, if only from lack of alternative — at a global level.

The implications of this are evident in Rorty's discussion of the profound economic inequalities in American culture — "the unending hopelessness and misery of the lives of the young blacks in American cities" — which prompts him to ask:

> Do we say that these people must be helped because they are our fellow human beings? We may, but it is much more persuasive, morally as well as politically, to describe them as our fellow *Americans* — to insist that it is outrageous that an *American* should live without hope. The point of these examples is that our sense of solidarity is strongest when those with whom solidarity is expressed are thought of as 'one of us', where 'us' means something smaller and more local than the human race.[19]

The most striking aspect of this denunciation of poverty is the elision of race, the fact that blacks are oppressed, not in terms of their nationality but by virtue of their cultural specificity *as blacks.* The reason for this omission is clear: Rorty is intent on establishing some kind of higher ground to maintain sameness, as against more manifest racial or religious differences. But why should solidarity, national or otherwise, depend on such thoroughgoing sameness? Though he makes a case for extending the boundaries of sameness into ever increasing circles abroad — "creating an ever larger and more variegated *ethnos*"[20] — it is difficult, as Bruce Robbins point out, to envisage what form this imagined global solidarity might take beyond existing national or patriotic boundaries.[21] If sympathizing with blacks at home requires an overarching American-ness, then it is likely that only those "others" overseas who behave like Americans will also attract similar benign attention: an argument, in fact, for recreating the world in the image of America through foreign policy and cultural expansionism. According to Rorty, civic solidarity may be:

> thought of as the ability to see more and more traditional differences (of tribe, religion, race, customs, and the like) as unimportant when compared with similarities with respect to pain and humiliation — the ability to think of people wildly different from ourselves as included in the range of 'us'.[22]

It is somewhat ironic, as we shall see below, that "humiliation" is brought under the auspices of sameness and physical pain in this passage, for this is, in effect, reintroducing the very concepts of "human nature" and universalism which Rorty claims to have obviated in his ethical and political theory. Rorty identifies a key aspect of humiliation when he writes that "the best way to cause people long-lasting pain is to humiliate them by making the things that seemed most important to them look futile, obsolete and powerless," but fails to acknowledge that this may often consist precisely in the tendency to belittle their deepest cultural ties: "the ability to see more and more traditional differences (of tribe, religion, race, customs, and the like) as unimportant."[23] As Edmund Burke pointed out in his indictment of colonialism in India over two hundred years ago, humiliation is never more debasing than when it involves the deliberate infringement of the most profound cultural differences — often the very taboos and customs that members of other cultures ridicule, or have the most difficulty in understanding, such as those having to do, in Mary Douglas's terms, with purity, defilement, and danger.[24] These customs and traditions are frequently dismissed by the Enlightenment as "superstition" or "prejudice," but as Burke recognized, it is only by extending the remit of the kind of sympathy and solidarity that is felt *within* a culture *to other cultures,* and precisely on the grounds of their difference, that the Enlightenment can hope to overcome the ethnocentrism and cultural chauvinism that often passes for civility and cosmopolitanism.

It is for this reason that those aspects of ethnicity that not only mark difference, but bear the scars and injuries of history, pose an even greater problem to Rorty's reworking of Enlightenment ethics. The task of purging all traces of the past from the public sphere, except when suitably embalmed for decorative ceremonial or heritage purposes, acquires even more urgency when tradition is not a stabilizing force (as in, for example, the foundation myths of British constitutionalism), but bears witness to the brute force of history. In terms of civic amnesia, to draw attention to one's oppression or the grievous injustices of the past is to engage in the unseemly act of licking one's wounds in public, indulging in a self-regarding culture of complaint. It is crucial for Rorty's argument that adversity and suffering produce this narcissism, throwing the injured individual or nation in on themselves:

> The tougher things are, the more you have to be afraid of, the more dangerous your situation, the less you can afford the time or effort to think of what things might be like for people with whom you do not immediately identify.[25]

This allows Rorty to make a finely tuned distinction between the progress of moral sentiments in Anglo-American and European culture, and the more restricted, insular codes of societies "outside the circle of post-Enlightenment European culture":

> Whenever tribal and national rivalries become important, members of rival tribes and nations will not so count...This is not because they are insufficiently rational. It is, typically, because they live in a world in which it would be just too risky — indeed, would often be insanely dangerous — to let one's sense of moral community stretch beyond one's family, clan or tribe...Such people are *morally* offended by the suggestion that they should treat someone who is not kin as if he were a brother.[26]

This is in keeping with John Stuart Mill's image of the insular Celt sulking on his rocks, the savage who loves his native shore but is not capable of lifting his eyes to other, distant horizons. On this reckoning, a history of oppression or adversity not only rules out a priori the capacity to identify with the plight of others, but may, indeed, be more likely to result in hostility to others, relapsing into the pathologies of xenophobia, atavism, and tribalism. The obverse of this is that only those cultures that have achieved certain levels of wealth and affluence are capable of true cosmopolitanism, as if, somehow, international solidarity in a market economy is the moral equivalent of duty-free goods, available only to those with the wherewithal to pass frequently through airport lounges.

Cries from Roger Casement: Humanitarianism and Postcolonialism

> ...the hearts we bring for Freedom are washed in the surge of tears;
>
> And we claim our right by a people's fight outliving a thousand years.
>
> — John Boyle O'Reilly, "The Exile of the Gael"

It is in this sense that postcolonial ethics, properly conceived, needs to be rescued from the enormous condescension of prosperity. Rorty's version of patriotism might be contrasted with that of another patriot and internationalist, Roger Casement, for whom love of one's country and love of humanity were inextricably intertwined. As Angus Mitchel writes, "whilst his [Casement's] humanitarian work in Africa and South America was seen as the greatest human rights achievement of his age,"[27] this did not prevent Casement dying for his own country, stigmatized not only in terms of his nationality but his religious persuasion (on account of his eleventh hour conversion to Catholicism) and sexual orientation (due to the official whispering campaign over his alleged homosexual *Black Diaries*). Casement's fearless humanitarian endeavours in the Belgian Congo and Brazil derived not from socially denatured conceptions of human rights, but from a discovery of his own Irishness, and his repudiation of a privileged imperial, Unionist upbringing: "In these lonely Congo forests where I found Leopold [King of the Belgians, and tyrannical ruler of the Congo], I found also myself, an incorrigible Irishman."[28] As Michael Taussig argues, it was Casement's immersion in Ireland's colonial past which allowed him to understand the Congo atrocities at a time when the British Foreign Office could not grasp their importance. In a letter to a fellow convert to Irish nationalism, the historian Alice Stopford Green, he wrote:

> I knew the Foreign office would not understand the thing, for I realized I was looking at the tragedy with the eyes of another race of people once hunted themselves, whose hearts were based on affection as the root principle of contact with their fellow men, and whose estimate of life was not something to be appraised at its market price.[29]

Instead of narrowing horizons and closing off sympathies, Casement's re-engagement with the history of oppression in his own culture induced a profound sense of human fellowship that enriched his awareness of the sufferings of other peoples. Nor was he alone in this. While there was no shortage of narrow-gauge nationalists who devoted their energies to Ireland, and Ireland only, many of the most radical currents in anticolonial struggles from the United Irishmen in the late eighteenth century saw Irish freedom as irrevocably committing nationalists to anti-imperialist and progressive causes across the globe. The great historian of the United Irishmen, R. R. Madden, distinguished himself while working in the colonial service by campaigning vigorously for the abolition of slavery in the West Indies, as well as for Aboriginal rights in Australia.[30] Later nationalist leaders like Michael Davitt related the defence of Jews against Catholic bigotry to a shared history of persecution: "Like our own race, they have endured a persecution the records of which will forever remain a reproach to the Christian nations of Europe."[31] In a similar vein, Davitt, who was the founder of the Land League in Ireland, wrote of the injustices suffered by the Aboriginal peoples under British colonialism during his visit to Australia in 1895:

> They are hunted off lands that are still the property of the state and only leased to pastoralists. Thus, with the game they lived upon gone and their hunting grounds fenced in they are forbidden to look for food where once it was found in freedom and abundance. The whiteman's law justifies him in stealing the black man's country, his wife, and daughters whenever he wants them; but to take a sheep from this moral professor of the ten commandments is to earn the penalty of the bullet.[32]

The ordeal of the Aborigines also figures prominently in the Fenian, John Boyle O'Reilly's, novel *Moondyne* (1879), based on the time he spent as a convict in Western Australia in the 1860s, and it is perhaps in O'Reilly's writings as editor of *The Boston Pilot,* and those of his more radical counterpart, Patrick Ford, who edited the *Irish World,* that some of the most forthright expressions of the solidarity between the Irish and other victims of racism and colonial injustice are to be found. Prominent among these in the case of American politics was support for abolitionism, the rights of Native Americans, the cause of Labour and, in Ford's case, the emancipation of all peoples under British colonial rule:

> If the people of Ireland have a right to their country, the people of India have as just a claim to theirs; if it is wrong to plunder the Irish, it is also wrong to plunder the Hindoos.[33]

The point of drawing attention to these examples is not to claim that Boyle O'Reilly and Ford spoke for the entire Irish diaspora — though it is worth noting that their newspapers were the largest circulation immigrant newspapers in the United States — but rather to contest the common Enlightenment assumption that preoccupation with cultural specificity and the past, particularly an oppressive past, militates against international solidarity and cultural diversity in a modern social polity. Patrick Ford did not address the plight of Asian Indians from a transcultural perspective, as one abstract human being to another, but specifically as an Irish person, steeped in Irish culture and history, to an Indian person, steeped in his.

Ford's status as an émigré also calls into question the tendency in many recent discussions of "hybridity" and "diasporic identities" to present attachment to the homeland, or one's "native" culture, as the disabling part of one's hyphenated identity, a nostalgic narrative awaiting redemption by the shock of the new. In a recent article in *Transition*, Manthia Diawara evokes powerfully the impact of American black culture and popular music on teenagers growing up in Mali in the 1960s, helping them to come out from under the shackles of Francophone culture, and its Eurocentric pretensions:

> For me and for many of my friends, to be liberated was to be exposed to more rhythm and blues, to be up to the latest news about Muhammed Ali, George Jackson, Angela Davis, Malcolm X, and Martin Luther King, Jr. These American heroes were becoming an alternative source of cultural capital for African youth. They enable us to subvert the hegemony of Francite after independence. [34]

This echoes the impact of the American civil rights movement on the early phases of the conflict in Northern Ireland, and is a clear reminder of the capacity of such cross-cultural influences to rock not just around the clock, but to rock history and maybe time itself. But it is when Diawara proceeds to argue that such transatlantic influences — the transmigration of soul, as it were — also liberated him from the shackles of his own native Mali culture that problems begin to arise. Cross-cultural interaction becomes strangely asymmetrical, for while the traffic from the metropolitan centre to the "periphery" is considered positive and liberating, the journey in the opposite direction, from Mali to America, is considered to be delimiting and disabling, if not something of an embarrassment for the diaspora. Recoiling during a visit home from an engagement with a griot — the equivalent of the bard, the keener, or perhaps the storyteller in Gaelic culture — Diawara writes that he "felt guilty for succumbing to the flattery of the griot woman".[35] This leads him to reflect ruefully on the "narratives of return" woven by the griots which help to assuage the sundering of the past in colonial societies, particularly the nostalgia for home experienced by migrant workers and the diaspora: "it makes people forget all the pain and humiliation they went through in exile":

> I thought about the griots' power to keep West Africans in the thrall of a heroic past, to evoke feelings that have not changed in seven hundred years. Despite our attempts to catch up with the modern world, they have trapped us in a narrative of return....They tell us...we are kings in Mande, even if we wash dishes or clean toilets in other lands. We are like disenfranchised clans when we travel overseas; foreigners have no idea how noble we are, how much history we have... [O]ur homeland is Mande, we must return to build our homeland; we must return to claim our inheritance ....I still ponder the injunction of the griots. They bar the door to any sense of cosmopolitanism, any profound mixing of cultures.[36]

But this raises the question: why are certain forms of cosmopolitanism only achieved at the cost of (usually hidden) guilt or embarrassment at reminders of the homeland, or one's personal past? As Ghassan Hage argues, this may often point to notions of "debt" and guilt in an unacknowledged moral economy of emigration. For the migrant who feels welcomed in a new country, "participation in the host community can be seen as repayment of the debt of belonging to it, [but] this same participation can accentuate feelings of guilt towards the original community" in the homeland — a guilt having more to do with resentment than reparation.[37] By contrast, the migrant worker who is exposed to prejudice and humiliation abroad has only the homeland to fall back on, even if this is at one, imaginary remove. These "obligations of the heart" (in Edmund Burke's phrase) are intensified rather than diminished through political persecution or oppression at home, for exile actively prevents one from repaying the debt to one's own community, thereby incurring an even greater need to make restitution. Not least of the ironies of such displacement is that home itself becomes elsewhere, and attachment to home a kind of cosmopolitanism in reverse, hyphenated in time as well as space. As Matthew Frye Jacobson points out, the Irish, Jewish, and Polish communities in the United States saw themselves as exiles rather than emigrants, leaving the homeland through political necessity rather than choice. Moreover, while this attachment to the homeland may have resulted in some cases in a narrow long-distance nationalism, in other cases, as we have seen, the sense of an injured identity engendered sympathy with the plight of other oppressed nations or sections of the community.[38] As Jacobson writes of the extraordinary success of Patrick Ford's *Irish World* and Michael Davitt's Land League campaign among those advanced sections of the Irish working class in mining communities and elsewhere which leaned towards international socialism:

> For these workers, the appeal of the universalist program rested largely in its resonance with the specifics of their national experience. The call to American working-class action rested on the basis of Irish colonial memory.[39]

It was not only the more insular forms of nationalism, however, which prevented Irish expressions of solidarity with other victims of colonialism: there were also the everyday pressures of participation in empire, the hidden injuries of cultural humiliation which encourage and reward the disavowal of one's own culture or homeland.

Postcolonial Abjection: Mimicking the Master's Voice

> Humiliation rituals have as an original assumption something of the hierarchical in them: a person is being put low either as a prelude to being raised on high or as a redefinition of continuing relations of dominance.
>
> — William Ian Miller, *Humiliation*

There is nothing automatic, still less instinctual, about postcolonial solidarity — the spark of sympathy between two beleaguered cultures is not a matter of spontaneous combustion, as if the experience of defeat or oppression could only enkindle concern for the plight of others in a similar predicament. It can indeed lead to a reverse movement where the humiliated of one culture become the shock troops of another, the ignominy of the slave prompting a need to retrieve dignity and self-respect by identifying with the master's voice and the very forces that gave rise to domination in the first place.[40] What is at stake here is the all too obvious fact of participation in, rather than resistance to, empire, the allurements of "the king's shilling" and upward mobility offering a means of social advancement even if, at another level, it meant the ultimate form of abasement and loss of face. It is striking that for the Irish, and "the Celtic periphery" of Britain, the king's shilling, in the form of military prowess and martial valour, became the most visible means of regaining lost pride — assertions of masculinity, moreover, that had their finest hour at the outposts of Empire, whether in Ireland, America, India, or Africa. Hence the fame of Scottish fencibles and the Black Watch, the Irish Connacht Rangers and, more recently, the Gurkhas, who provided the cutting edge of empire, often against rebels and insurgents whose grievances were akin to those of their own cultures.

The prototype of this colonial abjection can perhaps be seen in the transformation by which the Scottish Highlanders of the '45, in the front line of the genocidal purge of the battle of Culloden, became the loyal sons of the empire within a generation or two. As Robert Clyde puts it:

> Within a relatively short time, the service of the Highland regiments in the British army completed the rehabilitation of the Gaels in the eyes of the rest of Britain. During the seventy years between the Battles of Culloden and Waterloo, the common view of the Gaels as bloodthirsty rebels bent on the destruction of the British constitution had changed to a belief that they were among its most staunch defenders.[41]

Clyde might have pointed out that it was not just in the eyes of others that the Scottish Gaels sought rehabilitation — they needed to regain their own self-esteem (if not, as we shall see, their own self-respect). The battle of Culloden involved not just a military defeat but the crushing of the old Gaelic order, the loss of dignity and self-worth that follows the collapse of a culture. Part of the insidious logic of humiliation — the confiscation of one's self-image — is that it is only at the discretion of the perpetrator that the victim regains honour and pride. This, essentially, is what the erasure of cultural identity consists in: the alienation of one's self-image to another "superior" or more powerful adversary. Redemption then takes the form of heroic self-immolation — the "voluntary" reenactment of the original ordeal which led to domination and humiliation. Thus, for example, the gory spectacle of gladiatorial combat in ancient Rome — what one commentator refers to as classical antiquity's snuff movies — turned on a dramaturgy of sacrifice, in which despised slaves could regain their self-respect by audacious bravery, by staring defeat and annihilation in the face. As Carlin A. Barton describes this process, citing Horace:" 'The linen of honour is only bleached with blood.' Preserving one's honour required vigilance and bravery. Redeeming one's honour required ferocity."[42] Hence the fearless (and fearsome) reputation of colonial cannon-fodder — the Scots, the Iroquois, the Irish, the Sikhs, the Gurkhas — in the heat of battle. But, as with slaves in the Coliseum, such recognition as was achieved lay entirely in the hands of the audiences who savoured the carnage, or those who master-minded the theatres of war. Notwithstanding their contempt for the wretches in the respective arenas of slaughter, even the most hardened spectators felt compelled to applaud: as Carlin puts it, "It is hard to feel alienated from the man or woman walking a high wire *without a net*".[43] Built into the stereotype of the Celt, moreover, was the caveat that heroism need not even succeed, but may, like a comet, shine brightest in the moment of its own extinction: "They went forth to war, but they always fell," as Matthew Arnold noted of the cult of the doomed Ossianic warrior which launched Celticism in the eighteenth century.

In a lethal sense, therefore, the colonial foot-soldier — the more prosaic equivalent of the Celtic warrior — may be seen as doing the dirty work of empire, including his own self-destruction: as Carlin again describes this perverse identification with the master:

> The ideal expressed by these actions and attitudes was to be fiercer in destroying oneself than those who would destroy you ....In voluntarily punishing himself, the Roman took on the role and prestige of the punisher ....Self-destruction, then, could be a desperate form of self-determination, an indication of terrible (or miraculous) will and fortitude. Having lost honour, one imposed the most severe and artificial restrictions on oneself.[44]

This, perhaps, helps to explain the tragic paradox whereby the Irish or the Scots reserved their greatest rage and bloodlust for each other, or for those who resembled them most in battle. It was Government policy to place Highland troops in the front line of the butchery visited upon the Irish insurgents during the 1798 rebellion, just as, in a macabre denouement in 1811, an Irish regiment was let loose against those resisting eviction on the Sutherland estate in Scotland, declaring that they "would now have revenge on the Sutherlanders for the carnage of their countrymen at Tarahill and Ballynamuck" in 1798.[45] There was, of course, another rationale for this divide-and-rule policy, and that was to place colonial armies out of harm's way, as far as possible from their own locality or homeland. The perception here was that for all the staunch defence of empire, loyalty was suspect from the very outset, a matter of lip-service rather than fully internalized allegiance. Thus it was the Connacht Rangers in India, with "a reputation second to none for the way they handled the natives," who featured in the ill-fated mutiny against British Rule in 1920, protesting in their defence that "we were doing in India what the British forces were doing in Ireland." Private Joseph Hawes, who made this justification during his trial, had told the others in the regiment "of his indignation and humiliation at the breaking up of a hurling match in his native Clare while he was home on leave," and, as Tom Bartlett suggests, it may well have been this kind of festering resentment, precipitated by reports of Black and Tan atrocities in Ireland, which precipitated the revolt.[46]

The point of these examples from military history is to highlight the shifting boundaries between post-colonial solidarity with the oppressed, and complicity with the ideology of their oppressors. Roy Foster has drawn attention to what he refers to as "Micks on the Make" in nineteenth-century Britain, the indecent haste with which the Irish sought to make their way up the social ladder, but construes this as cultural tolerance on the part of the British establishment, whereas in fact it may also be seen as the cultural completion of colonial rule.[47] To this may be added the egregious process whereby the Irish "became white" in the United States, compensating for their own indignities by buying into the very white supremacist attitudes which discriminated against them.[48] Accommodation with the prevailing dominant ideology — hybridity under hierarchical rule — is often akin to the *ressentiment* of the humiliated in Nietzsche's terms, forced into outward shows of servility towards the humiliator who strikes them, but inwardly seething with resentment and the thirst for revenge. What is lacking in these circumstances is not the desire but the opportunity and weapons of resistance. But it is precisely this last line of defence — the domain of self-respect rather than the achievement ethic of self-esteem — which cultural humiliation seeks to extinguish, aiming for fully internalized loyalty to the dominant order so that the subject, literally, has no shame.[49]

This calls for an important qualification to discussions of humiliation which consider it as addressing preeminently that which is distinctively human, what (if anything) is shared in common by all human beings. "I claim," writes Avishai Margalit, "that humiliation is the rejection of a human being from the 'Family of Man'."[50] It is undoubtedly true that the most grievous forms of humiliation, such as racism, treat their victims as if they were nonhuman — colonial stereotypes of the Irish or Australian first peoples as apes, or Nazi depictions of Jews as vermin — but it is by virtue of their *cultural or group specificity* that they are so degraded. Though the humiliation may be taken to heart, and strike at the innermost part of the individual, it is not as an individual that one is shamed, but through one's membership of a despised group or culture. As Margalit himself describes it, in relation to sectarian conflict in Northern Ireland:

> Shame involves humiliation only when one is ashamed of a feature of her self-definition connected with her belonging to a group. If a society, through its institutions, causes people to feel ashamed of a legitimate 'belonging' feature of their self-definition — for instance, being Irish, or Catholic, or a native of the Bogside area of Belfast [sic] — then it is not a decent society.[51]

Were nationalists or Catholics to identify themselves primarily as human beings, and disavow their identities, there would be no grounds for discrimination. But it is this option which was closed off through equating "Irishness" with simian or subhuman behaviour, as if their brutishness was an intrinsic part of their cultural condition[52] The only path open — if, indeed, there was an escape route — was to renegotiate access to humanity in terms of the dominant colonial culture, which for the Irish meant embracing unionism or empire, or White Anglo-Saxon supremacy, whether at home or abroad. As Margalit points out, however, such gains in self-esteem — through social advancement or mobility — may be accompanied by an equally profound loss of self-respect, the psychic cost of such Faustian pacts with one's overlords brilliantly explored in Tom Kilroy's play *Double Cross*.[53]

As Margalit goes on to observe, the difficulty with universalizing humiliation as "rejection from humanity" is that only physical cruelty seems to obtain for human beings at this general level. Once mental or symbolic cruelty is involved — which may leave deeper scars in the long run than even physical pain — cultural specificity is encoded into the crime. What is not sufficiently emphasized, however, is the extent to which gross infringements or violations of what is valued most in a culture, extending to a denial of the importance of one's cultural identity, constitutes one of the gravest forms of humiliation — a violation of cultural rights for which well meaning Enlightenment universalism is as much responsible as more crass forms of cultural imperialism. But the response to this need not be colonial abjection, of the kind which forces the victims, as Rorty would have it, in on themselves, incapable of identifying with the plight of others unless they hide their own cultural wounds. "Mad Ireland hurt you into poetry," wrote W. H. Auden of the "honoured guest," W. B. Yeats, but it could just as well hurt many more Irish people into identifying with other less honoured guests — the recent arrival of refugees, asylum seekers, and guest workers from Eastern Europe and Africa.

Much of the rhetoric around the recent resurgence of racism in Ireland has attributed it to xenophobic nationalism, or an undue attachment to Irish identity. Such rhetoric makes it seem as if "Irishness" itself is part of the problem, and not, as seems more likely, the gradual integration of Ireland into the European Union, with its habits of authority and racial and ethnic superiority inherited from the colonial past. It is "Fortress Europe," the new restrictions of the European Union ironically decided at the Dublin convention in 1997, which poses the greatest problem to refugees and asylum seekers, not just the backwoods mentalities of rural Ireland, the urban underclass, or others marginalized by modernity. What is often overlooked is the extent to which cultural intolerance, in keeping with the universalism of the Enlightenment noted by Higgonet above, is a product of the metropolitan centre, and of the modernization that was supposed to render it obsolete. It may not be those aspects of Irish culture which have yet to be assimilated to mainland Europe that are the problem, but the uneven process of integration itself. Rather than lagging behind, the emergence of racism and related forms of virulence may be signs that Ireland is catching up with its advanced European neighbours, and so displaying (to however minimal a degree) the kinds of cultural fissures and conflicts that have long been part of advanced industrial societies. The underlying reasons are not too difficult to see: Ireland's newly created image as the "Celtic Tiger" of Europe brings with it the law of the jungle, at least where the economics of ethnicity and race are concerned. Mr. Deasy's remark in *Ulysses* (a remark, characteristically, often mistakenly attributed to the chauvinist "Citizen" in the Cyclops episode) that the Irish never persecuted the Jews "because she never let them in" is often cited as an example of Irish racism, but the reason Ireland did not "let them in" had less to do with xenophobia than with its own chronic economic underdevelopment under colonial rule. After all, if the post-Famine economy gave rise to the greatest emigrant outflows in Europe, and was subject to long-term cycles of acute unemployment, it was hardly in a position to act as a magnet for other immigrant populations. Modernity in its many guises may welcome the shock of the new, but it would seem that, at least where the legacy of colonialism is concerned, it has yet to find ways of negotiating the shock of the other.

ENDNOTES

1 "Time to Stamp Out Racism in Irish Society," *The (Dublin) Sunday Tribune*, 10 October 1999.

2 ibid.

3 "Ireland of the Welcomes?," Irish National Teachers Organization statement, <http://www.into.ie/touch/items/edmay.htm>. "Gaeltachts" refer to the Irish language speaking districts in Ireland.

4 Nuala Haughey, "Government Aims to Tackle Asylum-seeker Crisis While Reducing Numbers Arriving Here," *The Irish Times*, 13 December 1999. Romanians (1369) and Nigerians (895) constituted the largest ethnic groups of the approximately 9000 immigrants who applied for asylum in 1999.

5 Clifford Geertz, "Thick Description," in *The Interpretation of Cultures* (New York: Basic Books, 1972), 22, cited in Richard Rorty, "Human Rights, Rationality, and Sentimentality," in *On Human Rights: The Oxford Amnesty Lectures, 1993*, ed. Stephen Shute and Susan Hurley (New York: Basic Books, 1994), 112.

6 For an important reworking of cosmopolitanism in cultural terms, relating it to affective commitments and allegiances rather than attenuated abstract ideals, see Bruce Robbins, *Feeling Global: Internationalism in Distress* (New York: New York University Press, 1999).

7 Cited in Joseph Morrison Skelly, *Irish Diplomacy at the United Nations, 1945–1965: National Interest and the International Order* (Dublin: Irish Academic Press, 1997), 22. Skelly also cites Patrick Keatinge: "An instinctive sympathy for other 'small states' — occasionally amounting to a belief that "smallness" (usually undefined) is a guarantee of virtue — can be found in many public policy debates through the history of the state." (Patrick Keatinge, *A Place Among the Nations: Issues of Irish Foreign Policy* [Dublin: Institute of Public Administration, 1978]).

8 John Stuart Mill, *Considerations of Representative Government* [1861] (Indianapolis: Bobbs-Merrill, 1958).

9 See Fiona Stafford, *The Last of the Race: The Growth of a Myth from Milton to Darwin* (Oxford: Clarendon Press, 1994).

10 Patrice Higonnet, *Goodness beyond Virtue: Jacobins during the French Revolution* (Harvard: Harvard University Press, 1998), 221.

11 Zygmunt Bauman, *Modernity and the Holocaust* (Cambridge: Polity Press, 1991).

[12] For Foucault, see James Schmidt, *What is Enlightenment: Eighteenth Century Answers and Twentieth Century Questions* (Berkeley: University of California Press, 1996). For Lyotard, see Anthony J. Casciardi, *Consequences of Enlightenment* (Cambridge: Cambridge University Press, 1999).

[13] Richard Rorty, "Human Rights," 122, 129.

[14] Richard Rorty, "The Intellectuals and the Poor," *Harpers* (June 1996): 15.

[15] For such affective ties in the foundation of the United States, see Andrew Burnstein, *Sentimental Democracy: The Evolution of America's Romantic Self-Image* (New York: Hill and Wang, 1999).

[16] Richard Rorty, "The Unpatriotic Academy," in *Philosophy and Social Hope* (London: Penguin, 1999). See also the more extended treatment in *Achieving Our Country: Leftist Thought in Twentieth-Century America* (Cambridge, Mass.: Harvard University Press, 1998.

[17] John Stuart Mill, *Considerations on Representative Government*, 230, 233.

[18] Hence for all his postmodern suspicion of "meta-narratives," American-ness functions as a meta-narrative of progress and social advancement in Rorty's fusion of Dewey's pragmatism and Darwinian "adaptable" evolutionism. See "Rationality and Cultural Difference" in *Truth and Progress: Philosophical Papers, Volume 3* (Cambridge: Cambridge University Press, 1998).

[19] Richard Rorty, "Solidarity," in *Contingency, Irony, and Solidarity* (Cambridge: Cambridge University Press, 1989), 191.

[20] Richard Rorty, "Solidarity," 198.

[21] Bruce Robbins, "Sad Stories in the International Public Sphere: Richard Rorty on Culture and Human Rights," in *Feeling Global: Internationalism in Distress* .

[22] Richard Rorty, "Solidarity," 192.

[23] Richard Rorty, "Private Irony and Liberal Hope," *Contingency, Irony and Solidarity*, 89.

[24] See, for example, Edmund Burke, "Speech on the Impeachment of Warren Hastings," *Works*, vol. vii, (London: Bohn, 1900), 187 ff. For Douglas, see *Purity and Danger: An Analysis of the Concepts of Pollution and Taboo* (London: Routledge and Kegan Paul, 1966).

[25] Richard Rorty, "Human Rights," 128.

[26] Richard Rorty, "Human Rights," 125.

[27] Angus Mitchel, "The Diaries Controversy," in *The Amazon Journal of Roger Casement*, ed. Angus Mitchell (Dublin: The Lilliput Press, 1997), 24.

[28] Cited in Michael Taussig, *Shamanism, Colonialism and the Wild Man: A Study in Terror and Healing* (Chicago: University of Chicago Press, 1987), 19.

[29] Ibid., 19.

[30] Madden was the key defence witness in the trial which followed the seizure of the Amistad by slaves in 1839, travelling over 1000 miles of his own accord to give crucial, damning evidence about slave conditions in Cuba.

[31] See Dermot Keogh, *Jews in 20th Century Ireland: Refugees, Anti-Semitism and the Holocaust* (Cork; Cork University Press, 1998).

[32] Bob Reece, "The Irish and the Aborigines," *Quadrant* (January — February 1998): 32.

33 *Irish World,* 12 August 1877, cited in H. M. Brasted, "Irish Nationalism and the British Empire in the Late Nineteenth Century," in *Irish Culture and Nationalism, 1750–1950,* ed. Oliver MacDonagh, W.F. Mandle, and Pauric Travers (London; Macmilllan, 1983), 88.

34 Manthia Diawara, "The Song of the Griot," *Transition* 74: 21.

35 ibid., 30.

36 ibid., 26–27.

37 Ghassan Hage, "On the Differential Intensity of Reality: Migration, Participation and Guilt," in *Arab-Australians: Citizenship and Belonging,* ed. Ghassan Hage, (Melbourne: Melbourne University Press, 2000).

38 Zionism, as against the more culturally sensitive cosmopolitan strands in Jewish thought, may be a significant exception here. The longing for the homeland in the case of Zionist Jews was not for the country they left behind but for the projected state of Israel. This lack of attachment to their original countries, and the consequent absence of a discourse of "native rights" or even cultural inheritance, may partly explain the readiness to deprive Palestinians of their national territory, and their related cultural and political rights.

39 Matthew Frye Jacobson, *Special Sorrows: the Diasporic Imagination of Irish, Polish, and Jewish Immigrants in the United States* (Cambridge, Mass.: Harvard University Press, 1995), 28.

40 Zionism again maybe a case in point, where the experience of catastrophe encouraged identification with the previous forces of oppression in Palestine — the Anglo, now Anglo-American power bloc — rather than with other victims of British colonialism such as the Palestinians. It is difficult to imagine such a keen alliance with previous colonial rulers emanating from a nationalist movement that directly experienced dispossession, and for whom territory was a lived historical reality. Israeli nationalism is more akin in this respect to the patriotism of settler colonies; the Palestinians to indigenous peoples whose lands were confiscated. As Yael Zerubavel indicates, the powerful sense of official shame felt by the Israeli state towards the perceived passivity of the victims of the Holocaust may have influenced the need to redeem national honour through strident militarism, as in the recovery of the memory of the Masada revolt against Roman imperialism ("The Death of Memory and the Memory of Death: Masada and the Holocaust as Historical Metaphors," *Representations* 45 (Winter 1994)). As argued below, this aggressive masculinity was also proffered as the means whereby humiliated "Celtic" peoples could regain their honour in the service of their masters.

41 Robert Clyde, *From Rebel to Hero: the Image of the Highlander 1745–1830* (East Linton: Tuckwell Press, 1995), 151.

42 Carlin A. Barton, "Savage Miracles: The Redemption of Lost Honour in Roman Society and the Sacrament of the Gladiator and the Martyr," *Representations* 45 (Winter 1994), 46.

43 ibid., 55. As Carlin elaborates: heroism "was not intrinsic but imputed. Honor was withheld or bestowed, even to the gods; it could only be bestowed by those who observed, by the testators. The criminal, like the gladiator, redeemed himself...*and the*

audience with his own blood — but only if he had their sympathy — only if they acknowledged his 'gift.' The criminal's redemption was effected in the mind of the observer." ("Savage Miracles," 53; my emphasis) The most telling aspect of this formulation is that by redeeming themselves, the victims also absolve their masters of the original crime — as if the Scots' subsequent heroism in the service of their British overlords atoned for the butchery of Culloden.

44 ibid., 49–50. It may be that within a carefully orchestrated theatre of revolt, such rituals of voluntary self-immolation may prove to be formidable weapons of resistance, "cutting off the nose," in Erving Goffman's astute formulation, "to destroy the other's face" (Erving Goffman, *Interaction Ritual: Essays on Face-to-Face Behaviour* (Aldine: Chicago, 1967), 222, cited in Carlin, "Savage Miracles," 54. The most notable example of such anticolonial endurance through self-destruction is, perhaps, the practice of hunger-striking in Irish and Indian culture.

45 Robert Clyde, *From Rebel to Hero*, 172.

46 Thomas Bartlett, "The Irish Soldier in India, 1750–1947," in *Ireland and India: Connections, Comparisons, Contrasts* ed. Michael Holmes and Denis Holmes (Dublin: Folens, 1997), 22 ff.

47 R.F. Foster, "Micks on the Make" in *Paddy and Mr. Punch* (London: Penguin, 1991).

48 Noel Ignatiev, *How the Irish Became White* (New York: Routledge, 1995).

49 For a discussion of the need to differentiate self-respect from self-esteem, see Avishai Margalit, *The Decent Society*, trans. Naomi Goldblum (Cambridge, Mass.: Harvard University Press, 1998), 44–48. As Anthony Quinton points out, following Kant, the opposite of self-respect is shamelessness: someone could lose self-esteem in the eyes of others through official humiliation — e.g., Captain Alfred Dreyfuss — and could still feel no shame over his or her actions and maintain his or her self-respect. (See Anthony Quinton, "Humiliation" and Frederick Schick, 'On Humiliation" in *Social Research* 64, no. 1 (spring 1997). This is a special issue devoted to responses to Margalit's *The Decent Society*).

50 Avishai Margalit, *The Decent Society*, 108.

51 ibid.,132–133.

52 As Rorty puts it in relation to Bosnian atrocities: "Serbian murderers and rapists do not think of themselves as violating human rights. For they are not doing these things to fellow human beings, but to *Muslims*. They are not being inhuman, but rather are discriminating between the true humans and the pseudohuman" (Richard Rorty, "Human Rights," 112). Group identity is recognized, but only to demarcate it as the part of the individual that is not human — and to the extent that members of the group identify with being Muslims, Irish, etc., they are animals.

53 Tom Kilroy, *Double Cross* (London: Faber and Faber, 1985). Kilroy's play deals with the concealed, anguished Irishness of William Joyce, Lord Haw-Haw, who was executed as a British traitor for broadcasting Nazi propaganda during World War Two (having already informed against his Irish compatriots to the British), and the equal inner shame of Brendan Bracken, the so-called Australian who became one of Churchill's closest advisors, but who was the son a revolutionary Fenian organizer.

PART 2

LOGICS OF LABOR

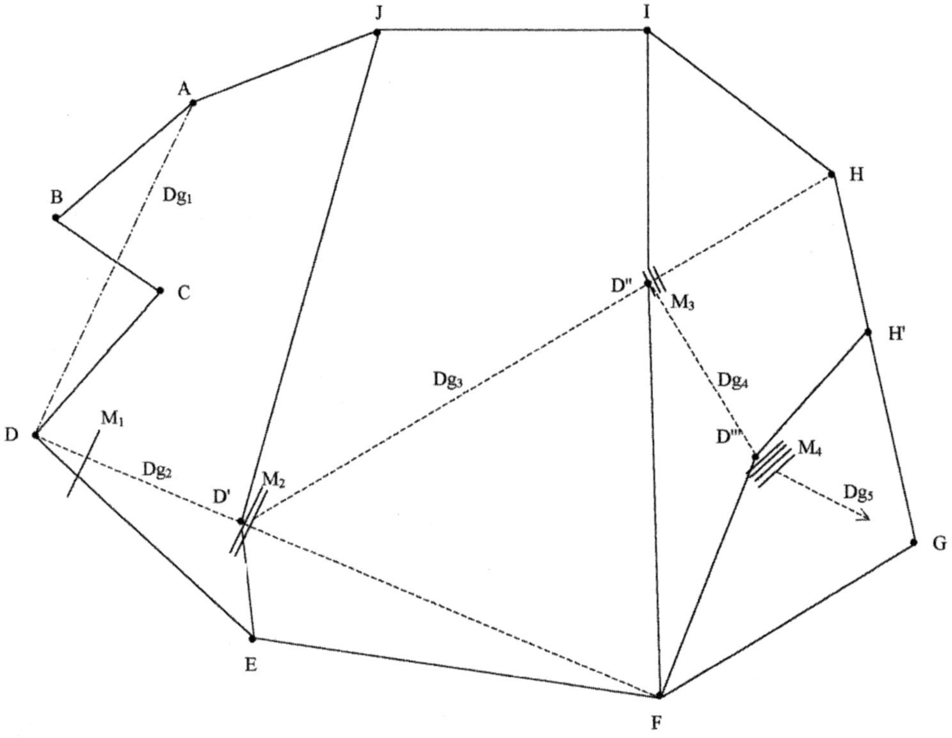

Dg_1, Dg_2, Dg_3, Dg_4, Dg_5 = diagonal of mobility

A, B, C, D, E, F, J, I, H, H′ = obligatory path to reach point G

M1, M2, M3, M4 = wall, obstacle, racism

Between the Hatred of All Walls and the Walls of Hate: The Minoritarian Diagonal of Mobility

Yann Moulier Boutang
— *translated from French by Bernard G. Prusak*

Questions of Method

Allow me to begin with a preliminary reflection on memory, since the subject of this colloquium is the memory of immigration. Memory, all memory, comprises two levels. The first is constituted of the givens susceptible to registration, whose various traces make up the archives, the records. For migrations, these givens cover material that extends from the lists of passengers on boats, to the letters or postcards sent by the immigrants to their families, to books where the immigrants signed their names — not to pass over the forms used by the border police, the registration cards, the court proceedings, and the stories of strikes, disruptions to the public order, and the appearance of strange diseases where reference is made explicitly or implicitly to the presence of foreigners, to non-nationals, to mobile populations. "Objective" material, these traces give witness to the representations and practices not only of the migrants themselves, but of the societies from which they were departing, the societies into which they were arriving, the descendants of migrants, and the "autochthonous." These givens, these traces, have nothing natural or factual about them. They are the products of an elaboration, of a construction — let us call it memory's second level. In order to be memorable and remembered, the history of migrations requires: (a) systems of language or of techniques that have been put to the service of the classification or codification of events into information (that is, transforming given facts into more complex and dynamic propositions); and (b) more general grids of interpretation, evident for example in the choice of techniques of codification, that give direction to the collection of information that is judged pertinent.

The historians of immigration, who as such are "guardians of memory," generally treat the archival deposits of human migrations as at once an objectively verifiable body of facts and a subjective representation by the actors implicated in a migratory system (the migrants, but also all those whose business was somehow or other migration or who interacted with it in some way).[1] They reflect much less rarely, however, on the protocols of rationality that preside over the construction of memory, that is, the schemas to which they have recourse in order to isolate their object and to remove the subjective representations of their subjects of study, or for that matter the subjective representations of their colleagues. I would like to bring my contribution to bear on this aspect of the study of the history of immigration, an aspect which is still largely to be explored. My contribution will be, then, more theoretical than bound to the presentation of particular empirical results.

I will proceed according to the following plan:

1. I will try to illustrate, first, the idea that human migration represents a distinctive trajectory in relation to the processes normally described as the rule in capitalist accumulation. I will refer to this trajectory by means of the image of the diagonal, over and against sequential, binary, or linear movements.
2. The collection of the most precise information on migration in historical capitalism (working here on the scale of the *longue durée*) reveals a repeating pattern, which we might well characterize as agonistic: the construction, bypassing, and then destruction of walls or of barriers. In economics, for example, this pattern is what we call the segmentation, de-segmentation, and re-segmentation of the labor supply.[2] If the movement of the diagonal brings, in general, something new into history, the resisting and renascent obstacles that oppose themselves to its progress rarely, themselves, present anything new to be considered. The accumulation of misfortunes from the migratory diagonal (I characterize thus the phenomena of racism, xenophobia, discrimination, marginalization, and exclusion) ought to have taught us something by now, cultivated in us an active memory and a capacity for effective response. But this is not always the case.

3. The hypothesis formulated here is that the traces of these obstacles to the diagonal, this coded information, have been packed away like dead memory, like cartons of archives or records whose classification and means of access have been lost to us. Something in the preparation of memory systematically effaces them. Is it a question here of a "classical prejudice," in the common sense of a poorly formed opinion? I think not, if only for the fact that quite often this error, these failures of memory, show up in the work of "engaged" historians who do not hide their indignation or disgust for manifestations of racism or xenophobia, but who can only identify the recurrence of racist prejudice without being able to explain it. We need, then, to uncover the reasons for this breakdown — which is not, however, a breakdown of memory as such. The breakdown is instead one of the practice of memory, in memory's power of transformation, here into a kind of pre-judgment, a prejudice in the formation of theoretical categories, an epistemological obstacle to the representation of the diagonal of movement.
4. I will illustrate this hypothesis by way of two concepts that have played and continue to play a crucial role in the collection of pertinent facts, in interpretation as well as in the actual strategies of the workers' movement and the radical critique of capitalism: I want to speak of the questions of proletarianization and the industrial reserve army. These two concepts have largely conditioned the theoretical prejudice that governs the apprehension of mobility, and consequently that of immigration. They have been used in two major conversions that we must see as intimately bound to the reduction of the subjective dimension of the immigrant experience, which is to say the inclusion of the immigrants in a mode of exclusion.[3] The two conversions are (a) the predominance of the *push* model in the holistic sociological tradition, to the detriment of the *pull* model, abandoned to the methodological individualism of liberal economics; and (b) the representation of the mobile or of the "nomad" or of the "diagonal man" (if we may introduce this term) as a danger for the advantages so painfully won by the "sedentary," in particular with respect to wages, working conditions, and the rights of citizenship.[4] The upshot is that the migrant finds himself doubly handicapped: according to these schemas, not only is he not an authentic subject endowed with an autonomy to react to the world, but non-migrants have reason to be suspicious of him, since he is an objective ally of the maintenance, and the exacerbation, of exploitation.

5. It will become clear that we need to generalize this result and effect what might well be called a Copernican revolution. This epistemological reversal consists in bringing the immobile to rotate around the mobile, in making the fixed points pivot on the diagonals, in short, considering immobility as a particular case, a specific declension, of the rule of movement.

The Diagonal of Mobility: Migration Is a Diagonal, the Diagonal of Freedom

The diagonal is not the mediation between two summits, but the way across, the shortcut. In a concave or convex polygon, the diagonal joins two nonconsecutive summits.[5] It cuts and crosses space, whether it be internal or external.[6] (See Diagram 1.)

Let us illustrate this rather abstract conception. In the passage of traditionally "raw" societies to "cooked" societies, and within these latter from low per-capita income to high per-capita income, there exist steps or links such as the development of a laboring class and of a market-based economy, the institution of money, internal rural exodus, and urbanization. We might also list the development of a wage-earning class, industrialization and its sectoring into a service economy, the rise of individualism, and more generally, according to Marx, the passage from a noncapitalist mode of production to a capitalist mode of production.

What is distinctive to both internal (national) and external (international) migratory movement is that it "diagonalizes," totally or partially, this passage from "raw" to "cooked." Thus internal migration or temporary international migration corresponds to the "diagonalization" of a part of the village community in order to procure, for the interests of the colonialist or by reason of economic pressure, the number of persons needed to keep or to allow the rest of the community to maintain its traditional relationships (for example, the *noria* analyzed by Abdelmalek Sayad in the case of Algeria, or the delegation of younger siblings in traditional African societies).[7]

Long-term international migration accordingly realizes one of the classic steps of proletarianization — namely, the transition of sizable portions of the economy from agricultural activity toward industrial or service activity — without the intermediary steps of the development of a wage-earning class and urbanization in the country of origin.[8] The objective of migrants to maximize their income is achieved without the mediation of industrialization in their former societies. Reciprocally, in societies receiving a structured immigration, originally peasant populations may increase their income and gain in social and professional mobility without the obligatory stop at the factory, whose labor is done instead by the flux of temporary or permanent migrants. The diagonal generates mixed states, hybrid rather than mediated, states that conserve and juxtapose, without dissolving or abolishing, the alternative paths of social mobility.

In its most important material dimension, freedom is the unshackled possibility, not so much to refuse all forms of constraint of an economic nature, but to withdraw from a type of work *in such and such a place* in order to choose another type of work, another activity, other means to make a living, *elsewhere* but always within the economy of exchange of money-for-work, whether as a dependent worker of some form or another, or in the more defined role of a wage-earner. (The possibility of the refusal of all constraint of an economic nature may nevertheless be significant; in much primitive accumulation, it disappears altogether in different ways.) When the freedom to sell oneself as a worker disappears, however, all freedom does not itself disappear.

Let us establish, as best as possible, the deviations of migratory diagonalization in relation to the nondiagonalized movements set forth on the left side of Table 1.

Table 1
The deviations of migratory diagonalization

Proletarianization	Semi-proletarianization
1. Generalized development of markets	1. Internal bartering, external markets
2. Internal rural/rural displacement	2. Rural exodus, internal urbanization
3. National urbanization	3. International exodus, international urbanization
4. Development of wage-earning class locally	4. Flight of the wage-earning class locally or nationally or abroad
5. The proletariat becomes the working class, locally or nationally and for the long term	5. The proletariat becomes the working class, internationally and but temporarily
6. Progressive social mobility in a single cultural and economic sphere	6. Rapid social mobility by insertion into a double cultural and economic sphere

If we characterize mobility in its fourfold global dimension of

a) spatial mobility,
b) inter-sector mobility,
c) professional mobility, and
d) social mobility,

we see that spatial migration, internal or international, is characterized by a strong deviance in relation to the expected trajectory. We speak of a diagonalization in order to highlight what, in this gap, is the result of an active behavior and does not simply track the purely passive result of economic forces. The diagonal spatial mobility of immigration corresponds to a localized excess of mobility (the agitation of the population, its "nomadification," and destabilization), a mobility that is either too long or too short in relation to what may be expected. Inter-sector mobility likewise frustrates the normal sequence, namely, from primary to secondary on the way to tertiary, or else from dependence toward independence (instead of working for a wage). This independence may be achieved in the primary sector (agriculture, mining, construction), or in the tertiary sector (clerical work, white-collar jobs), or for that matter even in the secondary (industry). We might note further that ethnic or regional groups who have migrated have historically experienced a much more rapid professional mobility than that allowed by the logic of professional competencies in force in sedentary groups. Instead of straightforwardly passing from the communal solidarity of the old society to the liberal individualism of the *homo œconomicus,* immigrants have hit upon a third way that is at once communitarian and individualistic: the egoism of the workers as a social class.

As is evident in Table 1, this diagonalization is significant both for the way in which the market operates (commercial transactions), and for its development over time. A rather subtle example of this *tertium quid datur* is found in the collective individualism of agricultural workers for the German aristocracy, the workers studied by Max Weber in his youthful writings.[9] The transition from collective solidarity to the individualism of the possessive and proletarian *homo œconomicus* who so much preoccupied, in 1892, the Association for a Social Politics (*Verein für Sozialpolitik*), which had financed Weber's study, is more complicated than the emergence of the class-conscious selfish individual of modernity. In tandem with this transition, there was a surge in emigration toward the United States and the cities of western Germany, on the one hand, and immigration from Poland, on the other. In both cases, Weber observed that individual passions came together in a way exactly contrary to Mandeville's *Fable of the Bees.*[10]

The diagonalization of movement is a law that is found in late capitalism as well as in market capitalism and primitive accumulation, and I have tried elsewhere to illustrate this diagonal of flight in all of its aspects.[11] The flight from dependence, slavery, serfdom, indentured servitude, the wage-earning class, and the countryside takes on as well, with the change in demographics, an intergenerational dimension. Diagonalization is multidirectional. But this characteristic is not yet sufficient to describe, correctly, the dynamic that accounts for the obstacles to this movement.

The Cyclical Return of the Diagonal in Reverse: The Obstacles to the Diagonal: Mediations, or Walls

This undesired, unprovoked movement is continually opposed. There exist two ways to oppose it. The first is the erection of barriers pure and simple, which interrupt the flow of the diagonals and force them to advance instead by way of the consecutive summits we evoked in our earlier geometrical description. These barriers can be direct or indirect. Let us take, for example, the checking or curbing of rural exodus. The lords who enjoyed rights over the person of the serfs wanted to prevent them from leaving their position — and so the laws and customs that forbade leaving the land and obstructed the freedom to come and go. But there are also indirect walls that close off the secondary diagonals mobility opens up (for example, the possibility of buying back one's freedom through savings); and it is thus that we can understand the interdiction applied to serfs and slaves, or in the twentieth century the peasants in "socialist" countries, against selling their agricultural and artisanal products in town.

The obligatory mediation, the necessary step, is a more subtle form of opposition. In appearance totally opposed to the wall, it amounts to a considerable check on movement, to its canalization not by deviation, but by reduction through the intervention of authority. Let us cite the regulation of voting rights; the limitation of days when contracts might be broken, as for example on St. George's day for the Russian para-serfs; and the administrative obstacles to the regularization and naturalization of immigrants.

The most demanding step, however, is strikingly captured in the celebrated phrase of François Pierre Guizot, the head of the French government under Louis Phillippe: *"enrichissez-vous,"* make money! We see here the return of the compromise invented by Cromwell's representatives in Putney's conversations with the Levelers over the criteria for political participation.[12] The Levelers wanted the people to have the power of decision, and thus that each man dispose of one vote (though only for those who were actually independent from their master, and so for servants only on condition that they did not live in their employer's residence). The criterion of the Levelers was then independence; Cromwell's adherents replied that only those who had "a stable interest in the Kingdom" could vote. Voting qualifications were born.

Two discourses confront one another in this example. The one wants freedom and access to government and makes property, of whatever quality, the condition for the exercise of freedom, predicated upon the capacity to escape subjection. The other, in order to cut off this access, also proposes property as the criterion, but property understood as the accumulation of wealth and the exercise of political prerogatives. This, too, is a discourse of enfranchisement (arriving at G in our diagram), but with a difference. It obliges those who would abide by it to pass through points B (the privation of all forms of property and the right of usufruct that guaranteed men's independence in the ancient world and was counted among the precious freedoms prized from the feudal order since the Magna Carta), C (dependent wage labor), D (the reconquest of wealth as measured by capitalist economics), and E (the status of a subject without active rights, that is, the status of passive citizenship). The discourse of power is a discourse of mediation; that of the crowds and of the people would cut immediately from beginning to end.

What I have called the two points of view on the market are formed in the gap between these two ways. There is the market of freedom, and then the freedom of the market. The market as a diagonal toward freedom is the invention of dependent workers to escape from servitude and slavery; the same holds for systematic hybridization, cross-breeding as well as the crossing of borders. This invention is taken over, however, and transformed into a process. As a result, the market of freedom provides the energy necessary for accumulation, but the free market never emerges. Capitalism, whether merchant or industrial, tends always toward the cartel or monopoly.

It is this "process" that was proposed to Europe's peasants, then to blacks enslaved for life in the New World. (Slavery was institutionalized in the Carolinas and in Virginia in 1633, and by 1695 had become a basic social institution in the North American colonies.) Voting qualifications were adopted by the French and American revolutions. Today, international migrants suffer the same long path (more or less long according to whether they find themselves in a decolonialized European assimilationist system, or in an integrationist system, in what have been countries of immigration since the period of colonialization). Naturalization is but another step in the process. Each link in this long chain, forged to repel the movement of the diagonal, is challenged by a new diagonal, which in its turn is countered by yet another roadblock and detour.

For us, it follows that what might be seen as opportunism obeys not merely an individualistic logic of the maximization of gain, but a logic of at once individual and collective liberation. (This holds for both wage earners and dependent workers.) We do not reject the economic (and "economistic") postulate of the pursuit of private and selfish material interests as too narrow, reductive, or amoral, but reinterpret it, set it within a new problematic, that of liberation. If the serf engages in deception in order to sell his products on the market, this is to gain for himself the document that will make him a "copy holder," a freeholder, a peasant who owns his own house, land, and tools, and accordingly a free man. If the slave works on his own and produces on his parcel of ground enough to amass some earnings, this is to buy his way out of his servitude. If the illegal immigrant works in the treacherous sweatshops of New York, Paris, or Milan, this is to be able to buy his papers and the freedom to sell his labor to the highest bidder. If the freshly arrived legal immigrant works overtime (which will make his longer-term colleagues resent him), this is to cut down the time that he is rootless, so that he might install himself in his new country as he will.

There is, in all historical periods, a relation between activity that is abnormal or against the norms, on the one hand, and the desire to escape from dependence, on the other. Money and wealth are pursued not only because they provide access to necessary goods, and make life comfortable and pleasant (as observed by Adam Smith), but because they make it possible to change the laws and status of property. Without this law of behavior, it would be impossible to understand the stakes of the marketplace, which is poorly grasped by the abstractions of supply and demand, mute and indifferent forces ever-so-slowly pushing up and under one another. To the contrary, the marketplace is a place of combat, full of sound and fury, between the accumulation of wealth and the power to command the work of others, on the one hand, and the flight toward freedom, on the other. That is, on the one hand, there is the market of dupes and of servitude; on the other, the possibility of a march toward freedom, of the free market. If this law is not understood, we also will not be able to understand, above all, the metamorphoses of dependent work and the institutionalization of the wage system.

Several laws govern these alternative or complementary systems of movement. To begin with, the stronger the current toward the diagonal, the more the walls (dams) or dikes must be powerful and their outlets effective, lest they all be overcome. The function of the various walls that block the shortcut of the diagonal is to redirect potential energy by creating forced passages. Accordingly, the more effectively blocked the path to wealth by independent work (the path of the peasants, the peasant "breach" admirably described by Sydney Mintz with regard to Caribbean slaves), the stronger the process of proletarianization, and furthermore the position of the wage-earning class and the liberal ideology of making it by making money. Economists would say: the stronger the motivation to private accumulation through the model of the market (unmediated by state intervention).

Having closely studied two historical examples of walls and detours, I have developed two convictions of a quasi-methodological value. First, when institutional walls are either on the point of being overwhelmed, or actually are overwhelmed, other walls are thrown up in front or behind. (For an example of walls on the point of being overwhelmed, take the impact of the massive transatlantic immigration to the United States. For an example of walls actually overwhelmed, take the liberation of blacks by the mixing of races in the Antilles toward 1760, and the urbanization of blacks in South Africa between 1910 and 1920). These new walls often put to use the energy of the white, or mixed-race, or immigrant European population in order to combat the black or Asian population. Racism, xenophobia, and anti-Semitism rush to compensate for the weakening of the old barriers. The invention of color as a political discriminant (like caste and ethnicity) is incomprehensible without reference to its role as a barrier of movement, and the same holds for the invention of labor statutes ("green cards," registration cards, and allowances). The underlying and methodical logic of municipal interdictions, of all those vexing hassles authorities throw up (while taking refuge behind the monstrous pretext of being unable to control the fury of the white mob), in particular of the famous laws in San Francisco specifying the ratio of air per person,[13] is lost on us unless we see that the movement of Asian immigrants was viewed as closing off the prospectors' opportunities. The authorities who wanted to keep these Chinese immigrants in agriculture or working on the railroad closed off to them the diagonal of gold. But they were unable to close off this diagonal to European immigrants. For without this particular white diagonal, there would have been another from the ranks of agriculture, which would have threatened the newly developing wage-earning class on the country's East Coast.

Such a schema, I believe, allows for a better understanding of the evolution of legislation in its detail, the tacking back-and-forth between tolerance and intolerance on the part of authorities, sudden bursts of racism, and interethnic incidents. But why, then, do these mechanisms remain unknown? Why does the analysis of migration and of labor movements (in the double sense of migratory movements and as a social movement) remain so timorous, so "academic," so defenseless in the face of resurgences of xenophobia? Ghassan Hage has exposed in an illuminating way the yawning hole in the theoretical analysis of tolerance and of democratic multiculturalism in contemporary Australia.[14] Without slighting the richness of his analysis, I would like to take a step back from it — which brings me to my second conviction.

If the institutionalized left of the labor movement (with several notable but isolated exceptions) has gotten itself into a fix over the phenomenon of racism, this fact is not, to my mind, by chance. There is in the vulgar, basic, Marxist *discourse* of the struggle against exploitation a formidable impasse on the question of liberation. (I am speaking only of this *discourse*, neither of practices that do not separate theory and practice, nor of Marx himself.) Feminism, black minority movements, Amerindians, minority nationalities (the Irish in England, the Basques and Corsicans in France, etc.), have pointed out this *differend*, which is often of a practical and political nature. But where is it rooted? To my mind, the root of this *differend* is to be found in the reduction of the active, subjective, and collective dimension of labor movements. The reduction of this dimension shows up in multiple ways: in the labor movement's "economism," in its blunderings on the peasant question and the question of national representation, and in its underestimation of internal, nonideological divisions. Two questions, however, illustrate this problem particularly well: the question of proletarianization and that of the industrial reserve army, two iron-bound laws of orthodox Marxism which, on closer inspection, reveal themselves to be fearsome "false friends."

Proletarianization: The Failure to Recognize Migration as an Active Phenomenon

The role played by the concept of proletarianization in Marx's analysis of the genesis of the capitalist system of production is well known. It is this concept that enables Marx to identify what distinguishes capitalist production from other historical forms of exploitation (servitude and slavery). The answer is that, in capitalism, work for another (dependence) is free.

Historically, including in the writings of liberal authors like John Stuart Mill, the triviality of this proposition is only apparent. For the total freedom of the economic subject is at once asserted and immediately limited by the systemic rule against selling oneself. The economic subject is asserted to be free in himself, in his activity. He is posited as the owner of his activity, of himself. But against Locke's theory of the unlimited nature of property, he cannot be the unlimited owner of himself. Now how to justify, to the "free" worker who must be the owner of himself in order to be able to exchange and to cede the use of his capacity of work to another, that he cannot sell, but only rent himself? How is this to be justified if property is by its nature unlimited? This discussion is not a mere intrigue; recall that in Russia, for example, the free person was free to sell himself as a slave in order to liberate himself from debt and that, until the middle of the nineteenth century, nonpayment of personal debts got one thrown into prison, that is, deprived of freedom in the strictest possible way. The legal system — which has never been exclusively governed by Roman law and has always limited property in one way or another — had subsequently to do away with this practice and reaffirm that, if the primary good of man is freedom, freedom is inalienable.

Marx's reply is also well known: this was the distinction between labor and labor-power, on the one hand, and the necessity of the remuneration of labor-power in the form of a wage, on the other. For Marx, the institution of the wage relation is the new form that exploitation takes, a fact about which there is no illusion, that appears as such and does not "seem." As merchandise bought and sold on the market, labor has a price like none other. As labor-power, labor has an exchange value. The use that is made of this power, however, does not itself have value, but is the preeminent source of value, not value as general equivalence, but the sole source of surplus-value in relation to the purely analytical cost of labor power's reproduction.[15]

According to Marx, in order for the money of the one who possesses cash to function as capital, he must turn to the proletariat. What is a proletarian? We can do no better than the exact definition of the poor given in the seventeenth century by the bishop of Besançon, Monsignor Camus: someone who has only his physical and intellectual capacities to live off. He must, then, sell his capacity to work and not the product of his work; he has no choice but to separate his labor-power from his actual production. As a simple bearer of labor-power (*Träger*), he must give up any and all claim to the product of his activity. The separation (*Trennung*) between his labor-power and his production deprives him of all ownership of the means of production (capital, tools, house, land, and manual labor), and thus renders him free for the labor market. Freedom here is not to have any other way to live than to sell oneself to the highest bidder as living labor otherwise comparable to that of machines.

From this analysis, which is to be found everywhere in Marx from the *Grundrisse* to *Das Kapital*, it follows that this separation must have been instituted in advance through primitive accumulation, the most often by coercive measures. That is, for the relations of capitalist production to be effective, and the wage relation established, the dumb pressure of economic relations cannot themselves be seen as the prime movers in the economy's organization.

Forced expropriation, the expulsion of small landowners driven into a corner from which the only way out was to go to work for their landlords or into the factories in the cities (think of Ireland) — these tactics become common currency as bourgeois freedoms were eagerly trampled underfoot. Racism and the systematic oppression of minorities also played a functional role in this proletarianization. Colonialism cunningly destroyed all the cultural elements that served to protect the fabric of traditional societies.[16]

Proletarianization is the hidden face of the rural exodus and industrialization at the end of the eighteenth century, the striking expression of which is the enclosures of communal lands. Another face of this proletarianization is rural/urban immigration (the principal population movement), as much local as national or international. The decision to immigrate is an individual decision, but the freedom that the lot-dwelling peasant manifests is an illusion, since it is constrained by structural laws of accumulation. Whether he likes it or not, his transformation into a proletarian is ineluctable.

But is this story — this superabundantly illustrated story where the proletariat is always, at the end of the day, crushed, dominated, beaten — is this story the final word? I am inclined to see here, instead, the story of the dominated told to the dominated by the dominated, when they have at last fallen totally under the sway of the dominant. And I propose, in Table 2, another story, other sequences of events, in short a diagonal.

Table 2
The orthodox schema and the diagonal in relation to proletarianization

Classical schema of proletarianization	Diagonalized proletarianization, proletarianization revisited
1. Stable, precapitalist regime	1. Internally unstable regime, with serfs, free peasants, freeholders seeking to become owners or to leave for elsewhere
2. External or internal fragilization; introduction of money into the market; parceling of property	2. With the desertion of villages, definitive destabilization of the means of agricultural cultivation
3. Determinative exterior constraint or shock (war, conquest)	3. Internal or external shock, figuring as a pretext or occasion
4. Change in the status of property; parliamentary enclosures	4. Piecemeal enclosure by agreement
5. Definitive destabilization of small land-owners	5. Transformation of the means of agricultural cultivation; development of animal husbandry, by peasants or landlords, on common lands
6. Loss of land and of the instruments of work	6. Taking of land, formation of a durable peasantry (yeomen or laborers); failure of proletarianization
7. Loss of homes; proletarianization achieved	7. Occupation of cottages; movement toward work as shepherds and, on a temporary basis, as wage-earning hands
8. Institution of the wage relationship	8. Movement toward the city; juridical liberation/regularization; access to independent work outside of the guild system
9. Rural/urban migration, predominantly of a *push* tendency; stable wages in factories; integration of the proletariat as the working class into the wage-earning class	9. Internal, then international emigration, predominantly of a *pull* tendency; introduction of self-employment, informal work, part-time wage work; limited proletarianization

This history is more complicated and for us more interesting inasmuch as it gives the dominated more space to maneuver, more autonomy.[17] Is this to say that the traditional schema is in itself false? No — but it tells only a part of the whole story, and inexact at that in many cases. (English proletarianization, for example, has to be understood in its full impact: upon the dangerous classes in London; the emigrants to the New World; and the Irish, the Scottish, and the Welsh in the factories of Manchester and Liverpool. It was slowed, moreover, by Speenhamland and the corn laws.) Historically, the proletarianization described in the left side of Table 2, the "classical schema," is the second proletarianization, which followed after the failure of the first, which itself had found its match in the peasants who had conquered their freedom after the "medieval liberation."[18]

What is essential for us is that the column on the left describes a process of unilateral domestication. Once active on its own, the pre-proletariat becomes an appendage of capital. After its defeat, especially its loss of "voice," the proletariat, now become the working class, is doomed forever to defeat. The rebelliousness of its subjectivity has totally disappeared.

The orthodox theory of proletarianization seems to inflate the independence or the subjectivity of the small landholder in precapitalist regimes, while refusing to see in dependent work any anticipation of the wage relation. It also annihilates the agonistic dimension of the proletariat, and treats the creation of all forms of semiproletarianization as holdovers from the feudal past. What it fails to notice is that it thus locates subjectivity exclusively in the nonproletariat "half." The upshot is that this purported "class" analysis is but a flat and derivative restatement of the facts of modernization and individualization. In short, this is an analysis of the capitalist assimilation or integration of the working class, but not the reconstruction of the interaction that would show the proletariat, the working class, living labor, in their subjective dimension as agents in both the evolution and the articulation of capital.

To return to the question of mobility, it will also be seen that emigration is presented in the left column as an essentially passive phenomenon, an accumulation of population that answers to the accumulation of capital. The analysis of working-class immigration is thus, not surprisingly, co-opted into a theory of, at best, integration or assimilation. At worst, peasants, women, foreigners, blacks, working-class minorities, the working class as a whole, suffer the indignity of being abstracted of all flesh, all subjectivity, by order of the canons of working-class whites already domesticated into unions.

In order to understand the model of white working-class integration, we must, however, take up another commonplace that has been used both to justify violence against the nondominant members of the wage-earning class, and to promote an attitude of "understanding" toward this violence.

The Industrial Reserve Army: A False Generalization, or the "Objective Responsibility" of Migration?

If the mobility of work is undesired, but structurally conditioned (whatever the position of the interested parties), in short if it is a function of capitalism, then there follows a formidable consequence: it is legitimate for the adversaries of capitalism, whoever they are, to be against migration. It is not difficult to understand that capitalism's irrational adversaries, or those who have not become conscious of its structural mechanisms, will oppose themselves sometimes violently, in any event firmly, to migratory movements: people from elsewhere are not welcome since the workers are at war against capitalism. But those who recognize capitalism's hidden laws, and who do not have this aversion for immigrants, victims as they are of proletarianization and primitive accumulation — these adversaries too will declare themselves for a limitation, a strict canalization of migration in order to avoid its foreseeable economic effect, which also threatens to foment explosions of racism. Here enters the famous law of the so-called "reserve army." According to this "law," if mobility is left unchecked, then the wages and the working conditions of the existing proletariat and working class will inevitably decline.

In this law's well-worn but most effective forms, its demonstration is based upon an implicit Malthusianism. If the level of wages is fixed by the market, which is itself governed by the law of supply and demand, it follows that a greater number of workers will lower remuneration and give to employers more power to exploit the wage-earning class as a whole. The relative "surplus population" will drive down wages to the minimum level of survival, a mere living wage. (The term "surplus population" was unfortunately given currency by Marx himself, even if he was careful not to speak of absolute surplus population and meant by it something subtler, namely, the relation between the introduction of machine production and the manual labor it requires. In point of fact, this relation speaks against the use some would make of the reserve army.)

Now, as with proletarianization, this totalizing economic narrative, despite its basis in historical precedent, rests upon a begging of the question, a vicious logical circle. It is my contention that leaving the private market unregulated is not at all the mechanism of construction of the industrial army. The sole mechanism of construction of a reserve army has always been in the past, and is yet today, the limitation of freedom by the state in its different aspects (civic, political, and even economic with respect to all that concerns mobility). The reserve army is the construction of the state in its role as the guarantor of collective capital, as a check upon subjectivity, the mobility of labor. It is not true that the mechanism of the free market leads *in itself* to a lowering of wages and favors the constriction of work to wage-labor.

In the paradigm switch we propose, we accept the well-documented hypothesis of neo-classical economists as to the scarcity of labor in relation to the abundance of capital — that is, that the rule is more the scarcity of labor than its superabundance. This want of labor appears to us to be a systematic feature of the capitalist system, as much locally as globally. Let us anticipate and say already what this means for the lowering of borders: exactly the opposite of what is normally said about this question from an overall, planetary point of view. In effect, if populations were not blocked or enclosed, both the cost of wage labor and real wages would rise and equalize to a considerable extent. For capital would be deprived of its most effective weapon apart from the division of labor, namely, the institutional and ethnic compartmentalization of the wage-earning class. Before making good on this point, however, let us first formulate the thesis of the "industrial reserve army" in its full implications.

The Thesis of the Industrial Reserve Army

Take any given economic entity, whether it be a business, an industry, or a local or national labor market. This entity is determined, on the one hand, by what traditional economic analysis calls the demand for and supply of labor; on the other hand, it is also determined by the requirement that it be possible to substitute one quantity of labor for another such quantity, that is, that labor be sufficiently homogeneous. We would do well to add to these determinations, however, another which Max Weber identified in his already mentioned youthful writings on the condition of agricultural workers in eastern Germany: the *Arbeitsverfassung*, or "constitution" of work.[19] Under this title we are to include the rules that govern labor relations (types of contract, the politics of migration and of manual labor, in short what the economist of institutions, R. Commons, calls "directive transactions"); likewise the field of social distribution, which is to say the ensemble of institutions that govern the diverse forms of wage negotiation; and finally the rules that govern market transactions themselves (goods, money, and credit). The thesis of the reserve army, in the classical argument by Malthus, appropriated by Ricardo and then by Marx himself, tells us that the abundance of manual labor and/or population — the two are not always distinguished — must lower the general level of wages. This conclusion is easy to demonstrate, *so long as one takes for granted,* as economists too often do in an analytic frame of mind that is deceptive when it comes to historical events, *that all things are otherwise equal* (*ceteris paribus sic stantibus*). The question we need to ask is what conditions would need to be fulfilled for such a lowering of wages to be verifiable.

The Conditions of the Realization of the Law

The first condition that must be fulfilled is that there must have been no loss to or movement from the entity under consideration, or in other words no movement *out* of it in net terms, no net emigration or exit of any kind, including no uncompensated inter-sector movement. There must also have been no break out of the wage relation, as exemplified by the peasant "breach" out of slavery or servitude, the move toward the liberal professions in nineteenth-century capitalism, and the surge in "autonomous" or independent work today. Further, variations affecting the regularity and the frequency of transactions must be foreseeable, recompensable, and compatible. Seasonal agricultural work at one place, for example, must not coincide with the harvest at another, or else the lack of manual labor is not relieved but redoubled, a problem that has long plagued the peasant or the serf.

To these demanding conditions, we must also add two others that prove determinative for the lowering or elevation of the cost of labor. (We leave aside the classic questions of the homogeneity of labor and of the reducibility of complex labor to a multiplicity of simple tasks.) The first is that there be, within the entity under consideration (business, state, trade, local market), an internal mobility. Such a mobility is indispensable for the transmission and equalization of prices;

without it, the value of labor-power would lack a common measure. As a second condition, however, this internal mobility must not in its turn lead to its own despoliation, whether this be toward a "cottage" industry, or toward the rest of the world by way of an indirectly induced emigration.

Now, when we examine these conditions, we see that they are as difficult to realize as the famous conditions of the Eckscher Ohlin Samuelson theorem on the equalization of pricing factors in international trade. Or, to put it another way, by wanting to prove the existence of a reserve army, what is proved rather is its highly improbable character. From the very beginnings of primitive capitalist accumulation (among the poor, the proto-proletariat, and the proletariat), free labor takes the form of a movement beyond the mechanisms of fixation and control.

These historical mechanisms show that capitalism normally develops in a setting that is precisely the contrary of that of the reserve army. A need for Malthusian or classical adjustments — rationing or organizing an overabundance of goods and a flexibility in prices according to property rights, static institutions, and stable demographics — arises but infrequently and is of short duration. Legal and institutional adjustments of price and limited goods, even demographic adjustments, constitute the rule.

The mobility of labor most often takes the form of a movement beyond the given economic entity (corporation, profession, business, industry, or the position of a slave, indentured servant, or apprentice), and most often by the employee's breaking of the work contract. The structural, permanent, and unyielding character of this movement again and again frustrates attempts to seal off the different types of labor markets, to extend temporary disturbances of a Malthusian kind into durable regimes of exploitation. In order to keep wages and income down, the complex ensemble of relations governing the exchange of money-for-work would somehow have to be frozen into a status quo — to which end unbending racism and sexual apartheid stand as historical examples of such monstrous attempts.

In fact, however, the fixing of prices, and indeed the limitation of goods, find themselves under constant attack, as much from the point of view of the employer as from that of the employee, the fund of capital. They are attacked by permanent modifications of institutional structures, of rules of the game, property rights, definition of the terms of contract, and the status of the contractors as well as of their spouses and their descendants. Historically, the medieval peasant "breach," the breach opened up by the mixing of races in slave societies, the breach opened by the poor when they conquered the right to income — all these crucial occurrences have counterbalanced the lowering of wages. To put it another way, historically, dependent labor has been on the winning side: at some times with respect to the price of labor, other times in liberty, other times again in loosening the bonds of dependence by gains of welfare or property rights. Considered on the whole, it is a rare period when there is a lowering of wages without some compensation on the side of freedom or of rights. Freedom, quality of life, and equality — these are the three terms to reckon with, probably in that order. The attainment of freedom has certainly been, and is yet today, the essential aspect of the "economic" struggle, if we take capitalism as an historical phenomenon of *longue durée* and the global economy in all its present-day extension.

If we return to our initial schema of the migratory diagonal, we can see that the thesis of the industrial reserve army has provided and continues to provide the principal presentable argument for the edification of walls toward checking the freedom of movement. This argument is presentable because it is rational, founded in the semblance of an economic analysis itself constructed on the basis of the sacrosanct law of supply and demand. It is always the fear of competition and of "degradation," however, that is at the bottom of disciplinary measures against the poor, the assimilation of foreigners, the inclusion of the immigrant population in a mode of exclusion from political participation, even from the elementary rights of association and coalition. When the consequences on wages or working conditions cannot be shown or brought to a point (which is most often the case, since the effect of the reserve army is extremely rare), talk turns to indirect consequences (the degradation of quality of life, of primary education, or of the neighborhood), or rumor invents phantasms whose only truth is the sedentary population's fear of the nomads.

I have shown elsewhere how to understand the charges against the Chinese, exposed to the outbreak of an extreme violence in Lambing Flat, Australia, during a moment of the gold rush (1856–1861) that they saved too much, sent too much of their savings to China, wasted water, lived in homosexual community, and stole the women of other prospectors.[20] (These charges replaced the old charges that they were the most stealing, lying, and immoral people on earth.) The answer is: we need to see these charges in relation to the state of the whites who were in the process of being proletarianized, a process the Chinese were escaping. By these hateful reproaches, the small white prospector was in effect saying: in contrast to the Chinese, I am not able to save; I do not send enough of my savings to Europe; I cheat myself out of lodes of gold by not using enough water; I am incapable of living in a masculine collective without falling under the suspicion of homosexuality; I lose the women I live with. Let us also take a more recent example: the *sans papiers*, or undocumented and illegal immigrants, and the question of regularization. In 1981, and then again in 1996–1999, the refusal of the French authorities, including a government of the left, to grant foreigners in this position unconditional regularization was essentially based upon the purported effect that such a lax entry policy would have: to invite new massive migrations and the degradation they would bring along. The far right developed the following argument: all immigration augments the reserve army. The republican right and left claimed, themselves, that an unregulated, uncontrolled immigration would play this role. But the problem for this argument is to explain how what holds for illegal migrants does not for legal immigrants. The most integrationist left explained, for its part, that illegal or uncontrolled migrants, though of no danger for white nationals, would play the role of a reserve army against the interests of those migrants who had legally entered the country. It therefore went along with the idea that these legal migrants or their descendants could succeed in integrating or inserting themselves into the citizenry and the working world only if borders were closed. The argument is always the same: that of the reserve army in its global dimension. "However much we would like to, we cannot welcome all the misery of the world," Michel Rocard pleaded when he was Prime Minister under François Mitterand.

A Reversal from the Ground up: The Point of View of Mobility

We have thus extracted from the heart of the theory of exploitation, such as it is generally accepted, two false totalizing narratives, false because they generalize on the basis of particulars. These narratives have been and remain heavily influential upon the male view of the movement of "other" populations, and in particular the male view of the entry of women into certain fields, including politics, with the aim of parity.

If movement is essentially the movement of capital, if it is the weapon of employers, then immobility is gifted, *a contrario*, with all the virtues. So we find believing Marxists making little-disguised apologies for the racism of the working classes, as in another epoch apologies were made for the racism of the guilds; or liberal politicians closing their eyes to racist exactions, or in South Africa passing electoral accords and governing with Afrikaners from the pro-apartheid regime.

In fact, as was suggested earlier, it is the exception when immobility contributes toward freedom and effectively resists the capitalist valorization of the market; more often its ambivalence serves rather as the best way to control the migratory diagonal. The immobility of labor and, still further, the immobility of the proletariat stand as particular cases of mobility.

In Albert O. Hirschman's celebrated distinction between voice versus exit — which cannot be praised enough for drawing attention to unrecognized movements of dissent or resistance — voice (the seizing of the word) retains a priority in fact and in principle over exit (mute defection).[21] It retains a priority in fact, since movements of defection, by refusing marginality, never bring any lasting transformation to the system of democratic conflict, which is regulated by the possibility for each and every party to express itself. It retains a priority in principle since, for Hirschman, wholesale defection proves catastrophic for the loyalty of wage earners to businesses and organizations (state, unions, mutual insurance companies, associations, and political parties). It follows that uncontrolled, noninstitutionalized movements must always be forced into conflicts, with the aim of explicit negotiations.

I wonder, however, if this priority should not be radically revised in two ways.

First, movements of defection, and movement *tout court*, seem to occupy, in the history of the complex system of capitalism, a dominant position in relation to open conflicts. Whereas such conflicts rarely gain much mass, and transcend elite or minority status only in revolutionary crises, defection seems to be the bread and butter of capitalism's daily functioning. Moreover, it seems that capitalism's system of agricultural production, and the movement of the "free" industrial wage-earning class it allows, have the advantage and the distinction of allowing a much larger dose of civic and social defection than traditional systems of complex human activity.

Second, Hirschman's postulate of the sterility of movements of defection and the constructive character of staying and fighting has been disproved. For the most important transformations of capitalism, its great inventions (such as the free wage-earning class), follow not from taking on the institutional structure that exists, but from an ongoing, nondialectical, diagonalizing interaction between the given system and the mobility of labor.

ENDNOTES

1 Y. Moulier Boutang and D. Papademetriou, "Typologie, évolution et performances des principaux systèmes migratoires," in *Migration et Développement, un nouveau partenariat pour la coopération* (Paris: OCDE, 1994), 21–41.

2 We use the term "agonistic" (from the Greek *agoon*, meaning "combat") to avoid the too dialectical and teleological term "contradiction," and the too phenomenological and neutral term "conflict."

3 I would like to acknowledge my indebtedness to the thinking of the late Abdelmalek Sayad on this point.

4 The term "mobile" has been too much associated with back-and-forth movement, and thus a movement that is foreseeable and capable of being tightly controlled. The "nomad" analyzed at length by Guattari and Deleuze in *Mille Plateaux* is, conversely, too erratic. It will be seen that, in the "diagonal man," there is at once the sense of the violence of constraint, inasmuch as his path is prescribed to him, and the force of resistance, in that he refuses to take the obligatory path and creates an alternative that cuts across it.

5 This definition is found in S. Baruk, *Dictionnaire des mathématiques* (Paris: Le Seuil, 1992).

6 Consider a polygon with summits A, B, C, D, E, F, G, H, I, J. To go from A to G the path must pass either through B, C, D, E, F, in order, or J, I, H (i.e., through the polygon's consecutive summits). I exclude from the start the direct paths from A to G or the semi-direct paths going through ADG, AIF, etc.

7 Abelmalek Sayad, *L'immigration et les paradoxes de le l'altérité* (Brussels: De Boeck, 1991). On African societies, see Claude Meillassoux, *Femmes, greniers, et capitaux* (Paris: F. Maspéro, 1974).

8 Y. Moulier Boutang and Georges P. Tapinois, "France," in *The Politics of Migration Policies*, ed. D. Kubat (New York: Center for Migration Studies, 1979) 127–143.

9 Sandro Mezzadra, "La communità dei nemici, migranti, capitalisimo e nazione negli scritti di Max Weber sui lavoratori agricoli nei territori prussiani al'est dell'Elba (1892–1895)", *Aut Aut* 275 (September-October 1996): 17–42.

10 In his 1892 work, *Die Lage des Landarbeiter im österlichen Deutschland*, Max Weber wrote that the reasons for migration extend beyond the attraction of high wages in the zones of immigration and include a more general desire for change, not only at a shop-floor level, but legislatively and in the ensemble of practices and customs governing labor relations. In the flight of agricultural workers and their families from the great estates, Weber saw a mass refusal of the patriarchal system. He observed that, although the emigrants quickly discovered that life in the city was anything but free from chains, they continued to leave for "the powerful and purely psychological magic of freedom."

For Weber, the subjective position of agricultural workers living through these profound transformations was marked by the emergence of a pronounced individualism: "Secession from the domestic community and the patriarchal economy is most pronounced precisely among the most capable of the workers, and this no matter what the price, even becoming part of the proletariat and severed from all homeland." He sees this as the context for the institution of a new kind of contract, not for an individual but for families — an arrangement like share-cropping, where monetary compensation is secondary. He sees the background for the degradation of this institution as a story, not of the "liberation" of manual labor and its subsequent proletarianization in the mines, steel factories of the Ruhr, or the developing food industry in the American Midwest, but of the beginning of a peasant liberation. When impeded, this liberation led on the one hand toward the birth of the individual (experienced as such in emigration), and on the other toward the birth of "class enemies," a superb demonstration of the indefeasible link between the birth of the modern classes and that of the individual. Methodological individualism is the translation into political economy of this transformation and the recognition of its power through reducing it to a demand for higher wages (according to the neoclassical theory of the mobility of labor). In a similar way, Locke's possessive individualism interprets the liberation of the peasantry in terms of the affirmation of property rights against proletarianization, in a bourgeois affirmation of the yeoman, and misrepresents the Levelers as destructive of all property and accordingly of every form of civil pact.

[11] See Y. Moulier Boutang, *De l'esclavage au salariat. Une économie historique du salariat bridé* (Paris: Presses Universitaires de France, 1998).

[12] Ibid., 326–335.

[13] In order to block the movement of Chinese immigrants into the cities, municipalities took racist measures on the pretext of health concerns. As an example, the immigrant was forbidden to bring his family unless he could provide a sufficiently spacious lodging.

[14] Ghassan Hage, *White Nation: Fantasies of White Supremacy in a Multicultural Society* (London and Sydney: Pluto Press, 1998).

[15] In this way, Marx simply takes over Ricardo's tautology defining the natural wage, in opposition to the current wage, by the quantity of standard goods (wheat) enabling the laborer to keep himself and his family alive. This idea of simple reproduction is intuitively and theoretically powerful: it can be reconciled with an historical approach to the question of what needs had to be satisfied in order for a given condition to be maintained; and it is the correlate of the postulate of equilibrium. But it is of very little use when it comes to actual questions of practice. In a dynamic society experiencing growth and surplus, talk of simple reproduction in isolation is absolutely unrealistic. It is like trying to determine surplus value by taking the value as an independent variable to which surplus value could be added *a posteriori*. In fact, value cannot be determined without surplus value, just as it cannot be determined before the system of prices and profits.

[16] For a recent, very complete, and synthetic point of view, see Theodore W. Allen, *The Origin of Racial Oppression in Anglo-America*, vol. 1, *The Invention of the White Race*, and vol. 2, *Racial Oppression and Social Control* (London and New York: Verso, 1994 and 1997).

[17] Y. Moulier Boutang, *De l'Esclavage au salariat,* 295–301.

[18] A book of fundamental importance on this subject is Pierre Dockès, *La libération médiévale* (Paris: Flammarion, 1980).

[19] See the interesting reflections of Sandro Mezzadra , op. cit.

[20] Y. Moulier Boutang, *De l' Esclavage au salariat,* 542–544.

[21] Albert O. Hirschman, *Exit Voice and Loyalty: Responses to Decline in Films, Organizations, and States* (Cambridge: Harvard University Press, 1972).

Recent Trends in Peasant Out-Migrations in Contemporary China

Huang Ping

— translated from Chinese by Erica Brindley and Joshua Goldstein

Introductory Remarks

The participation of rural populations in nonagricultural activities in contemporary China is becoming a widespread socio-economic phenomenon. This change is not only transforming the structures of cities and towns; in equally important ways it is also profoundly influencing agricultural development itself, as well as reshaping the overall urban-rural framework. Especially worth noting are the most recent trends since the 1990s. Large numbers of young people in the labor force have been leaving their villages, townships, and counties to search for a livelihood throughout the vast reaches of China. Their search for employment and attempts to open new spaces in which to live has become a social phenomenon of common concern to all. Today, the volume of people leaving their homes for work is historically unprecedented. In all likelihood these migrations are as much a component of the general socio-economic transformation as they are a significant consequence of that transformation.

As Philip Huang discovered in his research on the countryside of North China and the Jiangnan region, commercialization and subsistence farming have coexisted for several centuries in China. Then, in the several decades prior to the economic reforms of the 1970s, urban industrialization proceeded hand in hand with village underdevelopment.[1] Huang has pointed out that this sort of phenomenon runs counter to traditional theoretical models (which are actually based on conditions in England). His work has shown not only that Chinese scholarship is facing a crisis of paradigm; it has also demonstrated that China's rural development has quite likely been following a new and different path of its own.[2]

Philip Huang's research, which continues along the lines of what Fei Xiaotong had coined the "small towns, big problems" dilemma, goes even further than Fei's, embarking on a theoretical investigation of pioneering import.[3] While both Fei and Huang focus on the important implications underlying the sudden rise of Township Village Enterprises (TVEs)[4] in the midst of China's social change, Huang goes the next step to point out that the current flourishing of TVEs in the Jiangnan delta marks the first breakthrough in a trend which he calls "over-intensification/concentration of rural enterprises" (also known as "agricultural involution") — a phenomenon which had long characterized the Chinese countryside.[5]

We should note that Fei's and Huang's research is predominantly based on conditions and developments in rural Jiangnan prior to the mid 1980s. Since the late 1980s, however, as China's TVEs have continued to develop, their absorption of large quantities of the surplus rural labor force was clearly beginning to slow, and from the mid 1990s onward even more problems began arising (or, perhaps, merely began to capture our attention), including the following: 1) inefficient allocations of labor, monetary resources, and technologies; 2) the irrational opening up and utilization of natural resources; 3) serious environmental pollution; and 4) problems related to the break-up and voluntary restructuring of TVEs (including privatization, partnerships with outside companies, annexation, selling to private concerns, and bankruptcy). This situation was intensified by the increased competition in domestic and foreign markets. On the other hand, in China's vast interior as well as the northwest and southwest countrysides, the situation no longer tallies with the comparatively optimistic estimates of the 1980s which predicted that the TVEs in these areas would catch up with the fast-paced development of areas like Jiangnan and Guangdong. Of course, Fei and Huang, who are so familiar with the discrepancies in Chinese society, economy, and culture, never made such optimistic estimations. Fei clearly highlighted how the development in China's northwest differed from the model of small cities and towns in southern Jiangsu. But their research at that time could not precisely and flawlessly predict the various developments that would shape China's countryside in the 1990s. One of these developments is the large number of peasants leaving home seeking either seasonal employment or more permanent migration.

The vast number of peasants out-migrating for work include those leaving home for any amount of time or distance to engage in industry, agriculture, service, or commerce. These migrations have received a certain amount of encouragement and incentive from local governments because they are seen as a means of balancing and connecting the cities with the countryside, industry with agriculture, and the rich with the poor. Out-migration is seen as a channel enabling the continued development of Chinese society as a whole. Following the initial systemic reorganization at the outset of the reform era, this reallocation of the labor force has opened up employment opportunities to the growing surplus labor force (otherwise, their seemingly aimless wanderings throughout the country would be viewed with suspicion as a potentially enormous burden upon all levels of government and society as a whole). Out-migration also provides a crucial reserve labor force for newly flourishing nonagricultural industries. It is seen as a factor promoting the emergence of high-efficiency modern agriculture, a more rapid growth in wealth, and a growing diversification of lifestyles and income sources.

Beyond this, exporting labor is viewed as one of the primary measures for combating poverty. Local-level governments located in remote or ecologically inhospitable areas, as well as international development organizations, make both encouraging and promoting the out-migration of labor a primary focus of their work. They look upon out-migration as one of the fastest methods by which rural people can raise their standards of living, one that does not require large-scale investments nor the borrowing of money. Under many circumstances, it is actually the only viable mode of action. Moreover, those remaining behind in the villages also typically receive remittances, so that they also share in the enjoyment of the out-migrator's increased income. When other members of the family out-migrate, the standard of living for the whole family gradually rises as well.

This article is based on materials obtained in a case study led by the author from 1994–1995. It raises the following questions for discussion: 1) What Philip Huang has called the problem of "too many people with too little land" produced conflicts and pressures which forced peasants to strive for subsistence and survival rather than pursue the greatest comparative advantage. In facing such realities, these peasants made a variety of choices involving the prioritizing of their strategies and motivations. Along these lines, I raise in this essay the issue of "subsistence rationality" as opposed to "economic rationality" (a logic based on seeking profit maximization in the marketplace). This is to say that Chinese peasants, constrained by specific rules and resources, choose modes of living to provide for their families and themselves according to what is comparatively least detrimental to their survival. Primarily compelled by this subsistence rationality, these peasants often end up choosing paths that lead to agricultural involution, or to local development of commercial household handicraft industries, and later to the formation of TVEs. Some also out-migrate to find temporary employment or engage in business. The choices they make do not merely hinge on their own personal wishes but are constrained by social and historical environments — for instance, the structural framework of urban-rural relations, including institutions such as the labor market system, the household registration and identification systems, and food and fuel distribution systems.[6] 2) No matter how willful, realistic, or rationally calculated their decisions, these peasants' intentional actions, such as engaging in local TVEs or going elsewhere for employment, have many kinds of consequences — most of which they had neither hoped for nor predicted. Facing these unintended consequences, they reflexively monitor their actions, changing and adjusting their moves. As a result, they are continuously changing their subsistence environments and repeatedly rupturing the prevailing structure of rules and resources. Even though they may not be aware of it themselves, these types of unintended consequences always have their "positive" significance.

Part I

In surveying, describing, and analyzing China's growing peasant population and their search for nonagricultural work, both locally and through migration, I have come to believe that this trend cannot be adequately explained as exclusively constrained and driven by structural conditions. Nor can it be seen as arising exclusively from the rational choice of individuals seeking their best interests. Rather, the migration phenomenon must be seen as the result of the dialectic of agency and structure,[7] a process which is manifested in the form of over 100 million holders of rural household-registration papers seeking new employment opportunities and living space. If it were not for the limitations and possibilities provided by structural forces and conditions, then, even though peasants might have the impulse to migrate in search of profits and benefits, they would have no means by which to take any realistically meaningful steps in that regard; on the other hand, if peasants did not possess this impulse to seek nonagricultural work, then no matter what kind of structural planning existed, it would be meaningless as far as the peasants themselves were concerned.

The short-and long-term migrations of peasants are definitely not blind or random. On the contrary, peasants usually have clear-cut motivations and aims underlying their actions. At first, most peasants probably sought nonagricultural work as a way to earn some extra cash or supplement their insufficient farm incomes. But, no matter how clear their initial motivations and objectives, while in the process of out-migrating or relocating they are continually reinterpreting and recalculating their behavior, reflexively monitoring their movements and adjusting their tactics. In this way, over time they pass through a process of weighing pros and cons, at times persuading themselves they have made rational and appropriate choices, at others completely re-evaluating their initial aims or even changing these aims. In the end, it is precisely because the actors are reflexively monitoring and adjusting the "tactics" (*guize*) of their movements that the various consequences of these movements are not always predictable by the agents themselves, nor do they necessarily correspond to their original intent, nor do they all necessarily have "positive" or "rational" consequences.

For descriptive convenience, this paper advances the following hypotheses regarding peasants' migration and search for nonagricultural activity:

1) An "objective" reason for the occurrence of out-migrations lies in China's fundamental condition of "too many people, not enough land." Several tens of millions of peasants, or, to be more precise, a considerably large part of the rural population both in absolute and proportional terms, must eventually leave the agricultural sector and rural areas. If we compare the distribution of urban and rural dwellers according to current census registers, then no matter how great the statistical inaccuracies or blind spots, no matter how much low-grade land still remains to be improved and agricultural technology to be promoted, and no matter how many essays can be written in the service of agricultural development, the average amount of arable land per peasant gives us ample reason to say that the majority of the rural population and work force is overabundant and constitutes surplus labor. Realistically, this is probably China's clearest social reality and national condition.

Question: Since the problem of "too many people, not enough land" is by no means a new phenomenon, why were there no such large-scale peasant out-migrations over the past few centuries?

2) The relatively low profit from traditional agriculture, especially cultivation, brought the peasant labor force to the gradual realization that working on agriculture cannot compare to working in areas of industry and business. More and more of the rural population, including some that might not be categorized as surplus labor, have begun to turn toward the strong market influence of nonagricultural employment. Previously, there was always a minority who found it worthwhile to take the risk of nonagricultural activity. But until recently, though the average piece of farmland was very small, if from that sliver of land one could produce about as much income as through miscellaneous jobs in industry and commerce, and if this income was sufficient for rural families to maintain their basic living conditions, then, logically speaking, the majority of the labor force found no need to take such risks in the hope of higher wages.

Question: The diminishing returns in agricultural, especially grain, production did not just emerge recently. The decrease in comparative advantage was already quite apparent in the decades before the "household responsibility" system[8] was implemented. So why at that time (circa 1950–1980) was there not this "tide of migrant labor"?

3) Originally several systems — including labor allocation, household registration, food and fuel coupons, and the health care, welfare, and education systems — created structural conditions that prevented the peasant population (especially those involved in grain production and traditional sidelines) from leaving agriculture. Through various reforms undertaken in the 1980s, these systems were either abolished (like the grain coupon system), underwent massive restructuring (like the urban labor market system), or, whether advertently or inadvertently, collapsed or metamorphosed (like the household registration system which, to a greater or lesser degree, has been replaced by the identity card system). Previously these institutions all matched up and intertwined in such a way as to rigidly bind China's hundreds of millions of peasants and regulate their movements. They divvied up resources and the opportunities to utilize resources in a manner that successfully separated the provisioning of urban and rural populations. Hence — despite

being confronted with land scarcity, despite their consciousness that agricultural incomes were comparatively extremely low, and despite desires to switch to nonagricultural activities — the hundreds of millions who lived and produced in agricultural areas only began to act on these realizations and implement them at a very slow pace.

Question: If this set of systems created a rigid framework regulating movement and separately allocating urban and rural resources, then why were there no large-scale out-migrations prior to when these systems and regulations were implemented (before 1950, for example)?

4) Whether or not the vast rural population and labor force migrates, and how many do so, is greatly determined by whether nonagricultural employment opportunities are available in urban or rural areas. This is a crucial "external" environmental condition shaping migration. The problem of rural overpopulation and land scarcity was becoming increasingly serious during the Ming and Qing periods. But for quite a long time the organizational and systemic frameworks separating the cities and the countryside were not as clear and strict as they would later become. Moreover, because of innumerable "domestic crises and external threats", (*nei you wai huan*)[9] the rate of urban industrial development was relatively slow. Hence, most of the rural surplus labor force continued in traditional agriculture employments (grain production) and continued to contribute to the involutionary cycle; or they had no choice but to stay in rural regions, changing to more marketable crops (like cotton) or developing family handicraft enterprises and small businesses. They adopted these methods to supplement their insufficient agricultural incomes, especially those from grain production. These phenomena, which were more apparent in North China and the Jiangnan regions, demonstrate the so-called phase in which subsistence farming and commercialization coexisted.

Question: Given the serious pressures of overpopulation, land scarcity, and such a large surplus labor force, why did the majority of peasants choose paths leading to over-concentration or involution , without considering on their own the opening up and creation of nonagricultural employment opportunities?

5) Excepting what we have mentioned above as problems of "internal crises and external threats," as well as factors like the slow progress of urbanization and industrialization, there is one other crucial reason for the situation in

China during the majority of years since the Ming and Qing periods. Most of the peasant population resolved the problem of "too many people, not enough land" by adopting involutionary activities rather than going out in search of nonagricultural employment opportunities because, at a cultural level, they were not in a position to compare different occupational modes. Even more so, they were caged in by "traditional" principles of subsistence. Even though the problem of having a dense population and limited land existed at this time, there were also no strictly limiting and systemic controls on labor allocation, housing, or food distribution. Thus, nonagricultural activity did not become the principal mode of employment for most of the peasant population. This was because, under the pressure of overpopulation and land scarcity, peasants were not acting according to the principle of so-called "economic rationality." Rather, they were doing the best they could for the basic survival of their families. Under the egregious environmental conditions of "too many people, too little land" and frequent natural calamities, farming households had one primary consideration: how to preserve and maintain the existence of the entire family. They thus strove to attain the absolute minimum income to maintain survival. Escaping harm was foremost on their minds; only secondarily would they consider pursuing benefit. Moreover, many times these people dared not think of what might be of the greatest advantage to them, desiring but to have enough rice for the table. Traditional peasants were very unlikely to have considered risking and endangering themselves further by turning to new lifestyles and employment opportunities. For these traditional peasants, the countryside and soil were basic life securities from which they simply could not distance themselves psychologically.

Question: Why does this kind of "nightmarish" tradition not hold such sway over today's rural youth? What is it that allows these youth to pay less heed to "tradition" (including the rebuke of their elders)? What has made them so resolute about leaving?

6) The reforms of the 1980s marked the gradual opening up of the entire society. Today the majority of rural youth have at least an elementary education. Modern culture and its various manifestations are daily spreading through mass media technologies, and TV sets have slowly penetrated into villages and even peasant homes. Hence, for today's youth the horizon of vision and thought is already very unlike that of their parents. Through the values they

> have selected and rejected they have fashioned a distinct culture. This cultural background is essential to understanding the rural population's massive migration in search of new ways of life. This new generation is not only facing the problem of "too many people, too little land," they also face the added dilemma that farming delivers comparatively lower benefits. Moreover, ideas like "the village" (*xiang*) and "the soil" (*tu*) no longer have the same cultural meanings for this new generation. They have different lifestyles and value systems with which to compare their own lives. Further, urban development provides them with a greatly increasing number of job opportunities (unfortunately, most of these are in temporary and highly strenuous manual labor). Hence, given a system of increasingly loose restraints, it is not difficult to understand why more peasants would want to leave agriculture and the countryside.
>
> Question: Is this to say that the culture of consumerism that is sweeping through China's cities and coastal regions,[10] has now, in the wake of "the sending down of TV to the countryside" (*danshi xiaxiang*),[11] also started to influence the rural population, especially the youth? When these youth make choices about the nature of their future residences and type of work, are "cultural" (life-style) considerations also a factor that cannot be ignored?

No matter how ample the economic, social and cultural forces are that shape peasant out-migration, and no matter how clear migrants are about their aims and motivations, this type of large-scale, sustained, social phenomenon has a broad variety of consequences, most of which are unexpected or even undesired by the migrants themselves. From the perspective of rural development itself, large-scale peasant migration is not merely about the established goals of the migrants themselves (namely adding to their income). Objectively, migration also decreases the pressures associated with high population density. But as more people come to realize that the migrant labor force is earning more cash, it means that even more people, especially youths who have received some education, are following suit. Moreover, the theoretical distinction we draw between the "surplus" and "nonsurplus" labor force is in no way clearly visible in real life. It is entirely probable that the out-migrant populations also included a theoretically "nonsurplus" portion. And, to go a step further, since out-migrants are always ruminating over their actions and adjusting and "rationalizing" their efforts, they are always changing their aims: what was originally fixed as a short-term stay might become a medium-term one, what was once seasonal becomes annual, and so forth. In this way, rural development (including reforms in traditional agriculture), the promotion and application of modern agricultural technology, and the reorganization of rural districts and peasant households, all might be affected.

After out-migrants reach the city, they usually cannot "settle down" as quickly as they thought they could. Especially in times of economic depression, when markets have decreased and demand is insufficient, migrants do not necessarily find more satisfying work, nor can they start immediately leading an urban lifestyle. It takes them even longer to become accepted by their other city folk and, to a great extent, they simply become members of the urban underclass. Hence, at the same time that the rural population, due to the out-migration of labor, is slowly finding relief from a degree of poverty, in the cities a new and equally impoverished class has begun to emerge.

Part II

From 1994 to 1996 my colleagues and I conducted a survey in four provinces and eight villages, querying a total of 280 peasant households. On the basis of levels of socio-economic development and geographic location, we chose the provinces of Jiangsu, Anhui, Sichuan, and Gansu as general sites. From each province we then selected two villages, and from each village 35 households. The villages of this sample can be arranged according to the following types: 1) villages in which the level of TVE development is relatively high and peasants have basically realized the move to nonagricultural employment while remaining predominantly in their own region (Villages 1 and 2 in Jiangsu); 2) villages in which TVEs are somewhat less developed so that only a portion of peasants out-migrate for work (Villages 3 and 4 in Anhui); 3) villages in which the basic modes of production are traditional farming sideline occupations and where, due to the problem of high population density and little land, if more peasants did not out-migrate, there would be no means by which whole families could survive (Villages 5 and 6 in Sichuan); and finally, 4) villages in which harsh environmental conditions, especially drought, give rise to extremely low agricultural production yet, because the area is so remote, peasants primarily find work within provincial boundaries (Villages 7 and 8 in Gansu). None of these villages could be counted among the richest or poorest in all of China. Their populations and labor conditions can be seen in Tables 1 and 2.

Table 1
Eight Villages: Population and labor conditions

	Village							
Parameter	1	2	3	4	5	6	7	8
Total population	1121	1505	2250	1688	1805	841	2076	1720
Total number of households	244	438	467	470	484	240	480	350
Total labor force	627	896	1327	1060	1020	414	1324	1014
Average household size	4.6	3.4	4.8	3.6	3.7	3.5	4.3	5.0
Average number of laborers per household	2.6	2.0	2.8	2.3	2.1	1.7	2.8	2.9

Information source: The four province, eight village, 280 household interview survey. (Unless otherwise labelled the following information is all taken from this survey.)

Table 2
280 households: Population and labor power

	Village							
Parameter	1	2	3	4	5	6	7	8
Total number of persons	161	137	179	162	173	169	196	190
Total number of laborers	104	92	136	97	128	117	117	118
Number of persons per household	4.6	3.9	5.1	4.6	4.9	4.8	5.6	5.4
Number of laborers per household	2.9	2.6	3.9	2.8	3.7	3.3	3.3	3.4

The overpopulation/land scarcity phenomenon has been a key limiting factor in the socio-economic development of China's countryside for a long time. For the increasing rural population, there is an ever-decreasing amount of arable land. Not only does the land provide farmers with insufficient cash income, in some regions it does not even supply them with the necessary food supply for the year. Our investigations further demonstrate that if peasants are not utilizing various opportunities to increase and broaden their own farmlands, then they are thinking of ways to out-migrate or immediately find nonagricultural work.[12] In these eight villages, the number of persons transferring into the nonagricultural sector or out-migrating for employment varies greatly in both absolute and proportional terms. For instance, in the two Jiangsu villages, because the level of TVE development is relatively high, most of the labor force simply turns to nonagricultural work within their home village or township. The examples of the towns in Anhui and Sichuan show us that in most of the villages almost half of the labor force out-migrates or relocates. Village 6 provides us with an exception. Growth in recent years gave rise to the booming production of traditional sidelines, so the out-migrating labor force of that town was smaller. And in Gansu, geographic and cultural factors have shaped conditions so that despite the lack of growth in TVEs, the proportion of people out-migrating and seeking work is still only about 33% (Table 3).

Table 3
Eight villages: Numbers and ratios of out-migrating labor

	Village							
Parameter	1	2	3	4	5	6	7	8
Total number of laborers	627	896	1327	1060	1020	414	1324	1014
Number of agricultural laborers	42	40	676	582	503	289	916	683
Percentage of agricultural laborers	6.7	4.5	50.9	54.9	49.3	69.8	69.2	67.4
Number of out-migrating laborers	585	856	651	478	517	125	408	331
Percentage of out-migrating laborers	93.3	95.5	49.1	45.1	50.7	30.2	30.8	32.6

From Table 4 we can see that, excluding Villages 7 and 8, the average amount of farmland per person for the remaining six villages came to around 1.5 *mu* (*mμ* = 1/15th of a hectare). For three of the villages, the average did not even come to 1 *mu*. According to the 280 household interviews, the average amount of land per person in our surveys for the most part corresponded to prevailing village conditions (Table 5). Moreover, in all eight villages, due to the natural growth in

Table 4
Eight villages: Arable land (in *mu*)

Parameter	Villages 1	2	3	4	5	6	7	8
Total arable land	1211	1020	1860	2005	1299	1101	5067	2645
Average per capita arable land	1.08	0.68	0.82	1.18	0.72	1.31	2.44	1.51
Average arable land per laborer	1.93	1.14	1.40	1.89	1.23	2.66	3.82	2.61
Average arable land per household	4.96	2.33	3.98	4.27	2.69	4.58	10.56	7.56

Table 5
280 households: Arable land (in *mu*)

Parameter	Villages 1	2	3	4	5	6	7	8
Total arable land	282	54	182	168	105	203	437	301
Arable land per capita	1.75	0.39	1.01	1.05	.061	1.20	2.23	1.58
Arable land per laborer	2.71	0.59	1.34	1.74	0.82	1.73	3.74	2.55
*Arable land per household	3.70	1.50	5.00	4.50	2.90	5.60	12.50	8.90

* Household averages are based on medians rather than means because the 35 households in Village 1 included one from Zhejiang which specialized in farming and contracted out 150 *mu*.

the peasant population and an absolute decrease in the amount of arable land, the average amount of arable land per capita is steadily decreasing. The primary reason for the decrease in arable land is that a large portion is being used for nonagricultural purposes. The purposes include: the local and national governments laying or widening of roads or engaging in development projects, townships and villages starting up factories or commercial stores, and peasants themselves constructing new houses and buildings. Since 1993 arable land in Village 1 had decreased by a third. The same problem exists for Village 2 where, since 1990, 25% of the village's superior farmland had been used for building factories and houses and repairing roads. Arable land per capita in Villages 3 and 4 is not much more than in Villages 1 and 2, but in these two villages the problem lies not only in the quantity of land but in its quality. Peasants here must invest large amounts of money in irrigation if they are to insure their own provision, meet the state's purchasing quota, make sure they have a minimal amount of cash income, and achieve stability in their grain output. In Villages 5 and 6, population increases have also caused per capita arable land to decrease. In Village 5, for instance, it decreased from 0.81 *mu* in 1981 to 0.72 *mu* by 1994. In Village 7 mountain land is plentiful but flat land scarce: of the 6620 *mu* of farmland, 82.87% is infertile mountain terrain. Since the land is poor and output low, people in Village 7 have historically adopted the practice of "wide planting and thin harvesting" — planting on several extra *mu* of land so as to supplement the insufficiencies of low output. There is serious erosion as well. The village's unique geographical location (it is situated along the Longhai Railway line and is the capital of the local government), along with other space-occupying pursuits such as the laying of new rail lines and public roads and the construction of TVEs, all decrease the area's arable land considerably. At the same time, the frequency of marriages and births has increased the population of Village 7 sharply. Arable per capita land in Village 8 was 2.04 *mu* in 1981. However, such factors as population increase and the construction of schools, public roads, and homes had caused this number to decrease to 1.5 *mu* by 1994.

No matter how one views it, arable per capita land in these eight villages is far from sufficient for the needs of their ever-increasing populations. In other words, there exists a huge excess labor force in these regions, so large that it well exceeds anything Philip Huang had come across in his detailed regional studies of North China during Ming-Qing times. As Huang pointed out, the contradiction over the last few centuries of high population density and limited land caused peasants to engage in involutionary practices and hence forced them to endure the problem of steadily diminishing returns. Under such population and land pressures, peasants did not follow any "economic rationality" (the pursuit of maximum profit). For basic survival, they threw themselves into a mode of production that entailed consistently decreasing returns on their labor. Even though they were not simply seeking maximum profit, they were also not simply suffering exploitation either. Each individual peasant, still needing to provide for his or her family's basic expenses, turned to agricultural production (as well as to other sidelines like rural handicrafts).[13] After collectivization in the 1950s, agricultural production increased three-fold, but the labor force investment was also three to four times that of before. Collectivization was originally supposed to increase labor productivity, but due to the pressure of a swelling population along with the organization of certain government policies and systems, the outcome remained economic growth without economic development. Agriculture involuted as before and peasants, generally speaking, were still struggling bitterly for survival. China's countryside was still far from being a "modern society."

Here, the key unit of analysis is not the individual peasant but the peasant household. Many choices facing these peasants, including their decision to tolerate involutionary diminishing returns from their labor, if viewed exclusively from the perspective of the individual, seem very difficult to comprehend. This is especially true when thinking according to principles like so-called "economic rationality" or "maximization of profits." However, China's peasants have historically not participated in economic activities based on the interests of the single individual but in terms of the family or clan. Despite the fact that involution led to diminishing returns, as long as an activity translated into an increase in the household's overall output, then, from the perspective of family survival, it was worthwhile.[14] This is why this paper maintains that, at least for the vast population of China's peasants, subsistence rationality or, in other words, the weighing of choices according to that which is least detrimental to maintaining the survival of the entire family, is the most practical motivating force. In theoretical terms, no matter what the systemic or structural conditions, China's peasants have by no means completely lacked the power to act purposefully. On the contrary, according to the dictates of subsistence rationality they nearly always chose and acted so as to best insure the survival of themselves and their families, and were constantly evaluating, choosing, and acting. Still, there is no doubt that no matter how clear and purposeful their actions may be, these actions often produce a variety of undesired and unpredictable consequences. Of these unintended consequences, the consequences of greatest theoretical and practical meaning are those that bring about a reorganization in the rules and their structuring resources.[15] When we use this explanation to understand the contract/production responsibility system or the flourishing of TVEs in southern Jiangsu and Guangdong, they no longer appear anomalous.

Undoubtedly, the level of development of TVEs does not simply depend on whether there is a will and aim to achieve development; it also depends on whether a particular locality possesses the necessary rudimentary natural resources and conditions. This is to say that not every region could develop TVEs as smoothly as southern Jiangsu (and Guangdong, and other places where TVE development has been smooth). Even though the peasants of south Jiangsu and the coastal regions have accomplished this, it does not necessarily mean that the people of the interior regions, the northwest, and the southwest will be able to accomplish the same, regardless of how much will they muster or effort they expend. From this we can say that even agents acting with clear objectives cannot completely divorce themselves from structural conditions (rules and resources) in their search for subsistence and development. Since the late 1980s and early 1990s the "wave of workers" out-migrating from the countryside in search of employment has increased daily and is surging to flood levels. This is occurring for the following reasons: 1) the interior, northwest, and southwest regions do not have the ability to develop their own TVEs as smoothly as did southern Jiangsu and Guangdong, 2) the TVEs in the coastal areas are no longer able to absorb the outside rural labor force as quickly as they did initially, and 3) at the same time a new round of urban reform and development, particularly in the Southeast coastal cities, is exerting a forceful impetus.

Part III

It could be claimed that facing China's long-lasting, acute contradiction between population and land resources, an increasing number of peasants ultimately took the initiative and broke through the regulatory limits and resource constraints. That doing so would require they stride into a much vaster environment to search for or open up new resources, and that in the process they would create new rules for subsistence, was perhaps unavoidable. Especially against the backdrop of the reform of the land allocation system, and the relaxation of constraints in the household registration, grain coupon, employment, and other such systems, this process seems even more inevitable.

Still, the over-population/ land scarcity problem is only one of the causes underlying the recent migration of peasants in search of work and commercial activity. Another cause is that agricultural production is yielding such comparatively poor returns that peasants feel planting their fields is no longer worthwhile. Historically, and largely due to the effects of traditional folk culture, the bulk of China's peasants have been unwilling to leave their home villages unless it was a matter of life and death. Instead, they preferred to endure the strains of involution so long as the general output for their family or lineage as a whole could be raised by such means, and the family thereby sustain itself intact. Even after the 1950s, these traditional values and ways of thinking continued to affect the older generations of peasants. Still, even young people could not simply leave the countryside and abandon farming at will because, no matter how unprofitable agricultural production often was, the so-called dualistic structure of urban-rural relations in China was not anywhere as open as what Meier and others postulated for markets in the West.[16] Hence, the degree of agricultural involution had to reach a level where marginal returns were nearly zero before peasants began to break out of their pre-existing patterns and test new paths. The household responsibility system of the 1960s and the commune enterprises of the 1970s all serve to illustrate how, even under extremely fixed structural conditions, peasants still managed to exert their agency.[17]

Coming to the late 1970s and early 1980s, the Anhui peasants' experiment with the contract responsibility system and its subsequent rapid spread across the nation further demonstrated that agricultural involution had its limits.[18] Once this limit was approached or exceeded, the ability of the structure to restrict agency had reached its limit. That development now took new forms — the household responsibility system, TVEs, out-migration for employment — was because of the accumulated force of individual peasants' agency constantly breaking through the constraints of the existing system. Only half-conscious of their effects, peasants created new methods, restructuring rules and resources. The household responsibility system solved the problem of peasant enthusiasm for farming; TVEs finally started to counter the trend of agricultural involution.

Still, TVEs were something that peasants were compelled to create under the prevailing dualistic framework which had divided urban and rural, industry and agriculture in the 1980s. Even as involution was causing returns on agricultural labor to approach zero, and while comparative advantage was surely too low, peasants at this time still could not legally enter cities to work en masse. Hence local TVEs were a product of peasants' subsistence rationality: the least detrimental choice under unavoidable circumstances. At the time peasants began to forge the TVE path, they were merely reacting to the terribly low comparative advantage in agriculture by trying to find a way, in addition to traditional sidelines, to make some cash income to help meet their subsistence needs. It did not occur to them that this move finally marked the historic reversal of involution; nor did problems like depletion of land or environmental pollution occur to them.

Farming's low comparative advantage was a clear problem in all eight villages in our survey. The conditions of all 280 households we interviewed showed low wages for farming and traditional sideline occupations. In 1994, the overall average income from crop cultivation totalled about 2000 *yuan*, not quite 400 *yuan* per person, with traditional sidelines (pig, chicken, and duck farming) totalling even less (Table 6).[19]

Table 6
280 households: Income from farming and traditional by-employments (in 1000s of *yuan*)

	Villages								
Parameter	1	2	3	4	5	6	7	8	Total
Farming income per household	1.60	0.83	3.00	1.75	1.90	2.50	1.32	3.14	1.96
Farming income per laborer	0.35	0.18	0.50	0.40	0.39	0.56	0.22	0.56	0.38
By-employment income per household	2.00	–	1.40	1.30	1.43	2.15	1.60	1.88	1.90
By-employment income per laborer	0.40	–	0.22	0.29	0.34	0.52	0.25	0.34	0.34

Note: All numbers are derived from the median. Village 2 specialized in no traditional by-employments.

At the beginning of the 1970s, Villages 1 and 2 in Jiangsu started to form brigade-level enterprises. At first this was only to make up for the decreasing returns brought on by agricultural involution, but later, as TVEs really caught fire, agriculture itself gradually slipped to occupy a position of secondary economic importance. By the time of our survey, farming had already devolved into a small economic sideline. Taking Village 1 as an example, during the 30-year period from 1949 until the onset of the reforms, very few of this village's peasants had the opportunity to turn to nonagricultural production or move to other areas. If peasants here wished to earn a bit of cash through some nonagricultural work in order to supplement their incomes, then the only way to do so was by studying skilled manual arts such as carpentry, masonry, haircutting, tailoring, or cooking. Following the 1978 reforms, this village's TVEs began to emerge from what was originally a brigade-level sideline work team. At first these businesses consisted of small, family-sized workshops specializing in metal polishing, preparing concrete, and producing cardboard (boxes). Starting in 1985, the village quickly sprouted a sheet metal factory, a smelting factory, and a flame-plating factory.

In 1993 the village's total income was 1,720,000 *yuan*, of which TVEs brought in 1,687,500 and agriculture only 32,500, or less than 2% of the village's total income. From the onset of the economic reforms until the end of 1993, of the village's 627-person labor force, 246 (39.2% of the total labor force) had already entered into work units in the market sector, township-level enterprises employed another 85 (13.6%), village-level businesses employed 135 (21.5%), 119 people (19.0%) owned their own businesses in the village, and 42 people (6.7%) still engaged in agricultural and sidelines.[20] In previous decades, because of systemic or policy restrictions, peasants could not engage in occupations outside of agriculture, no less even breathe a word about issues like comparative advantage.[21] But since the reforms peasants have been permitted to engage in other types of work locally, and they quickly found that any form of employment was preferable to agriculture. For example, one peasant family farming a total of 6.7 *mu* faced annual expenses of 650 *yuan*, broken down as follows: 200 *yuan* for chemical fertilizers, 100 *yuan* for pesticides, 100 *yuan* for mechanisation, 90 *yuan* for water and electricity, 160 *yuan* farm tax. Peasant farmers do not usually count seeds and manual labor as production costs because these are counted as personal possessions already belonging to the family or oneself. If one were to take account of these two costs, then one should add another 100 *yuan* per *mu* of land for seeds for two seasons, and 100 *yuan* per *mu* for labor. The actual investment for seeds and labor, then, totals 300 *yuan* per *mu* annually. In 1993 the local value of grain was 0.50 *yuan* per *jin* (0.5 kilos) for rice and 0.40 *yuan* per *jin* for wheat. Calculated according to this village's average production levels, in a good year one *mu* yields 1000 *jin* of rice and 500 *jin* of wheat, so each *mu* annually produces 700 *yuan* in grain. If one were to subtract seed and labor expenses, each *mu* of land nets about 400 *yuan* per year. The average cultivated land per capita of this village is 1.1 *mu*, the average number of persons per household is 4.6, and the average amount of land per household is 5 *mu*. Figuring each household to consist of two laborers, husband and wife, then 5 *mu* of land sown to grain will earn them a net profit of only 2000 *yuan*, or an average of 1000 *yuan* per laborer annually (non-cash income included). By way of comparison, the salaries of workers in the village-run enterprises runs from 5000 to 7000 *yuan* while workers in independent market enterprises earn 6000–8000 *yuan*.

Similarly, the predecessor to the TVEs in Village 2 in Jiangsu was a tiny agricultural equipment repair station. In the late 1960s and early 1970s, under the banner of "preserving agriculture through engaging in industry," this village not only retained the workshop, but also made use of the special conditions prevailing under the campaign to develop rural industry. They utilized the skills and energy of the village's retirees and of urban laborers who had returned to the countryside. Taking advantage of the opportunity occasioned by the scarcity of machine goods at the time, the shop continually expanded. By 1980 it could already produce more than 700 spare parts used in photocopying machines. From 1978 to 1987, the number of enterprises in the village grew from two to eight, and the number of employees jumped from 77 to 812, eventually absorbing 95% of the entire village's labor force.

By the time of our survey, of the village's 896 member labor force, all but 40 persons still involved in agricultural work had transferred into TVEs, commercial enterprises, or service enterprises. In 1993 the total income from such enterprises for the entire village reached 230,690,000 *yuan*, while income generated by agriculture came to only 970,000 *yuan*, amounting to only 0.4% of the total village income. For the 35 households surveyed, the total income from nonagricultural enterprises came to 5,350,000 *yuan*, while the amount earned from farming was a bare 290,000 *yuan* — only 5% of the total income for those households.[22]

In Village 3 in Anhui 49.1% of the total labor force out-migrated to find employment. The cost-benefit ratio of working the land here has caused peasants to feel that "farming is not worth it," and that "picking up trash in the cities is better than growing crops in the countryside."[23] The average parcel of farmland per household in this village was about 4 *mu*, with the average expenditure, output, and related costs per *mu* roughly calculated as follows: under normal conditions one *mu* of land here produces 1000 *jin* of rice and 300 *jin* of wheat, equivalent to an income of about 800 *yuan*; each *mu* requires 24 *yuan* for seeds, 200 *yuan* for fertilizers and pesticides, 58 *yuan* for irrigation, and 18 *yuan* for agricultural tax. Calculating other village exactions and fixed expenses in terms of *yuan* per *mu* we come to the following: 10 *yuan* for road building and maintenance; 10 *yuan* for school facilities; 8 *yuan* for maintenance of rivers and lakes, 3 *yuan* for the local teacher training; and 2 *yuan* for birth planning, militia training, and welfare for veteran families. Finally, in 1994 each household was required to sell 20 *jin* of every 100 *jin* grown to meet a requisition by the state to aid the province's calamity-stricken regions.[24] The total for the above investment and other required expenses was 333 *yuan*. Calculated in this way, the income from one *mu* of land was not quite 500 *yuan*, in which is included the family's needs for food grain. Since peasants do not typically count their own food grain as income, the situation truly accords with their saying that "farming brings you no (cash) income."

Average arable land per household in Anhui's Village 4 was slightly more than 4 *mu*. Here we interviewed Household A, which had planted 9 *mu* of land, more than enough in comparison to the rest of the village. But they were also one of the few families in the village for whom farming was the primary source of income. In 1994 they harvested 8000 *jin* of rice and 1200 *jin* of rape. If the rice paddies yield 1000 *jin* per *mu* and the rape fields 150 *jin* per *mu*, then grain sales, including that purchased by state requisition, was 4000 *jin* sold for a total of 3000 *yuan*. After the state took its share of contracted rape, this left the family 150 *jin* of oil to sell at 5 *yuan* per *jin*, totalling 750 *yuan*. They also planted 1 *mu* of peanuts, harvesting 380 *jin*, of which they sold 250 *jin* (at 1.6 *yuan* per *jin*), pocketing 400 *yuan*. All totalled, then, they earned 4150 *yuan*. As for investments (for all 9 *mu* of land), various expenditures including pesticides, water costs, and so forth, totalled about 1000 *yuan*; seeds cost 200 *yuan*; and agricultural tax government exactions came to 600 *yuan*. In addition, at harvest this family hires temporary laborers, paying 60 *yuan* per *mu* and three daily meals. They pay helpers to transplant rice seedlings at 25–30 *yuan* per *mu* and three daily meals, and these people generally work for 4–5 days. All of the above expenses total about 2600 *yuan*. What they earn from their yield, on the other hand, is rather low; so, from working 9 *mu* of land their net income is no more than 1500 *yuan* annually (not even counting the family's own investment in labor). Household B in this village only farmed 5 *mu*, closer to the village average. They attested that in one year they shouldered the following costs (in *yuan*): seeds (100), fertilizers (500), hiring people twice to till the land (60/*mu*), pesticides (30), and agricultural tax (~80/*mu*). Their conclusion was that "farming expenses are too high; one does not get anything from it but a bit of food for the table."

The situation in the Sichuan villages was still worse. For example, in 1994 more than half of the labor force in Village 5 out-migrated and still the average arable land per capita was only 0.7 *mu*. If an average *mu* produces 1000 *jin* of rice at a price of 1.60 *yuan* per kilo, the gross income per *mu* is around 800 *yuan*. In Village 5, fixed costs of production include 120 *yuan* for seeds, fertilizer, pesticides, etc., and 25–30 days of labor per *mu*. If one is doing labor oneself, then at 5 *yuan* a day one would need anywhere from 125–150 *yuan* per *mu*. Taxes and other state exactions total about 210 *yuan* per *mu*. According to our calculations from the 35 households we queried, the net average income of peasants working in cultivation (grain, cotton, and rapeseed) and sidelines (raising pigs or domestic fowl) comes to no more than 370–380 *yuan* — just about 1 *yuan* a day!

Average per capita farmland in Village 6 (1.31 *mu*) is more than in Village 5, but the hilliness of the terrain, the scarcity of irrigated fields, the dearth of water resources, and the threat of drought combine to make agricultural producers shoulder an extremely high level of natural risks. According to provincial meteorological statistics from 1957–1985, in 28 years there were 21 spring droughts, 27 summer droughts, and 22 early autumn droughts. In 1993–1994 drought conditions were extremely serious, and agricultural production plummeted. In 1994, rice production of the entire village fell by 51%, corn by 64.3%, and sweet potatoes by 44%. In this way the investment in agriculture production was high while yield was low. In addition to suffering these harsh environmental pressures, peasants also have had to cope with the "price-scissors" effect between industrial and agricultural goods, driving the comparative advantage in the agricultural sector, especially in crop cultivation, even lower. According to the rough estimates of village cadres, farming one *mu* of land requires an investment of more than 100 *yuan* for chemical fertilizer alone. After adding in labor costs, there is simply no money to be made. And if the harvest is bad because of drought, then one will actually lose money. So villagers' incomes must come from sideline occupations (raising pigs and geese, pickling vegetables, and other pursuits).[25] Despite the contribution from sidelines, there are still many families who have trouble getting enough grain to eat and thus are hardly in a position to think of selling their crops for cash to meet their daily needs.

As for the two villages in Gansu, although there is far more land per capita, its quality is far worse, and the climate is dry and drought-prone, causing peasant incomes to be extremely low. In Village 7 farmland consists of loess, but due to the arid climate, the average nutrient and water levels of the soil are very low, and though the level of organic mineral deposits is high, the soil does not retain them. Furthermore, this soil qualifies only as low yield because total nitrogen content is lower than normal. The village is situated in the province's northern semi-arid region where rainfall is lowest, a mere 420–450 millimeters a year. Moreover, rainfall in winter, spring, and early summer is relatively low, peaking from July to September (accounting for 55% of the annual rainfall) and this produces a conflict over water supply among farming, forestry, and herding sectors. Vegetation is sparse and evaporation levels high, resulting in low rates of water use and frequent dry spells. Droughts occur most frequently in the spring, averaging once every two years. On occasion there is even continuous drought through the entire year. Even though hydraulic engineering has solved the village's problem of drinking water for people and livestock, there is no irrigation to the fields, and no pools, lakes, or rivers pass through the village. Hence, when there is a drought, grain supply decreases precipitously and peasants have to purchase grain or rely on government relief to survive. Living in this impoverished land and calamity-prone climate, the peasants of Village 7 not only suffer from insecurity over basic food supply in bad years; even in a fairly good year their grain output is not high: generally 95 kilos per *mu*. Among the 21 peasant households surveyed (information from 14 of the 35 households was unclear, so they are excluded), the following statistics apply: in 1993, 278 *mu* of contracted land was used for farming crops such as wheat, corn, potatoes, millet, sesame, and rape, and other crops. According to the market values in that year, the total wages earned from agriculture equalled 32,760 *yuan*, about 117.84 *yuan* per *mu* of land. However, subtracting the 16.56 *yuan* per *mu* needed for agricultural chemicals, 1.5 *yuan* for contracting the land, and 0.40 *yuan* for agricultural and forestry production tax, peasants realized 99.38 *yuan* per *mu*. This figure does not include the costs for seeds, human labor, animal labor, water, and other expenses. In a good year, then, peasants can earn no more than 100 *yuan* per *mu*, while more generally bad environmental conditions consistently threaten their survival. In the long-standing struggle against nature, village peasants have developed a mode of survival: in times of calamitous drought, government relief + going out to work = food to eat; in times of no drought or disaster, farming + going out to work = food to eat and a little spending money. The out-migrations of village peasants were thus driven by basic requirements for survival, like "getting a mouthful of food" and "earning some change to spend."

In Village 8, village peasants also believed that "money doesn't come from farming; it isn't worth it." First, this means that farmers cannot make ends meet. The 30 households surveyed in 1994 (the other five households' responses regarding their incomes and expenditures were unclear and so are not counted here), earned a total of 96,166 *yuan* from agriculture, while their living expenses totalled 96,473 *yuan*. Broken down by household, this means that the average income was 3205.53 *yuan*, while expenses were 3215.77 *yuan* — a deficit of 10.24 *yuan*. So, without even considering the educational or social conditions here, peasant yearly incomes were barely enough to meet daily living expenses. Second, while investments in agricultural production are high, the income from it is comparatively very low. Excluding the five households that gave inconsistent information, the 30 households surveyed contracted a total 265 *mu* of land. Given that the total annual income from agricultural work was 95,206 *yuan*, the average income per *mu* came to 359.27 *yuan*. These 30 households invested 26,610 *yuan* in fertilizer and pesticide (mechanisation costs not included), or 100.42 *yuan* per *mu*. Adding an average of 7.56 *yuan* per *mu* agricultural tax, peasants earned at most 251.29 *yuan* annually per *mu*.

As a result of the very low comparative advantage of agricultural production, farmers, especially young farmers, are not willing to farm the land and are far more willing to transfer to the nonagricultural sector or out-migrate to find work in industry, commerce, or even trash picking. In Village 1 there was a "farming strike" led by a small group of village folk. The households in this small organization believed that farming was a waste of time and demanded the village government take back their contracted land. The result was that the village council gave in and directly divided the land into "responsibility land" and "grain land," then recouped the land and contracted it to households from Zhejiang that specialized in farming. In both Villages 2 and 3 land was "abandoned," resulting in about 100 *mu* in Village 3 being left to waste. The village leadership clearly explained that they dare not redistribute the land again for fear that villagers would simply return their contracted plots one after another, thereby setting a precedent and creating a situation that could be impossible to control. Villagers had already expressed that they had no interest in farming the land which others had abandoned. In Village 4, 40% of the villagers expressed their willingness to return contracted land to the village government. Even in Villages 5 and 6, where the land shortage problem is obvious, peasants were unwilling to farm more land, feeling that the investment, local exactions, and various expenses simply made it not worth the effort. Village 8 is perhaps the only exception in our study. There, a regulation permitted the temporary adjustment of land: each time a household gained or lost two persons, that household likewise gained or lost one person's share of land. But even in Village 8 (as well as Village 7), only when a family's land was originally insufficient to provide for their basic sustenance did they express the hope that they could farm on this additionally supplied land.

Once systems started to loosen, especially as household registration was to a certain extent replaced by the personal ID system and grain coupons were no longer used, peasants, especially the youth, started to devise other plans of action. In this way, they went from the household responsibility system to TVEs, and then from local TVEs to out-migrating for work. China's peasants, step by step, transferred or migrated to realize their own goals (all along prevailed upon by the search for subsistence!), and in the process gradually, half-consciously, transformed behavioral norms and systemic constraints, and altered the comprehensive pattern of resources. If we wished to say that peasants do indeed act "rationally," carefully calculating investments and outputs, then when they are making their various choices, they are not primarily pursuing profit, but rather subsistence. Moreover, it is only when structural conditions permit (or at least are somewhat loose) that peasants, especially peasant youth, are able to act in this manner.

The above actions have lead to a variety of unintended consequences which, by and large, the actors themselves neither predicted nor desired. Most importantly, these actions do not always produce "positive" effects. The breaking down of the old framework does not necessarily mean that the new framework produced will be well-suited for the sustainable development of rural society.

The evidence of this micro-analysis of eight villages demonstrates that the villages themselves are subject to direct positive effects from out-migration. In line with the migrants' expectations, the average individual and household cash incomes in villages rose. Objectively speaking, out-migration also caused a certain slowing of the overpopulation/land scarcity bind. When these migrations first began, these outcomes were probably not clearly foreseen by migrants or their families as separate, discrete goals. However, in today's cramped countryside even the elderly are beginning to realize that, even if their sons and daughters are unable to mail any money home from their jobs, at least their out-migration can be considered a kind of escape.

Figuring for all eight villages, 280 households, and 1367 individuals, average arable land per capita comes to 1.27 *mu*, and the average gross income per person is 728 *yuan*. Following the transfer of 569 people to the nonagricultural sector, average arable land rises to 2.17 *mu*, and, even if out-migrants fail to remit a cent to their homes, the average gross income from farming rises to 1247 *yuan* per person. In reality, the incomes of migrants and those in TVEs and local businesses is far from negligible (see Tables 7, 8, and 9). We can see further in Table 10 that, according to the local nonagricultural and migrant workers themselves and their families, in 1994, of the 569 persons involved in local industry or migrant labor, nearly 90% made over 1000 *yuan*, and of those people, over 60% managed to remit over 1000 *yuan* back to their families.[26]

This is not to say that the land per person ratio is equitable or the average income plentiful. Because local conditions differ, the basic land and cash requirements of the people also differ. To figure out whether or not a labor surplus exists, one has to judge according to geographical conditions, the organization of labor, the mode of production, and the degree to which agricultural technologies are being utilized. Similarly, whether people are able to meet their basic cash needs must be estimated according to each locality's conditions of production, taxation, and exaction and the prevailing standard of living.[27]

Table 7
280 households: Changes in family size and number of laborers

	Village								
Parameter	1	2	3	4	5	6	7	8	Total
Prior to migration:									
Number of persons in village	161	137	179	162	173	169	196	190	1,367
Number of laborers in village	104	92	136	97	128	117	117	118	909
After out-migration:									
Number of persons in village	67	40	109	108	109	104	131	129	798
Number of laborers in village	24	9	67	49	67	59	63	59	397

Table 8
280 households: Changes in amount of arable land

Parameter	Village 1	2	3	4	5	6	7	8	Total
Total arable land	281.9	54.4	181.7	168.3	105.4	202.7	437.3	300.7	1,732
Before labor out-migration:									
Per capita	1.75	0.39	1.01	1.05	0.61	1.20	2.23	1.58	1.27
Per laborer	2.71	0.59	1.34	1.74	0.82	1.73	3.74	2.55	1.91
After labor out-migration:									
Per capita	4.21	1.36	1.67	1.56	0.97	1.95	3.34	2.33	2.17
Per laborer	11.75	6.04	2.72	3.43	1.57	3.44	6.94	5.10	4.36

Table 9
280 households: Income from industry and services* (in 1000s of *yuan*)

Parameter	Village 1	2	3	4	5	6	7	8	Total
Industrial work: Average per capita income	3.45	3.60	1.50	1.10	0.28	0.53	0.35	0.19	1.20
Industrial work: Average income per worker	5.00	5.75	2.00	1.63	0.39	0.83	0.79	0.31	1.78
Service work: Average per capita income	1.38	0.90	0.78	1.00	0.30	1.00	0.08	0.50	0.50
Service work: Average income per worker	1.50	1.13	1.25	1.00	0.75	2.00	0.20	0.60	0.75

* Industry includes: construction, transportation, maintenance, textile, etc. Service includes small shops, beverage stands, cleaning and sweeping, etc.
Note: all figures in this chart are derived from medians for each village.

Table 10
280 households: Cash earned and remitted by out-migrants

Cash earned		Cash remitted	
Amount (*yuan*)	Percentage of out-migrants	Amount (*yuan*)	Percentage of out-migrants
0	3.9	0	16.6
50 – 200	1.9	50 – 200	3.8
250 – 500	5.5	250 – 500	8.1
501 – 1000	12.1	501 – 1000	11.1
1001 – 3000	14.0	1001 – 3000	21.6
3001 – 5000	24.8	3001 – 5000	13.6
5001 – 10000	28.9	5001 – 10000	19.9
Over 10000	8.9	Over 10000	5.3

The following trends are of great importance: 63.82% of those out-migrating are between 18 and 35 years of age, while 62.49% of those left behind are over 36 years old (see Table 11). Tables 12 and 13 further reveal that over half those leaving are males, while nearly 70% of those left behind are female. Of the total number of villagers with middle or high school education, almost 70% out-migrate or transfer out of agriculture, while around 80% of the functionally illiterate stay behind. With over half (56.3%) of the labor force leaving agriculture or migrating, these villages have begun to be taken over by the so-called "3–8–6–1–9–9 Army:" a slang phrase referring to the fact that the majority of those remaining in villages now tend to be women, children, and the elderly, with women often managing sideline production and the elderly looking after the household economy. Previously, there was no strict line between the surplus and nonsurplus labor force — certainly no clear divide visible in real daily life. If we just consider quantity, the villages are still highly populated and, considering land per capita conditions, it is highly probable that many more will follow in the wake of the present migrations. But if those left behind to farm tend to be excessively elderly or less educated, or if the village population otherwise deviates greatly from an optimum balance, then the spread and use of agricultural technologies, the sustainable development of rural society and culture, and the stability and flourishing of rural families and communities, all loom as latent, pressing problems.[28]

Table 11
280 households: Age distributions among 1367 individuals (%)

Age	Out-migrants	Remaining at home
17 and Under	3.82	13.28
18–25	38.00	11.92
26–35	25.82	12.31
36–45	12.00	14.81
46–55	12.00	23.08
56–65	6.36	14.42
Over 65	2.00	10.18

Table 12
280 households: Gender distribution among 1367 individuals (%)

Location	Male	Female	Total
Out-migrants	52.14	30.57	41.65
Remaining at home	47.86	69.43	58.35

Table 13
280 households: Distribution according to level of education (%)

Location	Functional illiterate	Primary	Secondary	Higher/ specialty	Other
Out-migrants	18.56	44.38	69.78	71.08	18.9
Remaining at home	81.44	55.62	30.22	28.92	81.06*

* Among these 80.37% are children under 6 years of age.

Conclusion

The question before us is more complex than one of merely determining whether peasants have more or less agency in choosing strategies of migration and employment. Ever since the Qianlong era (1740–1800) in the Qing, one of the basic conditions restricting the development of Chinese society has been the acute contradiction between a constantly expanding population and ever more limited per capita resources. Moreover, it being the nature of history to bestow opportunities only once, China cannot follow the path of the early developing countries which managed to defer such problems by sending workers abroad or by colonizing foreign lands. The large rural population, the per capita scarcity of land and water resources, and the difficulties the surplus work force have out-migrating, when taken altogether, constitute a great limiting factor on contemporary Chinese development.

Against this backdrop, due to the combined effects of both international and domestic influences (political, social, economic, and cultural) over the past 50 years, the present pace of China's urban development not only lags far behind its population growth, it even lags behind its rate of industrialization. This is not merely manifested in the fact that, though industry now comprises the leading sector of our national economy and we are making great strides in the modernization of our basic industrial infrastructure, the majority of our 1.2–1.3 billion population is still of peasant status, engaged in the highly resource-limited realm of "food production," and thereby forced to endure increasingly severe agricultural involution and diminishing margins of return. It is also manifested, under the current system, by the so-called over-burdening or "overloading" of the cities. Even though urban areas contain at most only one-third of the total population, the basic transportation, communication, and housing infrastructure and the corresponding water, electrical, and sewage systems are extremely limited, as are the education, medical, and other forms of social services and insurance that permanent urban residents enjoy. It is precisely because of this that not only are urban reforms running into all sorts of difficulties, but, what is more, urban residents will try in any way they can to protect their own pathetically small share of these interests and will psychologically squeeze out and systematically limit rural people's access to work in the cities. Since the late 1990s, all the important large cities, one after another, have passed regulations restricting the entrance of rural populations and their search for work. With the arrival of every big holiday in the cities, there is a special effort to clean out "the three undocumenteds" (people lacking personal ID, housing permit, and work permit). Some local governments, in order to accomplish this task, simply deport migrants, even those who have all of "the three documents," without even a moment of routine questioning or investigation.

In light of the findings of our survey, this author believes that at present — as our country's vast rural areas embark on the process of shifting out of agriculture (through both sector transfers and out-migration) — structural economic and systemic influences play a particularly huge role. More specifically, with the land system already transformed, the restraints of the housing-registration and grain-rationing system relaxed, and given the dilemma of high population and land scarcity, it is unavoidable that the rural population's search for alternative channels into the nonagricultural sector would shatter the original regulations. Problems like drought and famine further explain why many villagers chose the nonagricultural path; some migrants are fleeing truly barren and desolate land.

But this is not all. Limited land and natural resources, compounded by the detrimental influences of certain state policies and structural planning, have driven returns on agricultural production to extremely low levels, and this is also an extremely important "push" factor. It is precisely because of the long-standing trend of diminishing returns in agriculture, exacerbated by policies and structures that severely lower returns on staple crop production, that more and more villagers see farming as a losing proposition. In particular, those involved in grain production make so little income that they need to find other ways to make ends meet, like leaving their home village, district, or even province in search of some nonagricultural employment to make up their "losses." Simply put, the previous dual system (dividing industry/agriculture, and urban/rural), which resulted in markedly inferior benefits in agriculture, has not yet been reformed on a basic, systemic level. Hence, the rural population, and the youth most of all, are an unstoppable force; they will increasingly forge their own paths in search of work, increased income, and improved social position.

Regarding so-called "pull" factors, certainly urban development offers job opportunities, especially in China's southern, coastal, and developing regions, attracting the bulk of the labor force. What is more, the lifestyles in the cities, the "urban magic" of the city's powerful consumer culture which reaches directly into the rural regions through TV and so forth, is also an extremely powerful influence attracting rural workers, and is especially seductive of rural youths. Urban development and urbanization not only draw the great mass of labor power out of their remote villages into the flourishing southern and coastal areas like Guangdong, they also lead to structural changes in peasant households and on the village level.

If we look at the overall structure shoring up our shifting social system as an organic integration of rules and their organizing resources, then individual agents, including peasants "with only a sweet potato in their pockets," can not be seen merely as impotent cogs in this social structure. On the contrary, they always have goals: first to scrape out a basic existence for themselves, and second to take a step towards self-improvement. However, no matter how crystal clear an agent's motivations may be, in the process of acting agents are reflexively monitoring their moves and adjusting their targets. Individual villagers simply evaluate and select modes of employment and lifestyles based on their own interests and experiences. In this respect they are very realistic and calculating. But it is highly unlikely that they know beforehand the broader social consequences which will spring from their actions. Of these unintended outcomes, the one which is of the greatest theoretical and practical import is that actions result in changing the rules and thus inevitably produce a restructuring of resources, or, more simply speaking, change the social structure.

The household responsibility system and the TVEs have been dubbed the two great inventions of China's peasantry. Yet, in light of the strict division of urban/rural residence and employment systems, they are "creations" about which, to a great degree, the peasantry had very little choice. Household responsibility helped resolve the problem of peasant initiative; TVEs began reversing involution, and, from the vantage of modern industry, have improved the allocation of labor, money, and technology. But with regard to resources and the sustainable use and protection of the environment, they pose many problems. Moreover, the real "secret" behind the great success of southern Jiangsu's TVEs since the mid 1980s has been the cheap labor supplied by migrants from Anhui and northern Jiangsu.

As more and more peasants migrate and search for employment, on a national scale they are invisibly, unpredictably, and powerfully shaking up the system. Goal-oriented individual peasants at first are pursuing some extra cash income, but they have few ways of predicting the consequences of their actions. By going to other areas to work in industry and commerce they help widen the gap between agriculture and industry, by cutting across provinces they shatter regional divisions, and by settling in cities and seeking work they blunt the urban-rural divide. Moving from household responsibility to TVEs and now to out-migration, China's peasants are themselves, step by step, blazing a new road to realize deruralization.

We found in our survey that the amount of TVE development, especially on the village level, strongly influenced the extent to which peasants out-migrated for employment. Basically, the more developed a village's TVEs, the smaller the out-migrating population and the greater the number of laborers attracted into the village from outside. But the level of TVE development is far from merely determined by motivation or goals. It largely depends on whether a locality possesses the necessary basic resources and conditions. Not every area can achieve the type of smooth development enjoyed by the Jiangnan region; people of the remote mountainous areas in the southwest, northwest, and interior will probably not achieve this, no matter how great their efforts.

A more serious problem remains that even in the Jiangnan region TVEs can only absorb so much labor power. If TVEs are to continue to prosper and develop in the increasingly competitive market economy they must make the transition from labor-intensive to cash- and technology-intensive production. Going into the 1990s, many TVEs underwent a hurried "restructuring" (from collective enterprises to joint-venture, share-holding, private, or outside-owned enterprises). They are no longer dominated by the original goal of absorbing rural surplus labor. Now, in an average year, rather than absorbing labor at break-neck speed, many TVEs are letting workers go (through retirements and layoffs). Even after "restructuring," their rate of efficiency is not as high as was hoped. Under the more serious conditions of domestic and international competition, restructuring alone will not simply solve an enterprise's present and developing difficulties. Management, finances, technology, labor, resources, government policies, and external environmental factors such as consumer tastes and habits (which are not merely "natural givens") are all key issues.

There is also no guarantee that the agricultural sector, especially crop cultivation, will share in the benefits associated with the high-speed development of TVEs. On the contrary, in some of the villages we surveyed, because TVEs have absorbed most of the village's young and educated work force while also occupying and even polluting sizeable amounts of arable land, the farming ecology, crop production, water, irrigation, and soil protection have been adversely effected.

Returning to the large-scale transfer and migration of the rural population, the present problems include the following: 1) All forms of enterprises in the southeast (Jiangsu, Zhejiang, and Guangdong) are facing a decrease in demand; the scale and pace with which they absorb labor has dropped off. Yet at the same time most peasants over the last several years have seen a steady slowing, if not an actual decrease, in their agricultural income, so that the number of rural youth (including youth from the northwest, who until recently very rarely out-migrated) searching for nonagricultural employment is a rising trend. 2) It would seem that high population and the scarcity of arable land should make land more precious; but given the relatively low returns on farming, most peasants feel farming is not worthwhile, and some even let their fields go untilled. 3) The large quantity of surplus labor in the vast countryside necessitates that many seek other paths of subsistence. Yet, ironically, due to out-migrations and transfers, some village families actually face a shortage of labor, and many village communities are in decline. 4) Following the extension of the information age into new territories, it has become exceedingly difficult to devise policy measures that can discourage China's hundreds of millions of peasants from going out to find new means of subsistence to improve their quality of life. Yet, from another angle, under the current, limited, development of basic infrastructure in this recent phase of structural adjustment, these migrants have great difficulty setting down roots in their new urban environments and in rationally and lawfully realizing their transition out of agriculture. 5) Chinese society for quite a long period has depended on its native agricultural sector to support and nourish its enterprises and its population of over 1.2 billion. But the sustainable development of agriculture is now facing a profusion of new challenges, including many ways in which so-called "globalization" excludes and ignores the peasant population (migrant or not).

Clearly, at the present stage it is too early to predict what the long-range social, economic, or cultural effects will be of these massive shifts between agriculture, industry, and commerce and these huge migrations between city and countryside among a population of 1.2 billion (most of whom still live in the countryside!). The first clues are only now emerging and being analyzed. The micro-level data here is only partial, based on interviews in eight villages in four provinces, marked by very different scales of migration and levels of socio-economic development. China's countryside is vast, its socio-economic differences huge. Even in the same district, different villages or families can be quite dissimilar. Indeed, the circumstances in the same village or the same household can change greatly in the course of a single year. In the process of attempting to analyze and generalize about overall ramifications, especially when it comes to trying to explain the various unintended consequences produced by these peasants' search for subsistence, the author strongly wishes to underscore the following: the various differences between localities, even down to the village level, ceaselessly remind us that we must be extremely cautious to avoid taking a strategy that seems successful in a specific locality and simply applying it to a locality with quite different conditions. On the academic level, this holds true for Western-derived models like rational choice, or for the urban/rural duality migration model, and even for the Jiangnan-derived model for realizing the shift away from agricultural through TVE development. Further, if we wish to understand what models the peasants in a certain locality will deem useful or will adopt, then the first issue we need to look at is whether it will improve their basic conditions of subsistence. At this stage, no matter how great the constraining force of systemic conditions, the ultimate force in breaking through and changing the overall structure of rules and their organizing resources is still the daily goal-oriented behavior and reflexive monitoring of the people themselves. Whether or not the great mass of peasants purposefully moving into nonagricultural activity will produce a new structuration of rules and their organizing resources to replace the previous structure, and whether this will lay a foundation that fosters conditions of sustainable and harmonious development, is to a great degree dependent upon the behavior of the social actors: China's people, both urban and rural. Moreover, given its current effects on poverty, migration, and development, globalization does not seem to promise future social transformations that are either "sustainable" or "inclusive."

Acknowledgments

The author of this article and his colleagues received a grant from the United Nations Agricultural Office to conduct an interview survey of 280 households in eight villages in four different Chinese provinces in 1994–1995. This article is based on that survey. Others who participated in designing the survey questions, performing interviews, and analyzing data included: Ying Tiankui, Guo Yuhua, and Yang Yiyin of the Chinese Academy of Social Sciences; Cheng Weimin of the Beijing University Sociology Department; Xu Ping of the Sichuan Women's Federation's Women's Studies Bureau; Xie Shenzan of Sichuang University's Philosophy and Sociology Department; Feng Shiping of the Gansu Academy of Social Science's National Affairs Office. Participants in conducting and initial organization of the survey data: Qiu Yonghui and Yang Minghong of Sichuan University for the southwest portion; Wei Xiaorong, Xu Meixiang, Shi Zhaohou, and Zhang Yanzhen of the Gansu Academy of Social Sciences for the northwest portion. Chinese Academy of Social Sciences Ph.D. fellow Chen Xin helped code the data. S. Erozer of the United Nations Agricultural Office and E. Croll of London University helped and guided the formulation of survey questions. For more detailed information based on this survey please see Huang Ping, Guo Yuhua, and Yang Yiyin, *In Search of Subsistence* (Kunming: Yunnan People's Publishing Company, 1996).

In the process of surveying, analyzing, and writing, I and my colleagues received no small help from the following: Chen Yuan, Shen Chonglin, Zhe Xiaoye, Cheng Yingying, Liu Dong, and Wang Hui of the Chinese Academy of Social Sciences; Xun Liping, Wang Hansheng, and Liu Shiding of Beijing University; Bai Nansheng of the Agricultural Bureau Agricultural Studies Center; Qin Hui of Qinghua University; Yuan Yayu of Sichuan University, and many other scholars. All contributed suggestions, criticisms, and caring attention.

Finally, and most importantly, the author wishes to express his heartfelt thanks to all the work units and individuals that gave their assistance and support in carrying out the local investigations on which this essay is based, especially the local provincial, district, and village officials on all levels and the peasant families and individuals we interviewed. If it were not for their help and support this study could never have come to fruition.

Bibliography

Castles, S., and M. Miller. *The Age of Migration*. London: MacMillan, 1993.

Castles, S. "Causes and Consequences of Asia's New Migrations." In *Transnational Migration in the Asia-Pacific Region*. Bangkok: Asian Research Center for Migration, 1995.

Chayanov, A. *Nongmin jingji zuzhi*. Translated by Su Zhegang. Beijing: Zhongyang Bian Shi Press, 1996. Published in English as Chayanov, A. *The Theory of Peasant Economy*. Madison: University of Wisconsin Press, 1996.

Chen Jieyuan, Yu Dechang. *The Migration of China's Agricultural Labor Force* (in Chinese). Beijing: People's Press, 1993.

Chen, T., and M. Shelden. "The Origins and Social Consequences of China's Hukou System." *China Quarterly*, no. 139 (September 1994): 644–668.

Chinese Academy of Social Sciences, Organization for the Analysis of the National Situation. *Subsistance and Development* (in Chinese). Beijing: Science Press, 1989.

Chinese Academy of Social Sciences, National Organization for Analysis of the National Situation. *Cities and Villages* (in Chinese). Beijing: Science Press, 1994.

Croll, E. *From Heaven to Earth*. London: Routledge, 1994.

Croll, E., and Huang Ping. "Migration Against and For Agriculture in Eight Chinese Villages", *China Quarterly*, no. 149 (March 1996): 128–147.

Eades, J. *Migrants, Workers and the Social Order*. London: Tavistock, 1987.

Fei Xiaotong, et al. *Small Cities, Big Problems* (in Chinese). Nanjing: Jiangsu People's Press, 1984.

Geertz, C. *Agricultural Involution*. Berkeley: University of California Press, 1963.

Giddens, A. *Central Problems in Social Theory*. London: MacMillan, 1963.

Giddens, A. *The Constitution of Society*. Cambridge: Polity Press, 1963.

Huang, Zong zhi. *Hubaei de xiao nong jingji yu she hui bian qian*. Beijing: Zhong Hua Shu Ju, 1986. Originally published as Huang, Philip C. *The Peasant Economy and Social Change in North China*. Stanford: Stanford University Press, 1985.

Huang, Zong zhi. *Changjiang Sanjiazhou xiaonung jiating yu xiangcun fazhan*. Beijing: Zhong Hua Shu Ju, 1992. Originally published as Huang, Philip C. *The Peasant Family and Rural Development in the Yangzi Delta*, 1350–1988. Stanford: Stanford University Press, 1990.

Huang, Zong zhi. *The Crisis of Paradigm in Chinese Studies* (in Chinese). Hong Kong: Oxford University Press, 1994.

Huang Ping. "The Impulse to Search for Subsistence." *21st Century* (1996): 12.

Huang Ping, Guo Yuhua, Yang Yiyin, and others. *In Search of Subsistence* (in Chinese). Kunming: Yunnan People's Press, 1996.

Mallee, H. "China's Household Registration System Under Reform." *Development and Change* 26, no.1 (1995).

Meier, Gerald, ed. *Pioneers in Development*. Oxford: Oxford University Press, 1987.

Meier, Gerald, ed. *Leading Issues in Economic Development*. Oxford: Oxford University Press, 1989.

Parnwell, M. *Population Movement and the Third World*. London: Routledge, 1993.

Popkin, S. *The Rational Peasant*. Berkeley: University of California Press, 1979.

Schultz, T.W. *Gai zao chuan tong nong ye*. Beijing: Shang Wu Ying Shu Guan, 1987. Originally published as Schultz, T.W. *Transforming Traditional Agriculture*. New Haven: Yale University Press, 1964.

Scott, J. *The Moral Economy of the Peasant*. New Haven: Yale University Press.

Shanin, T. *Peasants and Peasant Societies*. Oxford: Blackwell, 1987.

Wu H. Xiaoying. "Rural to Urban Migration in the People's Republic of China." *The China Quarterly* 139 (September 1994).

Yuan Yaou, et al.. *The Social Movement of China's Peasants*. Chengdu: Sichuan University Press, 1994.

Zhao Shukai, "Peasant Migration, 1995." In *1996 China Bluebook, #78-96,* Beijing: Chinese Social Science Press.

ENDNOTES

[1] Huang's research is presented in Philip C. Huang, *The Peasant Economy and Social Change in North China* (Stanford: Stanford University Press, 1985) and Philip C. Huang, *The Peasant Family and Rural Development in the Yangzi Delta, 1350–1988* (Stanford: Stanford University Press, 1990).

[2] Philip C. Huang, *The Crisis of Paradigm in Chinese Studies* (in Chinese)(Hong Kong: Oxford University Press, 1994).

[3] Fei Xiaotong and others. *Small Cities, Big Problems* (Nanjing: Jiangsu People's Press, 1984).

[4] [TVEs are local enterprises that emerged in towns in the countryside in the early 1980s. They began as relatively simple industries, often thriving by providing cheap goods (from construction materials to soda pop) to nearby urban areas. They were initially usually fully owned and controlled by commune or local administrative units, but through the 1980s and 1990s they were by far the most dynamic and fastest growing sector of the Chinese economy. Trans.]

[5] Philip C. Huang, *The Peasant Economy*, 8. "Involution" refers to a situation in which each additional unit of labor yields increasingly diminishing returns. This type of involution explains why there can exist growth without development, for even though there is a rise in the quantity of output, still efficiency (the ratio of output to labor) does not rise. Huang borrows the term "involution" from C. Geertz, *Agricultural Involution* (Berkeley: University of California Press, 1963).

[6] For information on the household registration system and its social consequences see T. Chen and M. Selden, "The Origins and Social Consequences of China's Hukou System," *China Quarterly*, no.139 (September 1994): 644–668. On the relationship between household registration and peasant out-migration, see Huang Ping, "The Impulse to Search for Subsistence," *21st Century* (1996): 12.

[7] On the dualism of agency and structure see A. Giddens, *The Constitution of Society* (Cambridge: Polity Press, 1984).

[8] [In the late 1970s, communes were broken up and individual households were given responsibility for farming their own plots of land. This was called the "household responsibility" system. After delivering a certain amount of their produce to the state they were allowed to keep the surplus for themselves and to do with it as they wished. This policy resulted almost immediately in a great burst of agricultural productivity that only began leveling off around 1985. Trans.]

[9] "*Nei you wai huan*" describes times of turmoil both domestic and international. Here the author uses the term to refer to the period from 1840–1949 when China was wracked by rebellions, foreign invasion, and civil wars.

[10] For a discussion of the manifestations and impact of consumer culture in China's cities and countryside, see Huang Ping, *Expectant Pursuits* (*Qiwang de yu qiu*) (Jiangsu People's Publishing Company, 2000).

[11] "The sending down of TV" is part of the government-initiated, "three send downs" (culture, technology, and sanitation). As this article was being written around the time of Chinese New Year in 2000, the national news repeatedly reported on how a great many remote rural areas were installing TV reception systems.

[12] What this paper terms "nonagricultural activity" includes two types of phenomena: 1) people migrating to other localities to find employment, and 2) peasants achieving a shift into the nonagricultural sector without having to leave their home villages. Most of the data discussed here does not distinguish between these two phenomena. For a discussion of their distinction in relation to this study see Yang Yiyin, 1996.

[13] The provinces Lu and Ji in the early Ming (14th century) averaged about 20 *mu* of arable land per capita, but by 1800 this had shrunk to 4 *mu*. With the marginal returns on sidelines diminishing as well, peasants had to leave their villages in search of short-term work just to meet the family's basic consumption needs. But with such a glut of surplus labor, hired laborers were very poorly paid and their income was far from sufficient in itself to support a family, so people had no choice but to continue working their fields as well. Hence the mode in many rural areas centered on agricultural sidelines supplemented by short-term hiring out.

[14] See Huang, *The Crisis of Paradigm*. T. W. Schultz, in his study of traditional agriculture, asserts that traditional peasants, with their great familiarity with the land, calculated their marginal returns in feet and inches rather than in dollars and cents. Like rational economists, they were most concerned with improving the fate of themselves and their children, and in this pursuit are even more ingenious than so-called economic experts. Schultz therefore presumes that it is simply untenable that part of a poor country's agricultural sector could yield zero marginal returns. While this article concurs that peasants are not simply "stupider" than the so-called experts and that they meticulously calculate the returns on their labor, this fact does not eliminate the possibility that agriculture could enter an involutionary cycle of diminishing returns — particularly in China where the pressures of land scarcity and overpopulation have been so enduring. See T. W. Shultz, *Transforming Traditional Agriculture* (New Haven: Yale University Press, 1964). These historical processes are described in Philip Huang's books *The Peasant Economy and Social Change in Northern China* and *The Peasant Economy and Rural Development in the Yangzi Delta, 1350–1988*.

[15] Since the changes resulting from these actions are to a great degree not anticipated by the agents themselves, these changes often fail to tally with the agents' original intentions, nor do they always play out in "positive" outcomes that accord with economic rationality. This essay has been greatly influenced by the insights of Anthony Giddens's "structuration theory". This theory looks at agency as a process including clarification of motivation, rationalization, and ceaseless reflexive monitoring. In this way the action of agents can lead to various unexpected and undesired consequences and these consequences in turn can create conditions limiting future action in unrecognized ways. See A. Giddens, *The Central Problems in Social Theory* (London: McMillan, 1979) and *The Consitution of Society* (Cambridge: Polity Press, 1984).

[16] Gerald Meier, ed., *Leading Issues in Economic Development* (Oxford: Oxford University Press, 1987.)

[17] [Commune enterprises were fairly small local industries, often brick or concrete factories, that began emerging under the banner of local self-sufficiency during the early 1970s when the commune system was more or less the exclusive administrative economic unit in the countryside. They are predecessors of the TVEs. Trans.]

[18] The so-called "contract responsibility system" was instituted in an attempt to make the household responsibility system more flexible and amenable to marketization. Land was no longer distributed according to household size, and the percentage of production given to the state was variable.

[19] The gross income from agriculture and sidelines was calculated according to crop type, size of land, quantity of livestock, and that year's market price for various crops and livestock.

[20] Aside from this, the village also had about 200 laborers working in an urban work unit who had shifted to an urban housing registration. Also, 30% of the workers in the village's own TVEs hailed from outside the village. These two estimated population groups are not included in the above statistics.

[21] Before the reforms, peasant life in this village was relatively impoverished. Older peasants here recalled that during the collectivization period a work point was only worth 30 cents. A hearty laborer could earn 3500 points in a year, which was just enough for the family's food grain with almost no cash income left over.

[22] The income for the village was calculated according to figures provided to us by the village council and village accountant, while income for the 35 households was estimated according to the amount of land they held and the prices on the grain and produce they sold (this is also the case for the other seven villages.)

[23] The study team in this area once attempted to write a comprehensive article titled "Pick trash, pick trash, pick your way to prosperity."

[24] This village's public welfare and benefits are all subsidized by the village collective, otherwise the service fees would be still higher.

[25] Due to the recent developments of sidelines, especially goose raising, the population out-migrating was much lower that in Village 5, less than one-third. This demonstrates that even if local TVEs fail to develop, the rural surplus labor force can find other paths besides out-migration. Family animal raising can attract a large amount of labor power. The conditions in Villages 5 and 6 are very similar, with the same high population, land scarcity, and poor transportation, but because Village 6 has for a few years given every household geese to raise, they have not only raised their income, they also have less pollution, less usurpation of arable land, and less out-migration. Influences from outside the village have been important in guiding this development. It was because the county seat near this village started a duck processing factory and began purchasing large quantities of geese, that the villagers use of their hillsides for goose-raising could be "effective."

[26] Typically speaking, people tend to provide estimates that are lower than what they actually earn, and their families often are unclear about how much money they are earning.

[27] For more detail on this aspect of the 280 households see Huang Ping, "The Impulse to Search for Subsistence," and Huang Ping, Guo Yuhua, Yang Yiyin, and others, *In Search of Subsistence* (in Chinese)(Kunming: Yunnan People's Press, 1996).

[28] It could be said that for relatively prosperous villages, peasants out-migrating is merely a type of supplement to local agricultural and nonagricultural activities; for middle level income areas it is a subsidy, and for poor and remote areas it is a substitute. For more of this study's findings on the influence of out-migration on agricultural and nonagricultural production see E. Croll and Huang Ping, "Migration Against and For Agriculture in Eight Chinese Villages," *China Quarterly*, no. 149 (March 1997): 128–147.

The Politics of Gender and Nation Rebuilding

Jung Yeong-hae
*— translated from Japanese by Brett de Bary**

Labor Shortages Accompany High Unemployment: A Dilemma

In the year 1998, the aggregate birth rate in Japan plummeted to the lowest in its history: the national average birthrate was 1.38. Statistics for the city of Tokyo have been even lower; in 1997, the city's birth rate was 1.07 by contrast to the national average of 1.39. The total number of children born in the year 1997 was 1,191,665. This compares to approximately 2,700,000 children born each year during the first "baby boom" from 1947 to 1949, and about 2 million per year during the second baby boom from 1971 to 1974. There has been a drop in births by approximately half since that time. Regardless of whether or not trends toward decline in labor power and the aging of Japanese society continue at their present rate, they will certainly not stop. According to many predictions, at the

---

* The translator would like to thank the following colleagues at the Reischauer Institute, Harvard University, during the academic year 2000–01, for their help: Kazuko Sakaguchi, Director of the Japan Documentation Center, generously helped to identify government reports and legislation; I consulted with Professor Jin Igarashi, of Hosei Univesity, and Sumiko Otsubo, Post-doctoral Fellow, about translation problems. Thanks to Andrew Gordon, Director, and Staff Assistant Ruiko Connor for their hospitality.

current rates, the labor shortage will reach something close to ten million workers over the next 20 years.[1] Even if a very high degree of mobilization of the labor of housewives and the elderly is assumed, the shortfall in the labor force has been predicted to be about 6 million people. Despite attempts to call on the elderly to be "active throughout life," and utilization to the utmost of the labor of full-time housewives, there will still be a labor shortage of this magnitude.

Although the existence of a labor shortage has required a sudden policy shift emphasizing the build-up of less labor-intensive rather than more labor-intensive areas of the economy (and a corresponding effort to make the structure of production more efficient), we are, in fact, witnessing a long-term tendency toward the reduction of labor hours, while at the same time it remains difficult to bring about structural reforms that place the highest priority on efficiency. Furthermore, flying in the face of the new emphasis on less labor-intensive aspects of the economy, as the Japanese population ages there is a growing need for services of caregivers such as nurses and home caregivers. This is a need that cannot be met as if it were, for example, a routine demand for an increase in imported commodities. It will require an increase in the proportion of workers in the domestic economy involved in labor-intensive work. These factors have created the current dilemma.

The effects of the shortage of labor power in Japan, however, are not limited to the problems of lowered productivity and declining expectations for stable economic growth. This is because at the present time international economic interdependency is growing rapidly, and it is required of nations that they play a role in keeping with the size of their economy. Under such conditions, the question arises: how can a labor shortage be avoided? It appears that Japan has reached the point where it has realized that intensification of the industrial structure is not enough and a long-term plan is needed: Japan is now positively considering how to institutionalize an international division of labor and admit more foreign workers.

In an outline report on projected vital statistics released by the United Nations in January, 2000, it became evident that if Japan hopes to maintain a supply of labor in the area now rapidly shrinking (people between the ages of 15 and 64), it will need to accept more than 600,000 migrant workers a year into the country over the next 50 years.[2] The need for such a large yearly number seems to be predicated on the fact that not all of these workers will remain in Japan long-term, and that some may be expected to go elsewhere. This UN report on vital statistics was sponsored by the UN Department of Economic and Social Affairs and was the first such study to focus on the problem of how highly industrialized nations will absorb immigration. It projected statistics for both the total populations, and the population of laborers, in eight countries (including Japan, the U.S., and Britain) through the year 2050. It also calculated the number of immigrants each country would need to receive in order to maintain a necessary level of labor supply over a fixed period and then projected a yearly number of entrants needed to maintain that level.

A look at the report's more detailed analysis of labor supply, total population, and aging, reveals the following:

First, although in 1995 the population of workers in Japan was 87 million, by the year 2000 this will have dropped to approximately 86 million. It is clear that the rate of reduction will become even more drastic in the future, so that by the year 2050 this population can be expected to fall to 57 million. If the labor force in Japan is to be maintained at its 1995 levels, about 33 million people have to enter Japan between now and 2050. This is an average yearly influx of about 600,000 people a year.

Next, we may note that the total population of Japan is expected to peak at 127 million in the year 2005. After this it will begin to decline, reaching approximately 100,000,500 by the year 2050. If Japan were to maintain its peak population, it would have to bring approximately 17 million people into the country by 2050, averaging about 400,000 people a year.

Finally, if we look at statistics for aging, in 1995 there were 4.8 working people for every person over the age of 65 in Japan. However, in the year 2050 there will be only 1.7 working persons for each elderly person. In order to maintain the 1995 ratio, 553,000,000 people would have to enter Japan by 2050, or a yearly average of 10,100,000 thousand people.

The factors I have just listed make it clear that the aging of Japan's population (caused by fewer births) is the fundamental problem, and more significant than either the decline in the total population or the decline in labor force.

But there is another side to this story. The unemployment figures published on April 28, 2000, revealed that the unemployment rate of 4.9% is as high now as it has ever been in Japan since such statistics were recorded, and that the total unemployed population of 3,490,000 is also at an all-time high. This situation stands in stark contrast to that of the United States and Europe, where high unemployment, as a structural problem, has suddenly begun to ease up and where there is a strong possibility that unemployment will become lower still. If we disaggregate the Japanese unemployment rate for gender, moreover, we can see that the present 5.2% unemployment rate for males is at an all-time high. Unemployment for women, on the other hand, is 4.6%. If we disaggregate for age, we also find that unemployment of recent graduates is the highest recorded, at 320,000, reflecting the current trend in industry to limit the hiring of this group. In particular, unemployment of people in the 15 to 24-year-old age group is at an all-time high of 11.3%. Over the past few years, the level of unemployment in this age group has been particularly striking.

Delayed Structural Change and Social Unrest

Instability of employment in the current poor economic climate appears to have had a direct impact on the morale of young people. The Japanese government's Youth Affairs Administration Management and Coordination Agency released on January 2, 2000, its *Sixth World Youth Survey* [*Dai rokkai sekai seinen ishiki chôsa*], noting that 40.3% of those interviewed who were between the ages of 18 and 24 expressed their dissatisfaction with "frequent unemployment, due to difficulty in finding jobs."[3] This represents a dramatic increase in the 12.3% of interviewees who responded in this way 5 years earlier. Closely related to this is the fact that the problem most youth surveyed felt to be the most urgent for them was "finding a job commensurate with my educational background" (52.2%), while for 48.8% the topmost concern was "political mismanagement" in Japan. Furthermore, 73.5% described a desirable father as one who "gave priority to his family," compared with 40% who responded in this way 20 years ago and 58.4% ten years ago. What emerges in relief from this pattern is the increasing antipathy of young people toward a sexual division of labor where the father works outside, while the mother remains at home, and raises children.[4]

Thus, we can see that Japan's problems today do not stop with the serious labor shortage or the aging of society. A major problem has also been created by pervasive social instability and discontent with the status quo that has arisen from the fact that, despite the existence of such shortages, those who can work are not being utilized to the fullest extent. Another survey, released by the Prime

Minister's Office on April 29, 2000, *A Survey of Public Opinion on the Quality of National Life* [*Kokumin seikatsu ni kansuru seron chôsa*], revealed that only 9.1% believed their lives would improve in the future, the first time this group had dropped below 10% of the total population.[5] Those who felt things would worsen represented 24.5% of the total, a proportion second only to that of the 1974 survey that followed the first "oil shock." The newspaper *Nihon Keizai Shinbun* commented after the release of this report: "The report reveals that in actuality a growing number of people are not optimistic about the future, because of their anxiety about the slow rate of economic recovery and the increasing burden of social costs related to the low birth rate and increase of elderly."[6]

Also, on April 20, 2000, a Ministry of Health and Welfare monthly release of vital statistics revealed that, for the second year in a row, the number of suicides in Japan had surpassed the 30,000 mark. Over the years, the number of suicides in Japan has tended to fluctuate between 20,000 and 25,000, but as recession in Japan deepened in 1998, the number jumped to 8,000 higher than the previous year, and reached 31,700. Suicides among men in their fifties who have borne the brunt of restructuring and bankruptcies are the highest in recorded history and show no signs of abating. According to police records, suicides among middle aged and elderly men afflicted by "problems with finances and livelihood" or "work-related problems" are numerous, and the tendency for men, driven to despair by restructuring or business slumps brought on by the recession, to choose death rather than revealing their suffering to their families, does not seem to be slowing down. Deaths by suicide at present are three times higher than those caused by automobile accidents, which has prompted the Health and Welfare Ministry to declare that this is "on a scale that cannot go unattended," and to embark, at last, on measures to prevent suicide, including bringing facilities for the treatment of mental illness up to standard.

Thus, we can see that what is lagging behind in Japan right now is not just economic recovery or financial reform. The government has no choice but to undertake a drastic transformation of infrastructure in order to bring about a balance between the demand and supply of labor, and to construct a "system for facilitating smooth transfers of labor power" (as it has been referred to) that would be necessary to bring this situation about. Social unrest and dissatisfaction with the status quo can only be dispelled through such measures.

Yet, to simply admit migrant laborers on the basis of the projections of the

UN report, without addressing today's unstable social conditions and the discontent that pervades them, would be disastrous. This would simply and inevitably be to needlessly provoke those within the country who are already unemployed, increase their anxiety, and channel their discontent toward the admitted migrant laborers. We have already seen examples of this kind of panic, most recently in the statements on April 9, 2000, of Tokyo governor Ishihara Shintarô, addressing the Self-Defense Forces. Making flagrant use of the term *sangokujin* (literally, "third nation people", a derogatory word used to describe Koreans and Chinese just after the Pacific War, and eschewed by most Japanese today as blatantly racist. Translator's note.) Ishihara told the Self- Defense Forces, "Heinous crimes have been repeatedly perpetrated by foreigners and *sangokujin*, and we may assume that, in the case of a natural disaster, riots may even break out. Since what the police force can do is limited, I would ask you to assist us in such a case, and to make the maintenance of civil order a top priority."[7] Ishihara's words reveal that there is still latent in Japan the kind of xenophobia which led the government and army, at the time of the Great Kanto Earthquake of 1923, to purposefully deflect the brunt of the population's social discontent, anxiety, and mutual distrust onto the slaughter of more than 6,000 Koreans and Taiwanese colonial subjects. But in the case of present day and even future immigrants, we can never allow them to bear the costs of the government's policy mistakes by becoming scapegoats for the nation's fear and dissatisfaction.

For the sake of Japan in the future, it is vital for us to transform the attitude of Japanese citizens into one in which we see foreign migrants as people we invite to become members of a society that *all* of its members help to sustain. But this cannot be a matter of changing attitudes alone. Unless we first transform the contradictions of our society at present, there is no way we can avoid the panic that will accompany the arrival of migrants. What will this require? First of all, we need to cultivate the objectivity and mutual trust that will enable us, as members of this society, to come together — even in the face of these difficulties — for the mutual discussion and sharing of wisdom that will enable us to overcome them. In other words, before we begin to envision how Japanese and foreigners can coexist, we need to learn how to transform our relationships with each other as Japanese, and how to respect our "internal" differences. In addition, each citizen must be able to have hope that the present situation can be ameliorated — to carry out such a political practice will require that we be thorough-going in our commitment to democracy and to respect the people's sovereignty.

A New Call for Japan's "Total National Mobilization" as a Society Where Old and Young, Men and Women, Work Together

On June 6, 1999, the *Report of the Research Group on Health and Welfare Services for the Aging Society* [*Kôreishakai o sasaeru kenkoo, fukushi saabisu nado ni kansuru kenkyûkai hôkokusho*], published by the Commodities Bureau of the Economic Planning Agency, called for measures encouraging women to seek employment in the fields of nursing and childcare and to determine a price for this kind of service to society.[8] In the body of this report, it was proposed that "various institutions which encourage women to become full-time housewives should be reassessed with an eye to guaranteeing availability of women workers to care for the elderly." The idea being proposed here was to reassess practices that now encourage women to define themselves solely as housewives and to instead lay the ground work for an environment more conducive to women joining the labor force. Specifically, the report called for a reassessment of a feature of the current pension system called the "housewives' category" (*daisangô hihokensha*), which targets full-time housewives between the ages of 20 and 60 who are married to salaried workers with yearly incomes of under 1,300,00 yen. Under this system, such women may earn up to 1,030,000 yen a year (doing part-time work or some other way) without paying social security taxes, and if they earn less than one million yen, they are exempted from local taxes as well. The value of offering women such incentives for continuing to see themselves as full-time housewives is being reconsidered.

This new proposal for encouraging women and the elderly to join the workforce has its roots in what I have already suggested is a most serious problemæthat whenever the issue of Japan's aging society is taken up it is assumed that the entire nation must be mobilized to permit greater participation of women in the work force *before* immigrants are admitted. If the policy of recruiting full-time housewives into care-giving services is successful, it will represent a kind of "killing three birds with one stone." It will introduce a new labor force for care giving, will reduce social security costs, and will raise government income from taxes. In fact, as if in response to these schemes of the government, the proportion of full-time housewives exempted from paying insurance fees into a public pension fund suddenly declined to 33.79% at the end of March 1999. What this signifies is that, as the age of marriage gets later and as divorces increase, the number of women who are long-term workers paying into their own public pension plans has increased, and that we are seeing a trend where more and more women qualify for pensions, not as full-time housewives, but as independent business people, either because their husbands have become unemployed or because their husbands have started their own businesses, within which the wives participate.

A similar kind of thinking is apparent in the government's effort to encourage the elderly to join the work force, thereby gaining economic independence and an autonomous livelihood. If the government succeeds in this, there will be a corresponding reduction in the financial and manpower costs of social security and social services, as well as the appearance of a new labor supply, which should enhance productivity. If the government can minimize even slightly the shrinking pool of working people who pay taxes, it can hope to ameliorate the debt of national and regional governing bodies. At the present time, the Finance Ministry calculates that the balance owed on long-term debt nationally (including the debt of urban and rural prefectural governments and of regional, city, town, and village governments) will be 667 trillion yen by the end of fiscal year 2000. This amounts to a sum 1.3 times the gross domestic product (GDP) of Japan, which is estimated to be 498.9 trillion for the fiscal year 2000. Moreover, the portion of national debt per family has been calculated to be 14,680,000 yen. Japan can certainly be thought of as a chariot on fire, a "world king" of debt. Further reduction in income from taxes, or an increase in the cost of social security, will eventually result in insolvency on both the national and regional governmental levels.

It is against this background that voices advocating a "society based on teamwork" (young and old, men and women) have emerged, from the Economic Planning Agency and elsewhere. On June 15, 1996, the Lower House unanimously approved the "Basic Law for a Gender Equal Society," which for the first time provided a legal basis for ending gender discrimination and the uneven division of responsibilities for child care, housework, and other forms of care-giving, in an effort to enhance gender equality. Even male economists are now sounding the alarm, warning that, while the government will protect wages based on seniority and other vested interests of the portion of workers (mostly men) who are already working under the lifetime employment system, this system will stand in the way of the kinds of social transformations needed to deal with the low birth rate and aging of society. Japan's system of lifetime employment has been characterized by the intense discipline of employees within the firm, but the price paid for employment security has been long working hours and frequent transfers; also, the image of the man for whom "it is all thanks to my wife" has been tacitly assumed.[9] Such writers point out that, not only did this assumption about women sustain an employment system based on gender discrimination, it also made it difficult for women to maintain a job continuously. It thus stands in the way of the creation of an economic and social system that makes full use of market forces, allowing work to be chosen freely without regard for gender or age. Such economists propose that the overcoming of ageism and the creation of a gender-blind labor market offers a path toward prosperity in an era of shrinking births and growing numbers of elderly citizens.

Yet concern is also mounting that if the slogan of a society where "men and women work together" miscarries in any way, it could become a policy of "total national mobilization" — one that, far from allowing free choice of employment, removes from the lives of men and women alike the ability to make such choices. This is because the real aim of such a slogan is, as its advocates put it, to "create a society where women and the elderly are all gainfully employed" and where "it is possible to be employed but also to have a family (of 2 or more children) and carry out the responsibilities of housework, child-rearing, and caring for the elderly." Such a social vision hardly seems intended to expand the scope of individual choice, but rather to be an attempt save the nation state from a threat to its very existence. In such a society anyone who is not gainfully employed, who cannot bear children, or who does not engage in care-giving activities, would have to feel ashamed of himself or herself or, in a more extreme scenario, become an object of discrimination.

We need to also consider the possibility that, as a result of this slogan, the burden of gainful employment, in addition to the burdens of housework, child-rearing, and care-giving, would all fall to women, while the male-oriented aspects of such a planned society would not progress. One can expect that this would set up a vicious cycle, in which women delayed marriage by greater and greater amounts of time, and thus gave birth to even fewer children in a lifetime. Indeed, with the recent bursting of the economic bubble, we have seen a situation in which the restructuring necessitated by the economic downturn is proceeding apace and companies are trying to achieve greater productivity with a limited number of workers. The result has been a tendency for not only men, but women as well, to have less and less time for housework, child-rearing, and care-giving, and for people not to protest the deterioration of their employment conditions out of fear of losing their employment. It seems difficult to reverse these tendencies.

Admitting More Foreign Workers and the "Divide and Rule" Policy

Japanese modernization after the Meiji period strengthened gender-based role division, allowing the state and business to fully utilize the labor of males who worked with selfless dedication, while women provided free or low-paid labor in households and rural areas. When we consider that this system played no small role in providing the basis for Japan's high-speed economic growth, it is certainly ironic that today, quite to the contrary, its new side effects (late marriage and a growing number of single people) have created a scenario where Japan seems on the verge of demise. (Coincidentally, we should note that today Germany and Italy, together with Japan, have the world's lowest birth rates. It cannot be an accident that these are the former Axis nations.) Gender discrimination based on nationalism cannot be so easily recanted and converted into gender-blindness based on nationalism! Although Japanese society may appear to have reversed its direction, insofar as this new course is not based on individualism but on nationalism, nothing has changed. Herein lies the problem.

Up until this point, the Japanese government has simply been unaware of the pitfalls of its policies on gender. But this government, which previously regarded the entrance of foreign workers negatively — all the while lacking any vision of how Japan should be transformed to meet its future — has finally had to realize that a change in policy is unavoidable. This realization was reflected in the 15-point outline released as a basis for discussion for the next ten-year plan by an advisory body to the Prime Minister's Office in April, 1999, which included the proposal that admission of immigrant workers from foreign countries be "actively investigated."

Despite such proposals, however, this matter cannot be dealt with easily. There are differences of view among the various ministries and agencies and no coordinated plan for action among them. Views on admitting immigrant labor range, for example, from the comparatively positive view of the Ministry of Labor to the extremely negative outlook of the Ministry of Justice, and we can even glimpse a struggle for hegemony on this issue among government sectors with different views — including the Ministry of Health and Welfare, the Ministry of Foreign Affairs, and the Ministry of Education. In the early 1990s, a Ministry of Labor hopeful of increasing admissions of foreign workers attempted to introduce a system of employment permits (somewhat resembling that in use in Germany) which would have loosened restrictions on the entry of foreign workers (facilitating, one suspects, entry of workers who did not fit the "highly skilled" category). This attempt elicited whispered suggestions from those in the Ministry of Justice, as well as *Mindan*, the largest organization of Korean Japanese (who are still generally known in Japan as *Zainichi Chôsenjin*, "Koreans residing in Japan" and, as such deprived of Japanese citizenship) to this effect: "The Ministry of Labor is attempting to set up a system in which all foreigners working in Japan would require its approval, stipulating a specific period of work. If such a system is implemented the advantages now enjoyed by Korean Japanese workers will be jeopardized." (Because of their legal status as "resident aliens," Korean Japanese, many of whom were born in Japan, would be affected by policies concerning "foreign workers." Translator's note.) As a result of these fears, Korean Japanese expressed their opposition to such a system. In the face of this opposition from the largest group of foreign workers in Japan, the Labor Ministry did not implement its plan. In effect, the Ministry of Justice, which has tried as much as possible to limit new modes of participation by foreign workers, employed a tactic here which set "old-comers" (Korean Japanese and others) against "new-comers." They deployed a typical divide and rule strategy in getting these old-comers to oppose the new system: insofar as the new system, designed to increase the inflow of foreign workers into Japan, targeted new-comers (and by virtue of that very fact might have threatened the vested interests of old-comers) they were able to attack it. It appears they have been able to make allies out of the old-comers by using these tactics to block increasing participation in the labor force by foreign workers, and thus to claim they are "protecting" their interests and guaranteeing, of course, the continued status of old-comers as quasi-citizens.

This divide and rule strategy has been consistently pursued, whether in the case of the so-called "reform" of the immigration laws (the Immigration Control Ordinance and the Refugee Authorization Law) and the Alien Registration Laws in August, 1999, or in the law introduced to the Diet on January 21, 2000, by the Clean Government Party (Kômeitô) and the Liberal Party proposing that "foreigners who are permanent residents be given the right to vote for presidents and assembly members of local public bodies."

The Revised Alien Registration and Immigration Control Laws and the Significance of the 145th Obuchi Diet

On August 13, 1999, on the eve of its closing session, Japan's Diet voted to "reform" its Alien Registration and Immigration Control Laws. I will briefly describe the content of the changes below. First, in relation to the Alien Registration Law, the following changes were made:

1. The system of requiring fingerprints on alien registration documents was discontinued.
2. The penalty applicable to those who violate the law requiring that the alien registration be carried at all times was revised, and a distinction was set up between old-comers ("special" permanent residents from former Japanese colonies, who will be charged a "reminder" fee of no more than 100,000 yen), and newcomers (all other foreigners, who will be charged the existing penalty of no more than 200,000 yen.)

In relation to the Immigration Law, the following changes were made:

1. The period of time that must elapse before a foreigner who has been required to leave Japan may return has been increased from one year to five years.
2. The offense of remaining in Japan illegally had heretofore been subject to a three-year statute of limitations; this was removed and the offender may now be subject to criminal charges at any time.
3. Penalties for "illegal entry" have been strengthened (without compensatory adjustments having been made in the existing Refugee Authorization Law).
4. The period for which permits to re-enter the country are valid has been lengthened.

Overall, the changes have somewhat improved the way former colonial subjects are dealt with, but have meant much more thoroughgoing administration and control of newcomers.

One might also ask why these two laws were revised in tandem with each other since, although both deal with foreigners, they are independent pieces of legislation. Indeed, it has been striking that these laws were passed in one fell swoop together with a host of other legislative reforms undertaken by the 145th Diet, that of the infamous Obuchi regime, in what amounts to a historical watershed in postwar Japanese history. While previously power relations between conservatives and progressives in postwar Japan had never veered too much in the direction of one camp, with the establishment of the newly hegemonic "*Jijikô*" power structure (the alliance of the *Jiyûminshutô*, or Liberal Democratic Party, the *Jiyûtô* , or Liberal Party, and the *Kômeitô*, or Clean Government Party), a series of measures have been implemented with startling speed, producing a legal system which has the potential to transform the very structure of the Japanese state. These have included the "Law Concerning Surrounding Situations" (which reinterprets the Security Act of the Areas Surrounding Japan, Article 9), the "Law Promoting Decentralization," "Three Laws Dealing with Organized Crime" (such as the new law authorizing wire-tapping), the "Law Concerning the National Flag and National Anthem," the "Law Concerning the Basic Resident Registry System," and the "Law Establishing a Commission on the Constitution." This was certainly no accident and there is a clear intentionality that these measures embody — almost as if they were linked by a single will. Let me describe them briefly.

1. Law Concerning Surrounding Situations (passed on May 24, 1999). This law stipulates a "relaxation of existing restrictions on military cooperation with the United States under the U.S.–Japan Security Treaty, as well as of other legal and national restrictions, in such a way as to give the Japanese government a significantly freer hand in involving itself with logistical operations in wars initiated by the United States in any part of the world." This legislation will allow Japan to mobilize local governments, private airlines and transport companies, and hospitals for war efforts. It can be predicted that this will lead to significant restrictions of, and infringements on, local autonomy.
2. Building on this basis, the Diet also passed a Law Promoting Decentralization (July 16, 1999). While this law transfers to local governments the authority to make decisions about social welfare, urban planning, industrial annulment measures, and so forth, it reserves for the state exclusive control over foreign diplomacy and the military. Private citizens and local governing bodies are deprived of the right to express opinions about these matters.
3. The Law Intercepting Communications (passed on August 18, 1999) legalizes

wiretapping in the case of investigation of matters involving drugs, firearms, murders, and group stowaways. In effect, this makes it possible for them to use wiretapping in other cases, as well.

4. The Law Establishing a Commission on the Constitution set up a committee to study the Constitution, making it quite clear that the goal of the new legislation is ultimately to bring about revision of the Constitution.
5. The Law on the National Flag and the National Anthem (passed August 9, 1999) makes them legally defined entities and thus offers legitimacy to Japan's prewar system while providing a legal basis for isolating anti-establishment groups who refuse to betray their own beliefs by submitting to this kind of "loyalty test."
6. The Revised Law Concerning the Basic Resident Registry System (passed on August 18, 1999) sets up the basis for a system whereby every Japanese citizen will have an identification number which the government can make use of to maintain public security, national defense, or other modes of administrative control in the case of a national crisis. As mentioned above, although the fingerprinting requirement for foreigners was abrogated through revision of the Alien Registration Law, this relaxation was counterbalanced by the requirement that foreigners bear their alien registration cards with them at all times, a requirement explained by the Justice Department as "necessary for the detection of illegal immigrants." The Home Ministry explained that, in the case of any crisis in Korea, a system enabling identification of all citizens would be required as part of organizing relief efforts for refugees. The ministry is thus thinking of making it mandatory for all Japanese citizens, as well as resident aliens, to carry identification cards.

When we survey this panoply of measures, it appears that the Japanese government is steadily attempting to intensify a sense of nationalism in preparation for a national crisis (one might almost say to prepare Japan for participation in a war). On the one hand, facing a declining birth rate and the aging of the population, it is attempting to implement a contemporary version of the wartime Total National Mobilization Ordinance, yet it is clear that even its efforts to plan a society in which men and women work together will not completely solve this problem. At the same time, in the face of the other "threat of extinction" brought on by the prospect of a severe labor shortage, reduced income from taxes, and declining economic power, the government is attempting to increase the flow of laborers into Japan by revising its Immigration and Alien Registration Laws, in a kind of national rescue effort. At some point we can even expect to see a debate take place in Japan like the one now taking place in Germany over whether or not the Nationality Law should be based on country of birth or not. Even if such a debate took place, however, it seems likely that a policy will be adopted that simply — without making Japan in any way more open to "foreigners" — "lets Koreans stay here," in much the same way that the old colonial Korean Registration Law ceaselessly maintained a difference between Koreans and citizens of "Japan proper." These policies seem to reflect an attitude that believes that, no matter how multi-ethnic or multicultural Japan may eventually become, there is nothing to fear, and that as long as the Emperor System is maintained it might even be possible to recreate the dream of the "Greater East Asia Co-Prosperity Sphere." Or they suggest that if, hypothesizing an extreme case, a crisis on the Korean Peninsula or between China and Taiwan arose and created great confusion among the population, it might be possible to tighten up Japan's borders in a way most conducive to control over its people, and also beneficial to Japan's relationship with the U.S. As long as North Korea remains a remote, unfathomable society, it makes an ideal imagined enemy. Discrimination against Korean Japanese (and foreigners) remains an ideal means of unifying the Japanese people, one that seems to transcend the passage of time. What the government now seeks to keep in place is a system that never compromises the established privileges of Japanese citizens, yet uses the "bait" of quasi-citizenship to enlist the help of people from its former colonies in excluding newcomers and in keeping them from attaining a fully legalized status, so that they may be expelled at any time. There is really nothing new about using this hierarchy as the basis for a policy of shrewdly utilizing foreign labor in such a way that workers can be admitted when they are needed and let go when they are not. The array of new laws and reforms implemented by the 145th Obuchi Diet affords us a glimpse of such a future.

Women's "Quiet Revolution" and Changes in the Structure of Daily Life

As I discussed in the opening section of this article, a "revolution" which is dramatically transforming the contours of Japanese society is now being launched by women. This is not the kind of revolution carried out by a political party dedicated to changing society; it is a "battle-less revolution" brought about by individual women who are making choices very different from those they would have made in the past, on the basis of their personal worldviews or opinions about marriage. As the marriage age for women gets older, as some choose not to marry, and as the number of divorces increases, resulting in a larger number of single people in Japan, the function of the family as a "nest" where children may be born and reared is weakening.

Let me briefly explain this situation. First, the later marriage age for women is said to be the chief cause of Japan's declining birth rate. The average age of marriage for both men and women in Japan has been rising since 1970. In 1950, the average age of marriage for women was 23 and for men 25.9 years of age. In 1996, it was 26.4 years old for women and 28.5 years old for men. If we look at the number of unmarried people in Japan in 1995, broken down by age group, we find that in the 30- to 34-year-old age group, 19.7% of women and 37.4% of men are now single. Lifestyles of women are changing accordingly. In 1927, the average age of first birth for women was 24.4, but by 1968, it had become 27.9. As marriage age becomes more advanced, the age of first birth gets later, and the number of children born over the course of a woman's lifetime is correspondingly reduced. Thus, while it is true that late marriage age is a factor in the decreased birthrate, it is also the case that the total number of children born to married couples has been declining since 1950. Of course, it is also true that the tendency for a society to move from a situation of "many births but fewer children" to "fewer births and fewer children" is a universal phenomenon that accompanies economic development.

Attitudes of men and women about later marriage were detailed in a 1997 bulletin released by the Prime Minister's Office, entitled *A Society Where Men and Women Participate Equally: An Opinion Poll* [*Danjo kyôdô sankaku shakai ni kansuru seron chôsa*].[10] According to this survey, in the case of women, 66.1% felt marriage age was getting later "because more women work and women have gained more economic power," 35.5% said that "the single life offers more freedom," and 30.7% said that "it is easier to work when single." Among men, 59.6% said that "the single life offers more freedom," while 26.9 % said that "social disapproval towards those who do not marry is declining;" 26% said that "more women work and women have gained more economic power," and 23.3%

said that they "could not leave their parents." This bulletin also stated that the number of women who never married (who were unmarried by the age of 50) is 9.74% in the city of Tokyo, and is 15.74% for men. (Tokyo's rate of unmarried population is thus 1.8 times the national average).[11] Another 1997 report entitled, *Basic Survey of Birthrate Trends* [*Shussei dôkô kihon chôsa*] released by the Research Institute for Population and National Social Security reported that, among men and women from the ages of 18 to 35, 4.9% of women and 3% of men "never intended to marry."[12] When an identical survey was carried out in 1982, 4.1% of women and 2.3% of men said they did not expect to marry. Therefore, the trend toward staying single has increased more markedly in the case of men. We should also note that while the rate of children born out of wedlock is about 1% in Japan (much lower than the approximately 50% rate in North America and the 30% rate in Western Europe), by 1994 about 30% of respondents to a survey conducted by the Economic Development and Planning Agency (entitled *Survey of Attitudes and Actualities Relating to Families and Society* [*Katei to shakai ni kansuru ishiki to jittai chôsa hôkokusho*]) declared they did not have negative feelings about unmarried single mothers.[13]

The divorce rate in Japan is also continuing to grow, and last year climbed above that of France. In Tokyo in 1997, the number of marriages was 81,002 (about 6.9 per thousand of the population), while the number of divorces was 23,690 (two per thousand), equaling a divorce rate of 29.2% To make an extreme simplification on the basis of these figures, we may estimate that slightly less than one out of three marriages in Tokyo at present ends in divorce. A special report issued by the Ministry of Welfare on April 28, 2000, which took into account the effect of the distribution of this tendency across different age groups, concluded that, over the past thirty years, the divorce rate in Japan has risen 4.6 times. Hence, we can see that the decline in the number of births in Japan has intensified in response to the combination of two tendencies: late marriages, divorces, and an increase in the number of single people represent a movement away from marriage, while at the same time the norm that "the place to raise children is within the marriage system" tends to persist.

Another factor contributing to the rising number of single people in Japan is the aging of the population, and the growing number of those left alone by the death of a spouse. In 1960, 3,580,000 households consisted of a person living alone. By 1995, this number had risen three times, to 11,240,000. In other words, this is was an increase from a rate of 16.1% of single householders among the overall population to 25.6% in 1995. The numbers of those aged 65 or over left alone after the death of a spouse is now 1,660,000; this is an increase of 450,000 households over a ten-year period. Strikingly, women make up over 80% of these households (1,038,000), reflecting their longer life expectancy. Here again, we can estimate that about one of four households in Japan is single headed. Furthermore, the average number of household members has continued to shrink, so that it was 2.28 in 1995. It appears that a nuclear family consisting of parents and children is losing ground as the prototypical family structure.

As Japan becomes a society with large numbers of single people, commodities oriented to this life style continue to be rapidly developed. Various means of providing housekeeping services are also being promoted, and systems that excel at providing both commodities and services are being expanded. This means that, at the same time that it is becoming far less inconvenient to live alone, this very reduction in inconvenience accelerates the trend toward singleness. While we have not necessarily seen a strengthening of principled individualism, the sense of isolation has probably intensified. What lies in store for Japanese society as this sense of isolation grows hand-in-hand with trends toward social instability?

International Marriages and Nation-Rebuilding

The influence of women's choices about their lives is beginning to be felt beyond national borders. According to the Ministry of Foreign Affairs' recently released *Year 2000 Statistical Survey of Japanese Living Overseas* [*Nisennenhan kaigai zairyûhôjinsû chôsa tôkei*], the number of women with Japanese citizenship living overseas has exceeded the number of men for the first time in 2000.[14] Such statistics were first gathered in 1976, but what we are seeing in 2000 underscores the striking phenomenon of Japanese women going abroad which we have seen in recent years. On October 1, 1999, 790,800 Japanese were counted living abroad (as permanent residents or for stays of over 3 months). This showed an increase of 0.8% over the previous year and was the highest number in history. Among these, about 402,500 were women and about 393,200 were men. The Consulates Division of the Ministry of Foreign Affairs commented that, in the past, the majority of these have been wives accompanying their husbands on overseas assignments, but recently the number of women who go abroad alone for professional reasons is rising."[15]

Among these women, it is not rare to find those who go abroad and marry a foreigner, with whom they return to Japan. International marriages now account for 3% of marriages in Japan. In 1965, the number of marriages in Japan in which one partner was not a Japanese citizen was a mere 0.4 percent. After crossing the 1% level in 1981, the number shot up over the next fifteen years to reach 3.6% (28,372 marriages) in 1996. Since the total population of registered foreigners in Japan in 1998 was 1,512,000 (with another 271,000 staying on after their visas had expired), foreigners make up 1.2% of the Japanese population. Of this, a relatively high portion, 3.6%, are spouses in international marriages.

If we look at the statistics for international marriages broken down by nationality, women who are recent Korean immigrants and Korean Japanese make up the majority of women married to Japanese citizens, while American men make up the majority of men married to Japanese women. In recent years, these patterns are becoming more diverse. In fact, it is striking that, whereas in 1965 the number of Japanese women with foreign husbands was triple the number of foreign women married to Japanese men, by 1995 this pattern had reversed itself, so that Japanese men married to foreign women are more numerous. In other words, although we may assume that the high number of Japanese women travelling abroad has led to an increase in the number of Japanese women married to foreign men, the increase in the number of Japanese men marrying foreign women has been far beyond this. The latter increased threefold from 1965 to 1995. If we keep this rise in international marriages in perspective, it is possible that the trends toward later marriage, remaining single, and divorce among Japanese women do not so much reflect a "turning away from marriage" per se as a desire to avoid marriages with Japanese men. As a result, Japanese men experiencing difficulty finding a marriage partner must inevitably broaden their vision to include foreign women as well as Japanese women as possible marriage partners. This suggests that perhaps Japanese women are no longer seen as "ideal wives" for Japanese men.

Regardless of how we interpret these trends, the growth in international marriages means that the arrival of greater numbers of foreigners to Japan is following a new pattern. To wit, foreigners are no longer coming to Japan simply as a work force, but they are coming as family members of Japanese citizens. This means that what has heretofore been construed as an issue that concerned "nationalism versus humanism," when the entry of foreigners to Japan was at stake, is undergoing a shift in inflection as a new problem emerges: do sovereign Japanese citizens have the right to live with family members, the right to "family unity"?

The core of the opposition to the revision of the Immigration Ordinance in 1999 comprised not only migrant workers and Japanese citizens demonstrating solidarity with them, but Japanese women with foreign partners. The revised law, which increased from one year to five years the penalty of barring re-entrance to Japan by those foreigners who had overstayed their visas, threatened to sever family ties of those who had previously made Japan the base for their family life. In one actual case, a Japanese woman married to a Pakistani man (who had never been to Japan, much less overstayed his visa) had to wait more than 10 months to bring him to Japan. She asked those supporting the revised law, "One year is a terribly long time to wait, but how could one wait for five years? It seems that something completely self-evident — the ability of people to live with their all-important family members — is not being recognized."

In fact, there have been cases in which the Minister of Justice, at his own discretion, granted special permission to stay in Japan to a foreigner who stayed in Japan illegally and married a Japanese. On October 25, 1999, a man from Bangladesh who had married a Japanese–Brazilian woman and faced the threat of imminent deportation because he had overstayed his visa, appeared at the Tokyo Immigration Office and appealed for special permission to stay. This incident was worthy of note because it suggested that, even in the case of two foreigners married in Japan, if they "expressed a desire to continue their married life in Japan," special permission might be forthcoming.

Changes in women's worldviews and their views of marriage, therefore, have not only changed the structure of everyday life in Japan. As children of diverse nationalities begin to be born in Japan, and as their parents advocate that, no matter what their nationalities, they must be treated as family members, the boundaries of national citizenship are being shaken. By arguing that the right to form a family takes precedence over the nation state's logic of excluding foreigners based on the principle of the sovereignty of the ethnos, women are challenging nationalism head-on. Regardless of whether or not the Citizenship Law is eventually transformed so that country of birth is not decisive, we can predict that such actions by women will continue to revise the "common sense" assumptions about who is (or should be) Japanese.

Divorces of Foreign Women Living In Japan: Gender, Ethnicity, Class

While trends on marriages between Japanese and foreigners are such as I have just outlined, the problems of those involved in international marriages who decide to get divorced have suddenly come to the surface. In the previously mentioned instance of "Japanese husband and foreign wife," child-rearing responsibility tends to rest with the wife, and many difficulties may arise when that wife learns she cannot easily take her child and care for it in her home country, since the child has either dual citizenship or only has Japanese citizenship. This is causing growing numbers of foreign women to stay in Japan to rear their children as single mothers. Thus the number of foreigners residing in Japan who are not spouses of Japanese citizens, but mothers of Japanese citizens, is increasing.

It is said that, in the Ôkubo area of Tokyo (in Shinjuku Ward), nine out of ten Korean women who were spouses of Japanese men are divorced. Income in female-headed households in Japan is extremely low (on average, under 2,500,000 yen a year), and to balance work and child-rearing for these women is extraordinarily difficult. In the case of Korean women who lack citizenship and face a language barrier (since they are not Japanese-speaking), such hardships are compounded. The proportion of foreign divorcees of Japanese men who live in the Ôkubo area seems to be getting even higher, as the women who gather there have formed a community and share a sense of camaraderie.

A look at the statistics concerning divorce rates among Korean immigrants and Korean Japanese reveals something even more striking. In this group, 48.5% of marriages in which the husband is Japanese and the wife is from Korea or a Korean Japanese end in divorce, and 36.8% of those in which the wife is Japanese and the husband is from Korea or a Korean Japanese end in divorce. Moreover, outstripping the divorce rate even for these "international marriages" is that of marriages between those who belong to the population of Koreans and Korean Japanese. In 1997, there were 938 divorces by contrast to 1269 marriages among this group, and in 1999 there were 1094 divorces per 1279 marriages. In effect, this means a 74% divorce rate in 1997 and 89% divorce rate in 1999. This is more than twice — indeed, about three times — the divorce rate for Japanese marrying other Japanese, which was 29% in 1997 (6,024 marriages per 1,000 people and 1,752 divorces). However much the divorce rate among Japanese has increased in the past thirty years, that is, it does not begin to approach this figure.

By the early 1980s, the number of Korean immigrants and Korean Japanese in Japan who were marrying Japanese had exceeded five times the number of marriages within that group. By 1985, this number had reached 70%, and by 1989, it had reached 80%. We may speculate on the reasons for this, which are not straightforward but rather complex. First of all, in the case of Korean Japanese in Japan there is the fact that, even if they do wish to find a marriage partner who is Korean Japanese, it is difficult to identify one since most Korean Japanese in Japan use Japanese-language versions of their names (*tsûmei*) on a daily basis. Thus, places and occasions for getting to know each other are limited. It is also probable that some women seek Japanese husbands because of a distaste for the Confucian, sexist outlooks of Korean Japanese men. It is also possible that they seek Japanese men because they have higher, stable incomes, while earnings of Korean Japanese men are comparatively low, due to the effects of discrimination. This has been a factor in the process through which growing numbers of women from Asia (not simply from the Korean Japanese population) are now seeking marriages with Japanese men. (On the other hand, this would not explain why there has also been an increase in the marriage rate of Japanese women to Korean or Korean Japanese men.)

Despite all of this, the very high divorce rate for marriages between Japanese and immigrant Koreans or Korean Japanese in Japan has been attributed to a "higher level of friction and conflict than in the usual marriage." Among the factors leading to this discord, differences in nationality, differences in the class backgrounds within which the individuals were raised, and prejudice and discriminatory attitudes on the part of relatives have been cited. However, we are then left with an unanswered question: how to account for the even higher rate of divorce for marriages between members of the Korean and Korean Japanese community, who are not seen as characterized by such differences?

We must first consider whether an economic explanation for this is most persuasive. Even among Japanese couples, the bursting of the economic bubble and reduction in husband's income has led to an increase in divorces. These effects are felt all the more sharply by men who are Korean Japanese in Japan, in whose case employment opportunities are already limited because of discrimination, and who are therefore more vulnerable to unemployment and bankruptcy. Korean Japanese in Japan are shut out of the system of lifetime employment and thus experience frequent job shifts, as well as having few chances for salary raises or severance pay. Being without steady jobs and receiving low pay, Korean Japanese men find their status as patriarchs is reduced and their sense of self-esteem as men constantly injured. Many develop dependencies on alcohol. As a reaction against their inability to win greater respect within society, many — afraid that even within their own families they will lose their positions of strength and dominance — become abusive and violent within their homes. This fits a pattern of domestic violence brought on through the combined effect of racism and myths about masculinity that we can see all over the world. As Lisa Go and I have shown in the book *My Journey Within* [*Watakushi to iu tabi*], those Japanese men who marry Asian women tend to be from more or less lower class backgrounds in Japan.[16] Even in the case of these men who are Japanese citizens married to Korean Japanese women, the deeply corrosive forces of both class prejudice and discrimination against foreigners combine to make their families as vulnerable to breakup as families of minorities.

Children raised in such conditions learn first that violence is a method of solving problems. Once they reach adolescence, this is manifested as violence towards others (as well as themselves). Or, conversely, having learned that any resistance to the violence they live with is futile, they may fall into apathy and a sense of powerlessness in which they lose any desire to change the circumstances they find themselves in. In other cases, they mistakenly conclude that it is *because* of the violence they see that they are discriminated against, and they come to understand this violence as their own nature, rather than as an effect of discrimination. This leads to an even greater sense of self-hatred, which reduces their discomfort with discrimination. Children who come to feel that the source of their feelings of self-hatred is the situation within their own families, rather than discrimination, begin to view their families with contempt and to scheme about ways to "escape" them, having lost the ability to trust those to whom they are most intimately bonded. Because of this self-hatred and inability to trust, even those who succeed in escaping find it difficult to form new partnerships or family ties.

It is said that when a shelter for battered women opens in Japan, the first to flock to it are Korean women. This reveals both the actuality that Korean and Korean Japanese women are being exposed to significant levels of domestic violence, and that they have no one to rely on. They are discriminated against on the basis of both gender and nationality. While the situation for Japanese female-headed households is severe, the obstacles faced by Korean women who are "foreigners" in Japan, and who have no place to turn except to shelters, is even more grave. To maintain economic self-sufficiency while raising children, without unduly jeopardizing their own health, is very hard. The lasting impact of psychological scars left on both mother and child by the experience of domestic violence is even more difficult to calculate.

The fact that divorce rates among the groups I have noted above are so high is the result of the various factors in each case, and also affects the lives of the people involved after divorce. In this sense, we are dealing with a problem that will take a great deal of time to solve. However, in the case of Korean Japanese families, we must also take into account the way in which repetitive violence represents the displaced violence of colonial rule, of which it is a direct continuation. This violence is not only directed towards others but towards the self, leading to self-destructive behavior and suicide.

Lee Setsuko, who recently compiled a study titled *Fatherless Families Among Foreigners in Japan* [*Zainichi gaikokujin no boshi hoken*] noted that the number of suicides of Korean Japanese in Japan is twice as high as that of Japanese nationals.[17] In 1999, there were 108 suicides of men between the ages of 45 and 64 who were Korean or Korean Japanese in Japan, five times higher than that of women belonging to this group. To the number of men who died as suicides must be added many others who die of liver diseases caused by alcoholism. And we must ask why the suicide rate among Korean Japanese in Japan should be higher now (at least, according to our statistics for 1999) than in 1955, a year when they would have been living in considerably harsher conditions.

Japanese social structure continues to shift the brunt of many years of accumulated discrimination based on gender, ethnicity, class, and nationality onto the most disenfranchised social groups. How much longer will Japan preserve such a structure, which is sacrificing its own citizens (and especially its children) as well? It is only if we declare an end to this age in which a society maintains control by setting up subtle and complex distinctions among its members, only if we leave behind the sense of powerlessness that accompanies being subjected to such compartmentalization, and only if we search, in however tentative a manner, for ways to live together, that we will be able to live on in the society of the future. As Japan is being transformed before our very eyes by declining birthrates and growing numbers of elderly, we may be entering an age where it is possible to ensure that not a single person will belong to either the privileged "elect" or the "outsiders." And we must never lose sight of the fact that, if we are to do away with discrimination based on gender, ethnicity, class, and nationality, we must not only do away with economic distinctions and inequalities in social mobility and the ability to make choices, but heal the psychological wounds produced by violence related to discrimination.

ENDNOTES

[1] Nakamura Jirô, "Population Decrease and Labor Power — Some Thoughts on Foreign Workers, Part I" (*Jinkôgen to rôdôryoku: gaikokujin koyô o kangaeru, 1*), in *Nihon Keizai Shinbun*, May 31, 1999.

[2] United Nations, Department of Economic and Social Affairs, Statistics Division, *Population and Vital Statistics Report. Statistical Papers,* Series A, Volume 52, No.1 (New York: United Nations Secretariat, 2000).

[3] Japan, Tokyo, Youth Affairs Administration Management and Coordination Agency, *Sixth World Youth Survey* [*Dai rokkai sekai seinen ishiki chôsa*], NDLC:EC153, 2000.

[4] Ibid.

[5] Japan, Tokyo, Prime Minister's Office, *A Public Opinion Poll on the Quality of National Life* [*Kokumin seikatsu ni kansuru seron chôsa*], NDLC:EF11, 2000.

[6] *Nihon Keizai Shinbun*, April 30, 2000.

[7] An English-language report on this speech may be found in "Ishihara to Tokyo Garrison: Be Ready to Put Down "Foreign Riots" After a Disaster," *The Japan Daily Digest*, April 10, 2000. *The Japan Digest Archive On-Line* may be consulted at *http://www.japandigest.com/*

[8] Japan, Tokyo, Economic Planning Agency, Commodities Bureau, *Report of the Research Group on Health and Welfare Services for the Elderly* [*Kôreishakai o sasaeru kenkô, fukushi saabisu nado ni kansuru kenkyûkai hôkokusho*], NDLC-EG213-G350, 1999.

[9] Yashiro Naohiro, "Toward Overcoming 'Socialism Within'," Nihon Keizai Shinbun, November 29, 1999.

[10] Japan, Tokyo, Prime Minister's Office, "A Society Where Men and Women Participate Equally: An Opinion Poll" [*Danjo kyôdô sankaku shakai ni kansuru seron chôsa*], 1997.

[11] Ibid.

[12] Japan, Tokyo, Research Institute for National Social Security and Population Issues, *Basic Survey of Birthrate Trends* [*Shussei dôkô kihon chôsa*], 1997.

[13] Japan, Tokyo, Economic Development and Planning Agency, *Survey of Attitudes and Actualities Relating to Families and Society* [*Katei to shakai ni kansuru ishiki to jittai chôsa hôkokusho*], NDLC:EC82, Ministry of Finance Publications, 1994.

[14] Japan, Tokyo, Ministry of Foreign Affairs, *Year 2000 Statistical Survey of Japanese Living Overseas* [*Nisennenhan kaigai zairyûhôjinsû chôsa tôkei*], NDC8:334.3, Ministry of Finance Publications, 2000.

[15] *Nihon Keizai Shinbun*, May 21, 2000.

[16] Lisa Go and Jung Yeong-hae. *My Journey Within* [*Watakushi to iu tabi*] (Tokyo: Seidosha, 1999).

[17] Lee, Setsuko, *Fatherless Families Among Foreigners in Japan [Zainichi gaokokujin no boshi hoken*] (Tokyo: Igaku shoin, 1999).

"Welcome to Our Family"

Tessa Morris-Suzuki

Moving back and forth between Japan and Australia, I notice strange echoes in the fevered language of the media. In Japan, television stations run investigative documentaries on the "snakeheads" (*jatô*), Chinese organized crime figures who supposedly control the flow of illegal migrants into Japanese ports: in Australia the term "illegal immigration" is gradually displaced by the term "people-smuggling." Note the subtle change of focus. "Illegal immigration" draws attention to the immigrants themselves, the huddled masses towards whom media audiences are likely to feel at least an element of sympathy. But the label "people-smuggling" (like the term "snakeheads") focuses the spotlight on the exploitative organizers of the immigration trade, whom we feel free to regard with loathing. The migrants themselves are in the process reduced to the status of invisible human cargo. Australian newspapers link reports on "ethnic crime" to exposés of a recently renamed phenomenon called "home invasion" (to distinguish it from the more venerable local tradition of robbery with violence): a Japanese weekly magazine deploys the same images of violated domesticity as it captures readers' attention with headlines on the "gangs of foreign robbers" who may be "targeting YOUR home." And then (just as Australian politicians have sought to capitalize on paranoia) Tokyo Governor Ishihara mobilizes these fears with words which link the common anxieties of a globalized age to the long local legacy of racism against Korean residents in Japan.

These are echoes which resonate globally. Everywhere, new flows of human mobility are challenging the neat conceptual boundaries with which bureaucracies try to keep people in order. National immigration systems struggle to maintain the lines that supposedly separate the temporary *gastarbeiter* from the permanent resident and potential citizen. In an age when human rights are increasingly recognized as having economic and cultural — as well as political — dimensions, legal regimes strive to uphold the fiction of an impermeable dividing line between the refugee motivated by a "justifiable fear of persecution," and the mere economic migrant in search of a better life. At the level of community interaction, meanwhile, unruly human flows stimulate reactions which are at once encouraging and alarming. As Ghassan Hage points out in the final chapter of his study *White Nation*, recurrent media panics over immigration in a country like Australia obscure the less newsworthy "reality of an unproblematic and pervasive multicultural interaction."[1] At the same time, though, such panics serve to fuel the ugly overtones of violence which accompanied the Hanson phenomenon in Australia, just as they have more recently fuelled the rise of Jörg Haider in Austria and the outbreaks of mob violence against immigrants in El Ejido, Spain.

The transformations described in Jung Yeong-hae's paper must be understood against the background of these global phenomena. Yet the way in which changes are unfolding in the Japanese context marks, I think, a potentially profound shift in nature of Japanese society. Throughout the second half of the twentieth century the Japanese state relied, to a greater degree than most other national systems, on the mobilization of a myth of ethnic homogeneity as a key element in its discourse of identity. Tight restrictions on immigration were repeatedly justified by reference to the need to maintain national homogeneity, and so avoid importing into Japan the tensions seen as characteristic of more ethnically diverse foreign nations (most notably the United States). The myth, of course, required a forgetting of the history so vividly outlined by Komagome Takeshi: the history of the Japan which had ruled a multilingual and multiethnic empire where dividing lines between "self" and "other" were always fraught with irresolvable complexities and contradictions. It also required amnesia about the legacies of that colonialism — the presence of substantial communities of ex-colonial subjects and their descendants in Japan. It could be sustained, moreover, only by the deployment of an ambiguous notion of *minzoku* (nation/ethnic group) which served to obscure the presence of Ainu and Okinawans in Japanese society.

In the last couple of years, however, there have been clear signs that official consensus surrounding the discourse of homogeneity is breaking down. One sign, as Jung Yeong-hae points out, comes from projected shifts in Japanese immigration policy. The recently released report of the government's advisory committee on "The Structure of Japan in the Twenty-First Century" calls for the state to "embark on an immigration policy" (*imin seisaku e fumidasu.*) By this it seems to mean that Japan now needs, not only a set of rules on how to keep people out, but also a policy that explicitly recognizes the presence of immigrants within Japanese society. As Jung Yeong-hae's paper emphasizes, this shift is inseparably related to issues of generational change and gender discrimination in Japan. A more "tolerant" approach to immigration, in other words, is in many cases part of a policy for maintaining social and gender inequities by providing a pool of low cost female labor to care for the elderly. At the same time, though, the pressures for increased migration are generating new challenges to established ideologies of national identity.

Beyond the realms of immigration policy itself, therefore, change is also evident in the wider discourse through which official images of nationhood are constructed. This was vividly illustrated during the November 1999 celebrations marking the tenth anniversary of Emperor Akihito's accession. The celebrations were notable, not just for their efforts to associate the imperial family with the media glitz of rock stars and sporting heroes, but also for their attempts to add a "multicultural" gloss to the proceedings by (for example) giving prominent place to loyal statements by sports stars of non-Japanese ethnic origin. In an interview marking the occasion, the emperor also spoke at particular length about the issue of Okinawa and about his interest in "Okinawan history and culture."[2]

Yet cautious moves towards the construction of more "multicultural" versions of Japanese identity are fraught with their own complexities. For one thing, they are being accompanied by the racism represented by the comments of Governor Ishihara and his supporters. Besides, hesitant steps towards the recognition of a degree of ethnic or cultural diversity within Japan involve, not so much an acceptance of the haziness and arbitrariness of the lines surrounding national identity, as an effort to redraw these lines in a slightly different place. At one level, as Jung Yeong-hae rightly suggests, this may result in the creation of a sharper set of social distinctions between second- and third-generation Korean permanent residents (on the one hand) and (on the other) more recent migrants from Korea, China, and other parts of Asia.

I would suggest, however, that the emerging official "multicultural" rhetoric also embodies an urge to temper the effects of more inclusive ethnic boundaries by imposing more intense demands for public displays of loyalty to the nation. A small but significant illustration of this process was an advertisement, displayed on Japanese trains in the latter part of 1999, for a government-sponsored "tax awareness week." The advertisement featured a statement by Brazilian-born soccer star Ramos Rui, who has recently taken out Japanese nationality, about the civic duty of all Japanese citizens to pay their taxes promptly. On the one hand, the advertisement was notable for its conscious and positive portrayal of the changing ethnic complexion of Japan. On the other, it also carried an unmistakable subtext — the foreign immigrant earns his or her acceptance into Japanese society by visible and exemplary performances of the role of loyal, law-abiding, tax-paying citizen.

Seen from this perspective it seems neither ironic nor entirely coincidental that steps towards a liberalization of immigration policy and improvements in the legal status of long-term foreign residents in Japan should have been accompanied by the passing, in mid-1999, of a law enshrining the official status of the national flag and anthem, and by subsequent and remarkably heavy-handed efforts by the Ministry of Education to force all public schools and universities to fly the flag and play the anthem at entrance, graduation, and other ceremonies. In a sense, we may be witnessing a shift from a postwar rhetoric of nationhood based upon visions of ethnic homogeneity towards a new rhetoric of nationhood which has some features in common with the prewar colonial ideologies described by Komagome Takeshi. It is therefore interesting that the last few years have also witnessed an enthusiastic rediscovery by historians of the neglected legacy of prewar ideologies of cultural diversity.

During the first half of the twentieth century, the realities of rule over a multi-ethnic empire made it difficult for the Japanese state to sustain an ideology of ethnic homogeneity or racial purity. It is true that some prominent public figures espoused such an ideology. Ideas of racial purity, however, were at odds with efforts to persuade (or force) colonial subjects to assimilate and identify themselves with the Japanese nation. In general, therefore, there was widespread acceptance of the view that the Japanese people were the product of millennia of racial and cultural mixing, and some scholars even argued that Japan had demonstrated particular success in serving as an ethnic melting pot. Colonized populations (such as the peoples of Korea and Taiwan) could thus be represented as more "backward" variants of Japanese who would, through the processes of social evolution, be assimilated into the "mainstream" of national society.

The ideology of the colonial melting pot was combined with an emperor-centered vision of the national community as patriarchal family (*ie*) with the emperor as head. In this vision there was a constant slippage between notions of ethnic belonging and notions of political loyalty. Assimilation, in other words, meant acceptance into the fictive family: an acceptance which could be achieved by "adoption" as well as by "birth," but which always required submission to the authority of the patriarch. This imagery made it easy for those whose political loyalty was suspect (Marxists, for example) to be excluded from the family and defined as "non-nationals" (*hikokumin*), and conversely for visible signs of ethnocultural difference (such as "foreign" accents) to be interpreted as signs of potential political disloyalty. The result was a series of concentric circles of belonging, where the further one was removed from the center, the more one had to prove one's belonging by ritualized displays of loyalty to the state. So regular pledges of loyalty to the emperor were enforced in the colonies but not in "Japan proper," and the adoption of Japanese names was more rigorously imposed upon Koreans than upon Taiwanese because Korean subjects were seen as potentially more subversive to the order of the empire.

The plural society being created by rising levels of immigration in contemporary Japan is profoundly different from the prewar imperial order. The political and social structure has been radically transformed since 1945, and that transformation has weakened both the political power of the emperor and the social power of the patriarchal family. All the same, prewar experience reminds us that recognition of ethnic diversity is not necessarily a path to the recognition of equality or the creation of more flexible boundaries. As Japan enters a period of intense debate on proposals for revision of its postwar constitution, the post-1945 ideology of Japan as an ethnically homogeneous nation, too, appears to be being transformed in a complex way. Acceptance of the inevitability of cross-border movements of people has, in recent years, encouraged the emergence of new visions of Japan as a more socially, politically, and ethnically diverse society. On the other hand, growing immigration is clearly generating an ethnonationalist backlash evident in the popular support for Ishihara Shintarô's remarks on "foreigners."

In this context, one possible outcome is a form of "multicultural" ideology combined with efforts to strengthen the symbolic authority of the nation and the demands of ideological conformity. This ideology creates a social hierarchy in which the most marginal (the most recent migrants, the most visibly different) are always under the greatest pressure to demonstrate their submission to the symbols of national belonging. The symbols may no longer be ritual oaths of loyalty to the emperor, but may (among other things) include rituals of respect to the flag and anthem. They may also involve proving one's status as a suitable member of the "modern" national family by displaying one's membership of a "normal", stable, tax-paying family unit. It is striking that Ishihara, in an interview published in June 2000, spoke of the multiracial origins of the Japanese in terms which precisely echoed prewar ideology. He then went on to argue that Japan did indeed need increased numbers of migrants, particularly "because of the shortage of aged care helpers and nurses," but that it was desirable that these migrants should "as far as possible melt into Japanese life, marry and perform settled work here."[3] So admission of a degree of ethnic diversity can at the same time be a process of subjecting the visibly "different" to an increased degree of social control, and of excluding other sorts of social diversity: keeping out the politically suspect, the socially nonconformist, the single parent, the unmarried partner, the lesbian and gay.

And here I am reminded once more of cross-border echoes, and of Alistair Davidson's critique of a particular variant of Australian multiculturalism. This version of multicultural belonging was represented, a few years ago, by a series of government advertisements encouraging immigrants to adopt Australian citizenship. The advertisement featured a series of cheerful, articulate, assimilated and apparently prosperous migrants with a range of "ethnic" names and faces. The accompanying dialogue highlighted the contribution of the migrant as a stable and hard-working member of society, and always ended with the same words: "welcome to our family."[4]

ENDNOTES

1 Ghassan Hage, *White Nation: Fantasies of White Supremacy in a Multicultural Society* (London: Pluto Press, 1998), 233.

2 "Constitutional reform: the Yomiuri Newspaper Company's second draft proposal" (Kempô kaisei: Yomiuri Shimbunsha dainiji shikian), *Yomiuri Shimbun*, 12 November 1999.

[3] "A new immigration policy is needed" (Atarshii imin seisaku wa hitsuyô da), *Newsweek Japan*, 7 June 2000, p. 29.

[4] Alistair Davidson, *From Subject to Citizen: Australian Citizenship in the Twentieth Century* (Cambridge: Cambridge University Press, 1997.)

Part 3

Memories of State

Japanese Colonial Rule and Modernity: Successive Layers of Violence

Komagome Takeshi
— *translated from Japanese by Victor Koschmann*

Memories of the Forgotten "Empire"

In August 1945, the Japanese government surrendered by accepting the Potsdam Declaration that had been issued by the Allied Powers. This declaration confirmed the basic line of the Cairo Declaration, which had called for the reversion of Taiwan to China and the independence of Korea, thereby returning the territory of Japan to the status quo ante, prior to the Sino-Japanese War of 1894–1895. In effect, therefore, it brought about the dissolution of Japan's colonial empire. As of August 1945, some 6,500,000 Japanese were residing in Japan's former colonial territories — Taiwan, Korea, plus various islands in Micronesia — and the occupied areas of China and Southeast Asia. Some 3,500,000 of these were civilians, serving as government officials, businessmen, agricultural emigrants, or in other capacities. Indeed, some 10% of the total Japanese population lived in the occupied area outside of Japan proper, a region referred to by Japanese as *gaichi* (outer territories, as opposed to the inner territories, or *naichi*, i.e., Japan proper). In postwar Japanese society, however, it has been unusual for those who returned from the *gaichi* to speak publicly about their prewar or wartime experiences in those areas. Although some have reminisced nostalgically in alumni gatherings and other relatively intimate contexts, it has been extremely rare for someone to reflect self-critically on his or her experiences as a colonist in front of others who did not share those experiences. Overall, the colonial experience was thoroughly repressed, and in the process the event of forgetting was itself forgotten. Why did that occur? I'd like to explore the reasons for this phenomenon in three separate dimensions.

The most fundamental dimension of the problem is political. Even though the Allies, led by the United States, established the Far Eastern International Military Tribunal (Tokyo Trials) to demonstrate Japan's responsibility for military expansion from 1931 on, they did not seek to establish Japanese responsibility for Japan's colonial rule prior to that date. Of course, if we consider that at the time of the trials the United States was actually in the process of reestablishing its own colonial control over the Philippines, it becomes clear that the court's neglect of Japanese colonialism was less a matter of choice than of practical necessity. Moreover, Japan's relationship to the newly independent states that emerged in the formerly colonized and occupied areas was determined by Cold War strategy. In effect, therefore, in the postwar Japanese social structure and value system, issues related to postimperialism were immersed in the more salient processes of demilitarization and democratization; they were therefore neglected, and ultimately left "frozen" in an incomplete state.[1]

The second dimension relates to the consciousness of the participants in Japanese imperialism. Most former Japanese residents of the *gaichi* had experienced serious deprivation and other problems in the course of their repatriation, and those intense and bitter memories of repatriation tended to blot out any detailed recollection of the lives they formerly enjoyed as colonists. In the case of former soldiers, as well, memories of the rigors and mistreatment they experienced in the military interfere with their ability to confront the acts they committed. The "freezing" of the issues related to postimperialism at the political level allowed, indeed encouraged, individuals to "freeze" out their own memories of empire at the personal level.

Third is the dimension of intellectuals' responsibility. Most of the intellectual leaders of postwar Japan happily embraced the dismantling of the empire, and identified themselves with the construction of a democratized nation state. Very few expressed misgivings regarding the public's general failure to confront and deal critically with memories of "empire."

For example, in 1951 the leading postwar political scientist, Maruyama Masao, quoted Ernst Renan to the effect that modern nationalism should be founded upon a "daily plebiscite."[2] That is, in principle, each individual was obliged to choose daily whether he or she chose to be "Japanese," and their choices could be effective only when the ideals of democracy held sway. But who should have the right to "vote" in these daily "plebiscites"? Maruyama never addressed that question even though meanwhile, in the world of realpolitik, Koreans and Taiwanese were first denied the right to vote in general elections and then, once the San Francisco peace treaty went into effect, lost their citizenship completely. There were very few exceptions. People who formerly were obliged by colonial policy to live in Japan were now unilaterally excluded in the course of reestablishing the Japanese nation state. Intellectuals like Maruyama failed to see the contradiction implied in the gap between these rude political realities and the ideal of autonomous choice expressed in the notion of a "daily plebiscite." Needless to say, they also failed to recognize the rights implicitly claimed by these peoples by virtue of their history of being colonized. Thus, the discourse of intellectuals also reaffirmed and legitimized forgetfulness regarding the legacy of empire.

Of course, there were exceptions. In 1948, Takeuchi Yoshimi, the scholarly specialist in the works of the Chinese writer, Lu Xun, cautioned against the contrasts commonly drawn between the "success" of Japan's Meiji Restoration and the "failure" of China's 1911 revolution, and argued that whereas Japanese had quickly forgotten their defeat at the hands of European culture and accepted it facilely, Chinese had not only resisted their own cultural defeat but mounted "resistance against any forgetfulness regarding that defeat."[3] Takeuchi suspected that amidst the postwar reforms Japanese were again preparing willfully to forget their defeat and change their stripes; he argued that an alternative to this type of superficial turnabout could be found only by learning from the experience of other Asians.

In Takeuchi's 1961 essay, "Nihon to Ajia" [Japan and Asia], he developed this motif as a critique of the "unilinear view of civilization" (*bunmei ichigenron*). According to Takeuchi, this conception of a "one-way street from barbarism to civilization" took root as the de facto state ideology in conjunction with colonization following the Sino-Japanese War. Moreover, Japanese had never experienced the kind of intellectual developments, including "proletarian thought," that would have led them to reject imperialism, which he understood as the "forcible imposition of civilization."

Why, then, was Japan, which modernized rapidly after internalizing the "unilinear view of civilization," prosecuted at the Tokyo tribunal as a "rebel against civilization"? Takeuchi does not offer a very clear answer to this question, which he himself poses, but he does provide a way to approach it. He suggests that Japan was left out of the movement — which flourished in formerly colonized Asia — to "resist civilization and thereby help to reconstruct it." As an example of such resistance he recalls that, "when Gandhi took to the spinning wheel as a means of opposing the Lancashire textile factories, civilization increasingly found it impossible to punish such a rebellion against civilization." Yet "that change was invisible to the Japanese."[4] In the tones of a prophet who can perceive the future in such a seemingly insignificant event, Takeuchi writes that, "as American global policy is increasingly forced to protect pseudo-civilization, civilization itself will become increasingly devoid of principle and content;" in the meantime, however, the quickening of nationalism in Asia and Africa harbored a movement toward "the autonomous discovery of a more comprehensive value system."[5]

Takeuchi was most likely unaware of it, but in Algeria the same year, Franz Fanon wrote in *Wretched of the Earth,* "Let us decide not to intimidate Europe; let us combine our muscles and our brains in a new direction. The pretext of catching up must not be used to push man around, to tear him away from himself or from his privacy, to break and to kill him."[6] An effort to "resist civilization and thereby help to reconstruct it" was indeed emerging in Asia and Africa.

Although Takeuchi does not explicitly say so, he implies that Japan should have been tried as a rebel against civilization, not by the United States but rather by the peoples of Asia and Africa who were seeking to reconstruct civilization by resisting it. Nevertheless, the United States was in fact controlling the Tokyo trials. This subtle but decisively important fact allowed Japan to be exempted from prosecution for colonial rule and accelerated the onset of forgetfulness in postwar society regarding the legacy of "empire."

Even Takeuchi failed to address Japan's colonial rule concretely. Because he was preoccupied with the experiences of China and India, he made light of the fact that the Japanese "Asianists" who supported India's independence movement were also fervent nationalists who had ignored anti-Japanese movements in Taiwan and Korea. Nevertheless, his remark that the "unilinear view of civilization" provided the underlying ideology of colonial rule is worth reexamining, even in postwar Japanese society, and thus it is very important to rethink the relationship between colonial rule and modernity. The reason is that postwar Japanese forgetfulness is still half-unconsciously legitimated by a value system supporting the belief that, like Europeans, the Japanese bestowed the "blessings of civilization" upon those they ruled and contributed to their modernization. The postwar Japanese government has also helped reproduce that value orientation by refusing legitimate demands for reparations from former colonies and occupied areas while at the same time presenting itself as eager to provide "aid" to formerly colonized "developing countries."

Major studies of Japanese colonial administration tend to stress how different it was from Western varieties. Japanese rule is considered unique because of its "assimilation policy," by which it imposed Japanese language and Japanese names, and enforced Shinto shrine worship.[7] Of course, in some ways Japanese policies differed irreducibly from Western equivalents. Nevertheless, it is necessary to recognize from the outset that Japanese colonial rule also occurred in the midst of the enormous transformations attending political and cultural modernization and the truly global diffusion of the capitalist mode of production. In effect, imperialistic colonialism was pursued as a joint project by Japan and the Western powers. Therefore, rather than constructing a balance sheet so as to tally up and "compare" the good and bad points of the Japanese and Western regimes, it is important to make clear that multiple imperialisms mutually reinforced and overlapped each other vertically, in a process that was thoroughly penetrated by violence.[8]

More concretely, it is essential to unify the Japan-Taiwan and Japan-Korean relationships, which are usually considered in terms of the history of colonial policy, with the Anglo-Japanese and Japanese-American relationships, which are usually considered only at the level of diplomatic history. In this essay, I will attempt to extract from the various combinations that might result the relations among Britain, Taiwan, and Japan. While focusing on the Christian missionaries who were sent from Britain to Taiwan on the occasion of the Opium War, I will also consider their relations with the Japanese who, following their victory in the Sino-Japanese War, were ascendant as the new imperial rulers in the "Far East," and the Chinese residents of Taiwan, who were gradually coming to see themselves as "Taiwanese."[9] The British missionaries in Taiwan do not necessarily represent the Western colonial administrations, but we can situate them historically by means of an investigation of their social and cultural background.

In the first section, I will take up the process by which, in the era leading up to the Japanese takeover of Taiwan following the Sino-Japanese War, pressure for modernization penetrated Britain, China/Taiwan, and Japan, producing one "convert" to modern civilization after another and arranging them in a hierarchy of adaptation to the civilized order. While portraying in collage-like fashion several individuals who clearly manifested the qualities of such a "convert," I will attempt to reveal the "intertwined history" of Britain, China/Taiwan, and Japan. As Edward Said has suggested, "juxtaposing experiences with each other, letting them play off each other... [in order] to make concurrent those views and experiences that are ideologically and culturally closed to each other and that attempt to distance or suppress other views and experiences" is itself an important perspective in the study of imperialism.[10] It is precisely the work of parsing the threads of such "intertwined histories" that will allow the issue of responsibility for imperialistic colonialism to rise clearly to the surface.

While focusing on the relations between culture and imperialism, I will take up in the second section the history of the half-century following Japan's occupation of Taiwan. After clarifying the sense in which Taiwan has been designated a *colony,* I will use the microscopic case of the Tainan Presbyterian Middle School established by the British missionaries to show the process by which three orientations to modern education — British, Taiwanese, and Japanese — subtly differed, came into conflict, and finally generated a form of panic before bursting apart.

Areas needing to be problematized from the perspective of "culture and imperialism" are manifold, including literature, mass culture, architecture, and others, but in this essay I will focus especially on religion and education. Even in the modern world, religion continues to be an important dimension of the cultural realm. As Benedict Anderson points out in connection with the excellent example of the "tomb of the unknown soldier," far from a unilinear process of secularization, modernization is rather a process in which people's religious imagination is gradually absorbed by the modern nation state.[11] Religion becomes even more ideological than before, and ideology becomes religious. Moreover, rather than occurring in a self-sufficient manner within each nation state, modernization has developed as a process in which different cultures collide with each other, competing for hegemony. In the tense force-field that results, they have used violence to defend the illusion of their own culture's "purity" and fought to maintain cultural hegemony. Thus, in a manner of speaking, the objective of this essay is to join together and reconstitute the fragmentary vestiges of that violence.

"Converts" to Modern Civilization

The events that most vividly bore witness to the virtually seismic shifts that had transformed the face of 19th-century East Asia were the Opium War and the Sino-Japanese War. The Opium War began the dismantling of the classical community that comprised the Sinocentric empire, and the Sino-Japanese War completed the process. The inter-regional order that had formed through the mediation of the tribute trade system began to crumble in the late 19th century as a result of intrusions by the European powers and the United States; and the final link in the Sinocentric system of tribute trade — that with Korea — was dissolved by the Treaty of Shimonoseki that resulted from Japan's defeat of China. Japan's possession of Taiwan caused tremors in the balance of power system that had restrained the European powers and the United States, and opened the way for China's partition. Then, just at the turn of the century, the powers' (including Japan's) dispatch of troops to quell the Boxer Rebellion brought the final disintegration of the Sinocentric empire and signaled the establishment in East Asia of the modern imperialist system.

In the process, Japan rose to become the "military policeman of East Asia," and in that capacity contributed to the formation among the European powers of a system of "joint restraint." This was possible because the leaders of the Japanese government internalized the "white man's" perspective and disrupted the social order and value system of the existing society, striving instead to adapt to the order dictated by modern civilization. Those who feared the violence of the "white" overlord formed a "national subject" via the ordeal of "conversion" to modern civilization, and were themselves transformed into entities that exercised violence over subaltern others. In the course of this reversal, they took on a behavior pattern that combined cruelty toward others they viewed as uncivilized with coquetry toward the supposedly civilized. "Japanese" who shared this behavior pattern appeared in parallel with the Sino-Japanese War and Japan's takeover of Taiwan, and the importance of this pattern was self-consciously recognized by those in positions of power in the Japanese government.

The prime minister at the time of the Sino-Japanese War, Itô Hirobumi (1841–1909), said in a speech entitled "Administration following the Sino-Japanese War" that most residents of Taiwan were "ruffians from Guanzhou province and Fujian," and since this was a "half uncivilized" area whose residents included "aborigines,"

Japan should station there "sufficient troop strength" and use police to impose thorough-going control.[12] The same year as Itô's speech, Takano Môkyo, who had been appointed chief of the colonial administration's high court, reported in a letter to Itô that, "Among the natives arrested by our military or police forces, those deserving of the death penalty were hauled before the court and that evening taken out to the mountains or fields and executed. Their numbers were by no means small."[13] Itô's speech served to affirm and legitimize such a lawless situation.

On the other hand, in the midst of the Russo-Japanese War, Itô repeatedly appealed for the "sympathy of the civilized world," saying that "For the survival of the nation, especially in wartime, the sympathy of the civilized world is an extremely important, intangible form of support."[14] In the international politics of the time, when only a feeble form of restraint resulted from an untempered struggle for survival, Japan's hegemony over the East Asian world would have been impossible in the absence of the Anglo-Japanese Alliance (1902). In light of that, Itô's statements on the vital importance of the "sympathy of the civilized world" as a condition of Japan's survival in the international struggle for existence can be taken literally, as a serious statement indeed.

Those who fear violence are, at the same time, the ones who do violence to others. The position of the "Japanese" around the turn of the century aptly illustrates such ambivalence. However, it is also interesting to consider whether *some of* the British and Taiwanese, even if few in number, were not also "Japanese" in this sense. In other words, to the extent that there were among the British and Taiwanese those who actively promoted modernization, they must have included some who were forced to embrace the ambivalence of being simultaneously oppressor and oppressed.

Of course, by pointing that out I do not mean to argue that by virtue of their oppressor/oppressed ambivalence the British, Japanese, and Taiwanese necessarily all occupied equivalent positions. Such an over-generalization would dissolve all responsibility for domination. What I am getting at is not merely that they experienced a similar form of ambivalence, but also that as a result of differences in the timing of their adaptation to the order of civilization they came to be arranged in a political hierarchy, and out of the solidification of that hierarchy there emerged the regime of *colonial rule*. As Naoki Sakai has pointed out, modernity limits "the range of possibilities for thinking about the world historically and geopolitically;" by excluding the "possibility of coexistence between a 'premodern' West and a 'modern' non-West," it reinforces the imaginary identity of the West.[15] Therefore, in order to deconstruct that imaginary identity, it is necessary to be able to conceive of *some* British and Taiwanese also as "Japanese."

In order to consider this possibility, I will focus on three individuals. The first is Itô Hirobumi, already mentioned. The remaining two are Hugh M. Matheson (1821–1898) and Li Chun-shen (1838–1924).

Hugh Matheson was one of the managers of Matheson & Co., the London office of Jardine, Matheson & Co., which was famous in the opium trade. He was also the influential chairman of the East India-China Department of the London Chamber of Commerce, and served for more than thirty years as convener of the foreign missions committee of the Presbyterian Church of England, which dispatched missionaries to China's Fujian province and the southern part of Taiwan. As I will discuss below, when Itô Hirobumi traveled secretly to Britain in the late-Tokugawa period, Matheson served as his host.

Li Chun-shen was born into a poor household in Amoy, Fujian province. At the behest of his father, as a youth he was baptized a Christian. He cultivated his English ability at Ellis & Co. and other firms. When the business center of Amoy was destroyed in the mid-1860s as a result of the Taiping Rebellion, Li moved to Daidaocheng in Taipei and amassed a fortune in tea manufacture. Rather than resisting the modern transformation of East Asia, he was one who actively rode the waves of change. When Japan began its colonial administration, Li was among its active supporters, and in 1896 he was decorated by the Japanese government. The prime minister of Japan at the time was Itô Hirobumi.

Itô differed from the other two in his relationship to politics and evaluation of Christianity. Moreover, none of these men can be taken to "represent" the British, Japanese, or Taiwanese populations at the time. Matheson was little more than a parvenu in the eyes of English gentlemen. Itô was separated by a deep fissure of consciousness from the mass of the Japanese people who did not necessarily welcome "civilization and enlightenment;" and as a wealthy comprador, Li was isolated both from intellectuals who strove to preserve Chinese civilization and from ordinary Chinese. Indeed, the concept of "British" was multiply fissured from the beginning, and that of "Japanese" had only recently been manufactured; similarly, the term "Taiwanese" meant nothing more than a resident of Taiwan. These three men had in common only that, when modernization clattered over them like a falling line of dominos, they chose to hasten its advance. Of course, the precise varieties of modernization each espoused differed significantly, but in order even to locate such differences we must first trace their backgrounds.

Victorian Parvenu: Hugh Matheson

Britain in the Victorian era (1837–1901) was dominated by the view that along with science and technology the main pillars of civilization were free trade, Christianity, and the Western way of life, and that these should be extended as widely as possible to the "uncivilized" peoples of the world. However, those who would be the agents of the "civilizing mission" might themselves have only recently emerged from the realm of so-called "barbarism." Take the case of Matheson: He was born in Edinburgh, former capital of Scotland, and his father was born in the northern region of Sutherland, so Hugh was raised at the cultural backbone of the Celtic fringe.

Scotland had been an independent kingdom, but in 1707 for most purposes it merged with England. It lost its own parliament, and the Presbyterian Church, which was the Established Church of Scotland, was reorganized according to the Episcopalian system of the Church of England. In other words, contrary to the Presbyterian principle that ministers should be appointed by a congregation that included laymen, now the right of the landowning class to appoint ministers was guaranteed.

Culturally, Scotland was divided into the lowlands, where English culture was strong, and the highlands which, like Ireland, belonged to the Celtic cultural sphere. In the highlands the peculiar pattern of social organization called the clan had developed, and Christianity did not penetrate very deeply. However, in the mid-18th century, an increasing number of clan headmen sent children to school in the lowlands and accepted Christianity; moreover, "Like many converts, they made the most zealous evangelists in attempting to convert their social inferiors to what they now regarded as civilization."[16] Then, from the late-18th to the early-19th centuries, a large-scale process of enclosure, called the Clearances, was carried out for the purpose of securing grazing land for sheep. As a result, most highlanders flowed into the urban slums, or migrated to North America. For example, the first missionary sent to Taiwan by the Canadian Presbyterian Church, G. L. MacKay, remarked, in explanation of his parents' emigration to Canada in the 1830s, that "There had been dark days in Scotland — the dark and gloomy days of the 'Sutherlandshire Clearances,' when hundreds of tenant-farmers, whose fathers were born on the estate and shed their blood for its duke, were with their wives and families evicted."[17]

It was just another incident in the harsh advance of modernity. In Hugh Matheson's case, it appears that already in his grandfather's generation his family had begun to advance in the world via relatives as Presbyterian converts. Nevertheless, in his youth, Hugh's family spoke Gaelic and recalled their experience in the clearances. Hugh himself participated in the movement to preserve Gaelic and once declared that, "There is not a drop of blood in my veins that is not Highland."[18]

At age 15, Hugh joined a Glasgow firm and taught Sunday school in the church whose pews were the most expensive in the city. At that time, church pews were sold, and obtaining one at an expensive church was an indispensable means of attaining social respectability if one did not have prestigious bloodlines or educational credentials.[19] In 1843, Hugh experienced a remarkable incident. The Free Church of Scotland split from the Established Church and became independent in the course of the so-called Disruption. The main issue was distortion of Presbyterian principles since the Union with England. Included in the splitters' sense of "free," as in the Free Church of Scotland, was the ordinary sense of freedom from state rule. The supporters of this free church, including Hugh Matheson, were primarily from the middle class that had burgeoned in parallel with the rapid industrialization of Glasgow, and they were known for their belief in the orthodox Calvinist concept of predestination, along with hard work, frugality, educational achievement, and their zeal to spread the gospel overseas and among the poor. Armed with the doctrine of complementarity between laissez-faire and Christian morals, they rationalized social inequality in theological terms as the result of disparity between "those chosen by God" and the rest; "this theological rationalization of success and inequality prevented the rich and successful from feeling guilty about their wealth and success in the midst of the shocking misery and poverty about them."[20]

Perhaps the Scottish middle class was able to produce these aggressive proponents of the "capitalist ethos" because the "refined" cultural tradition of the English landed class had not accumulated there in sufficient depth. On the other hand, the rapid increase in Irish emigration as a result of the great famine of the 1840s led to prejudice and the circulation of stereotypes of the Irish as "monkeys" and "drunks." This dichotomy between the Calvinists, who embodied the capitalist ethos, and the Irish, at the other extreme, represented an originary form of the binary of civilization vs. barbarism that soon spread across the world. Of course, when they appeared in the "Far East," they were regarded equally as "whites."

Scots were numerous in the vanguard of the British empire. Hugh Matheson's grandfather, James, was among them. James established Jardine, Matheson & Co. in cooperation with W. Jardine, and when the East India Company's monopoly over the China trade was abolished, Jardine, Matheson & Co. moved aggressively into the opium trade. Hugh's elder brother Donald and cousin Alexander were active in the business along with James, and in 1839 all three were ordered expelled from China by Lin Ze-xu. In 1843, the same year as the Disruption, James, who had returned to England to serve in Parliament in the ranks of the Liberal Party, urged Hugh to join Jardine, Matheson & Co. In light of the opposition to the opium trade that was gathering even within Britain, Hugh initially declined. Eventually, however, he was involved in managing Matheson & Co. Thus, beginning with his father's generation, Hugh represented a progression from Sutherland, the northernmost point on the British Isles, through Glasgow to London, the "center of civilization."

In 1844 in London, the Presbyterian Church of England was established around a central core of Scottish immigrants, and, using funds provided by Matheson & Co., the young church began to dispatch missionaries to China. It was, indeed, a matter of opium in the left hand and bible in the right. Such a structure seems fraught with contradiction, but as J. A. Mangan points out, "they had to construct bulwarks against a possible sense of guilt produced by disjunction between their colonial actions and domestic practices." Precisely because the immorality of the opium trade was clear, they needed some way to regain their confidence as agents of the "civilizing mission."[21]

The Tientsin Treaty (1858) that ended the second Opium War expanded the region in which missionaries could operate, even as an anti-Christian movement flourished. From the perspective of the educated gentry, the missionaries were destroyers of the received social order, and little more than barbarian intruders. Yet it was difficult to stop activities that were backed up by gunboat diplomacy. In the clash of civilizations between China and the West, the Chinese side lost. This became evident in the historical process leading to the 1898 Reform

Movement at the end of the century. In the late-1880s, Matheson wrote, "The opening of China to the commerce of the world, and her adoption, in a large degree, of Western ideas, in the defence of the country, and in the development of her material resources, signalise one of the most remarkable and most interesting changes of modern times" and it called for "profound gratitude to God."[22] Hugh Matheson's death in 1898 elicited condolence letters filled with remorse from Chinese who belonged to churches in Amoy and elsewhere.[23] In them, we find confirmation "in the words of Chinese themselves" of the victory of modern civilization as a victory of morality.

"One of the Matheson Boys" — Itô Hirobumi

Those who zealously "convert" to modern civilization on account of what is thought to be their barbarian origins never hesitate to impose that civilization on others. Not limited to Hugh Matheson, this behavior pattern is evident all over the world and was shared by Itô Hirobumi as well. At the same time, it is noteworthy that Itô accepted constitutional government and industrialization as the content of modern civilization, while considering Christianity to be irrelevant. Therefore, in his case the religious metaphor of "conversion" is indeed no more than metaphor.

Itô was born into a poor farmer's family in Chôshû domain at the end of the Tokugawa period, but because his father was adopted into the Itô household, the family had entered the very lowest stratum of the samurai class. In May 1863, at a time when Chôshû had just turned to a policy of "expelling Western barbarians" (*jôi*) and began firing on Western ships, Itô, along with Inoue Kaoru and three others, received the tacit approval of their feudal lord, the *daimyô*, to travel secretly to Britain. The idea was that in order to fight one's enemy one must first know him, and as the ship left Yokohama harbor, Itô wrote, "Suffering the shame of unmanly behavior, I go for the sake of the divine country."[24] Apparently, it was considered shameful to travel to a country of "Western barbarians."

The group of samurai, who had boarded a Jardine, Matheson & Co. ship in Yokohama, landed first in Shanghai. Itô's biography says that, "Surveying the scene from the ship's deck, they could make out warships, steamships, and sailing vessels passing frequently in and out of the harbor, and along the shore were rows of magnificent Western-style buildings and other sights. They marvelled at this scene of prosperity." It also says that Inoue Kaoru rapidly changed his views in favor of opening the country to the West.[25] Their visit occurred toward the end of the Taiping Rebellion, just as General C. G. Gordon led the Ever-Victorious Army to victory against the Taipings, causing crowds of desperate refugees to stream into Shanghai. Itô and his shipmates must have encountered such tragic scenes even amidst the splendor of Shanghai, an urban show-window displaying the strength and appeal of modern civilization.

The travelers landed in London in September, and, according to the *Westminster Gazette*'s later account, "had the good fortune to be commended to the care of a Christian man of sturdy common-sense, a member of the firm which had arranged their escape — Mr. Hugh Matheson, to whose wise counsels and fatherly care Japan owes not a little today. 'Yes, I was one of Mr. Matheson's boys', said the Japanese Premier [Itô] to me the other night."[26]

Hugh Matheson not only took charge of Itô's personal well-being, but opened the way for the party of Japanese to study at the University of London's University College. Unlike Oxford and Cambridge, this school was open to those outside the Church of England, like the Presbyterians, and was willing to tailor its curriculum to offer natural sciences and foreign languages, while leaving out theology. Matheson's background, including his Scottish origins, conformed well to the desires of Itô and his party.

In March of the year following, news from Japan caused Itô hastily to return there and devote himself to persuading Chôshû to abandon its expulsionist policy and make peace with the European powers and the United States. Having directly experienced China's distress and Europe's wealth in close succession — what Matsuzawa Hiroaki defines as the "combined experience of China and the West"[27] — he had promptly become a "convert" to modern civilization.

In 1872, following the Meiji Restoration, Itô visited London again as a member of the Iwakura Mission. This time, he enlisted Hugh Matheson to help recruit faculty for the Imperial College of Engineering (later the College of Engineering of Tokyo Imperial University). Matheson consulted with the professors at the University of Glasgow, and negotiated on Itô's behalf with Henry Dyer.[28] Under Dyer's direction, the College of Engineering became a progressive, high quality institution of technical learning, and its products achieved rapid industrialization from above. Meiji Japan was thus able to defend itself against massive intrusions of foreign capital and grew into a state that behaved much like a large-scale trading company with its own military support.

Japan succeeded quite well in erecting a barrier against domination by foreign capital, but pell-mell introduction of modern civilization also caused confusion in the realms of religion and morals. In order to prevent negative reactions against modernization from turning into a full-scale "revolt against civilization," it was necessary to bring about a "mass conversion" to the civilized order that would include even those of Itô's generation who had no experience of Shanghai and London.

What was fashioned in place of Christianity to meet that political need was the pseudo-religion of the emperor system. In 1887, at the outset of deliberations on the draft Constitution, Itô Hirobumi emphasized that in the West, Christianity unified the minds of the people as the "axis" of the state and thus supported the Constitutional order, whereas in Japan, Buddhism was in "decline" and Shintô lacked the "power to guide the minds of the populace;" thus, "only the imperial household" was capable of constituting the state's "axis."[29]

Just as Itô planned, Article One of the Meiji Constitution (1889) announced that "The Empire of Japan shall be reigned over and governed by a line of Emperors unbroken for ages eternal," thus appealing to the creation myths as the basis for imperial legitimacy. Despite the archaic aura in which the emperor was cloaked, this "invented tradition" was essentially an adaptation to modern civilization. In its essence, it had the characteristics of a new religion, offering this-worldly benefits. Emperor worship actually began to function effectively as a means of mobilizing mass consciousness after the Sino-Japanese War. During that war, the Emperor Meiji was ensconced in an imperial headquarters in Hiroshima so as to make it look like he was personally commanding Japan's military forces. This imperial performance was effective in disseminating the image of the emperor as a beneficent entity who brought home such "spoils of war" as monetary reparations and Taiwan.[30]

In the end, the Japanese government succeeded in warding off Europe and America in the realms of both industry and religion, and while appealing to the "sympathies of the civilized world," completed its adaptation to the modern order. The politician who consciously steered such a course, while sensitively comprehending trends in international politics, was Itô Hirobumi. Even Itô's comment that he was "one of Mr. Matheson's boys,"was made during a newspaper interview in March 1895 in the midst of peace negotiations for the Shimonoseki treaty, and was calculated not only to excoriate the barbarism of the Ch'ing court, which had obscured the locus of war responsibility, but also to pointedly inform the Chinese plenipotentiary, Li Hong-zhang, of Itô's knowledge of the West. In other words, the comment represented Itô's pride in keeping a step ahead in terms of modernization and his calculated appeal for British favor.

At the very moment the interview took place, a reaction was occurring in Britain against Japan's dominion over Taiwan, and there was even an effort by Matheson to buy Taiwan back within the syndicate headed by Jardine.[31] But although the Shimonoseki treaty's award of the Liaodong penninsula to Japan invited the Triple Intervention, Japan was able to gain the powers' understanding regarding its appropriation of Taiwan, and was able to avoid intervention by giving highest consideration to "sharing benefits" with the government and merchants of Britain via the most-favored nation provision. Jardine Matheson had already withdrawn from investment in Japan in the 1870s, but on the basis of the most-favored nation provision was now able effortlessly to obtain industrial rights in China and begin full-scale investment there.[32] Hugh Matheson's solicitous care of the young Itô Hirobumi had paid off handsomely.

In 1901, a series of articles in the *China Mail*, an English-language paper published in Hong Kong, criticized the monopoly over the sales of camphor and other goods exercised by the Japanese Government-General in Taiwan. W. C. Campbell, a missionary sent to Taiwan by the Presbyterian Church of England, took the Government-General's side, arguing that even though the monopoly disadvantaged certain Western merchants, it was not an egregious abuse of the "spoils of war." Moreover, in response to the proposal made by the author of the articles that pressure should be brought to bear on the British government by way of the London Chamber of Commerce, Campbell commented that, "those connected with such important Corporations, like our own Mission Convenor, the late Mr. Hugh M. Matheson of 3 Lombard Street, are also sensible men of honour, who believe in both sides of the 'live and let-live' principle."[33]

It is true to a certain extent that both British and Japanese adhered to a principle of "live and let-live." However, the effective scope of that principle was limited, and toward Chinese and Taiwanese it was more a matter of "joint oppression."

"Castaway" of the Qing Dynasty: Li Chun-shen

The residents of Taiwan had nothing to do with the decision that led to Japanese rule over their island. This lack of consultation was legitimized by the view that political self-determination was appropriate only for "nationals" who had gone through the process of adaptation to a civilized order.

However, as they moved to occupy Taiwan the Japanese military were confronted with stubborn resistance by anti-Japanese guerrillas. Cruel suppression visited upon those viewed as guerrillas succeeded only in encouraging others to resist, contributing to a vicious circle. Kabayama Sukenori, the first governor-general of Taiwan, frankly expressed his uncertainty to Itô Hirobumi in a cable, which said that the "Righteous Army," which is what the anti-Japanese guerrillas called themselves, "frequent mountain roads, disrupt rail and power lines, and pounce upon villages, causing casualties among our troops." Therefore, he requested permission to delay the advance of Japanese forces southward toward the cities of Anping (Tainan) and Dagou (Takao).[34] In reply, Itô wrote that because, "Foreigners in Anping and Dagou are facing an emergency, and we are frequently subjected to inquiries even from the British government regarding the scheduling of our military operations," the troops should advance south no matter what, and Kabayama finally succeeded in occupying Tainan/Takao in November.[35] In this case, Itô consistently adhered to his policy of placing priority on "the sympathies of the civilized world."

Even several years later, the Government-General continued to worry over how to respond to anti-Japanese guerrillas, but it also benefited from the cooperation of certain powerful Han Chinese, and somehow succeeded in establishing the colonial administration on an even keel. One of those Han Chinese was Li Chun-shen. In July of 1895, Li successfully proposed that the Government-General establish a Bureau for Preserving Peace and Order (*horyôkyoku*). In a report to Itô, Kabayama wrote regarding the Bureau that, "We haven't had the time to gain a complete knowledge of the feelings, customs, etc., of the indigenous people, but even though we find administration here extremely difficult, it is fortunate that a wealthy merchant and others have established a Bureau for Preserving Peace and Order, and we have communicated our views on it, with the result that both colonial government and Japanese people rely upon it."[36] Also, the chief of the Civil Government Bureau, Mizuno Jun, made an award to Li and some others on account of "their frequent help in hunting for bandits," etc.[37] From this, it is clear that the Bureau also played an important role in rounding up anti-Japanese guerrillas, so Li also cooperated in the process of "joint oppression."

From Li's point of view, one can imagine that as a capitalist his highest priorities were "the preservation of order" and the security of his own assets. However, the Government-General had allowed a two-year period of grace during which colonials could decide on whether or not they wanted to take Japanese citizenship, so Li had the alternative of selling his assets and returning to the mainland. Why did he decide to become a Japanese "subject"?

One key to this issue can be found in his "travels to the East" of February 1896. Li was invited by Governor-General Kabayama to accompany him on a "triumphal return" to Japan proper (*naichi*). The *Tokyo asahi shinbun* introduced Li as follows:

> A rich merchant from Daidaocheng (outskirts of Taipei) who deals in tea and camphor, Li Chun-shen was one of the first of his countrymen to show goodwill toward the Government-General and has often exerted himself on behalf of our military forces. Brisk and alert in temperament, he is a master of Mandarin and nearly fluent in English as well. He turns sixty this year. He says that when he gets to Japan proper he intends to cut his pigtail and dress entirely like a Japanese.[38]

From Governor-General Kabayama's perspective, Li's journey "east" served, no doubt, to show off the civilized contours of Japan proper and impress him profoundly. The propaganda effect of demonstrating to ordinary people the successful subjugation of a "new subject" might also have entered into his calculation. Kabayama and his party were given a grand welcome, and met by an imperial messenger and Prime Minister Itô Hirobumi. The young man who, thirty-some years before, had stolen away on a ship to London, the center of civilization, could now welcome an important visitor to Tokyo, the new center of civilization in East Asia. In June of the same year, Itô visited Taiwan, and this time Li's congratulatory article was published on the front page of the *Taiwan shinpô* (later changed to the *Taiwan nichinichi shinpô*).[39]

Li's account of his visit to Japan proper, *Tôyû rokujûyonichi*, was serialized in *Taiwan shinpô*, and later published as a book in Fuzhou. In that account, he records how impressed he had been to find the various institutions of civilization, such as schools, factories, newspapers, etc., in completed form, but he also mentions the powerful influence of Christianity in Japan. As he understood it, in Japan — contrary to the situation under the Qing — there was now complete "freedom of belief." Yet, as research by Huang Jun-jie and Ku Wei-ying has revealed, Li's itinerary was completely controlled by Japanese officials, and he could not observe situations in which Christianity had been suppressed.[40]

In his address at Azabu Church in Tokyo, Li introduced himself by saying, "I was born in Lujiang, and as a youth obeyed my father, had faith in God, and followed the teachings. After moving to the east (Taiwan) I obeyed my teacher, McKay (the Canadian Presbyterian missionary), followed the Way, and observed the rites." He then raised the question of why the small country of Japan had defeated the much larger Qing empire, and by way of an answer, suggested that in Japan, "government is lenient while customs have profound effect; people worship Jesus and clearly serve the Lord;" in Qing China, on the other hand, "government is anachronistic and the people are recalcitrant," so that "sovereign and people are of one mind in seeking to destroy the sacred faith."[41]

Li's comments were delivered in a Japanese church and must be evaluated in that context. Nevertheless, his beliefs that Christianity is the foundation of the strength and wealth of civilization and that the defeat of the Qing was determined by its persecution of that religion appear to be sincere, and based on his own experience. In the 1870s, missionaries in Taiwan worked out a division of labor in which Canadian Presbyterians began their proselytizing in the north and English Presbyterians took the south. Li became a central figure in the northern sector. However, his activities in conjunction with both missionaries and foreign business interests made him the object of considerable popular antipathy.[42] Thus, Li, who was isolated and vulnerable under Qing rule, had grounds for his charge that Qing "rule was anachronistic and the people recalcitrant."

Another possible reason why Li chose to become a Japanese subject was the shallowness of his identification with the Qing. Li was a resident of Taiwan on the periphery of the Qing empire and held no rank or title under the bureaucratic examination system. In this, he differed markedly from intelligentsia on the mainland, but was typical of his class in Taiwan. In the late Qing, the local elites in China, including landowners, merchants, landlords, and others, tended to arrange by various means to obtain titles as degree holders and thus to gentrify themselves, even though their social status depended less on cultural respect that on actual power, which was based on assets and private armies.[43]

For Li, it was most important to promote industry and spread Christianity, so as long as the new Japanese rulers were patrons of modernization, they were acceptable to him. Clearly, he placed certain very optimistic expectations on the modern era, but, at the same time, it would be a mistake to conclude that he was simple minded.

Li was not only a prominent merchant, but an early introducer of modern thought to Taiwan. From the mid-1870s, he drew upon his profound knowledge of the international situation to contribute a number of opinion pieces to papers like Hong Kong's *Zhongwai xinpao* and Shanghai's *Wangkuo gongpao*. When Japan dispatched troops to Taiwan in 1874, he rang the alarm bells regarding an invasion, saying, "Those concerned about Ryûkyû (Okinawa) and Korea would be well advised to mount a defense at the earliest opportunity. We should never adhere tenaciously to established ways, or just sit and await a Japanese invasion."[44] At the same time, he argued for the necessity of expanding defenses, promoting industry, abolishing the traditional examination system, and propagating Western-style school education, and when the Western affairs movement occurred in the 1880s under the governorship of Liu Ming-zhuan, he offered his cooperation in constructing a modern infrastructure, including the railway from Taipei to Keelung. From Li's perspective, Japan constituted a threat, and at times even an outright enemy.

During his visit to Japan, Li was keenly conscious of being the "castaway of a defeated country." His most vivid ordeal occurred as he disembarked in Hiroshima and was called "Chankoro" — a disparaging epithet — by a Japanese child.[45] Indeed, only a policeman's intervention saved him from having a stone hurled in his direction, and the incident shocked him so profoundly that he cut off the pigtail that marked him as a subject of the Qing and changed to Western clothing. This is what lay behind the *Tokyo asahi shinbun* report that "when he gets to Japan proper he intends to cut his pigtail and dress entirely like a Japanese."

Moreover, when he went to see a performance of "Battles of the Sino-Japanese War" (*Nisshin suiriku sentô no geki*) in Asakusa, he was unable to bear it so got up in the middle and left. As he reveals, the incident had a deep emotional impact: "Although my recently-acquired obligations toward the Japanese empire are profound, it is difficult to forget a debt to the Qing Dynasty. Although it is shameful to lose one's country, it was my decision to change nationality. At the same time, it was excruciating to see others enjoying those heart-rending scenes."[46] No doubt, the drama portrayed "peerlessly brave and loyal Japanese soldiers" cutting down "timid and fearful Chinese soldiers." Even though he was a "castaway," Li clearly took pride in having chosen voluntarily to become a Japanese subject. Meanwhile, in the eyes of Japanese who were in a frenzy over their victory and admission into the club of "civilized nations," Li was just a "Chankoro."

After his return to Taiwan from his visit to Japan, he virtually stopped his commentary on current events, devoting himself instead to activities related to the dissemination of Christianity and education. He produced a series of books explaining Christian doctrine that were published in Fuzhou, and one can imagine that these publications embodied his fervent hope that the Chinese people under Qing rule would finally embrace Christianity.

In regard to education, it is noteworthy that when he traveled to Japan he gathered seven young men from among his grandchildren and relatives and requested that they be allowed to study for a period of time at Japanese schools. This clearly symbolizes the high expectations he placed on modern education under Japanese rule. Although his request was granted, it soon became clear that this was an exceptional case. Not too long after Li returned to Taiwan, the following article, entitled "The Education of Taiwanese," appeared in the *Tokyo asahi shinbun*:

> Even in the Ministry of Education there is an atmosphere of caution regarding the education of the people of that island. Some say that we should select outstanding students and educate them in Japan proper, but often when unenlightened people are rapidly imbued with a civilized education the results are contrary to intent. We have, in fact, educated Okinawans in Japan proper and spread an enlightened atmosphere among them, but in not a few cases they have advocated Ryukyuan independence and impeded provincial administration. Some argue that educating Taiwanese in Japan proper will produce similar results. Thus, the issue of temporary study (*ryûgaku*) requires further deliberation.[47]

It is difficult to confirm the facts behind the contention that students from the Ryûkyûs advocated "Ryukyuan independence." Nevertheless, it is true that Jahana Noboru, who went from Okinawa to Tokyo in 1882 as the first exchange student supported by the prefecture, returned to Okinawa as a higher civil servant after graduating from the College of Agriculture, Tokyo Imperial University and soon — just as the above newspaper article was published — became embroiled in a confrontation with the governor of Okinawa prefecture over official appropriation of land formerly held communally by farmers. Jahana, who resigned from the government in 1898, subsequently devoted himself to the movement to obtain suffrage rights for Okinawans. Finally, he became deranged after failing to achieve his objectives and died in a fit of anger.[48]

What is important here is not the question of whether figures like Jahana actually advocated "independence for the Ryûkyûs," but the fact that their oppositional discourse was taken that way in the metropole. In its first part, the selection quoted above suggests that Taiwanese and Okinawans are "unenlightened" people so "civilized education" should not be imparted to them. However, the second part of the article makes it clear that this is merely the inverted expression of a hidden logic. That is, as we can see from the example of Jahana, there was concern that arguments made by Okinawans would "impede prefectural administration," hence "civilized education" of the sort that might encourage such arguments should be avoided. As a further extension of this logic, it was necessary to tag the Okinawans as "unenlightened" in order to legitimize such a policy. It is characteristic of this hidden logic for problems arising in the realm of political and economic conflict to be reduced to a matter of the civilizational level of a particular group — that is, to an attribute. In other words, education and culture were being mobilized in order to rigidify imaginary "natural differences." It was a logic admirably suited to the realities of *colonial rule*.

Most likely, Li was incapable of imagining the true nature of *colonial rule* under a regime of modern imperialism. In fact, at the juncture of 1896, the gap between Lee's expectations and those of the Japanese had only begun to emerge in the "Chankoro" incident and minor newspaper articles like the one above. Nevertheless, in parallel with the development of colonial rule, this gap was destined gradually to mature into bitter conflict.

The Construction of Colonial Rule

The first decade after Japan took possession of Taiwan was characterized by trial and error, as the Japanese gradually formulated colonial policy. "Castaways" of the Qing, like Li Chun-shen, were unable to participate in policy formation; it was clear, above all, that as the victors in war, Japan's government leaders were able unilaterally to determine policy, but even they had no blueprint for colonial rule. The two main sources upon which they based their policy decisions were the experience of governing Okinawa and the information that had been collected on colonial administration by the European powers and the United States.

One who played a major role in establishing the main institutions of rule over Taiwan was Gotô Shinpei, who in 1898 was appointed chief of the Civil Affairs Bureau and later, Director of Civil Administration (*Minsei chôkan*). In a memorandum he wrote around the time he was first appointed, Gotô said, "In an era of competition among nations, successful colonial administration seems to be a major factor in recent imperialist development;" and "In Taiwan, it will be difficult to apply the legal system of Japan proper; we must proceed with close attention to world trends."[49] The success or failure of colonial policy impacted on the "struggle for survival" among the imperial powers, and in order to succeed in that struggle, it was disadvantageous to be bound by the "legal system of Japan proper." Japan should seek a colonial policy that conformed to the "trends of the world."

As one who saw colonial policy as merely a part of diplomatic policy more broadly, Gotô felt it necessary to be attentive primarily to the perspective of the European powers and the United States rather than those of the people of Taiwan. The *Fifty Years of New Japan* (*Kaikoku 50-nen shi*), published in both Japanese and English, observed that "Experienced men of other countries, who had practical experience of the difficulties in governing a new territory, were inclined to predict that Japan would, like Sparta of old, certainly fail as a ruler in peace."[50] This was just when negotiations with the European powers and the U.S. were at the most crucial stage, and Gotô's colonial policy, including the elements focused on political administration, economics, education, etc., gave highest priority to meeting the skeptical gaze of the Europeans and Americans.

The same orientation is evident in Takekoshi Yosaburô's *Japanese Rule in Formosa* (*Taiwan tôchi shi*), published in 1905 in both English and Japanese, with a preface by Gotô. In his own preface, Takekoshi announced, "Western nations have long believed that on their shoulders alone rested the responsibility of colonizing the yet unopened portions of the globe, and extending to the inhabitants the benefits of civilisation: but now we Japanese, rising from the ocean in the extreme Orient, wish as a nation to take part in this great and glorious task."[51] While comparing the colonial systems of various nations, he explains the system of rule on Taiwan as follows: "The power vested in the Governor-General is similar to that held by the Governors of the British Crown Colonies, while, with regard to military matters, it more closely resembles that of French Colonial Governors."[52]

Takekoshi's observation regarding the Taiwan Government-General is not mistaken. Among the Japanese leaders there had been a debate regarding whether or not the colonial government should be granted comprehensive powers, free from the constraints of the Constitution, but in the end, just as Gotô had intended, the government took the option of cutting Taiwan off from "the legal system characteristic of Japan proper." The Government-General was granted by the emperor the power to issue edicts that had force equivalent to law, and its only political responsibility was to the emperor as sovereign. The road to obtaining rights to participate in politics was closed almost entirely to Taiwanese. Of primary importance here is not how this colonial regime compares to others, but the political implications of the very task of comparison itself. It was through comparison that Takekoshi sought to legitimize Japan's rule over Taiwan in the eyes of Europeans and Americans and to appeal to the "sympathies of the civilized world." Toward the Japanese people, on the other hand, Takekoshi sought through comparison to demonstrate that denial of the Taiwanese right to participate politically was consistent with practice in all colonial administrations; he also aimed to whitewash the violence committed under this autocratic system of rule.

Having clarified the dependent status of the Taiwanese politically, Gotô turned to the economic task of completing the basic projects necessary to allow capitalism to penetrate, such as surveying the land, constructing railroads, digging harbors, etc. These were absolutely necessary in order to convince people at home and abroad that the leaders of Japan were agents of *la mission civilisatrice*. Indeed, the missionaries showed unconcealed pleasure at completion of the rail line traversing Taiwan on the West, and Li also extolled Gotô's virtues in "A Biographical Sketch of Baron Gotô Shinpei," where he also wrote, regarding the railroads and harbor facilities, that "the Taiwan of ten years ago hardly differed from a village of barbarians, while today it has been transformed into a world where civilization prospers."[53]

Capital for the various projects to advance civilization came largely from monopoly sales of opium, camphor, salt, tobacco, and other products. The sale of opium was suggested and initiated by Gotô when he was head of the Hygiene Bureau of the Ministry of Home Affairs, before he was appointed chief of the Civil Affairs Bureau. Gotô opposed a complete ban on opium, as that would drive habitual users to their deaths; he hoped that by selling officially produced opium only to those with licenses to buy it, he could eventually eliminate the evil habit of opium smoking and at the same time increase the Government-General's revenue. Indeed, it appears to have been an ingenious policy, but of course there was no guarantee that the Government-General would not issue excessive numbers of licenses in order to further increase revenue. In fact, during the Russo-Japanese War, the missionary Dr. P. Anderson who was engaged in medical activities in Takao reported that, "I do hear often enough of their hunting up those who have ceased to smoke (temporarily at least), with a view to their renewing their licenses," and added that, "the local authorities are under great temptation to almost any methods that will bring in revenue."[54]

Opium smoking had been strictly prohibited in Japan proper ever since the opening of the country to the Western powers in 1858. It was 1898 before the government monopoly system was initiated with experimental sales of tobacco. In economic policy as well, Taiwan was able to take exceptional measures for securing revenue because of its colonial status. From Gotô's perspective, these were consistent with "the trends of the world" and were efficient means in carrying out the "civilizing mission."

In the field of education as well, differences from Japan proper were quite evident. The educational system Gotô set up while he was Director of Civil Administration placed Japanese and Taiwanese schools in different tracks; the Japanese went to "elementary schools" that conformed to the system in Japan proper, while Taiwanese went to "public schools" with a special curriculum. Coeducation of the Japanese and Taiwanese ethnic groups was forbidden. There were no middle schools to provide liberal education, so the Government-General's Japanese Language Schools (*Kokugo gakkô*) and Medical School provided the extent of post-elementary education available to Taiwanese. The consistent orientation underlying these facilities was that there should be no disruption of the status order between peoples and thus Japanese superiority over Taiwanese should be guaranteed. In the state of social fluidity that followed dissolution of the prescribed status order of the Tokugawa era in Japan proper, the education system served as the means of selecting a national elite, but people in the *colony* were excluded from that process.

Gotô Shinpei's tendency to restrict the spread of education naturally conflicted with Li Chun-shen's conception. Chen Pei-feng has characterized Li and Gotô as "lying in the same bed but dreaming different dreams," showing that they were at odds, especially in regard to education.[55] As the basis for his argument, Chen refers to the fact that Li made handsome contributions to promote the spread of education in the 1910s, but contributed nothing during the era when Gotô was Director of Civil Administration. He also points out that Gotô wrote critically regarding Li in "Monthly Comments on Gentry in Taipei" saying, "He is bigoted in his opinions and miserly by nature. Ever since Taiwan became part of the empire, he has calculated his own interest but coldly spurned the public good."[56] For his part, Li might have meant his refusal to make further donations as a tacit protest against Gotô's restrictive approach to education. Despite his praise for Gotô in "A Biographical Sketch of Baron Gotô Shinpei," their relationship seems to have been cool; as Chen points out, Li's initial hope for "salvation by faith" (*tariki hongan*) — that is, his naive trust that his support for Japan would be rewarded with modernization as he interpreted it — was snuffed out early on. He also gradually realized his mistake in wishfully seeing Japan as a state that protected Christianity.

Emperor Worship as Racism

In his contribution to *Fifty Years of New Japan,* Gotô writes in a self-satisfied vein regarding the restoration of public order following suppression of the anti-Japanese guerrillas and the preparation of infrastructure resulting in industrial development as signifying the "success" of Japanese rule in Taiwan. On education, however, he resorts to the awkward comment that, "As regards education in Formosa, it is as yet a matter of study and consideration what measures may be the best to adopt."[57] He seems to recognize religion's importance, by saying, "How far religion affects colonization it is needless to conjecture here," but then writes frankly, "The question therefore arises whether Japan had any such religion to rely upon. To this the answer, I am sorry to say, must be in the negative."[58] No doubt he was keenly aware that, in as much as Christianity has been viewed as an important element in the construction of civilized values, Japan could not in this regard be viewed as a "civilized country."

How, then, did Western missionaries evaluate Japan's administration of Taiwan? In 1896, Thomas Barclay, a missionary sent by the Presbyterian Church of England, wrote in a report to the London headquarters that, "One cannot but sympathise with the people, dissociated without their consent being asked from the ancient Empire of China, with all its traditions, of which they are so proud, and handed over to form a despised Empire.... In the meantime, there seem to be some advantages to be hoped for. The change will improve the conditions of life for missionaries, and the greater facilities of communication will greatly help our work. The destruction of the Mandarinate and perhaps still more of the literary class as a body, involving the discrediting of Confucianism, will remove many obstacles out of our way."[59]

In the eyes of this missionary of Scottish origin, Japan was nothing more than a "despised Empire." On the other hand, his posture of naive faith in modernization and its development of the means of communication, along with his assignment of top priority to the dissemination of Christianity, caused him, like Li, to prefer Japanese rule to that of the Qing empire. That is precisely why Gotô Shinpei sought to win the missionary's favor by such measures as supporting their school for the blind. Nevertheless, that alone was insufficient as a means to wipe away the image of Japan as a "despised Empire" and demonstrate the "high morality" of the Japanese rulers. To the extent that political discrimination and economic exploitation — as symbolized in the pattern of "opium in the left hand, bible in the right" — dominated the realities of colonial rule, it was necessary to fabricate some kind of morality to obscure those realities. With his keen insight into Western imperialism, Gotô must have been painfully aware of that necessity. Yet, although he demonstrated clear vision in other areas, on these points he could only respond ambiguously. Why was that so?

When Gotô writes modestly that in Japan there was no religion that could be relied upon, hidden behind his words was his evaluation of modern Japan's favored pseudo-religion, emperor worship. In principle, that is, he could have adopted the alternative of propagating in Taiwan, and establishing at the nucleus of religious and educational policy, the same pseudo-religion of emperor worship that obtained in Japan proper. That he did not suggests that, unlike the Government-General bureaucrats of later years, Gotô was skeptical regarding the probable effect of such a policy.

As noted above, emperor worship was devised as an equivalent to Christianity in order to aid in national unification. An important role in instilling such worship was played by school rituals carried out on the imperial holidays that were institutionalized in the early 1890s. Consisting of such elements as obeisance to the imperial couple's portrait, reading of the Imperial Rescript on Education, moral admonitions by the principal, and the singing of "Kimigayo," these ceremonies produced an atmosphere appropriate to a place of worship. Then, in 1898, the Ministry of Education banned religious education from all formal schools and sought the basis for moral education not in the bible or Buddhist sutras but the Imperial Rescript on Education. Moreover, although not provided for by law, shrine worship organized through the schools began to be encouraged.[60]

Shrine worship originates in Shintô, an amalgam of various religious customs based on animistic conceptions of the sacred. However, Shintô changed markedly in the course of the Meiji government's efforts to consolidate and standardize it as emperor worship. The newly formed state Shintô situated the emperor at the top as high priest, and although there was no unified doctrine, government-employed priests were made to carry out rites prescribed by the government. According to the government's official view, shrine worship was not religious activity and therefore did not contradict the "freedom of belief" provided for in the Imperial Constitution. Aside from what people believed, shrine worship was considered desirable as patriotic behavior. At the same time, the methods and extent of coercion varied with time and place, although in most cases it was encouraged through tangible or intangible measures via the school system.

In the process of forming state Shintô, many folk practices associated with Shintô were suppressed, and sometimes actively persecuted as evil rites or heresy. Of course, no matter how wrenching were the changes they were subjected to, in Japan proper the original shrines still continued to exist in most areas, whereas in Taiwan there were no shrines to begin with and unique local beliefs associated with Taoism were the most prevalent. For that reason alone, it would have been difficult to transport Japan's system of emperor worship wholesale to Taiwan. In addition, there were the following obstacles.

In the first place, there was concern that importation of emperor worship would be criticized by Christians as an infringement upon "freedom of belief." Of course, such criticism occurred in Japan proper as well, but it was especially dangerous in the colony, where it was always difficult to recruit collaborators. We need to remember that, for missionaries like Barclay as well as Taiwanese Christians like Li, the perception that, unlike the Qing, Japan was tolerant of "freedom of belief" was a major element in their support for Japanese rule. Also, as Wu Wening's research has shown, even though Taiwan's Christian population was less than 1% in 1900, one out of every four graduates (1902 to 1906) of the Government-General's medical school was the descendent of a Christian, and

Christians were among the few who welcomed the Government-General's new educational policy.[61] Introduction of emperor worship would only antagonize this important minority.

Second, there were issues related to factors intrinsic to emperor worship, such as its relative lack of the kind of systematic doctrine that was typical of Christianity and Buddhism, and also the fact that it was a new religion that emphasized this-worldly benefits while lacking a transcendental, otherworldly perspective. The problem here was that unless there was some basis for the claim of tangible benefit, it would not attract adherents. In Japan proper, victory in the Sino-Japanese War had contributed to an image of the emperor as a beneficent entity who provided the "spoils" of war, but clearly it would be difficult to sell the same concept to people who were themselves part of those "spoils."

Third, as another problem intrinsic to emperor worship, one can point to its fundamental reliance on a rhetoric of consanguinity. For example, as in the formulation by the legal scholar Hozumi Yatsuka, if the "Japanese race" (*Nihon minzoku*) traces its origins back far enough they will find that all are ultimately descended from the imperial household. Thus, "sovereign and people have common ancestors" and form a "group based on blood" (*kettô dantai*). Thus, at the foundation of emperor worship were myths impervious to all rational argumentation. According to these myths, the question of whether or not an individual belonged to the "Japanese race" was to be determined on the basis of the "natural" attribute of blood line, and this attribute was institutionalized in the form of the ubiquitous family register.

When Gotô Shinpei rejected any direct application of the Japanese Constitution to Taiwanese, he wrote that it was impossible to "bring new people under the blessings of the Constitution on a basis equal to those who for three thousand years have loyally served the imperial household."[62] The logic by which he legitimates his exclusion of Taiwanese from the Constitution's "blessings" relies on the "fact" of mutual connections centering on the imperial household for the past "three thousand years." Here, exclusive links to the imperial household constitute the "family circle" (*uchiwa*) of the rulers and function as a system to legitimize discrimination against others; therefore, it was best to refrain from publicizing it to the colonized peoples.

What, then, was the standard for determining who were to be included among those who "for three thousand years have loyally served the imperial household"?

In day to day life, one's name played an important role, but when it came to determining legal rights and duties it was the family registration system that was relied upon. The family register was the basis for determining matters of conscription, taxation, education, hygiene, etc., and the criterion for arbitrating within the fixed realm of kinship any changes in an individual's status on account of birth, marriage, or death. In the same year that Gotô went to Taiwan, a new family registration law was promulgated along with the civil code in Japan proper, but rather than extend this law to Taiwan, the authorities established a different system there.

The primary means of moving from one family registration system to another were marriage and adoption, but a number of obstacles blocked these processes. In the case of marriage, domestic partnerships in which one partner was governed by the registration system of Japan proper and the other by the system in Taiwan were until the 1930s considered merely common-law relationships. Transfer of registration from one system to the other by means other than marriage or adoption was prohibited until the collapse of the empire. In effect, the categories of "Japanese" and "Taiwanese" were differentiated on the basis of consanguinity and reproduced in a manner that precisely corresponded to the rhetoric of emperor worship.

Emperor worship with the above characteristics should be considered as an equivalent to racism or, indeed, as racism itself. If we define racism as discrimination based on skin color, then Japanese as part of the "yellow race" will be classified solely as the objects rather than the subjects of racism. In fact, even at the present time it is common for Japanese to see themselves merely as the victims of "racial discrimination," which they interpret in light of the distinction in Japanese language between the term "race" (*jinshu*), based on biological differences, and the cultural category of "ethnic group" (*minzoku*). However, according to Robert Miles's definition, racism selects as an important standard some arbitrarily chosen characteristic such as skin color, and on the basis of that characteristic categorizes human groups and applies to them negative (or positive) stereotypes. Usually the arbitrarily chosen characteristic "is a phenotypical feature (e.g., skin colour, hair type, shape of the head), but genetic and other less immediately visible biological phenomena (e.g., blood) are also signified."[63]

Michael Weiner, who has studied the history of Koreans in Japan, invokes Miles's definition, but treats the racial/cultural discrimination perpetrated by

Japanese as a variant of racism. As he points out, the important issue in defining racism is not whether it is to be based on biological or cultural characteristics, but how those characteristics are employed. What is important is that, "the possession of these supposed characteristics may be used to justify the denial of the group's equal access to material and other resources and/or political rights."[64] Based on this point, the process by which a cultural tendency to despise Taiwanese as "Chankoro" spread in conjunction with the institutionalization of colonial rule should be considered tantamount to the process by which emperor worship begins to function as a variant of racism. The Taiwan Government-General sought to foster an image in which all were equal as recipients of the imperial benevolence and in order to give substance to this rhetoric, repeatedly claimed that eventually Taiwanese would be thoroughly assimilated. But it was thought necessary to make such claims precisely because in its essence, emperor worship is a mechanism for racial and ethnic exclusionism.

The source of headaches for the Japanese colonial administrators was that this emperor worship might indeed, on the one hand, substitute for Christianity as an "axis" of national unification but simultaneously, on the other, would act in the dimension of colonial rule as an equivalent to racism. Agents of Western imperialism found it possible to obscure the cruelty of their strict discrimination between "white" and "non-white" by relying on the pseudo-universalism of Christianity. However, such a strategy was difficult in the Japanese case, at least to the extent that emperor worship was formed as a defensive reaction to "universalistic" Christianity. Their inability to make the same distinctions as the Western imperialists made it difficult for the Japanese rulers to demonstrate their "high morality."

Skepticism regarding the effects of introducing emperor worship directly into Taiwanese schools did erupt during Gotô's tenure as Director of Civil Administration. One Japanese teacher in a public school pointed out that the content of the ethics curriculum was discouraging and unbearably "confused and inconsistent," adding that "to harp on sentiments of kinship" — such as, that "sovereign and people have common ancestors" and form a "group based on blood" — "could lead to dangerous results;" therefore, he suggested, it might be best not to teach the Rescript on Education for a while.[65] Gotô proved unable to come up with a positive solution to this problem. The regulations for public schools set forth in 1904 stipulated that the Rescript should be the basis for ethics instruction, but the textbook that was to give specificity to the Rescript's principles was never compiled during Gotô's term in office, nor were regulations established to regulate school ceremonies on holidays.

While ambiguously shelving issues related to the ideals of education, Gotô did set out a policy of thoroughly pursuing Japanese language education from the elementary level onward. This was because by elevating Japanese language to the level of a formal ruling culture, it was possible to portray the Japanese as "competent" and the Taiwanese as "incompetent." Among Taiwanese, demands for modern education gradually manifested themselves, and the supression of Taiwanese language and Chinese writing were criticized, along with the inadequacy of institutions for secondary education. Moreover, the hidden confrontation between emperor worship and Christianity inevitably came to the fore.

The Anti-Japanese Movement and Tainan Presbyterian Middle School

Considerable pressure for change was put on the education policy of the Taiwan Government-General in the 1910s and 1920s. In 1911, Kumamoto Shigekichi, chief of the School Affairs Section, wrote regarding that policy that, "On the surface we act as though we place great importance on education, but in fact we take no action to encourage it." Schools had been established only to the extent deemed necessary under the watchful "eyes and ears of the Western powers."[66] No new facilities for secondary education were set up, and those that existed were just low-level vocational schools. Thus, the colonial officials had deemed it important just to establish sufficient facilities to avoid Western criticism, and their conscious decision not to develop secondary education suggests that at this stage they were still following the line established by Gotô.

However, dissatisfaction with the Government-General was spreading among powerful Taiwanese. In 1912, forseeing that an application to establish a private middle school of the new type would be denied, they went to the missionaries with funds to expand the existing Tainan Presbyterian Middle School so as to offer a full liberal education. This school had been established by missionaries prior to the Japanese takeover of Taiwan and retained many aspects of its original mission as a preparatory school for those going on to seminary. Sponsors of the proposal numbered twenty-eight in all, among whom only Li Chun-shen was a

Christian, but the application said, "We offer the money, but have no intention of meddling in Christian educational policy." This was clearly an attractive proposal from the viewpoint of the missionaries, and in his letter to the London headquarters Barclay quoted the Taiwanese benefactors as saying, "If you can get $20,000 for rebuilding a broken-down temple, surely we can get it for a school; the idols are all very well, but not so important as a good education."[67]

The endorsers of the proposal included some, like Li, who had adapted early to his sense of world trends by converting to Christianity, but in the eyes of most of these influential men the missionaries, who despised as mere "idols" the deities worshipped in temple halls, were disturbers of social peace. Nevertheless, at a time when on the Chinese mainland the traditional examination system had been abolished, and then in 1912 momentous historical changes accompanied the establishment of the Republic of China, even conventional local gentry had no choice but to conclude that " idols are all very well, but not so important as a good education."

In the end, the Taiwan Government-General, which disliked any extension of Christian power, decided to establish a public middle school. The Government-General had no choice but to concede, since it needed the support of influential Taiwanese in the war to subjugate the aboriginal population. Of course, at the level of the Government-General, this decision faced powerful opposition when official permission was sought from Tokyo. The home government opposed the idea because "efforts to raise the level of general education needlessly contribute to developing the civilized consciousness of indigenous society and might bring results injurious to colonial rule." Additional arguments were that schools should be low level because of local concerns about the length of the school year and entrance qualifications.[68] Here, one can easily detect refrains of the colonialist logic underlying the statement in *Tokyo asahi shinbun*, quoted above, to the effect that "often when unenlightened people are rapidly imbued with civilized education the results are contrary to intent."

In response to the home government's tendency to adhere closely to the logic of colonial rule, Kumamoto argued that, "In our view the safest way to maintain control is to provide appropriate education," but in the end the Government-General had to comply with the home government's demands.[69] It is worth noting that the Government-General had turned away from the view that the spread of education should be restricted in favor of the theory that under rigid control it was best to disseminate education as a "safety valve." According to this view, the demands for modern education on the part of influential Taiwanese should not simply be suppressed but should rather be encouraged and guided. It was as if they would be told, we'll provide you with a chance for modern education, but in return you must accept Japanese as the "national language" along with emperor worship. Indeed, during Kumamoto's term as School Affairs Section head, an ethics text was finally compiled and holiday ceremonies were introduced in the public schools. Even though the Taiwanese were not going to become whole-hearted "believers" in the cult of emperor worship, the condition of a modern education was to be their acceptance of a value system that situated the Japanese as a superior people.

In the 1920s, when it was necessary somehow to respond to the world trend toward "national self-determination," the home government itself took the initiative in carrying out reforms in the above direction. That is, in 1922 the Government-General issued the Taiwan Education Ordinance, which stipulated that although in principle Japanese and Taiwanese would continue to be educated separately at the elementary level, they would now go to the same secondary and higher schools. At the same time, the entrance examinations and curriculum in secondary schools would still be almost entirely in Japanese, and in order to pass the entrance exams it would be necessary to memorize the Imperial Rescript on Education. Moreover, the provisions of the Taiwan Public Secondary School Regulations, passed in conformity with the Taiwan Education Ordinance, stated explicitly that on the regular festival days, students should visit Taiwan Shrine for worship. Thus, while these regulations aimed at a certain level of equality, they also clarified relations of subordination in the cultural realm and constituted a "new concept" in colonial rule.[70]

Enactment of the Taiwan Education Ordinance placed the Tainan Presbyterian Middle School in a difficult position. Because it was not an official middle school, its graduates were not qualified to go on to higher schools; therefore most of those students who did aspire to continue their education dropped out and transferred to middle schools in Japan proper. On the other hand, the Government-General was afraid that recognizing the Presbyterian School as a formal middle school would open a breach in the rampart of educational control. Contrary to the case in other public middle schools, this school was aimed solely at Taiwanese and promoted bible study in their own language, so it had the potential of gaining the overwhelming support of the Taiwanese. Consequently, the Government-General resorted to financial hurdles as a pretext for nonrecognition, and demanded a very large donation for purposes of establishing an endowment fund.

In order to qualify their school to send students on to higher education, in 1925 people connected to the Presbyterian Middle School organized a supporters' organization to carry out a five-year campaign with the objective of raising ¥100,000. Playing a central role in the organization was Lim Bo-seng (Lin Mao-shen in Mandarin). The missionary, Edward Band, who was principal of the Presbyterian school from 1912, wrote that, "Mr. Lim Bo-seng, our head teacher, is occupied in touring the country, giving lectures, writing scrolls, and seeking to enlist subscribers.... So eloquent are Mr. Lim's powers of persuasion that within a few months he has received £2,000 in promises."[71]

Lim Bo-seng was born in Tainan in 1887. After graduating from the Presbyterian Middle School, in 1907 he continued his education in Japan proper, eventually graduating from the College of Literature, Tokyo Imperial University. Thus, he was Taiwan's first Bachelor of Arts under Japanese rule.[72] He became head teacher at his alma mater, and in 1921 participated as a lecturer in the newly established Taiwan Cultural Association (Taiwan Bunka Kyôkai) which functioned as part of the anti-Japanese movement. When the Association's publication, *Taiwan minpao,* took up the question of the Presbyterian Middle School, it reported that "On the basis of their different beliefs, up to now many people have refused to contribute to Christian schools, but as the result of Lim Bo-seng's reputation now a substantial number of people from all walks of life are offering support." The paper speculated the rather than "wasting" money on old-fashioned idolatry these people were choosing to invest in "raising the level of Taiwanese culture."[73] In the early 1910s, the influential Taiwanese donors had stipulated that "idols are all very well" and at that time foreign religion had come to be viewed negatively. So, clearly, there was change over time. Lim Bo-seng was similar to Li Chun-shen in his Christian belief and enthusiasm for the dissemination of modern education, but he differed in being active at a time when he could attract many supporters among Taiwanese. On the other hand, the Taiwan Government-General, which from the outset of Japanese rule had presented itself as a proponent of modernization, was now clearly in the position of intervening in that process.

Lim Bo-seng's plea for aid in expanding the Presbyterian Middle School and making it into a normally accredited institution was appealing to many Taiwanese, whether Christian or not. This seems to suggest clearly that feelings of frustration with the colonial education system had spread widely. While it is true that the Taiwan Education Ordinance had opened up opportunities for Taiwanese to receive a secondary and higher level education, it was still extremely difficult to qualify for such schools. Because from the beginning there had not been a system of compulsory education, the rate of advancement to public school was very low. Fewer than 1% were able to enter secondary schools.

Lim's efforts bore fruit, and although the Presbyterian Middle School had not yet succeeded in raising the entire amount that had been stipulated, in May 1927 the Government-General recognized its establishment of an endowment fund. The founders were Edward Band and Lim Bo-seng. They also formed a Board of Managers, with five representatives each from the Mission Council, the South Formosan (Taiwanese) Church Presbytery, and the supporters of the School Endowment Fund.[74] However, the same month, Lim left for Columbia University as a foreign researcher under the auspices of the Government-General. This all too timely appointment might have resulted from a destructive strategy on the part of the Government-General, but Lim tried to turn it to his own uses. At Columbia he selected "Public Education in Formosa under Japanese Administration" as a thesis topic, and clearly outlined the various problems involved in the exclusive use of Japanese language and the system of jointly educating the two ethnic groups. In his conclusion, he states, "Modern education aims to develop the individual from within, not impose a development from without for fear that it would spoil the creative power on the part of the child. Assimilation sets out to impose standards for its own from without which are not desired."[75] This selection aptly suggests what kind of *modernity* Lim sought. It should be noted that even the seemingly naive assertion that education should "develop the individual from within" calls sharply into question whether or not the Government-General's colonial education policy could indeed be called *modern.*

On the above point Band, the school principal, had the same views as Lim. In a report he wrote in 1930, he remarked critically that, "A state in which all Formosans think, speak, and act according to the same standardised Japanese pattern, may be very pleasing to imperialistic politicians, but hardly satisfactory to the more thoughtful Japanese educationalists." He then remarked more reflectively that, "Even we Christian educationalists, in spite of our alleged emphasis on the things of the spirit, in our desire for quick results and in a slavish conformity to government methods, may be tempted to educate by 'reforming from without' rather than 'transforming from within'."[76] It is easy to detect behind his use of the phrase, "slavish conformity to government methods" a critical consciousness with respect to the Government-General's educational policy.

Of course, Band's approach was also contradictory. At the December 1928 meeting of the supporters' association the opinion was expressed that a Taiwanese should be elected principal, and Band understood this desire, in the sense that "This Middle School should be rendered independent by Taiwanese themselves in accord with the demands of the time, and it is therefore natural that the job of principal should also be held by a person from the island." But he did not come out and say this clearly at the time.[77] In propagating Christianity the missionaries in Taiwan upheld the principles of "self-government, self-support, self-propagation" in line with the parliamentary spirit of the Presbyterian Church, and they had actively pursued the principle of self-support in the sense that the school had become less dependent on financial aid from London. Yet, they had shown less concern to actualize "self-government." In opposition to this tendency on the part of the missionaries, the Taiwanese in the supporters' organization adopted a "Declaration" that plainly set out the need for change in the nature of the school, saying that, "Although support comes from the British and its creed is Christianity, in essence this is a purely Taiwanese educational institution. We hope and pray that it can be a Taiwanese school in every way."[78]

Dissension in relations with the missionaries had arisen because non-Christian Taiwanese had risen to important positions in the supporters' organization. However, more seriously, disagreements had also appeared in their relations with the Taiwanese Christians. The younger Taiwanese tended to exceed the intentions of the missionaries in criticizing the status quo of church affairs.

This tension was clearly revealed in the circumstances that arose in conjunction with the Young People's Conference held during summer vacations at the Presbyterian Middle School beginning in 1929. For example, in reflecting on the third such Conference, held in 1931, the young and only recently appointed missionary, F. Healey, wrote, "Electrons and instincts and social reform; Einstein and Kagawa and Marx; Beauty, Truth and Goodness; these were some of the catchwords which they wanted to relate to the gospel.... A Formosan who is trying to secure adequate political rights for his countrymen" spoke with prophetic fire mixed with irony, humor and enthusiasm, and "even when his attacks on the sluggish church somewhat offended older pastors," his words firmly gripped the hearts of the young people.[79] L. Singleton, a missionary who taught chemistry at the school, reported as follows:

> [T]here are the very rich and the very poor. This and the Japanese-Chinese race feeling give rise to a form of Communism different a little from that *in* China or Japan proper. Christ and Marx are held to preach one gospel. Inequality of material wealth and the power rising therefrom are the real evil. The rich are to be disposed by violence, that all may be equal. How men may get rid of the lusts of their hearts, that all may walk equally as brothers in Christ, such thoughts do not arise, or are considered as opiate dope.[80]

Around 1930, not only in Europe and North America but in Japan, as well, theology such as that of Karl Barth, which was skeptical of the existing state of the church, was gaining influence and it was a time of activism on the part of a Christian student movement that yearned for social change. Among the young Taiwanese were some who had brought such ideas back from their studies in Japan proper.[81] However, Singleton's report suggests that the understanding of Christianity embraced by the young people of Taiwan was not merely an imported theory but a conviction rooted in and nourished by the realities of colonization. Moreover, as indicated in Singleton's final sentence, the missionaries were on the whole quite cool toward this tendency. For them, an orientation to social change through violence deviated from the orthodox faith, which aimed at "conformity with love."

If we think about this in conjunction with Takeuchi Yoshimi's dictum on "reconstructing civilization by resisting it," we can understand the Taiwanese youths as attempting to "reconstruct the church by resisting it." Amidst the realities of colonization there was germinating in Taiwan a brand of Christianity completely at odds with what had originally been brought "with opium in the left hand and bible in the right." The missionaries were being left behind by that movement. And for the Japanese bureaucrats, a tangible threat appeared when Lim Bo-seng and the others associated with the Presbyterian Middle School cleared the financial hurdles and in conjunction with the anti-Japanese movement became, in substance, a "Taiwanese educational institution." The unstable relationship among the Government-General, British missionaries and influential Taiwanese was now clearly sundered, and a force field of sharp tension was forming.

It was in the midst of this situation that the Government-General made shrine worship into a prerequisite for obtaining recognition as a private middle school. In this manner, the card of emperor worship that had been embossed at the outset of Japanese rule over Taiwan was now being played in support of repression.

Shrine Worship as Violence

In 1929, Band mentioned the shrine worship issue in a yearbook read by missionaries in Japan proper, Taiwan, and Korea:

> My own impression is that if we could see our way to confirm the shrine worship, recognition would soon be granted, but of course we have no intention of doing so.... Merely to satisfy a few over zealous Shintoist officials, it would be mistaken in colonial policy to impose unduly a Shintoist Cult upon the Formosan people. To demand the attendance of pupils at the shrines as a necessary condition would be more than a mistake. It would be religious tyranny, subtle and refined, but none the less cruel.[82]

While criticizing shrine worship in this manner, Band also held that, "So long as Christian principles are not infringed, the Christian schools in Taiwan should sincerely cooperate with the Government-General in cultivating loyalty among the people of Taiwan." He was only concerned about the means of expressing such loyalty, which was clearly prejudicial to "freedom of belief."

Minutes of the Mission Council meeting of January 1931 recorded that, "The Council unanimously agreed that as long as elements of religious significance were still retained in connection with the shrines it could not recommend the Board of Managers to apply for recognition."[83] Nevertheless, following the "Manchurian Incident" and the process leading to Japan's withdrawal from the League of Nations in 1933, nationalism rose as the counterpart to uneasiness rooted in Japan's international isolation, and pressure for enforcement of shrine worship rose precipitately. Held up as the scapegoat to this nationalism was none other than Christianity, which was inseparable from the "the West." In Japan proper, in 1932 the military attacked the Catholic-denominated Sophia University on the pretext that its students were failing to engage in shrine worship. The university authorities subsequently accepted shrine worship as an expression of patriotism and loyalty, as it was put by the Minister of Education, and took the grave step of conforming to both educational policy and shrine worship.

In May 1933, having considered the viewpoint of the Ministry of Education, the Board of Managers of Presbyterian Middle School asked the Mission Council to review the matter of whether or not to allow shrine visits. The non-Christian Taiwanese — whose sense of crisis was mounting as, amidst cries of "emergency," the school's chances of accreditation seemed to be slipping further away — had concluded that the school had to accept shrine worship. In September, after intense struggle, the Mission Council recommended to the Board of Managers that shrine worship be accepted. Singleton, who had argued against the measure, wrote the London headquarters separately, saying that, "for members of the native Synod to express their opinion frankly on Shrine attendance would mean running some risk at present." He argued that despite the argument that it merely signified an expression of patriotism, shrine ceremonies clearly contained religious meaning, and that when it came to forcing shrine worship on Taiwanese Christians, "we cannot remain neutral, or unwillingly acquiescent. It should be remembered that 90% of the Formosan population has not the historical background even of the masses in Japan proper."[84]

No final decision emerged from the Board that received the Mission Council's recommendation. The reason was that the Taiwanese church representatives could not agree. The chairman of the Board at this time was Lim Bo-seng, who had returned from the United States. No final decision was made to institute shrine visits, but those opposed to the measure were eventually reduced to a minority, and dissension was beginning to occur even among those associated with the school.

In January 1934, while Band was in Britain on vacation, a rather trifling matter provided the occasion on which the shrine worship issue became a social problem. The immediate issue was the Board's firing, after a series of incidents, of the Japanese teacher, Uemura Kazuhito. Singleton, who was acting principle, said regarding the reason for the firing that, "Due to promises unfilled etc., he had already lost the confidence of our Old Boys, their parents, contributors to the Endowment Fund." He then added that, "we learnt afterwards that there had been words better left unsaid between this teacher and the Chairman of the Board, Mr. Rin Mosei [Lim Bo-seng in Japanese]."[85] It is expressed ambiguously here, but one can imagine that Uemura might have hurled a term like "Chankoro" at Lim, and that he had exploded in response.

According to Band's account of the incident, when Uemura heard he had been fired he, "linked it up with the burning question of Shrine attendance, and cast aspersions on Dr. Lim's loyalty as a Japanese subject, thereby enlisting sympathy from the Japanese, among whom nationalism has now attained feverish height."[86] Toward the end of February, the remaining seven Japanese resigned en masse and simultaneously sent a petition to the Education Office of Tainan district, demanding that "the Board be reconstituted with five new Japanese members," that "a Japanese be nominated as principal," etc.[87] With this, the problem escalated beyond the question of whether or not to accept shrine worship, and now involved fundamental issues of school governance and general educational policy. The same day, the Tainan Dôshikai (Tainan Comrades Association), an organization of influential Japanese residents of Tainan, met and devoted its energies to an attack on Presbyterian Middle School; the Japanese language newspaper also began a campaign against the school.

Meanwhile, at Presbyterian Middle School, on March 3 Lim Bo-seng issued a statement saying that, "ceremonies of the state should be participated in," thereby adopting a policy of recognizing shrine worship as nonreligious behavior, adding that "in order to unify residents of Japan proper with those of Taiwan, all spiritual discrimination should be completely eliminated."[88] Discreetly hiding the fact that it was precisely "spiritual discrimination" on the part of the Japanese that touched off the incident, Lim attempted to dispose of it by agreeing to carry out shrine visits. However, in fact, the incident had only begun. On March 4, the Tainan Dôshikai held an extraordinary meeting and decided to urge the Government-General to exercise its jurisdiction and abolish the Presbyterian Middle School, which "cannot be recognized for even one day as an educational institution of the Japanese empire."[89]

In the meantime, the Japanese teachers who had resigned en masse charged in the press that "when they had spoken about the superiority of, and the need for reverence to, Japan's national essence (*kokutai*), Taiwanese students would invariably whisper to each other in a rebellious manner. And when the teachers would mention the Japanese spirit, the students would murmur about the Taiwanese spirit." The teachers also stated that when they had "aggressively enforced the use of Japanese," acting principal Singleton would make statements to the effect that, "if they imposed Japanese too coercively it would be like the imposition of English on Ireland, and be counter-productive." On the pretext of such cases, they demanded the resignation of Lim Bo-seng, abolition of the position of Professor of Taiwanese language, and other changes.[90] Then, on March 6, Tainan Provincial Governor Imagawa Fukashi issued the statement that, "those who oppose the guiding spirit of this island [Taiwan] under cover of religion will be strictly censured."[91]

When the Tainan governor formally showed support for the campaign, the racial and ethnic feelings of the Japanese mounted to a fever pitch. In Band's words, this loosed a "terrific storm of hate and the fierce floods of nationalistic feelings."[92] Band cut short his vacation in England and sped back to Taiwan. Based on the judgment that survival of the school was top priority, he accepted a set of school "reforms" that almost entirely met the demands of Governor Imagawa. This meant not only explicitly legislating shrine attendance, but appointing a Japanese principal and Board members, and abolishing the professorship of Taiwanese language. Band's line of defense was to argue that the Japanese principal and Board members should be Christians. Board chairman Lim Bo-seng and Ng Su-beng (Huang Si-ming in Mandarin), who had taken charge of the students' religious instruction as School Chaplain, were forced to resign all school positions they held.

Thus, the Government-General succeeded in violently forcing the Presbyterian Middle School, which had sought to evade control, back under close supervision and subordination. Under historical circumstances in which it was no longer necessary to cultivate the "sympathy of the civilized world," the Japanese authorities no longer attempted to ignore emperor worship because it stimulated Taiwanese opposition, but instead actively promoted it as a means of reminding the colonials of their subordinate status and threatening them in such a way as to dampen their enthusiasm for resistance.

Ng Su-beng, who felt that he had been betrayed by the British missionaries, went in the midst of his disappointment to visit his son, Huang Zhang-hui, who was studying at Tokyo Imperial University, and began a life devoted to reading the Book of Job. As a result of this experience, Ng Chiong-hui wrote of how deeply his father had respected Principal Band and how he had loved being chaplain at the Presbyterian Middle School; he continued,

> It was indeed a very heavy blow to find himself thrust out from the school and for what were basically political reasons too. Partly it was because of his involvement in the Shinto Shrine controversy, and his strong opposition

> to 'emperor worship', which was at the centre of the dispute. Partly it was because of his inability, or unwillingness, to teach the Scriptures in Japanese.... It was one of the most painful experiences of my life to hear and see the one whom I loved and respected in such suffering, mental, physical and above all spiritual.[93]

In 1935, the following year, Ng Chiong-hui returned to Taiwan for a rest, and met with Lim Bo-seng. Lim had been extremely angry at the treatment meted out to Ng Su-beng.[94] On the other hand, Edward Band wrote in a report to London that,

> Fortunately there was little anti-foreign feeling against the missionaries, the main attack was directed against the Formosan members of the Board who — it was alleged — had actually interfered with a Japanese head teacher in his laudable efforts to promote national education among the Formosan pupils.... Many Formosans are disappointed that in this affair we missionaries have not stood out as the champion of Formosan independence against the authorities. We have no desire or right to do that. As missionaries, if we can secure an official guarantee that no infringement will be made against perfect freedom for Christian education we must be prepared to carry out the colonial policy of the Japanese authorities.[95]

Here we have a clear statement of the reason Band compromised. In the same manner as the Japanese in the colonies gave absolute authority to the framework of "Japanese/non-Japanese," for Band the distinction "Christian/non-Christian" had exclusive supremacy. The Free Church of Scotland, which was the direct ancestor of the Presbyterian Church of England, was originally formed in protest against domination by the secular state, but what that gave rise to was the attitude that so long as the state did not interfere with freedom of belief, the church would loyally obey the state's commands. Such a principle could even lead the church into union with imperialism.

As Band correctly sensed, his compromises had caused many Taiwanese associates to be disappointed in him. Dai Ming-fu, one of the teachers at the time in the Presbyterian Middle School, wrote that, "I am in complete despair about the direction of the school."[96] Band himself later reflected that, "in the light of subsequent events, those who have watched the religious situation in Japan may now be regretting that the Christian and Buddhist Churches did not make a definite line somewhere, and at some time earlier make a definite uncompromising stand against this system of State Shinto Shrines."[97]

The Tainan governor, Imagawa, became governor of Taipei district in 1936, and by the same methods attacked and overcame the Tamsui Middle School, which was run by the Canadian Presbyterian Church. In 1937 he was promoted to the prestigious post of chief of the Monopoly Bureau. Considering that the one who profited most from the whole series of events was Imagawa, one might be tempted to believe that he planned it from the beginning. But even if this supposition is correct, it is instructive to remember that his plan could not have succeeded without support from the anxiety-ridden Japanese colonists.

Successive Layers of Violence

Expanding upon Jacques Derrida's *Monolinguality of the Other* (1996), Ukai Satoshi writes,

> The colonist imposes on the colonized a culture that forcibly assimilates them, but is that culture really the colonists' culture? Is it not the case that the colonist himself was originally assimilated, and that in order to forget, or at least avoid recalling, the pain of his own assimilation process, he imposes that culture, as "mine," on the other? Does not colonialist violence originate precisely in the lack of identity between the colonist himself and the culture he imposes, and through diverse linguistic behavior designed to divert attention from that gap — and by constructing through sheer force the conditions that support that behavior — do they not make the other believe in that unity, and by means of the other's belief make themselves believe as well?[98]

Those who wield colonialist violence against others have themselves had violence wielded against them. The very act of wielding violence helps the colonists to forget the pain of their own assimilation, and to believe that what they impart is "their own culture." What Derrida calls "violence" is not necessarily the sort of thing that corresponds to a specific historical event, but he points to an important dimension of colonial rule.

I have attempted to show that, in the midst of pressure for modernization, which advances like huge dominoes falling one after the other, Hugh Matheson and Li Chun-shen manifested the same sort of ambivalence as did Itô Hirobumi.

Matheson's relatives lived through the violence of the Highland Clearances, which heralded the onset of modernity. Li Chun-shen aided in the wielding of violence against the anti-Japanese guerrillas. The kind of double standard that allowed him to flatter those who were thought to be civilized and deal harshly with those he viewed as uncivilized was typical of someone like Itô Hirobumi, Japan's top government leader, but that pattern was not limited to Japanese. That is, there were such "Japanese" among the British and even the Taiwanese as well.

However, that each of the above three individuals was the object as well as the subject of violence does not mean that they were all at the same level. They were rather arranged in a strict hierarchy, and the system of colonial rule was devised precisely in order to rigidify and sustain that hierarchy. In Derrida's case as well, although he takes for granted the historically formed hierarchy of French colonial rule over Algeria, it is important to recognize that his writing incorporates a critique of the identity of "French culture." Derrida's argument is important because he makes clear that this hierarchy has only the most arbitrary basis. He shows it is not the case that such identities as "French culture" and "Japanese culture" exist from the beginning, along with the distinction between "civilized people" and "uncivilized people"; rather, these concepts are formed ex post facto and used in order to translate political domination and social disruption into problems of "culture." He also makes it clear that colonial rule calls forth, stimulates, and employs the desire for modernization, while also preventing its actualization and distorting its direction.

It is always dangerous to step lightly over the circumstances peculiar to each case of imperialism and thus overgeneralize. However, it is also true that, as this essay sought to make clear, Japanese colonial rule was certainly not unique. Rather, in the midst of the seismic shifts caused by modernity, Japan sought to navigate by imitating the Western imperialist models, and developed its colonial rule according to the principle of appealing to the "sympathy of the civilized world." If a major difference existed, it was that by depending upon the pseudo-universalism of Christianity the agents of Western imperialism found it possible to cover up their discriminatory behavior to some extent, while in Japan's case it was difficult for the colonial rulers to develop a "high morality" that suited them. This was inevitable in that the pseudo-religion of emperor worship was ethnically and racially exclusivist in its essence.

In the 1920s and 1930s, the principle of appealing to the "sympathy of the civilized world" receded into the background and deviation from civilization became increasingly characteristic of Japanese colonial policy. Yet, the civilization that Japan feared and viewed antagonistically was not the modern civilization spawned by Western imperialism but rather the new civilization being produced by colonized peoples as they grappled with the realities of their situation. Although only in the early stages of development, a process that can only be called "reconstructing civilization by resisting it" was emerging among the people of Taiwan, and Japan carried out its deviation from civilization in the process of reacting against this trend. As the vehicle of that reaction, the Japanese imposed the litmus test of shrine worship. Of course, even shrine worship constituted an imposition of "Japanese culture," so there was supposedly no problem. Yet, if we remember that the Japanese had achieved their adaptation to the civilized order precisely by internalizing the gaze of the "white" Westerner, this formulation itself demonstrated just how far they were from any kind of "cultural unity." Moreover, in order to divert their own attention from that inconsistency, it was essential that they force the colonized others to believe.

The Taiwanese people were liberated from imperial Japan in August 1945. On October 25, Chen Yi was dispatched as the governor of Taiwan province in order to incorporate Taiwan into the Chinese Nationalist government, and ceremonies marking Japanese surrender were held. On the anniversary of the reversion to China, Lim Bo-seng, wearing Chinese dress and an expression of excitement and confidence, said to his son, "Finally, the era has arrived in which we can be the masters of our own fate."[99] However, the Nationalist government also denied rights of political participation to Taiwanese on the pretext that they "know nothing of China, nothing of culture, and nothing of the resistance against Japan." Once he realized that the "era in which we can be masters of our own fate" was an illusion, Lim Bo-seng became increasingly depressed and blurted to his son that, "since the end of the war Taiwan is completely isolated and helpless. We have nowhere to turn in our dissatisfaction and anger."[100] Then, in the midst of the February 28th Incident in 1947, he was arrested for inciting the students of Taiwan University, planning rebellion, and "having delusions about Taiwan's independence;" and then he "disappeared."[101] His modest desire to establish an "educational institution for the Taiwanese people" was crushed by the Japanese, he was betrayed by the British missionaries, and killed by the Nationalist government. This was "modernity" for Lim Bo-seng, and the outcome for him of "colonial rule."

The Taiwanese movement that is seeking an apology and compensation from the state for the February 28th Incident, led by Lim Bo-seng's son among others, is putting pressure on the Nationalist Party to recognize its responsibility. Band and Singleton returned to the Presbyterian Middle School after the war and finally turned over major authority to Taiwanese, and even appointed a Taiwanese principal. As for the Japanese government and Japanese people, it must be said that far too much has been forgotten, including the "spiritual" damage done by the litmus test of shrine worship. Perhaps that is because even today in Japanese society the ideals of freedom of thought, belief, and conscience remain formalistic. And finally, the violence that is "subtle and refined, but none the less cruel" is spurred by the spread of racist attitudes and continues to wield destructive force.

ENDNOTES

1 Mitani Taiichirô, *Kindai Nihon no sensô to seiji* [War and politics of modern Japan] (Tokyo: Iwanami Shoten, 1997), 76. Mitani uses the common term "post-colonialism," but because this term does not usually include the perspective of the colonial rulers, I have used "post-imperialism" instead.

2 Maruyama Masao, *Zôhoban Gendai seiji no shisô to kôdô* [Thought and behavior in modern Japanese politics: revised and expanded edition] (Tokyo: Miraisha, 1964), 161.

3 Takeuchi Yoshimi, *Nihon to Ajia* [Japan and Asia] (Tokyo: Chikuma Shobô, 1993), 18.

4 Takeuchi, 260–263, 283–284.

5 Takeuchi, 285.

6 Frantz Fanon, *Wretched of the Earth* (New York: Grove Press, 1965), 313–314.

7 For a critique of past studies of Japanese colonialism, one which is especially critical of facile reliance upon the analytical category of "assimilation policy," see my *Shokuminchi teikoku Nihon no bunka tôgô* [Cultural unification under the Japanese colonial empire] (Tokyo: Iwanami Shoten, 1996). The present essay is more or less a synthesis, from a single perspective, of this book and two of my essays: "Bunmei no chitsujo to misshon" [Overseas missions and the civilized order] in *Nenpô: Kindai Nihon kenkyû 19: chiikishi no kanôsei* (Tokyo: Yamakawa Shoten, 1997), and "Tainan chôrôkyô chûgaku jinja sanpai mondai" [The problem of shrine visits at Tainan Presbyterian Middle School], *Shisô* 915 (September 2000). See these works for more detailed coverage of previous research and documentation.

8 For a comparative study of Japanese and European colonial rule, see Lewis Gann, "Western and Japanese Colonialism: Some Preliminary Comparisons," in *The Japanese Colonial Empire, 1895–1945*, ed. Ramon H. Myers and Mark R. Peattie (Princeton, NJ: Princeton University Press, 1984).

9 Because of this emphasis, I will be forced in this essay to leave out a number of other important topics. In connection with domestic affairs in Taiwan alone, I am unable to discuss such issues as gender and relations between the Han residents of Taiwan and

the aboriginal minorities. I also neglect the Okinawan issue, which is so intimately connected to the administration of Taiwan, and Japan's rule of Korea as well; nor am I able to discuss the role of the United States which displayed an overwhelming presence in East Asia in place of the British. As a cooperative effort in the intellectual arena of *Traces,* I should like to bring these other elements into focus as well.

10 Edward W. Said, *Culture and Imperialism* (New York: Alfred A. Knopf, Inc., 1993), 32–33.

11 Benedict Anderson, *Imagined Communities,* revised edition (London: Verso, 1991), 9.

12 Komatsu Midori, *Itô kô zenshû* 2 (Tokyo: Itô kô zenshû kankôkai, 1927); Seiji enzetsu [political speeches], 49–50. Speech delivered in the ninth session of the House of Peers, January 1896.

13 Takano Môkyo to Itô Hirobumi, Oct. 1900, in *Itô Hitobumi kankei monjo* 6, ed. Itô Hirobumi Kankei Monjo Kenkyûkai (Tokyo: Hanawa Shobô, 1978), 125.

14 Komatsu, *Itô kô zenshû* 2, Gakujutsu enzetsu [Academic speeches], 231.

15 Sakai Naoki, *Shisan sareru Nihongo — Nihonjin* [Still-born Japanese language, Japanese people] (Tokyo: Shinyôsha, 1996), 5.

16 T. C. Smout, *A Century of Scottish People: 1560–1830* (London: Fontana Press), 322.

17 G. L. Macay, *From Far Formosa* (Edinburgh and London: Oliphant Anderson & Ferrier, 1896), 14.

18 Ann Matheson, ed., *Memorial of Hugh M. Matheson* (London: Hodder and Soughton, 1899), 260.

19 Callum G. Brown, "The Costs of Pew-renting: Church Management, Church-going and Social Class in Nineteenth-century Glasgow," *Journal of Ecclesiastical History* 38.3 (July 1987): 359.

20 Donald C. Smith, *Passive Obedience and Prophetic Protest: Social Criticism in the Scottish Church, 1830–1945* (New York: Peter Lang Publishing, 1987), 112.

21 J. A. Mangan, "Images for confident control,' in *The Imperial Curriculum: Racial Images and Education in the British Colonial Experience,* ed. J. A. Mangan (London and New York: Routledge, 1993), 10.

22 W. S. Swanson, *The China Mission of the Presbyterian Church of England: Its History, Methods, Results* (London: Presbyterian Church of England, 1887), 2.

23 Ann Matheson, 305–308.

24 Shunzekô Tsuishôkai, *Itô Hitobumi-den* [Biography of Itô Hirobumi] I (Tokyo: Tôseisha, 1943), 105.

25 Shunzekô Tsuishôkai, 106.

26 "The Making of New Japan," *The Westminster Gazette,* March 4, 1895.

27 Matsuzawa Hiroaki, *Kindai Nihon no keisei to seiyô keiken* [Foreign experience and the formation of modern Japan] (Tokyo: Iwanami Shoten, 1993), 76.

28 Ann Matheson, 206.

29 Shimizu Noboru, *Teikoku kenpô seitei kaigi* [The drafting conference for the Japanese constitution] (Tokyo: Iwanami Shoten, 1940), 88.

30 Hisaki Yukio, "Meiji-ki tennôsei kyôiku kenkyû hoi" [A supplement to research on education under the Meiji emperor system] *Bukkyô daigaku kyôikugakubu ronshû* 6 (1995).

31 Leonard H. D. Gordon, "Taiwan and the Powers," in *Taiwan: Studies in Chinese Local History*, ed., Leonard H. D. Gordon (New York and London: Columbia University Press, 1970), 109.

32 Ishii Mayako, *Kindai Chûgoku to Igirisu shihon* [Modern China and English capital] (Tokyo: Tokyo Daigaku Shuppankai, 1998), 290–293. Also see Ishii Kanji, *Kindai Nihon to Igirisu shihon* [Modern Japan and English capital] (Tokyo: Tokyo Daigaku Shuppankai, 1984).

33 W. Campbell, *Sketches from Formosa* (London, Edinburgh, New York: Marshall Brothers Ltd., 1915), 298–300.

34 "Anping Dagou senryô subeki keikaku ni tsuki Kabayama sôtoku denpô" [Telegram from Governor-General Kabayama concerning plans to occupy Anping and Dagou], July 2, 1895 (Itô Hirobumi ed., *Hisho ruisan Taiwan shiryô [Classified Collections of the Private Documents: Sources Related to Taiwan*](Tokyo: Hisho Ruisan Kankô Iinkai, 1936), 25.

35 "Sôri daijin yori Anping Dagou o shikyû senryô subeki mune Kabayama sôtoku e denpô" [Telegram from the Prime Minister to Governor-General Kabayama regarding the urgent need to occupy Anping and Dagou], July 3, 1895, in Itô ed., 26.

36 "Taiwan sôtokufu jôrei happugo minsei shikô gaikyô hôkoku" [General report on the situation of civil administration after proclamation of the Taiwan Government-General's regulations], September 23, 1895, in Itô ed., 259.

37 "Horyô sôkyoku e no kôfukin" [The grant for the Bureau for Preserving Peace and Order], September 1895, in Itô ed., 303.

38 Kurosaki Michio, "Sôtoku jôkyô" [The Governor-General's visit to Tokyo], *Tokyo asahi shinbun*, March 3, 1896.

39 Li Chun-shen, "Zhu Taiwan xinbao chuangkan" [Celebrating the first issue of the *Taiwan shinpô*], *Taiwan shinpô* 1 (June 17, 1896).

40 Huang Jun-hie, Ku Wei-ying, "Xinen yu jiuyi zhi jian", in *Li Chun-shen de sixiang yu shidai*, ed. Li Ming-hui (Taipei: Zhengzhong shuju, 1995), 254.

41 Li Chun-shen, *Donyou liushisi ri suibi*, (Fuzhou: Fuzhou meihua shuju, 1896) , 41.

42 Lai Yong-xiang, *Jioahui shihua*, (Tainan: Renguang chuban, 1995) , 117–118.

43 Harry J. Lamley, "The Younkai of 1900: An Episode in the Transformation of the Taiwan Elite during the Early Japanese Period," in *Rijushiji Taiwan shi guoji xueshu yantaohui lunwenji* (Taipei: University of Taiwan,1993), 116, 126.

44 Li Chun-shen, "Lun riba youguan shiju", in *Juzhu jinxin* (Fuzhou: Fuzhou meihua shuju, 1894) vol.1, 27.

45 Li Chun-shen, *Donyou liushisi ri suibi*, 4.

46 Li Chun-shen, *Donyou liushisi ri suibi*, 51.

47 *Tokyo asahi shinbun*, May 9, 1896.

48 For biographical information on Jahana, see Arakawa Akira, *Han kokka no kyôku* (Tokyo: Shakai hyôronsha, 1996). According to Arakawa, rather than the fact that Jahana quit the government and developed the movement for political rights, it is his derangement in the course of that movement and his death in a fit of anger that should be problematized. See Arakawa, 209.

49 Tsurumi Yûsuke, *Gotô Shinpei*, Second edition (Tokyo: Keisô Shobô, 1965), 35.

[50] Simpei Goto, "The Administration of Formosa (Taiwan)," in *Fifty Years of New Japan* 2, ed. Shigenobu Okuma (London: Smith, Elder & Col, 1909), 530.

[51] Yosaburo Takekoshi, *Japanese Rule in Formosa* (London: Longman, 1907), vii.

[52] Takekoshi, 77–78.

[53] Li Chun-shen, "Gotô Shinpei kô shôden hatsu" [Biographical sketch of Gotô Shinpei], *Taiwan jihô* 8 (February 1910).

[54] "Takow," *The Monthly Messenger* 709 (April 1905).

[55] Chen Pei-feng, *'Dôka' no dôsôimu* (Tokyo: Sangensha, forthcoming 2000).

[56] "Taihoku shinshi jinbutsu gettan" [Monthly comments on gentry in Taipei] (Kokkai toshokan kensei shiryôshitsuzô Gotô Shinpei monjo, R33–88).

[57] Gotô, *Taiwanshi*, 818.

[58] Gotô, *Taiwanshi*, 808.

[59] Thomas Barclay, *The Church in Formosa in 1895, the War: Mission Work: The Outlook* (London: Publication Committee, 1896), 3–5 (The Presbyterian Church of England Archives, Microfishe No.153, School of Oriental and African Studies, University of London; hereafter cited as PCEA Microfiche No. 153).

[60] On the function in Japan of emperor worship and "modern myths," see Carol Gluck, *Japan's Modern Myths* (Princeton, NJ: Princeton University Press, 1985), Chapter five.

[61] We Wenxing, *Rijishuji Taiwan shehui lingdao jiecheng zhi yanju* (Taipei, Zengzhong shuju, 1992), 141.

[62] Gotô Shinpei, *Nihon bôchô seisaku ippan* [A sketch of Japan's expansion policy] (Tokyo: Takushoku shinpôsha, 1921), 10.

[63] Robert Miles, *Racism after "Race Relations"* (London: Routledge, 1993), 63.

[64] Michael Weiner, *Race and Migration in Imperial Japan* (London and New York: Routledge, 1994), 11.

[65] Maeda Takerô, "Kôgakkô no shûshinka o ikan ni subeki ka" [What is the proper content of the ethics curriculum in public schools?], *Taiwan kyôikukai zasshi* 8 (November 1902).

[66] Kumamoto Shigekichi, "Taiwan ni okeru kyôiku ni taisuru hibun no ichi ni nami ni gimon" [A few questions regarding education in Taiwan] (Tokyo daigaku kyôyô gakubu shozô Kumamoto Shigekichi monjo, 0102).

[67] Letter of Barclay to Maclagan, March 21, 1912, PCEA, Microfiche No. 2033.

[68] "Kôritsu Taichung chûgakkô setchi mondai," Kumamoto Shigekichi monjo, 0301.

[69] "Kôritsu Taichung chûgakkô setchi mondai."

[70] On reforms of the colonial regime in the early 1920s, see Haruyama Meitetsu, "Kindai Nihon no shokuminchi tôchi to Hara Takashi" [Modern Japanese colonial rule and Hara Takashi], in *Nihon shokuminchishugi no seijiteki tenkai*, ed. Wakabayashi Masahiro and Haruyama Meitetsu (Tokyo: Ajia Keizai Gakkai, 1980). The expression "new concept in colonial rule" is Haruyama's.

[71] E. Band, "Report of the Presbyterian Middle School Tainan, Formosa," 1924, PCEA Microfiche No. 153–154.

[72] Li Xiao-feng, *Lim Bo-seng Chen Jin he tamen de shidai*, (Taipei: Yushan chubansha, 1996) , 18–28.

[73] "Tainan Changlaojiao zhongxue de jibenjin ji muji shiwan yuan," *Taiwan minbao,* No.113 (July 1926).

[74] "Shiritsu Tainan chôrôkyô chûgaku zaidan hôjin kifu kôi," *Shiritsu Tainan chôrôkyô chûgakkô yûkai zasshi* 4 (1927).

[75] Mosei Lin, *Public Education in Formosa under the Japanese Administration; A Historical Study of the Development and the Cultural Problems* (New York, 1929), 168.

[76] E. Band, "The Educational Situation in Formosa," *The Japan Mission Yearbook,* ed. Paul S. Mayer (Tokyo: The Meiji Press, 1929).

[77] "Houyuanhui dahui jilu," *Shiritsu Tainan chôrôkyô chûgakkô yûkai zasshi* 4 (1927).

[78] "Tainan Changlaojiao zhongxue jiang wei minzhong zhi jiaoyu jiguan," *Taiwan Minbao,* No. 236 (November 1928).

[79] F. Healey, "The New Generation in Formosa," *Presbyterian Messenger* 1041 (December 1931).

[80] L. Singleton, "Evangelizing in Formosa," *Presbyterian Messenger* 1042 (January 1932).

[81] Hugh Macmillan, *Then Till Now in Formosa* (London: English and Canadian Presbyterian Church in Formosa, 1953), 90.

[82] E. Band, "The Educational Situation in Formosa," *The Japan Mission Yearbook,* ed. Paul S. Mayer (Tokyo: The Meiji Press, 1929), 274. Previous studies of the shrine worship problem at Tainan Presbyterian Middle School include Cha shijie, "Huangminhua yundong xia de Taiwan Changlaojiaohui" in *Zhongguo Haiyang fazhanshi lunwenji* (Taipei: Zhongyang yanjiuyuan sanminzhuyu yanjiusuo, 1988) , Zhang Hou-ji, *Tainan Changrong Zhongxue bainian si* (Tainan: Tainan sili Changrong zhongxue gaoji zhongxue, 1991); Hamish Ion, *The Cross and the Rising Sun 2: The British Missionary Movement in Japan, Korea and Taiwan, 1865–1945* (Ontario: Wilfrid Laurier University Press, 1993). Those by Ion and Zhang Hou-ji are especially rich in a documentary sense and were valuable references for the present study. Nevertheless, a comprehensive study that employs English, Chinese, and Japanese sources so as to present a multilayered account of the facts of the issue remains to be written.

[83] "Minutes of the Mission Council," January 27, 1931 (PCEA Microfiche No. 11).

[84] L. Singleton, "Objections to Shrine Attendance," October 1934 (PCEA, Microfiche No. 19).

[85] "Letter from Singleton to Maclagan," March 10, 1934 (PCEA Microfiche No. 21).

[86] Edward Band, "Tainan Presbyterian Middle School 1934" (PCEA Microfiche No. 20).

[87] *Taiwan nichi nichi shinpô,* February 28, 1934.

[88] *Taiwan shinpô,* March 2, 1934.

[89] *Taiwan shinpô,* March 6, 1934.

[90] *Taiwan nichi nichi shinpô,* March 5 and 6, 1934.

[91] *Taiwan shinpô,* March 6, 1934.

[92] Edward Band, "Tainan Presbyterian Middle School 1934" (PCEA Microfiche No. 20).

[93] Shoki Coe, *Recollections and Reflections* (New York, 1994), 66, 69.

[94] Coe, 71.

[95] Edward Band, "Tainan Presbyterian Middle School, 1934" (PCEA Microfiche No. 20).

[96] Dai Ming-fu, "Guanhu qianhou de huiyi," in *Tainan sili changrong zhongxue,* ed. Xiaozhang huijilu (Tainan: changrong zhongxue, 1956) , 49.

[97] Edward Band, *Working His Purpose Out: The History of the English Presbyterian Mission, 1847–1947* (London: Presbyterian Church of England, 1947), 183.
[98] Ukai Satoshi, "Koroniarizumu to modânitei," *Tenkanki no bungaku* (Tokyo: Mineruva shobô, 1999).
[99] Lin Zong-yi, "Wo de fuqin Lim Bo-seng," in Hu Hui-ling ed. *Daoyu Ailian* (Taipei:Yushan chubanshe,1995), 8.
[100] Lin Zong-yi, "Wo de fuqin Lim Bo-seng," 17.
[101] Li Xiao-feng, *Lim Bo-seng Chen Jin he tamen de shidai*, 282–288.

Sexual Politics of State Violence: On the Cheju April Third Massacre of 1948

Kim Seong-nae*
— *translated from Korean by Jiwon Shin*

Introduction: Violent Order in the New-Old World

Crossing over "the age of extremes," as Eric J. Hobsbawm referred to the twentieth century, the new millennium has dawned on the world today; yet, the world still remains at the boundary between the ghost of the Cold War era and the utopia of the post-Cold War era. The post-Cold War morass has resulted from an ongoing justification of violence at an institutional level, under the pretext of recovering national and racial, as well as religious, utopias. While the vision of achieving multiracial, multicultural, and transnational world peace is gaining prevalence, why do the human dreams for utopia produce intractable violence and catastrophic myths like genocide? Why, in other words, do the desire for peace — and the ceaseless movements to materialize that desire — create a world of destruction and death, such as conflicts and wars, and why, in the end, do they result in the production of war and death as a way of life? An answer to these queries can be

* This paper is the newly revised version of a paper originally presented at the Cheju April Third Uprising's Fiftieth Anniversary East Asia Peace and Human Rights Conference, Cheju-do, Korea, 21–24 August, 1998. Various versions of the original paper were published elsewhere.

found in the fantasy of identity politics rooted in *otherness*, which, by constantly producing and expunging the other, seeks the existence and survival of the self.

Zillah Eisenstein has regarded the present new world order as the "new old" world, in which nation, race, and sex as the representative categories of *otherness* reemerge as the central axes of this identity politics.[1] The "new old" world order is a legacy of the modern nation state, and it might also be referred to as the order of fascist violence represented through genocide and collective sexual violence.[2] Nationalism and the growth and expansion of the nation state through a monopoly on public authority and law have been the fundamental characteristics of modernization. Engineering the category of membership to the state through inclusion or exclusion is part and parcel of this process of modernization. Political violence by the state in this process presents itself as the "constitutive element" in the formation and the existence of the modern nation state. Thus, in every case political violence toward the bodies of those regarded as alien is not an incident deviating from modernity, but is rather its main event.[3] Fascism, as a political technology characteristic of the modern nation state, refers to the politics in which violence is exercised with the human body as its medium; namely, "bio-politics" in Foucault's term. In "bio-politics" state sovereignty is constituted by extensively regulating the bodies of its population through the tactical process of inclusion or exclusion.[4]

Giorgio Agamben, who analyzes the juridico-political structure of the concentration camp during the Nazi period, explains that the camp, which had initially been the space born out of the state of exception for political prisoners, was transformed into a stable space, a means of establishing an order of racial purification toward constructing the national identity of Nazi Germany. A decisive and irrevocable "threshold of biological modernity" in the construction of national identity is the point at which "bare life," a simple living body of people, becomes subjected to the political strategies of the nation state. Agamben argues, therefore, that the camp must be recognized, not as an historical fact or an anomaly belonging to the past, but as the virtual political space created every time "bare life and the juridical rule enter into a threshold of indistinction."[5] To put it another way, state sovereignty consists of the state of exception in which "bare life" can be easily displaced as decisions concerning the living bodies of people are gradually expanded beyond their limits, toward decisions on death. Agamben, by extending the Foucauldian concept of "bio-politics" to the new old world order of the post-Cold War era, in which growing numbers of internment camps are sprouting up from regional conflicts all over the world, regards *the camp* as the paradigm of contemporary bio-politics.

Massive killing of the population by the state has been ubiquitous in the formative process of the new third-world nation states which emerged under the Cold War world order. The case of Korea is not an exception in this regard. Korea, which is today alone in maintaining the Cold War system in the post-Cold War world, is a typical case of Agemben's so-called political space of "the camp" where modern bio-politics is in practice. The history of contemporary Korea was set in place following the end of the Second World War, upon the division and the occupational rule by military regimes of the United States and Soviet Union on either side of the thirty-eighth parallel, and with the outbreak of the Korean War in 1950. In the present situation in which one nation is divided into two state systems (the communist and the anticommunist states of North and South Korea, respectively), unification of the nation state has become a shared modernization project in both the North and the South. To put it more boldly, the history of contemporary Korea has been a constant "state of emergency" in order to accomplish the modern task of national unification. This continuous state of emergency has provided the opportunity for both North and South Korea to legitimize the use of political violence toward their populations for the sake of safeguarding the unstable state system. In North and South Korea, where the project of national unification had to be propelled under the condition in which the "nation" and the "state" are split, the category of the "nation" or *minjok*, which has been sanctified as the absolute symbol transcending the category of nationality or *kugmin*, has allowed the states to exercise their extensive authority, respectively, without hindrance, to all citizens under the pretext of "national" unification.[6]

State violence, in the case of South Korea, was violence based upon an anticommunist ideology, manifested and carried out through a tactic of "red hunting" of communists, often referred to as "reds" or *ppalgaengi*. The "red hunt" had already begun, even before the birth of the anticommunist state in South Korea on August 15, 1948, during the three-year interim period under the regime of the American military government beginning in 1945. Subsequently, during the past fifty years since the Korean War in 1950, it has developed into political tactics legitimating the oppressive anticommunist rule under the banner of "modernization."

The April Third Incident on Cheju Island broke out on April 3, 1948. The Incident grew out of the Cheju people's collective protest against separate elections south of the thirty-eighth parallel scheduled for May 10 of that year. Separate elections, proposed first by the United States, meant a permanent national division along the thirty-eighth parallel, and the news of the United Nations commission's decision (the official title of this commission was "United Nations Temporary Commission on Korea") to supervise the election was thus received with dismay by a great majority of Koreans. The April Third Incident initially flared up when a few hundred communist guerrillas attacked police stations and the rightwing youth organizations on the island. In the beginning, government retaliation targeted the guerillas who had organized the attack. However, within a brief period of less than six months after the establishment of the new government in the south in August of the same year, over 30,000 of the island's inhabitants were massacred in "screening operations" and house-to-house searches in a campaign, supported by American military aid, to weed out dissidents and their sympathizers. These were the victims of the so-called "red hunt."

Described by the American historian and political scientist Bruce Cumings as "a magnifying glass, a microscope on the politics of postwar Korea," the April Third Incident was the very first "red hunt" executed in Korea.[7] Like the Holocaust, it resulted in the massacre of innocent people. As in the paradigmatic political space of the newly emerged modern nation state, referred to as the "camp" in Agamben's analysis, the Cheju Incident put to the test the governing ideology of the newly emerged anticommunist state. The April Third Incident occurred at the juncture in which the state of emergency during the American military occupation, when the rule of law had been temporarily suspended, was transforming into the permanent political space of the anticommunist state. The incident, moreover, accelerated the transformation that had already been underway. To put it differently, the state violence embodied in the massacre of the innocent people on Cheju Island in 1948 was an advanced political tactic instrumental in accelerating the passive modernization of a Korea entangled in the powerful international political conditions of the Cold War system.

In this article I shall explore the issues pertaining to the technology of "bio-politics" through which state violence is applied, in connection with the Cheju

April Third Incident. In particular I shall attend to the framework of the sexual politics of state violence, and thereby examine the issues of the technology of "bio-politics" along the axis of gender. What concrete effects did the formation of the anticommunist nation state have on the lives of individuals under the Cold War world order, and how did it determine the forms of their lives? The "people" upon whom state power inflicts injuries by applying violence is not a unitary subject, but is fractured within. In other words, the "people," the concept ambiguously referring to the individuals within the nation state, does not represent the homogeneity of the group, but always oscillates between two mutually contradictory poles: the absolute and total inclusion of all people and those who must be excluded in order to produce the total inclusion of the "people" in the nation state. Ironically, state power applies violence when a group of people has to be eliminated for the sake of the well-being of the "people."[8] This is why state violence is carried out discriminatingly according to the collective characteristics of the people. As shall become clear in this article about Cheju Island in 1948, categories such as gender, geographical region, and adaptability to the state ideology prescribe the criteria for people's inclusion in or exclusion from state power. In this context, it might be said that the atrocities suffered by Cheju Islanders began as they were utterly alienated from the sphere of membership among "people" in good standing of the anticommunist state. From the time of the April Third Incident of 1948 until recently, the island had to bear the mark of the "red island." This paper pays special regard to the injuries suffered by women of Cheju as distinguished from those suffered by the island's men. First, by looking closely at some of the less-told facts about the Cheju April Third Incident, I shall examine how, in the process of constructing the Cold War order, state violence took the forms of genocide and sexual violence toward the "reds." What is the nature of state violence inflicted upon women, and how does this type of violence silence women and utterly destroy them? What adverse effect does it have on the women's recovery from their injuries, when men in a male-centered society politicize sexual violence? This set of inquiries will, then, lead this writer to link the issues of political discourse on gender with concrete cases of pain and resistance of women's bodies.[9] And to conclude, I shall expand the issues of state violence toward a discussion of human rights in relation to women.

The Cheju April Third Incident: The "Red" Genocide and Sexual Violence[10]

In 1998, on the fiftieth anniversary of the founding of the Republic of Korea which had established a separate government south of the thirty-eighth parallel, the newly inaugurated president Kim Dae Jung called for the "rebirth of the state." Even on the occasion of the rebirth of the state, however, the truth of the Cheju April Third Incident still remained unresolved. This is because the Cheju April Third Incident remains branded as the "incident of original sin" that impeded the birth of the anticommunist state in 1948. Two opposing positions have, until now, prevailed in the historical characterization of the Cheju April Third Incident. The official position views this incident as a product of the ideological conflict between the left and the right during the period of American military occupation, and thus, as a rebellion or insurrection by the communists. The "unofficial" position regards it as a national independence movement opposing the unilateral election in South Korea scheduled for May 10, 1948, which would (and, as it turned out, did) solidify the North–South division. According to this latter view, the April Third Incident was an act of resistance of the people of Cheju against the tyranny of anticommunism under the American military government.[11] But, as summarized, both the official position, which treats the April Third Incident as a Communist rebellion, and the unofficial position, which regards it as a people's resistance movement, explain the injury of the Incident in such a way that the cause and effect relationship of the violent acts is transparent. Although the two positions are in opposition to each other in their points of view regarding the Incident, in understanding the state of violence in the April Third Incident, they both are predicated upon a discursive structure that legitimizes violence itself, be it state violence or the antagonistic violence of the people.

The great majority of the victims of the Cheju April Third Incident were *innocent* civilians. I emphasize their "innocence," for neither did their ideology and behaviors offer cause for violence nor did they respond to violence with counter-violence. Yet they still fell victim to the massacre by such violence. The victimization of the guiltless civilians in the course of the development of the April Third Incident resulted from a scorched-earth campaign that labeled the entire population of the island enemies of the state, or "reds," and Cheju Island a "red island." This operation is considered to have been in compliance with the martial law declared by Syngman Rhee, the first president of the Republic of Korea. But since this preceded the enactment of the law regarding martial law, the operation was actually an illegal use of violence, and the massive deaths of the islanders resulting from the scorched-earth campaign were, in fact, an *innocent* victimization.[12] In this sense, the incident was, simply stated, the Cheju April Third *Massacre*.[13] In the discursive politics of recent years surrounding the public demand for the truth about April Third, however, those innocent victims remain invisible. They cannot be located within the structure of the hierarchical relations of power, such as the conflict between the state and the "people" or the ideological struggle between the left and the right. They are displaced as the *other* in the discourses of struggle for power, and thus, are still kept invisible. The parties involved in the discursive politics of April Third — be they the leftists or those who claim to represent the voices of the "people" — failed to bring the victims to the fore and to rescue them from their status of invisibility. Instead, the very invisibility of the "innocent" victims has often been used merely as a sign marking the boundary in the binary structure of the struggle for power in the discursive politics of the Cheju Incident. How to make their guiltless deaths visible? To answer this requires a structural explanation beyond merely relating the facts about the massacre of the innocent. Still, the facts leading to the massacre demand clarification. In this section, I shall first clarify some facts about the Cheju April Third Massacre, then examine the political technology of state violence that legitimized that massacre as it unfolded through the tactics of genocide and sexual violence toward the "reds."

Located about 100 kilometers south of the Korean peninsula, the 1,800 square-kilometer island of Cheju is dominated by a volcanic cone, Mt. Halla. Mt. Halla forms the core of the island and the villages are scattered on the middle to lower slopes of the mountain and in the coastal areas. The slopes of Mt. Halla were crucial for both the guerillas, who initially attacked the police stations and later fled to the hills, and the punitive forces sent by the government. The government's counterattack was at first unsuccessful in detecting the insurgents' base areas on the upper slopes. Frustration with the initial failure led those in command of the punitive forces to surmise that the guerillas had to be hiding out in the villages. During the four-month period of the scorched-earth campaign by the paramilitary and constabulary forces, from the proclamation of martial law in mid-November of 1948 until March of the following year, the Cheju Massacre was concentrated in the middle slopes of Mt. Halla. As the separate government was established in South Korea the disorder in Cheju Island became conceived of not as a simple regional instance of communist rebellion, but rather as a challenge to the legitimacy of the state, and thus its suppression was total. The entire interior of the island, up to five kilometers inland from the shoreline, was declared an enemy zone. And while the scorched-earth campaign of the punitive units of paramilitary and constabulary forces was underway, over 130 of the 300 villages in the middle ranges of the mountain were burned to the ground. The inhabitants of these villages were forced to disperse to the coastal villages. In the worst cases, they were subject to suspicion of being "red" or "family of the insurgents" and were slaughtered indiscriminately, regardless of gender or age.[14] Those inhabitants of the villages in the middle slopes of the mountain, who had naively believed that they would return home shortly and had left their belongings at home to temporarily take refuge in other villages, began to flee from the encroaching scorched-earth campaign to the hills and caves. Those who fled into the hills were labeled *ipsanja* or "hill-fugitives," and were subject to suspicion of being "reds" or "insurgents" along with the guerillas who carried out the attacks on police stations. If their hideouts were found, they were massacred in tens or hundreds at a time, and any family members left behind (mainly children, women, and the elderly) were tortured or slaughtered for being the family of the "hill-fugitives." For the aggressors, the martial law that legitimized the killing of the innocent meant the "law of killing people."[15]

The atrocities committed by the punitive forces upon the Cheju Islanders appeared also in the form of collective sexual violence. Beyond the rape of young women and forced marriages, from inhumanity and perversity in shooting pregnant women or those in childbirth, to the brutality of gathering villagers stripped naked and randomly forcing men and women, heedless of family relations, to perform sexual acts, and then shooting them to death — all these can be seen as collective sexual violence against the Cheju Islanders as a whole.[16]

The massacre of and collective sexual violence against the islanders were products of hatred toward the "reds." At the forefront of the "red hunt," the operations to exterminate communist guerillas, were paramilitary forces like the Northwest Youth League, comprised of anticommunist refugees from the northern part of Korea. The motto of these perpetrators of atrocity was "Rooting out the reds and drying out their seeds." As can be seen from the brutal description, "rooting out and drying out" the "reds," the objects of these acts were construed as less than human, and were treated as a weed-like, inferior species, subject to elimination. That the term "red," which had initially meant the probable ideological tendency of the guerillas who took to arms to protest against the unilateral election proposed and supported by the American military government, gradually came to designate a certain species of people inhabiting a particular region, is indicative of the peculiarity of the "red hunt." It was not only the individual communists who were targeted in the extermination campaign, but anyone who fell under the category of "red," be they the entire extended family of someone who fled to the hills or the inhabitants of villages unfortunately located in the middle slopes of Mt. Halla. In this sense, it might be said that the "red hunt" during the April Third Massacre was genocide along the lines of the Final Solution of Nazi Germany that systematically sought to eliminate certain groups of people deemed "undesirable" to the German race. The inhabitants of the island stigmatized as the "red island" were deemed to be an inferior race that would contaminate and pollute the identity of the new anticommunist state. Even after April Third, once it had been given, the mark "red" or "insurgent" persisted as a burden on the surviving family members or relatives who where thereafter known as the "red family" or the "rebel family," and were persecuted under the Law of Complicity. These practices and policies are none other than organized acts of terrorism originating from the hatred of a certain species. What lurks behind these acts of terrorism, to put it another way, is the kind of collective hatred that is structurally parallel to *racial* hatred. This kind of hatred prompted degradation of surviving members of families of the victims of April Third into mere objects. In the eyes of the perpetrators they were seen as nothing but "bodies of the reds" that reproduced and would continue to reproduce the "red" race. According to the same logic of hatred, the entire population of the island came to symbolize the "body of the reds." Moreover, the hatred for the red went hand in hand with fear of the reproductive potential in the bodies of the victims' families. This suggests that the "bodies of the reds" also represented "gendered bodies" fraught with the danger of reproducing more reds, and consequently, Janus-faced terrorism of hatred and fear made the victims of the "red hunt" the victims of double-pronged violence: anticommunist terrorism and sexual violence. As I shall discuss in detail, the women victims of April Third, as more clearly visible entities upon which such forms of violence are exercised and exhibited, suffered triply, because they experienced the violence of patriarchy in addition to the violence of everyday life.

The injuries experienced by the victims of the Cheju April Third Massacre, the island's inhabitants as a whole, and the women in particular, were concrete instances of the technology of sexual politics of state violence with which the state racializes and sexualizes its population on the basis of being "red." That which I refer to as the technology of sexual politics here is the technology that transforms the bodies of the population into a signifier for a "gendered body." As a gendered signifier, a body indicates the location in which state power is brutally exercised, and it also provides the agents of state violence with free political resources. As I shall show, the instances of torture in the process of carrying out the "red hunt" and the cases of injuries suffered by women clearly demonstrate how the racialized hatred toward the reds and sexual violence are interrelated. In what follows I shall show how the racialized *otherness* and the sexual *otherness* of Cheju Islanders, as they came to bear the label "red," became interwoven within the structure of state violence. Furthermore, by examining the cases of torture and sexual violations during April Third, I shall argue that the fascist violence of the state, including genocide, perpetrated under the wartime structure, corresponds to the violence of patriarchy imposed upon women in everyday life within family relationships.

The Body of the Reds: The Matrix of the Anticommunist State

The hatred against the reds was legitimated as the cornerstone establishing the identity of the anticommunist state and the social order of ethical anticommunism. At the same time, it was precisely the hatred for the reds that rationalized the massacre by the public authority of the state in such a case as the Cheju April Third Incident. For the past fifty years, this type of hatred has, moreover, been materialized in the form of continuing tortures, terrorizing, and murders of leftists and other dissidents. The practice of labeling someone "red" went so far as to be applied *en masse* to those segments of the population considered either politically radical or dissident, and as a result, it might be said that the anticommunist state of South Korea established its identity with the tactic of *racial* annihilation of the "reds." It is an undeniable fact that, as the basis for social regulation of South Korean society, anticommunism and the ideology of national security could not be criticized or questioned. This explains why the truth about the Cheju April Third Massacre was silenced until 1987, when the testimonies of the victims first emerged as a public discourse. It might also be said that the formation and existence of the modern state in South Korea were made possible by continual acts of political violence towards the people by the state; and that to legitimize those acts, more victimization of the people ensued.

Michel Foucault explains that it is in the characteristic antinomy where the "bio-politics" of a modern state inevitably accompanies "thanatopolitics" that the process of legitimization of state violence can be understood. He states:

> [The state] wields its power over living beings as living beings, and its politics, therefore, has to be a bio-politics. Since the population is nothing more than what the state takes care of for its own sake, of course, the state is entitled to slaughter it, if necessary. So the reverse of bio-politics is thanatopolitics.[17]

Here, "thanatopolitics" is one aspect of "bio-politics," the regime by which the state controls and organizes the lives of the population, and by which state violence and the killing and injuring of the population are rationalized.[18] The state power responsible for the lives of its population conducts, with the continuous mechanisms of control and correction, a standardization that determines, evaluates, and ranks the qualifications for nationality and citizenship. The basis for this normative regulation in the Republic of Korea is anticommunism. Hatred and slaughter of the "reds," the means by which such standardization of the population was conducted, is the technology of power of the anticommunist state in practice; at the same time, by subjecting the population to "bio-politics," the hatred and slaughter are rationalized. The slaughtering of the innocent in the Cheju April Third Incident was, thus, a systematic act of murder in accordance with the normative ideal of anticommunism. Even for this reason alone, the state as an independent social body can (and must) be held responsible. The contradiction between the state as a living entity and its slaughtering its own population for the sake of its existence can be referred to as the "carceral side of modernity."[19]

The state that holds the power over the life and death of its citizens utilizes the "body of the population" as the "fundamental political resource" for this bio-politics. In a modern state, the "body of the population," as it is subsumed under the "body of the state" where life and death coexist, comes to be subjected to political technology. The goal of its politics, in this case, is nothing more than to strengthen the state itself. To put it differently, the state comes to be conceived as a material entity, a living being, existing in and of itself, and in its very being becomes the order of things. As can be seen in the Nazi's Final Solution or in the ethnic cleansing of the Serbian nationalists, even within the state system, those groups of citizens who represent a challenge to the power of the state become the combatant target for bio-politics. In the course of organizing and establishing the order of the anticommunist state, Cheju Island was chosen to be the place for the extermination of the reds; and as a result of a successful suppression of the Cheju April Third Incident, the "bodies of the inhabitants" of Cheju, brutalized by torture and slaughter, turned out paradoxically to be the matrix in which to establish the structure of order of the anticommunist state.[20]

Why must "reds" be exterminated? The destructive power that the state authority exerts maintains its legitimacy by transforming itself into a productive power. If the Nazis' Final Solution was a biological control aiming at purifying the blood of the German race and at the same time was a political technology deployed for the sake of the lives and welfare of the German people, then, along similar lines, the extermination of the reds during the April Third Incident was a political technology, an instrumentality of discipline and control, used for the sake of the founding of the anticommunist state and the guarding of liberalism. During the Incident, the members of an extreme right-wing anticommunist paramilitary group, the Northwest Youth League, were brought in to Cheju Island to execute the "red hunt." These youths reportedly explained that they came to the island because "Cheju Island was tainted in red." As can be detected in their words, Cheju Island was conceived of as a red camp and a kind of living body tainted in red.[21] The "bodies of the Cheju Islanders" were thus none other than the "bodies of the reds." Soon after the outbreak of the April Third Incident, Cho Pyŏng-ok, who was the chief of the police force under the U.S. military government, presupposing that "it was the reds who instigated the incident," dispatched the members of the Northwest Youth League, several hundred in number, ordering them to take the vanguard position in the "extermination of the reds." He once boasted that "We must, for the sake of the Republic of Korea, spray gasoline over Cheju Island, light it, and burn 300,000 islanders all at once." Colonel Pak Chin-gyŏng of the ninth regiment, who commanded part of the scorched-earth campaign, reportedly said, "This country can do without the Cheju people," as he commanded a merciless "cleansing" of the "red." It was a project of creating the anticommunist order by seeking to transform Cheju Island, conceived of as the "red island," into an outpost in the battle with communism. The Cheju Massacre revealed the functioning of thanatopolitics in which the deaths of those "bodies of the reds" had already been programmed from the beginning in the project of anticommunism. At the same time, it was a technology of politics of life that allowed the "body of the state" to go on living. That is to say that it was by means of massacre that a new order for the state centering on anticommunism was created.

Anticommunist violence by the state, as a programmed political technology, transforms the population into a "docile body" submissive to the governing ideology of the state. This technology, while naturalizing its population into a docile body on the one hand, assigns a new meaning to the "body of the red." This new meaning assigned to the body makes it possible to sexualize the bodies of the "red" suspects. The "body of the red" is the place where the fear of communism and desire for conquering it can be "felt and seen" and becomes, therefore, a part of the spectacle of performance in the violent politics of anticommunism. Moreover, the physicality of this body (its visibility and materiality) offered, for the performers of violence who desire to defeat and to humiliate the reds, powerful resources in the political struggle toward the sanitized order of the state. When a piece of firewood or a whip in the hands of the members of the punitive force or the Northwest Youth League is thrashing the red suspect, the body of the suspect is no longer that of an individual, but the "species body" labeled "red." In the acts of the members of the Northwest Youth League, described as "wielding a bamboo spear and, like a matador, bravely shattering to pieces the leftist hideout," one can glimpse the very aspect of violence resembling sexual pleasure.[22] The physical pain of torture and violence makes the victims succumb to self-abandonment and despair, and subsequently makes them plunge into submission toward the coercion of the state that is the agent of violence. That a survivor of the April Third Incident still recalls, "I have been living with a weight of April Third on my back. Sometimes remembering it becomes so painful that I even wish I had died then," is indicative of a resigned attitude of self-abandonment and utter despair, an attempt to forget about the very experience of violence. For the aggressor, the pain in the victim's body when starved, cut open, raped, and killed, and his or her submission stemming from complete resignation provides, reciprocally, the resources for pleasure that can defeat the fear of the red and can satisfy the desire for life.

The novelist Hyŏn Ki-yŏng describes this intimate and reciprocal relation between the victim and the aggressor occurring in the contradictory amalgamation of death and pleasure as a kind of "consensual sexual relation." With the publication of his short fiction, "Aunt Suni" in 1978, in which the truth of April Third was first exposed to the public, Hyŏn Ki-yŏng was taken into an intelligence agency facility and tortured. Hyŏn, in his statement, testifies that the pain of bearing the label of "red writer" was greater than the physical pain of being beaten. In recalling his experience of being tortured, he stated, "my body was tainted in ink-color."[23] Due to the wounds of torture (both physical and psychological) he then remained silent for nine years, and began to speak out about his experience again only in 1987. When he gained an objective distance from the immediate experience of his torture, Hyŏn described the humiliation he had felt at the time as "crawling like a dog." When his torturer, after three days of beating him, consoled him, though with an unexpressive and indifferent attitude, saying, "Shall we go out for a drink when you're on the outside?" Hyŏn states that he could not avoid the feelings of absolute defeatism and impotence. He explained that his torturer's invitation had the effect of annihilating his own pain as if it had "never been there." In his short story he depicts the humiliating relationship between the torturer and the tortured as like that between the "consensual sexual partners." In order to erase the fact of the torture, to make it as if it had "never happened," the torturers would wait until all traces of torture had disappeared before letting their victim out. The victim, without the trace of torture, would then begin to doubt the truth of his own experience. Moreover, since the humiliation of having been tortured evokes disgrace regarding his person, the tortured victim resorts to silence. The complexity of this violence in torture, compelling the victim to forget the fact of the torture, emerges in the form of sexual violence that breaks and tames the body of the tortured to turn it into the "docile body." The torture that sanitized Hyŏn's body, the "body of the red," through its transformation into the "ink-colored body" within the order of anticommunism must be understood as a manifestation of a technology of sexual politics and political violence, which forces the population to succumb to state power.

Women's Body: Sexual Fantasy and the Violent Spectacle of Anticommunism

What the so-called "red writer" Hyŏn Ki-yŏng describes as the pain of sexual violence inflicted upon his body and the submission stemming from the sudden feeling of annihilation of pain resembles the experiences of women victims who were raped and who suffered from other forms of sexual assault during April Third. Condemned for being "red bitches" or "red family," the innocent women of Cheju were often tortured and slaughtered in place of their husbands, fathers, and brothers who had fled to the hills and mountains. Nevertheless, what seems to be more salient is a particular cruelty in the materialization of their suffering that is different from what men experienced. Beyond the added suffering of the sexual violence that women were forced to endure, they were forced to be silent about their injuries inflicted by the system of patriarchy which required their silence for the honor of the family and the village community. The technology of politics in state sponsored violence where the "red" hatred and male sexual fantasy intersect also makes it possible to imagine the woman's body as a representation of the "bodies of the reds." More precisely, this means that the woman's body becomes an embodiment of all that is abhorred and feared in the "bodies of the reds." In the cognitive representation concerning the tortures sponsored by the anticommunist state, the bodies of women victims are the place to inscribe the danger of the "red" by means of a gendered sign and thus, they represent the fear of this danger. In other words, the body of a woman "red" suspect is a *spectacle* where the antagonisms between anticommunism and procommunism cross swords and clash with each other.

The injuries suffered by Hyŏn Ki-yŏng or the women of Cheju demonstrate that the target of state violence becomes a signifier for a gendered and sexualized body.[24] This phenomenon is rooted in the biology of a woman's body. A woman's body, due to its characteristically warm and flowing menstrual blood and its reproductive quality, is often used as a metaphor for the "docile body" in bio-politics. In the cases in which Cheju Islanders were displayed (and quite literally so) as the gendered and sexualized body, a frequent torture-method for "crushing the reds" was to strip suspected rebels (regardless of whether it was a man or a woman) naked, hang them by the heels from a ceiling, and beat them with a horsewhip or burn them with red-hot iron rods. Why, though, strip them naked? The wounded body of the tortured suspect, where the act of violence is exhibited, that is, where the flesh has been cut open by the whip, is a place where the torturer can "see and feel" his power with his own eyes. The naked body with cut open flesh, in addition, appears as a "sexualized body" where the sexual desire of the aggressor is inscribed. The corporeality of a woman's body where the display of violence is transposed as sexual desire shows precisely the sexualization of the "body of the red" and it is, itself, a signifier for the body of the red.

In the following case, violence against a pregnant woman's body demonstrated the technology of politics, materialized by the sexual fantasy of the aggressor. Ahn Insun (age 75) of Hagwi village on Cheju Island gives the following account of the death of her brother-in-law's wife, a woman named Mun, (twenty-one years old at the time) who was murdered during childbirth:

> The tragedy of Ahn's family originated from her brother-in-law Hong. Hong had returned from his studies in Japan upon Liberation, and followed the armed rebels or *mujangdae* as they fled to Mt. Halla as the April Third Incident broke out in 1948. He seemed to have been taking part in communist party activities. The tragedy begins after Hong left for the mountain. In December of that year, when Hong's wife, Mun, returned to her parents' home in Hagwi village for childbirth, and was beginning to go into labor in a room covered with barley straw, the Special Attack Corps of Hagwi Village — a local youth organization formed in the village after the initial outbreak of the April Third to assist the police force — suddenly barged in. Two men said, *"Let's dry out the seeds of the commie's family,"* and dragged Mun out to the open field behind the village. When Ahn heard about this and ran to her rescue, Hong's wife had already been killed, stabbed thirteen times with a metal spear, including eight times in the chest. Hanging from her vagina was the baby, half-delivered. Fearing other people might see her wretched body, Ahn buried her temporarily by loosely covering the corpse with soil. Two years later, after the raging winds of the massacre had calmed down, Ahn called in a shaman and had a shamanic ritual, *kut,* performed. This was done because Hong's wife kept appearing in Ahn's dreams. During the ritual, the spirit possessed Ahn's niece. The spirit in her niece's body earnestly appealed to her to "please cut open my belly." It said, "Because the baby is hanging between my legs, neither can I walk nor

> can I be admitted to the other world." The spirit also screamed, saying that the person who killed her was one she had called "brother" and followed around when she was alive. After the *kut* ceremony, Ahn exhumed her corpse and moved it to the present site of her grave and took proper care of it. She also separated the blood-covered newborn from the corpse and buried it by her side.[25]

In the words of the two young men of the Special Attack Corps, Hong's wife had to be killed because the reds must be stripped of their "seeds." What was it that led them to murder a woman during childbirth? It was because hers was the body pregnant with life, that is, the body fraught with the danger of reproducing another red. The danger of the "body of the red" is drawn, first, from the symbolism of the color red itself, and the symbolism of the "bleeding" and "open" body that the body in childbirth evokes. The color red is also the color of rebellion and of communism. It stands for the color of a political taboo in an anticommunist state, and combined with another, the associational image of blood, it is to create a more composite net of signification. The "body of the red" is the body in danger of contaminating, that is, the body, from which the flowing blood could taint the society red. At the same time, the body in red associated with the fluid and permeating property of blood is a lascivious and bewitching body that spreads a subversive air over the society. The "open body" of the "red bitch" is an object of sexual desire for the aggressor and is, simultaneously, an object of anxiety regarding the aggressor's own repressed sexual desire. By torturing or murdering the object of desire, the aggressor liberates his repressed sexual desire. The infectiousness and lasciviousness of the "red bitch's open body" is taken to be the political danger of the reds, and the fear of that danger led to the killing of Ahn's sister-in-law by the young men, her neighbors in the village. Brutality inflicted upon the pregnant "body of the red" indicates a genocidal act, an elimination of the red-species. By eliminating the object of sexual desire, the anticommunist state rebuilds itself with a soundly purified healthy male body.[26]

In this way, violence against the "body of the red," a genocidal act against the body pregnant with a potential survival of the red species, is manifested as racialized and sexualized. Another atrocity was the death of a woman, the wife of a man who fled into the hills, who was dragged in front of other villagers who had been imprisoned on suspicion of being communist sympathizers and were being held in the village yard. There in public, she was forced to perform sexual acts, and at the end, a live grenade was inserted into her vagina, which exploded, shattering her body into unrecognizable pieces.[27] In yet another case, the wife of another "hill-fugitive," one who was making horsehair hats for a living, and living in a remote area out of fear of the young exterminators, was literally blown away without a trace after volley after volley was fired at her. All of these cases suggest that these acts mean something beyond the cruelty committed toward the "body of the red." In the former case, the insertion of a live grenade into the vagina was a punishment for an assumed crime of adultery. Raped by the constabulary officer who was spying on her home, waiting for the possible return of her husband who had gone off to the mountains, the woman was accused of adultery, stripped naked in public, and in utter humiliation was forced to performed sexual acts with her rapist.

The individual body of the woman is a signifier for the "social body" of the entire population on the island. The disgrace of an individual woman is the disgrace of the population as a whole, and the demolition of her body foreshadows the atrocious death of the social body of the prisoners detained in the village yard. A despicable act like exploding the genitals of a woman accused of adultery is a political instrumentality, which seeks to elicit the moral disgrace of the entire population by setting forth an ostensible moral reason for the punishment of the crime of adultery. This suggests a thoroughly deliberate technology of politics, which, by semantically transfiguring the perpetrator's antihumanistic violence into a legitimated act of violence against the victim's presumed act of adultery, seeks to deny or evade the ethical responsibility of the perpetrators themselves. In this process, the shame and victimization of the individual woman are completely ignored. The most visceral pain of the woman's injured body, eclipsed behind the shadow of the perpetrator's legitimated act of violence, becomes invisible. In turn, it is precisely that invisibility of the woman's "body in pain" that makes the power of the state visible.

The Body in Pain and the Limits of Language

Even today, six years after the opening of the April Third Damage Report Center under the Cheju Provincial Assembly in 1994, those who have been labeled as so-called *insurgent families* hesitate to report their injuries. The majority of the testimonies on the April Third casualties have been made not by the victims themselves, but by third parties, such as family, relatives, or neighbors. In particular, there has been no direct testimony in any case involving the sexual assault of women who are still alive. In such cases, the testimonies regarding sexual assaults, including rape, are made mostly by men. Almost as a rule, the indirect experiences of male eyewitnesses attest to the injuries from sexual assault on women.

In women's silence, men begin to speak. While women try to speak in vain with their injured bodies alone, men with their language tell the stories of women's experience of sexual assaults. As I described earlier, in a common method of torture during April Third, women were stripped naked, hung by their heels from the ceiling and flogged with a leather whip. A certain Kim Ho-gyŏm, one of the core constabulary officers of the punitive force, testified as an eyewitness to the brutality of Ch'oe Nan-su, a commander of the Special Investigation Team during the Incident.[28] In the collection of testimonies, Kim Ho-gyŏm's account is followed by an account given by a woman who fell victim to this form of torture. But the part about "being naked" is missing from the record of the woman's account. While Kim Ho-gyŏm emphasized "hanging the woman naked," the woman's firsthand account simply notes that she was cleared of all the charges and was spared her life even though she had been suspended upside down from the ceiling and flogged.[29] Her account, in other words, emphasizes the fact of survival. Between the woman's silence and the man's testimonies lies a difference in the perception of the sexual torture or sexual assault. While a woman *is* in pain, a man remains an observer of someone else's pain. Woman cannot see her own torn, naked body. She only feels the pain of the naked body, as she holds in herself the pain of the injured body. The subject and the object of pain are not split. Thus, the body's pain can only speak with the body itself. Herein lies the limit of the representation of pain.

On April 1, 1998, on the occasion of the fiftieth anniversary of the Cheju April Third Incident, an island-wide shamanic ritual, the *haewŏn sangsaeng kut* or "ritual for the resolution of resentment and mutual living" was held for the citizens of Cheju. Kim Yang-hak (male, age 58), representing the surviving families of the Incident, spoke out about the injuries of April Third. Along with the massacre of the 157 inhabitants of T'osan village, he noted the collective sexual assault that the women of the village suffered for nine days at the hands of the punitive forces. Hoping that one of the victims might leave evidence in the form of a voice recording before she passed away, Kim remarked, he approached his friend's mother. But whenever he brought up anything regarding the incident, she would immediately become agitated and refuse to speak. Once she even fainted during one of the conversations with him. Kim never did receive her first person testimony. Kim also reported that the women victims refuse to speak because the incident was "so heinous that it makes my whole body tremble even to think about it."

Why are the women so upset by even the mention of an incident of sexual assault? It is because of the horror that the pain itself evokes. According to a German historian, Reinhart Koselleck, who conducted a comparative analysis of the dreams of concentration camp survivors before and after internment in the Nazi camps, when extreme horror becomes a part of everyday experience during custody, an inmate becomes so numbed to the terror that their dreams become devoid of image or action. That is, one reaches the point where it is no longer possible to talk about or otherwise represent the horror. [30]

Pain imprisoned in a body is torture. Elaine Scarry contends that pain resists verbal objectification, and is impossible to express in relation to anything other than pain itself. She argues that in the process of rendering pain in language, the most fundamental place of pain is lost — that is, the body, as the object of violence is lost or destroyed. Instead, in the process of verbal representation of the pain of the *other* by the subject who inflicts it, the place of pain is fantasized as the place of desire.[31] In dramatizing sexual assault as a plausible incident to be expected in a patriarchal society, the stories of men who testify to the women's experience of sexual assault threaten to legitimize the very act of sexual violence. Regarding the case of the woman who was accused of adultery and blown up, the way in which this story was told, with its "excessively detailed and explicit descriptions," suggests that the male witness is taking a certain amount of pleasure in the act of telling. The speech of the men who shamelessly testify to the brutality committed on women's bodies, whether those women are already dead or are silently imprisoned in their injured bodies, is a performance of patriarchal violence. This is because their words alienate the victim's physical pain as well as the moral indignity that she suffered.

Women's Bodies in Wartime and Peacetime: Patriarchal Violence

Why do the women victims not testify to their experiences by themselves? What forces them into silence? I shall cite one case:

> The Northwest Youth League turned an elementary school building into a prison and detained people for over a month and ceaselessly tortured them in various ways. There was a couple, A (man) and B (woman), both schoolteachers in the village, who were engaged to be married. One day A was arrested and imprisoned, and B asked the Northwest Youth League for permission to see him. Taking advantage of her desperation, men in the Northwest Youth League raped B. At that time, to be a woman schoolteacher on the island was to have a considerable position, and for that reason, she was raped by not one, but several members of the Youth League. In the end, A's life was spared through B's sexual sacrifice. Moreover, another core member of the Northwest Youth League, coveting A's niece, came to know of this story about A, and kept threatening to kill him if he couldn't have A's niece. At this, A's family held a family meeting and decided to marry her off to secure A's protection. A, who was able to maintain his life on the basis of women's sacrifices, is known to be living in wealth and honor today.[32]

A in this case was able to live and maintain peace in his family through his former fiancée's, B's, sacrifice. Nevertheless, because she lost her chastity to men of the Northwest Youth League, she was abandoned by her family, forced to marry her rapist, and is known to be living out of sight of her former acquaintances. Even today she is silent about her experience, but her story is being told by her former fiancée.

In instances like this, it is the patriarchal ideology regarding women's purity and chastity that is accountable for the women victims' silence about their experiences. Women's chastity and maternity are like soil and earth necessary to fortify a community's identity, and since a woman's body is irrevocably subsumed under the patriarchal "social body" — the family or village community — her dishonor or the destruction of her motherhood also mean dishonor and loss to the entire community. In the case above, since publicly disclosing the fact of a gang rape implies the collapse of patriarchal society, a tacit agreement from within demands the silence of the woman victim in order to prevent the shaming of that society. It might be said that the persecution of women in the wartime conditions of April Third is a continuation or extension of the *tacit agreement* that silences and wounds women in a patriarchal society in times of peace.

The women of Cheju who suffered from wartime violence, and are forced to endure the tormenting burden of that experience in patriarchal society in times of peace, share their affliction with the women who became the target of the ethnic cleansing of the Serbian nationalist rebel army, the victims of gang rapes, but are forced to keep silent about that experience. Maria Olujic, a Croatian woman anthropologist who published a collection of testimonies by gang rape victims, studied the structure of patriarchal ideology imposed upon women during wartime and times of peace. She found that the patriarchal ideology of peacetime in Bosnia and Serbia, which takes women's chastity as a symbolic repository for the honor of family and relatives, uniformly applies to wartime.[33] According to her study, the shame brought to women by wartime rape and sexual torture is considered a disgrace to family and relatives, and women are inhibited from publicly denouncing the agents of their suffering. She explains that the ideology of honor and disgrace, which is upheld uniformly during wartime as in times of peace, causes the women's bodies to be subsumed under units of the social body of men, representatively within the family and kinship structure. She points out that rape and other forms of sexual violence are the means by which one ethnic group can disgrace the other, and are thus the symbolic mechanisms with which two ethnic groups of Serbia and Bosnia compete with each for the honor of each patriarchal society.

Silence about the fact of wartime rape is often demanded at the state level. A typical case is that of the Korean comfort women, wartime rape victims during the Japanese colonial period. The sufferings of the comfort women are now known publicly and a three-volume collection of testimonies has been published. However, two important forms of patriarchal violence can be discerned as reasons why the victims were silenced for fifty years, until the first testimonies were taken in 1991, and also why the two states, Korea and Japan, maintained such a passive attitude in the course of the unfolding testimonies and the demands for the truth. One is the internalized ideology regarding chastity, which causes women victims to feel shame; the other is the fact that such individual shame is seen as a nationwide shame, in which Korea is represented as the victim vis-à-vis the perpetrator, Japan. The nature of the debates that occurred within the nationalist camp regarding the comfort women attests to the fact that the matter of the injuries to women during the Cheju April Third Incident and their testimonies about them are directly connected to the structural violence of patriarchal power.[34]

As long as women are subsumed under the structure of the patriarchal power of family, relatives, village, nation and state, the experience in the woman's body is violently alienated from the patriarchal language of domination. For the women victims of Cheju, those who refuse to speak out in the first person, because "it makes the body tremble", or who deny the veracity of the experience itself, "body" and "speech" are split. Veena Das who analyzed literature on the subject of the war of partition between India and Pakistan bitterly criticized the sexual violence contained in the ideology of Indian nationalism. She contends that in their writings, nationalist writers attempt to render women's pain as representation of an Indian nationalism wounded by British imperialism, but they keep silent regarding the fact of the women's injuries of rape and terrorism.[35] The language of nationalism or that of patriarchy cannot adequately speak for the "body in pain," for as soon as the injured body enters the regime of that language, it becomes a textual body, an object of that language to be grasped and interpreted. Consequently, such a language erases all traces of the *lived experience* of pain. As the state, or the experts representing the state, reorganize and textualize the memories of the incidents of sexual assault, their voice alone will be materialized and will gain a kind of eternal life. In such a text, the experience of the victim herself is lost in silence and invisibility.

If language does not adequately represent the experience of the victim of sexual violence, it is her injured body, her silenced body, that speaks to that experience. Words betray the body. When the body and speech are separated, the women's words are muffled. Nevertheless, too much is spoken about a woman's body. An abundance of words on women's bodies — in particular, those discussions that strip and dissect the injured bodies of women, on the contrary — mute the *cries* of the bodies in pain, which try to speak out about their brutal scars and deaths, the deeply carved pain of anticommunist violence and sexual violence. This is yet another form of sexual violence. Albeit muffled, the cries of the bodies in pain, the commonality in the experiences of those women victims in pain, *do,* however, suggest the solidarity among women, the women victims of the Cheju April Third Incident, the rape victims of ethnic conflict and ethnic cleansing in Bosnia and Serbia, the comfort women under the Japanese colonial regime, and the women victims in the war of partition in India and Pakistan. This is the solidarity of pain, which will come about as they commit themselves to cooperative activities of testifying to the facts of atrocities and their suffering. This solidarity of pain will be the voice of those who have been dispossessed of the language, and will thus come together in inarticulate and nonverbal forms such as dreams, laments, or spirit-possession.

Solidarity of Pain: Dreams, Lament, and Spirit-possession

Giving testimonies about the suffering of violence requires courage to confront violence itself as well as the fear of violence. Such courage may be obtained collectively through the solidarity between the victim and other women who recognize and acknowledge her suffering. The solidarity of pain can be achieved when a woman, by means of her body, can bear the pain of another, that is to say, in the words of Emmanuel Levinas, "when one is willingly taken as a hostage for the other."[36] When she can take the place of someone else, she can give meaning to that other's pain just because it is "for the other." Levinas refers to this pain as the pain in substitution. It is, of course, not the case that all pain in substitution is laden with significance. The solidarity of pain may not come together until one can expose herself to the "possibility for injury" such as that which the other experienced.[37]

When the language that expresses pain is monopolized by state power and patriarchal men, the solidarity of pain may be sought in laments and dream-images, the forms of expression prior to language, and in spirit-possessions, the supernatural and religious forms of expression in the imaginary realm. In the case of Ahn In-sun's sister-in-law, it is the woman murdered during childbirth who appears in Ahn's dream, tells Ahn of her death, and demands her resentment be appeased. But in the nonimaginary realm, this dream expresses the courage and ethical will of Ahn, a witness to her sister-in-law's murder, who perhaps unconsciously seeks to identify with the pain of the dead.

In Korean shamanic practice, the spirit of one who died an "unnatural" death cannot depart to the other world, but must wander around as a spiteful soul in this world. Such spirits, it is believed, try through dreams to tell the true circumstances of their deaths to the family members or neighbors to whom they were closest in life. The spiteful soul will speak to one who has suffered pain and therefore seems able to understand and convey her story.[38] In the patriarchal family structure, those who are most often possessed by the spirits are the marginal beings with the least power, that is, married women or children. Ironically, what is manifested in the fantastic and supernatural world that substitutes for the historical reality can be described as something "more genuine" than the phenomena of the real world where one often cannot speak the truth of the lived experience, or where the truth can easily be subjected to distortion. At least in folk religious traditions, the *truth* of the dream images and lamentation of spiteful souls is guaranteed, more than anything, by faith.

Because the historical character or truth of testimony of the Cheju April Third has not been classified under a single conceptual title — whether "rebellion," "resistance," or "massacre" — one must pay special heed to the "non-obvious acts and moments of resistance, a kind of diffuse consciousness that is never further explored as a set of ideas, practices, and feelings," in other words, the mode of representation of pain manifested in dreams and lamentation.[39] The violent pain of the victims of April Third is revealed in the real world by the secret agreement between the victims and the survivors, such as that made in an ambiguous state of consciousness like a dream or spirit-possession. The survivor endures a living death, the pain of forced silence. It is sometimes too painful a process for the survivor to express in words her physical wound and the memory of that injury. Depending on who is the subject of a ritual mourning unjust deaths, and depending also on who controls the language of that mourning, the truth of April Third can be either brought out or distorted. The pain of the living is the legacy of the dead. The dead and the living perceive their pain identically. This is because as long as the pain of the dead remains unhealed, the living cannot go on living in peace.

In a *kut* ceremony, the shamanic ritual of Cheju Island, the phenomenon of spirit-possession is an opportunity for the spirit of the dead to borrow the body of the shaman to begin speaking spontaneously in "whatever words come out of her mouth." The words that the shaman conveys are referred to, in the Cheju dialect, as *yŏnggye ullim* or "lamentations of the dead." The shamans of Cheju Island claim that when they put on a shaman's robe and sit at the *sin chari*, or the "place of the spirit," the words come spontaneously out of their mouths and they begin to "see things." This is because "the spirit has something to say." The lamentation that the shaman conveys through the *kut* ceremony is a testimony to the injuries of the April Third.

In the *kut* ceremony, by making the lamentation of the spirit of the dead and the testimonies of the survivors stand in parallel, without one voice quelling the other, the ritual dialogically reconstructs the violence of April Third. During the *kut* ceremony, at one stage the spirit of the dead speaks through the shaman while the survivor also speaks out an untold story while communicating with the spirit through the shaman; at another stage, the shaman assumes the role of a priest, or a master of ceremonies, to console both the dead and the living. In transmitting the testimonies of the victims and the survivors of April Third in multiple voices, the *kut* ritual produces plural subjects for the narrative: one of the *simbang* (the local dialect referring to shaman), one of the dead, and one of the living. They denounce and testify to the injustice of anticommunist violence by exposing the wounds and the pain in "bare life." The lamentation of the spirit, which the shaman transmits through her plural subjectivity, is a language prior to discourse of either "rebellion" or "resistance." It is precisely the "body in pain" which was shot and stabbed by the spear and is bleeding; it is the visible, "physical body."

The lament of the spirit of the dead, however, is too naïve and powerless to contest the truth of April Third against the ubiquitous misrepresentations of the Incident. Nevertheless, the laments of the spirits, even in their powerlessness, challenge the grave historical reality in which the truth of the Incident has been stifled by the official language of state power. Although obscure and feeble, these representations of pain were the only way to resist the firm and violent order of the modern nation state of South Korea until 1987, when the victims' testimonies were first discussed publicly. Even after 1995, when the Cheju Island Provincial Assembly published its first report on the investigation of the damage of April Third, and even now, after the 1999 promulgation of the special law for the investigation of the truth of April Third, these imaginary representations remain recognized as a truthful source where the memories of April Third are preserved and testified.

"Let the Women Speak": The Issues of Human Rights

But now is the time to let women speak not in their dreams, but in the real world, in broad daylight. How can women speak in their own language about their own bodies being crushed, torn, and murdered? The testimonies of pain are the political forum in which the woman's body in pain and the body thrust into silence can be made visible. Women's pain is a product of the sexual fantasy of the men the state represents. To deconstruct the signifier for the sexual fantasy of state violence inscribed on the body of woman, she must now tell her experience with her own voice. To tell the story of long-suffered injuries is to rewitness the wordless and objectless void of memory imprisoned beneath layers of patriarchy, and to revisit the imaginary realm occupied only by spirits of the dead and their laments. It is, in other words, "a form of action of confronting and changing the painful reality and also a struggle for survival."[40] For an individual woman victim to tell her experience directly is to liberate the pain imprisoned in the body and to take possession of the power over her own life and death. At the same time, it is to erase the boundary of power that the state, as the community inscribed in women's bodies, holds. In this sense, the state is a nonentity for women.

Materializing the pain experienced by the women of Cheju in their own words will lead to making the innocent victims, virtually the entire population of Cheju Island whose lives (and deaths) have been affected by the Incident, visible. This is because the "red" genocide was executed by means of sexual assaults and patriarchal violence against actual women's bodies and those bodies of Cheju people taken to be "women's bodies." On December 16, 1999, in the National Assembly of the Republic of Korea, the "Special Law on the Cheju April Third Incident" was enacted, and official legal proceedings for the investigation of the truth of the Incident, as well as the recovery of the Cheju people's honor, have been ensured. Going beyond the erstwhile scope of the unofficial efforts at clarifying the truth of the incident, which had consisted of investigations based upon intermittent testimonies by the victims, the task of excavating the official documents that will formally establish the evidence of the cause and the course of April Third, along with more objective facts about the injuries, will begin. But in disclosing the facts about the incidents of massacre that took place, unless the state as the perpetrator acknowledges these facts and makes reparations to the Cheju people, there is the possibility of falling back into unilateral concealment of the event itself. The need for such a concern has already been demonstrated by the failure to include representatives of the surviving victims or any of the civilian experts on the "Committee on April Third" or the "Planning Team for the Investigation," the members of which were appointed to execute the special law. Instead, the committee and the team are filled mostly with government bureaucrats and military experts assigned to the task by the Department of Defense.

The objective of this paper is to create hope for a new century of peace by bringing to light the Cheju April Third Incident from a perspective of human rights, to argue specifically for the punishment of such crimes against humanity as the massacres of the innocent and gang rapes, and to call for reparations for injuries and damage. Despite the various obstacles and difficulties in the process, the objectives of the Special Law on the Cheju April Third Incident point to the acknowledgment of the individual's right to life, in other words, towards a recovery of human rights. The perpetrators of the massacre and sexual violence of the Cheju April Third Incident, the rightwing groups including the Northwest Youth League who participated in the acts of violence directly and indirectly, and the government of the Republic of Korea — as the organization that commanded and legitimated such attacks — must share the responsibility for the atrocity. This responsibility begins with listening attentively to the individual stories of each victim, and ultimately will lead to the task of public disclosure of the facts and making reparations for the guiltless victims. Such a task is the debt owed to the body in pain, and the solidarity with those in pain that will emerge from it will become an opportunity for breaking down the violent order of the new–old world.

ENDNOTES

[1] Zillah R. Eisenstein, *Hatreds: Racialized and Sexualized Conflicts in the 21st Century* (New York: Routledge, 1996).

[2] Barbara Ehrenreich, foreword to Klaus Theweleit, *Male Fantasies*, Vol.1, *Women Floods Bodies History*, trans. Stephen Conway (Minneapolis: University of Minnesota Press, 1987), ix–xvii.

[3] German sociologist Zygmunt Bauman views the Holocaust as a characteristically modern phenomenon. He suggests that the Holocaust was a unique outcome of the emancipation of the political state, with its monopoly of the means of violence and the practice of rational administration under scrupulous engineering, from traditional social control. Zygmunt Bauman, *Modernity and the Holocaust* (Ithaca: Cornell University Press, 1989). Also, Peter Fritzsche, in describing how the experiment of modernism in Nazi Germany unfolded in various areas including science and technology, arts, scholarship, and social welfare, explains that the Holocaust was a product of the political technology of the Fascist modern state of Nazi Germany. Peter Fritzsche, "Nazi Modern," *Modernism/Modernity* 3, no. 1 (January, 1996): 1–22.

[4] Michel Foucault, *History of Sexuality*, Vol. 1, *An Introduction*, trans. Robert Hurley (New York: Pantheon Books, 1978; Vintage Books, 1990), 137.

5 Giorgio Agamben, "The Camp as the 'Nomos' of the Modern," in *Homo Sacer: Sovereign Power and Bare Life*, trans. Daniel Heller-Roazen (Stanford, California: Stanford University Press, 1988), 166–180.

6 See Kim Se-gyun, "Kukka kwŏllyŏk ŭi p'ongnyŏkchŏk kich'o" (Violent basis of state authority), *Silch'ŏn munhak* (Seoul), no.15 (fall, 1989); and Han Chi-su, "Pan'gong ideollogi wa chŏngch'i p'ongnyŏk" (Anticommunist ideology and political violence), *Silch'ŏn munhak* (Seoul), no.15 (fall, 1989).

7 Bruce Cumings, *The Origins of the Korean War*, Vol. II, *The Roaring of the Cataract, 1947–1950* (Princeton: Princeton University Press, 1990), 251.

8 Agamben, *Homo Sacer*, 176–180.

9 Kim Eunshil's comments have been extremely helpful in raising these questions. See Kim Eunshil, "P'ongnyŏk kwa yŏsŏng" (Violence and Women), in *Tong asia ŭi p'yŏnghwa wa inkwŏn, Cheju 4.3 che 50 chunyŏn kinyŏm che 2 hoe tong asia p'yŏnghwa wa inkwŏn haksul taehoe pokosŏ* (Peace and Human Rights in East Asia: Report for the Second International Conference on Peace and Human Rights in East Asia on the Fiftieth Anniversary of the Cheju April Third Incident), ed. *Cheju 4.3 yŏn'guso* (Institute for Research on the Cheju April Third Incident) (Seoul: Yŏksa pip'yŏngsa, 1999), 182–185.

10 The first scholarly discussion on the cause and the background of the outbreak as well as the development of the Cheju April Third Incident was John Merrill's study, "The Cheju Rebellion" in *Journal of Korean Studies* 2 (1980): 139–197. But if Merrill's view provided an American perspective and characterized the April Third Incident as "communist rebellion," another study, which precedes Merrill's by almost twenty years, offered the perspective of the victims on Cheju Island. Kim Min-ju and Kim Pong-hyŏn, eds., *Cheju-do inmindŭl ŭi 4.3 mujang t'ujaengsa charyojip* (Materials on the history of the April Third armed uprising of the Cheju people) (Osaka: Munch'osa, 1963). The authors of this study are Korean–Japanese historians who had been residents of the island at the time of the incident. They managed to escape to Japan during the course of the Incident. Currently, the most reliable source in and outside Korea on the Incident is *4.3 ŭn malhanda* (April Third speaks), 5 vol. (Seoul: Chŏnyewŏn, 1994–1998). The volumes contain the materials researched and collected by the special investigation and report team of the island's local newspaper, *Chemin ilbo*, which had been serialized in the same newspaper prior to the publication. These volumes comprise the reports on the series of field investigations based upon references contained in *G–2 Periodic Report*, intermittent recordings of the events that unfolded on the island during a one-year period between 1948 and 1949, published by the American military administration and the United States Armed Forces stationed in Korea (USAFIK, *G–2 Periodic Report*). The five volumes by Cheju Island's newspaper give more objective facts about the state of affairs during the Incident as well as the situation of injuries and damage. An accurate count of the death toll from the April Third Incident is still unavailable. Presumably, the number varies from 30,000 to 80,000 depending on the researcher; but according to the testimonies by Cheju Islanders and the publication by the Cheju newspaper's special investigation and report team, *4.3 ŭn malhanda* (April Third speaks), it appears to have been approximately 30,000. This number is about

11% of 270,000, the total population on the island at the time. By contrast to previous studies, the publication, *4.3 ŭn malhanda* (April Third speaks), attends to the views of the direct victims of the Incident and, in particular, it illuminates the characteristic aspect of the "red hunt," the massacres that claimed so many innocent lives. The debates on the characterization of the April Third Incident are in progress even today, and I have analyzed the discursive politics of these recent debates in an article, "Kŭndaesŏng kwa p'ongnyŏk: Cheju 4.3 ui tamnon chŏngch'i" (Modernity and violence: Discursive politics of the Cheju April Third Incident), in Yŏksa munje yŏn'guso (Institute for Historical Studies), *Cheju 4.3 yŏn'gu* (The study of the Cheju April Third Incident) (Seoul: Yŏksa pip'yŏngsa, 1999).

11 Ko Ch'ang-hun, "4.3 minjung hangjaeng ŭi chŏn'gae wa sŏngkyŏk" (The development and the character of the April Third people's resistance), in *Haebang chŏnhusa insik 4* (Understanding the history before and after liberation, vol. 4) (Seoul: Han'gilsa, 1989).

12 Kim Sun-t'ae, "Cheju 4.3 tangsi kyeŏm ŭi pŭlpopsŏng" (Unlawfulness of the martial law during the April Third Incident), in Yŏksa munje yon'guso (Institute for Historical Studies), *Cheju 4.3 yŏn'gu* (The study of the Cheju April Third Incident) (Seoul: Yoksa pip'yŏngsa, 1999), 147–179.

13 In accordance with each of the various perspectives claiming a different historical characterization of the Cheju April Third Incident, it has been classified under various conceptual titles, such as "Cheju Communist Rebellion," "Cheju April Third People's Uprising," or "Cheju April Third Massacre." Since the historical truths about the Incident are still to be clarified, Cheju Islanders often refer to it simply as 4.3 or "April Third Incident." The title, "Cheju April Third Massacre" is most appropriate for this paper, which analyzes the mechanism of state violence as the main force responsible for the pain and sufferings of the victims. In addition to this I shall make use of two other titles: "Cheju April Third," which is broadly used today to demand and urge the clarification of the truth about the Incident, and "Cheju April Third Incident," a neutral designation simply referring to an event in history.

14 According to "Che il ch'a Cheju-do 4.3 p'ihae chosa pogosŏ" (The first report on the investigation of damage of the Cheju April Third Incident) published in 1995 by a special investigation committee appointed by the Cheju Provincial Assembly, approximately 15,000 cases were filed as death reports related to the Incident. But as I have explained in my earlier note, the accurate death toll is yet to be known and the researchers estimate around 30,000.

15 Kim Chong-min, "Cheju 4.3 hangjaeng — taegyumo minjung haksal ŭi chinsang" (Cheju April Third resistance: The truth about the massacre), *Yŏksa pip'yŏng* (Seoul), no. 42 (spring, 1998): 30.

16 Chemin ilbosa (Cheju Daily News), *4.3 ŭn malhanda* (April Third speaks), vol. 3 (Seoul: Chŏnyewŏn, 1995), 81.

17 Michel Foucault, "The Political Technology of Individuals," in *Technologies of the Self: A Seminar with Michel Foucault*, ed. Luther Martin et al. (Amherst: University of Massachusetts Press, 1988) 160.

18 Michel Foucault, *History of Sexuality*, 137.

[19] Alan Milchman and Alan Rosenberg, "Michel Foucault, Auschwitz, and Modernity," *Philosophy & Social Criticism* 22, no.1, 1996:103.

[20] April 1, 1949 entry of *G–2 Periodic Report* by the United States Armed Forces in Korea describes the activities of the South Korean punitive forces during the Incident as a "red hunt." This entry also states "a program of mass slaughter among civilians" as the chief reason for the successful suppression. This description and the statement help to establish that the "red hunt" during the Incident was a programmed slaughter of civilians and thus genocide by the United States and the pro-American anticommunist regime in South Korea. Chemin ilbosa (Cheju Daily News), *4.3 ŭn malhanda* (April Third speaks), vol. 4 (Seoul: Chŏnyewŏn, 1997), 361–363.

[21] Formed on November 30, 1946, the Northwest Youth League or *Sŏbuk ch'ŏngnyŏndan* was composed of extreme rightwing, anticommunist refugees from North Korea who came to be known for their brutal methods of terrorism in fighting the South Korean Labor Party and other communist forces in the south. Having been driven from their homes in the Northern provinces, they harbored strong resentment toward the Korean Communist Party and perhaps equally strong discontent with the Soviet occupational regime. With an outbreak of March First demonstrations in 1947 (the protests against the formation of the South Korean Interim Government, which started with a series of meetings to commemorate the March First anniversary of the Korean independence movement against Japanese colonialism in 1919) about 700 of the Northwest Youth League members were brought into the island to assume the role of emergency police. After the establishment of the South Korean government, they were absorbed into the military brigade and police force on the island and were dispatched for the scorched-earth campaign. As an agent of anticommunist terrorism, the Northwest Youth League was given much privilege and, for the civilians, their privilege represented terror of the omnipotent public authority. The prevailing opinion is that their cruelty served as one of the fundamental origins for the outbreak of the April Third Incident. Since the Northwest Youth League members, who received little financial support from the government, took up residence in the villages, they lived entirely off of the land through the means of confiscation of civilian property. Also, for this reason, rape and other forms of sexual assaults on the island's women occurred in their daily contact with the villagers.

[22] Yi Kyŏng-nam, *Pundan sidae ŭi ch'ŏngnyŏn undong* (Youth movement in the period of division) (Seoul: Samsŏng munhwa chaedan, 1989), 70.

[23] In the presentation of his paper at the "Seminar on Women's Rights and Peace" in March 1998, Hyŏn Ki-yŏng discussed the agony of representing the pain of torture in his writings and the limits of the language of such representations. He argued that the limits of representing pain are in the gulf of difference between the person in pain and the one who represents it. The difference arises in the process of representation when the addresser or the storyteller recreates meaning in the reality of pain for the sake of the specific addressee or audience. This representation is meaningful only within the relationship between the addresser and the addressee, and this *meaningfulness* can thus misrepresent the pain and the actual event that took place.

[24] Eisenstein, *Hatreds*.

[25] In April of 1997 when this writer visited the April Third Damage Report Center under the Cheju Provincial Assembly, I was able to listen to this testimony directly from Ahn. The despicable cruelty represented in this testimony is a typical case of violence against women during the Incident.

[26] Klaus Theweleit, *Male Fantasies*, Vol. 1, *Women Floods Bodies History*, trans. Stephen Conway (Minneapolis: University of Minnesota Press, 1987). Theweleit analyzed the diaries and other documents recorded by Freikorps, the predecessor of the Nazi and the radical antisemitic, anticommunist terrorist group. He explains the fascist violence in Germany as the product of male fantasy toward other races and women. The Freikorps members responded toward women's sexuality with fear of their own sexual desire and feeling of the putative danger of contamination by that sexual desire. They conceived of a woman's body as both the object of men's sexual desire and an uncontrollable and destructive entity of threat, which stimulates sexual desire to contaminate men's bodies. According to Theweleit, these men rationalized their violent acts as a self-defense mechanism to eliminate women's bodies in order to maintain their own health.

[27] Han Rim-hwa, "4.3 tangsi sŏbuk ch'ŏngnyŏndan e ŭihae haenghaejin Cheju yŏsŏng e taehan t'erŏ" (Terrorism against the Cheju women by the Northwest Youth League during the April Third Incident), a paper originally presented at the "Seminar on Women's Rights and Peace," and published in *Tto hana ŭi munhwa* (Seoul; May 1998). The case was presented as follows: "Sexual assault on the wives of the men who fled to the hills occurred frequently. This woman victim was married to the police officer, but he, too, fled to the mountains. At the time, quite a few people were blamed for being friends or family of a "red," and to escape constant harassment, some people sought to survive by taking flight into the mountains. After her husband's flight, her house was under surveillance by an officer who was waiting for the possible return of her husband. This officer coveted her and one day, as he was about to rape her, the infamous Northwest Youth League barged in. They dragged both of them out, detained them in the village prison, and forced them to perform a sexual act in front of the entire village. When they disobeyed, they were severely whipped. They had to perform. After that, the Northwest Youth League had a hand grenade inserted into the woman's vagina with a piece of string tied to a safety pin and then they ordered her to run. Her body fell apart into unrecognizable pieces."

[28] *4.3 ŭn malhanda* (April Third speaks), vol. 4 (Seoul: Chŏnyewŏn, 1997) 223.

[29] According to the reporter Kim Chong-min who recorded the woman's account, the woman victim might actually have mentioned the fact about being naked. Nevertheless, he rationalized that the reason for this omission was his concern for the woman, in other words, his unconscious act of self-censorship as he was writing it down; since the witness's name was to appear in the article, he was concerned that the fact of having been stripped naked would become publicly known and consequently become a disgrace to the woman.

[30] Reinhart Koselleck, "Terror and Dream," in *Futures Past: On the Semantics of Historical Time*, trans. Keith Tribe (Cambridge, Massachusetts: The MIT Press, 1985), 223.

31 Elaine Scarry, *The Body in Pain* (New York: Oxford University Press, 1985), 161–162.

32 Han Rim-hwa, "4.3 tangsi sŏbuk ch'ŏngnyŏndan e ŭihae haenghaejin Cheju yŏsŏng e taehan t'erŏ" (Terrorism against the Cheju women by the Northwest Youth League during the April Third Incident). See note 28.

33 Maria B. Olujic, "Women, Rape, and War: The Continued Trauma of Refugees and Displaced Persons in Croatia," *Anthropology of East Europe Review* 13, no. 1 (spring, 1995): 40–43.

34 See Chŏng Chin-sŏng, "Chŏngsindae p'ihae wa inkwŏn hoebok undong" (Injuries of the military comfort women and the recovery of human rights), *Kyegan sasang* (Seoul) (winter, 1996): 138–151; and Hyunah Yang, "Remembering the Korean Military Comfort Women: Nationalism, Sexuality, and Silencing," in *Dangerous Women: Gender and Korean Nationalism*, ed. Elaine H. Kim and Chungmoo Choi (New York: Routledge, 1998), 123–140.

35 Veena Das, "Language and Body: Transactions in the Construction of Pain," *Daedalus* 125, no. 1 (winter, 1996): 67–91.

36 Emmanuel Levinas, *Autrement qu'être, ou, delà d'essence* (The Hague: Martinus Nijhoff, 1974), 94, quoted in Yongahn Kang, "Levinas on Suffering and Solidarity," *Tijdschrift voor Filosofie* 59 (1997): 482–504.

37 Borrowing the words of Stanley Cavell, Veena Das rephrases the expression "a hostage for the other" as "pawning of voice of the other." Veena Das, "Language and Body: Transactions in the Construction of Pain," *Daedalus* 125, no. 1 (winter, 1996): 69, quoting Stanley Cavell, *A Pitch of Philosophy* (Cambridge, PA: University of Pennsylvania Press, 1992).

38 Seong Nae Kim, "The Lamentations of the Dead: The Historical Imagery of Violence in Cheju Shamanism, Korea," *The Journal of Ritual Studies* 3, no. 2 (summer, 1989). Most frequently, the spiteful soul possesses a married woman living among other family members. This is because the spiteful soul which is barred from entering the "ancestors' world" due to the abnormal condition of its death and is therefore excluded even in *chesa*, the formal ancestor worship ceremony, tends to identify itself with the marginal and obscure status of women in the patriarchal order.

39 James Scott, "Domination, Acting, and Fantasy," *The Path to Domination, Resistance, and Terror*, ed. Carolyn Nordstrom and J. Martin (Berkeley: University of California Press, 1992).

40 Dori Laub, "Truth and Testimony: The Process and the Struggle," *Trauma: Explorations in Memory*, ed. Cathy Caruth (Baltimore: The Johns Hopkins University Press, 1995).

Narratives Engendering Survival: How the Muslims of Southwest China Remember the Massacres of 1873

Jacqueline Armijo

Preface

Those that survived the initial attacks by government soldiers fled up into the hills, hiding in the forests. If they dared to return to their homes to collect food or supplies, it was only at night under cover of darkness. Some of their neighbors had helped them escape from the soldiers, promising to take care of their homes and land while they were hiding, but others had assisted the soldiers in hunting down the Muslims, and had taken over their homes, mosques, and businesses. The Muslims had been labeled "outsiders" despite the fact that they had lived there all their lives, and their ancestors had migrated to that region more than half a millennium earlier.

This is not an account of recent events in the Balkans, but rather events that took place in southwest China in the 1870s. What is striking about this description is that with only a few slight changes it could also describe a myriad of other persecutions of the last century, a century which witnessed the Holocaust and promises of "never again." The comparison with the situation in the former Yugoslavia is especially compelling because in both instances government officials were able to create a myth of age-old ethnic tensions, and to combine that with the dissemination of racist stereotypes and panic-inducing rumors, in order to implement a campaign to destroy an entire population.[1] That the Muslim populations in both cases had settled there centuries earlier and intermarriage was so extensive as to have blurred any racial categories did not seem to make any difference. For different reasons strangers, neighbors, friends, and even family turned on those now designated as "outsiders," killing them or driving them away.

In 1873, in the aftermath of the Qing government's successful defeat of an independent multiethnic Islamic Kingdom based in Southwest China, Qing troops carried out a systematic and brutal massacre of the Muslim population (Hui) of Yunnan. This government-sponsored ethnic cleansing is estimated to have resulted in the death of as much as 90% of the Muslim population.[2] Most of the estimated one million Muslims living in Yunnan during this time were the descendants of Muslim officials and soldiers from Central and Western Asia who had first settled there during the Yuan Dynasty (1271–1368). Despite their centuries-long residence in the region, Qing officials were able to manipulate common xenophobic attitudes to gain the support of many of the recent Han Chinese immigrants from Central China in carrying out attacks on the Muslims. In many respects, the attacks and subsequent persecution of the Muslims are reminiscent of the treatment of the Armenians of Turkey, the Jewish population in Nazi Germany, the Muslim population of the former Yugoslavia more recently, as well as the Tutsi population of Rwanda. In all these cases — the list is emblematic, not exhaustive — the systematic dehumanization of a minority ethnic group enabled members of the dominant ethnic group to justify murder, confiscation of economic assets, and targeting of women for brutalization. Based on interviews with the survivors' descendants, this article discusses the incorporation of collective memories into present-day conceptions of ethnic identity, the creation of Islamic religious rituals to commemorate the lives of the victims of state-sponsored violence, and the idealization of the role of women in collective memories of community survival.

By studying the historical experience of Muslims in southwest China who survived state-sponsored massacres, we gain insight into how attacks based on ethnic and/or religious identity break out, and how some communities survive these catastrophes. Moreover, by concentrating on the experiences of women in this particular case of ethnic cleansing, and how their role is remembered by present-day descendants, we can see how the brutality and sexual violence perpetuated by men on women can be transformed into a collective badge of honor rather than a source of individual shame. Although women have been targeted throughout history during times of war and mass violence, their experiences have, for the most part, been either ignored by historians or manipulated by men to justify further violence. Recent events in Bosnia and Kosovo, however, have been well documented and have forced us to acknowledge the systematic violence perpetuated against women in times of conflict. These reports have also enabled us to re-examine earlier periods of mass violence in order to better understand the consequences for women and the roles played by women.

This article will focus on present-day collective memories of the massacres among the Hui of Yunnan, and individuals' own understandings of how it was that Muslims survived. It is not meant as a comprehensive examination of the Muslim uprising and the events leading up to it, nor does it include the perspectives of the non-Muslim peoples of Yunnan.[3] Although historical sources about this period in Yunnan history are available, most are based primarily on reports written by government officials or written from the perspective of immigrant Han Chinese. Recently, however, several Chinese scholars based in Yunnan have made important contributions to the study of this period. The surviving accounts of the Muslim population are primarily oral accounts passed on from generation to generation. What few personal written accounts may have existed were most likely destroyed during the Cultural Revolution when the Muslims were once again the objects of persecution by government forces. Many of the Hui with whom I spoke were quite concerned about the general lack of knowledge among the Hui of their own history. As one man explained, "We don't control our own history; our history is in the hands of others. Since few Hui of the older generation can write, it is inevitable that our history is written not by those who know it, but by those who don't."[4]

My own interest in this event is the result of many years living among the Muslims of Yunnan. From 1993 to 1998 I lived in Kunming, the provincial capital of Yunnan, carrying out research on the early history of Islam in southwest China. During these five years I traveled throughout the region interviewing Muslims in many different communities. Over time my contacts within these communities grew wider and increasingly close and varied due to the length of my stay. In many respects this paper reflects these relationships, and I have chosen this opportunity to give voice to the memories that have been shared with me.[5]

Introduction

With a Muslim population conservatively estimated at 20 million, China today has a larger Muslim population than most of the Arab countries of the Middle East, and yet even specialists in both Chinese studies and Islamic studies know little about this important population.[6] The Muslims of China are divided into 10 different ethnic groups, nine of which are concentrated in the northwest, while the tenth and largest group, known as the Hui, is spread throughout the entire country.[7] Despite their long history in China, only a handful of scholars have focused their research on China's Muslims.

In many ways, the Hui of Yunnan share a history similar to that of other Muslim communities in China. However in other ways their history is unique. For centuries the region that is now known as Yunnan was able to resist conquest by China. It was only under the Mongols in the 13th century that this formerly highly independent region was finally brought under direct control. In 1253, after personally leading a military expedition to Yunnan as part of a concerted attack on the Song empire, Qubilai Qan left the region under the military control of the Mongol general Uriyangqadai. Subsequently, shortly after the establishment of the Yuan dynasty and his taking the title of emperor, Qubilai deputed one of his trusted officials to establish a civilian government and begin settling the region. The official chosen was Sayyid 'Ajall Shams al-Din, a Muslim from Bukhara who had been kidnapped during the Mongol conquest of Central Asia and brought back to Mongolia to be raised within the Mongol Court.

Sayyid 'Ajall's accomplishments during his tenure as governor of Yunnan were considerable, and thus to this day he is considered to be an almost mythical character by both the Muslims of China and the indigenous peoples of Yunnan. His extensive service under the Mongols was characterized by his extraordinarily humanitarian approach to governing. In Yunnan he showed an unprecedented commitment to improving the lives of the local peoples. And while traditional Chinese historians who have examined his life have portrayed him as a paragon of Confucian values, Chinese Muslim scholars have described him as being simply an ideal Muslim official. In many respects his career was very similar to that of many of the thousands of other Central and Western Asians who played such an important role in assisting the Mongols after their massive campaigns of conquest.

More than any other Muslim who migrated to China during this period, Sayyid

'Ajall appears to have played an active role in recruiting other Muslims from Central and Western Asia to settle in China, as well as being an active patron of Islam.[8] In addition to the Muslim soldiers and officials who had arrived with the Mongol forces in Yunnan in 1253, many other Muslims settled here as well, and within 50 years the Muslim population of the region was sufficiently large to be noted by both Rashid al-Din (the Persian historian) and Marco Polo in their writings.[9]

Although some of the higher ranking Muslim officials may have been able to arrange marriages with Muslim women from their places of origin, it is generally assumed that most of the soldiers, officials, craftsmen, and farmers who settled here during this early period married local women. Despite centuries of intermarriage, both the Mongols and the Muslims who arrived at this time were able to establish communities which survived with many of their cultural and religious traditions intact over a period of more than 750 years.[10]

Among Sayyid 'Ajall's twelve sons and numerous grandsons, many served throughout China and there are Muslim communities scattered across the country who can trace their genealogies back to him. The largest number, however, remained in Yunnan. His eldest son, Nasir al-Din (Ch. Na-su-la-ding), also held a high office in Yunnan, and is commonly credited with providing the source for the traditional Han Chinese surnames that all Muslims were required by the state to adopt during the Ming period (1368–1644). In Yunnan, after Ma (the surname which derives from the transliteration of the name of the Prophet Mohammad) the most common surnames for Muslims are Na, Su, La, and Ding.

During the early part of the Ming period, the emperor Yongle ordered Zheng He, a Muslim eunuch from Yunnan, to lead a series of massive naval expeditions to explore the known world.[11] In all, between 1405 and 1432, seven major expeditions were launched, involving hundreds of Chinese vessels and thousands of tons of goods and valuables to be traded throughout the southeast Asian archipelago, the Indian Ocean, and as far as the east coast of Africa. The success of these trading expeditions was no doubt in part due to Zheng He's religion and his ability to interact with many of the Muslim rulers and merchants encountered along the way. However, shortly after the death of the Yongle emperor, China's cosmopolitan and international initiatives gave way to a period of conservatism and the redirection of imperial resources toward domestic issues and projects. During this period numerous laws were passed requiring "foreigners" to dress like Chinese, adopt Chinese surnames, speak Chinese, and essentially to become Chinese in appearance. It was also during this time that Ming officials changed the character used to denote the Muslims (Hui), by adding the "dog" radical to the character. Although historically the "dog" and "insect" radicals have been incorporated into the names given to many of the non-Han Chinese peoples living within and bordering on China, this is the only case I know of in which a derogatory radical was added to an ethnonym.[12]

In 1644, the Qing dynasty was established by the Manchu, marking the second time China was ruled by "barbarians." Having succeeded in conquering China, the Manchus seemed determined to become "more Chinese than the Chinese." However, at least during this period, travel restrictions were lifted, and the Hui were once again allowed to make the pilgrimage to Mecca and study in the major centers of learning in the Islamic world. During this period several Hui scholars from Yunnan studied abroad and when they returned they started a movement to revitalize Islamic studies in Yunnan by translating the most important Islamic texts into Chinese and thus making them more accessible.

Population Explosion and the Arrival of "Avaricious" Han

The Qing dynasty in Chinese history represented a period of unparalleled growth and expansion, both in terms of territory and population. Partially as a result of the introduction of food crops[13] from the New World, China experienced a massive population explosion resulting in the migration of millions of Han Chinese from Central China into the frontier regions and other areas that had previously been considered undesirable, and thus had remained inhabited primarily by indigenous peoples.[14]

As a border region known for its abundance of natural resources (including timber, precious metals, and fertile land), Yunnan became a popular destination for millions of Han Chinese migrants. According to the calculations of historical demographer James Z. Lee, between 1775 and 1850 the population of Yunnan more than doubled, from 4 million to 10 million. Fueling this large scale migration of Han Chinese were government incentives such as tax remissions, travel funds, and land grants.[15]

As large numbers of Han Chinese immigrants moved into Yunnan, there were increasing numbers of clashes between them and both the indigenous peoples and the Hui (who had already lived there for almost seven hundred years at that point in time). It appears that Han Chinese from the heartland viewed the border regions as uninhabited, since the majority of the population there were not Han.[16] Perhaps, like white settlers throughout much of the world, these new immigrants felt entitled to the resources of "their" state, regardless of whether or not "others" were already in possession of them.[17]

One well-documented case involved the Lisu people who lived in heavily forested regions of Yunnan. As a result of land alienation and the destruction of the forests in which they lived by immigrant Han, the Lisu saw their way of life threatened. The Han immigrants had discovered that the trees of the forests, when cut down, served as excellent growing beds for mushrooms, which once harvested could be transported north to the cities of Jiangsu and Zhejiang and sold at a significant profit. In this way, entire mountainsides were deforested, and the consequent soil erosion left the land permanently barren. Complaints to local Han Chinese officials were ignored, and eventually the Lisu, together with Tai and Yi villagers, organized an attack on the Han settlers in which hundreds were killed.[18] Their attempt to regain control of their land and lives was quickly and brutally suppressed by the state.[19] The significance of the multi-ethnic component of this uprising has been noted by Christian Daniels:

> Although this uprising did not last long, and was soon put down by the Qing army, the fact that a multi-ethnic force was raised, almost spontaneously, within such a short period bespeaks deep-seated common grievances against Han settlers among different ethnic groups. Moreover, since the Lisu and the Yi practised swidden agriculture on hill slopes, while the Tai engaged in wet rice cultivation on the valley floors, it also shows that the grievances were so ubiquitous that they transcended the great variations in elevation, a topographical factor which historically helped to reduce ethnic conflict between groups engaged in different forms of agriculture.[20]

During this period the immigrants also came into conflict with the Hui of Yunnan. Most of these conflicts concerned mining rights in rural areas, and economic disputes in towns and cities. When the Hui brought their grievances to the attention of local officials, the officials repeatedly sided with the immigrants, who like themselves were Han Chinese from the heartland (China's traditional "law of avoidance" policy required that officials not be assigned to their place of origin). Although many of the other non-Han peoples who came into conflict with the new immigrants chose to retreat up into the hills or further afield,[21] the Hui were determined to remain where they were, insisting that they receive equal protection under the law.

As disputes escalated into violence, more and more Hui were killed. Officials not only stood by, but in several instances participated in the killing of the Hui and the confiscation of their property. Local Muslim leaders sent envoys to Beijing to petition the emperor to investigate the escalating violence, but to no avail. Between 1839 and 1856 there was a series of massacres of Muslims in Yunnan in which thousands of men, women, and children were killed.[22] The last of these took place in the provincial capital of Kunming, and was carried out with the assistance of the local government officials.[23] Only 40 or 50 individuals are said to have survived from Kunming's Muslim population of 20,000. Men, women, and children were indiscriminately murdered by government forces under the pretext that reports had been received that the Hui were plotting against the state. The carnage was such that the mother of an official is reported to have reprimanded her son for his role in the slaughter. After noticing a fetus which was still moving among a pile of naked dead bodies, she sought him out and demanded to know: "All these things were done by men, why do women have to suffer the consequences? How could you have been so viciously cruel?"[24]

At this point in time the Muslims of Yunnan decided to organize themselves into an army to defend themselves and overthrow the government. They chose as their leader Du Wenxiu, a local well-educated Muslim who had already passed the first level of the civil service examination. He took for his title "Sultan Sulaiman" in Arabic, and "Generalissimo" in Chinese (*zongtong bingma dayuanshuai*). For their capital they chose the city of Dali in northwest Yunnan.[25] Located in the center of a long narrow fertile plain alongside a large lake on one side and high mountains on the other, Dali could be approached only through two mountain passes, each of which was guarded by a walled city at the northern and southern tips of the plain.

The Muslim rebels quickly recruited not only other Muslims, but indigenous peoples who had also suffered at the hands of Han Chinese immigrants and local officials.[26] In addition, they were able to gain the support of many of the Han Chinese who, like themselves, had settled in Yunnan centuries earlier. Within a short period of time half of the province was under their control, and their state developed their own system of government, intermixing Islamic traditions and Chinese offices.

The state survived for almost 16 years, and in many respects was a model of a multi-ethnic government. During this period Du Wenxiu and his followers were able to resist the advances of the Qing army because the bulk of the government forces had been deployed to even more serious rebellions in other parts of the country. By the early 1870s, however, having quelled the other uprisings, the emperor decided to concentrate his forces on crushing Du Wenxiu and his independent state. As the Qing forces marched across the province towards the rebels' capital in Dali, the Hui communities they encountered were decimated, and hundreds of thousands of Muslims were killed. In January of 1873, government forces were finally able to penetrate the city of Dali. Du Wenxiu, acknowledging imminent defeat, decided to surrender to the Qing forces in the hopes of convincing the Qing officials to spare the civilian population. The Qing military commander, Yang Yuke, promised to honor the terms of his surrender and soldiers were billeted in Muslim homes. For three days the cease-fire was enforced, but when the military leaders of the rebellion were invited to a banquet, they were beheaded upon arrival. Immediately thereafter a prearranged signal was given to begin the massacre of the Muslim population of Dali. The soldiers began by first killing the Muslims with whom they had been living, and then proceeded to kill every Muslim they could find in the city. Thousands were killed over the next few days.[27]

Only the Muslim followers of the rebellion were killed; Yi, Bai, and Han Chinese followers who surrendered were spared. Some Muslims fled to nearby Thailand, and their descendants still live there,[28] while others fled to Burma or neighboring provinces. Scholars estimate the prerebellion Muslim population to have been between 800,000 and one million, of whom it is estimated as many as 90% were killed. Of those who survived many fled the region.[29]

Another consequence of the rebellion was a series of government regulations severely restricting the lives of the Muslims who survived. Those who lived in villages lost their homes and land and were forced to become tenant farmers; those who lived in the main cities lost their homes, businesses, and communal property and were no longer allowed to live within city walls. The Hui of Dali still refer to the sign which appeared over the main gate of the city after the final defeat of the uprising: "Traitorous Hui Not Allowed" (*buzhun ni-Hui jincheng*). It was not until a Hui from Kunming happened to be appointed to an official position in Dali in 1917 that the sign was finally taken down.[30] There are also reports that students in Hui communities were forbidden to sit for the civil examinations.[31] Many Muslim villages throughout the province became ghost towns and were occupied by immigrant Han and the soldiers whom the Qing government had recruited to suppress the uprising. Today these villages are Han villages, but in several cases if you look closely at the gravestones along the hillsides you can see that they all face in one direction, towards Mecca. (Han Chinese gravestones, by contrast, usually face in a variety of directions given the particular *fengshui* of individual grave sites.)

With limited access to land and resources, many Hui returned to occupations that they had dominated for centuries in China: trade, transport, and caravansaries. The Muslims of China have always been part of extensive travel networks throughout the country as well as into the neighboring regions of Southeast Asia and Central Asia. In the past (and down to this day) these networks have been used by Muslims traveling for trade, on pilgrimages, and to study under prominent Islamic teachers in other regions. It was through these trades that many Hui sought to reconstruct their communities and their lives.

When first interviewing Muslims in this part of China, I was struck by the frequent references to their historical experiences. This phenomenon was especially common in the region around Dali which had borne the brunt of the fury of the Chinese imperial troops. Residents of Dali today describe in graphic detail the slaughter of women and children, as if they are remembering something they had witnessed in their own lifetime. Outside Dali there is a place along a riverbed known as "The Pile of Ten-thousands." According to local residents and historical documents, it is the site at which a large number of the Muslim civilian population of Dali were brutally executed. After the city had finally fallen, the Qing officials announced they would spare the lives of those who had survived the first wave of massacres (mostly women and children) if they agreed to come out of hiding and vacate the city. Believing the officials, the Hui women and children left their hiding places and surrendered. They were then ordered to march north of the city, and by the side of a river they were murdered and their dead or dying bodies thrown in. Every year, on the anniversary of the date of the massacre, services are held at that site and prayers said to honor those who lost their lives there.

Understanding Survival

In every region I visited, when discussing the Du Wenxiu uprising, I always made the point of asking individual Hui why and how they thought their communities had survived this catastrophe. The most common response to "why" was, "because of our faith" or "because of Islam." The most common response to "how" was "because of the sacrifices made by Hui women." Among the small number of Muslims who were able to survive the massacres, it seems the majority were young women. Apparently government soldiers, officials, and other men allowed these women to live for the sole purpose of forcing them into concubinage. Others, on the other hand, chose to profit from the massacres by selling off the survivors as chattel. One eyewitness account by a Westerner traveling through Yunnan at the time describes witnessing, "Muhammadan women and children and booty all sold together in a veritable bazaar outside the governor's yamen."[32]

Although many of the women refused to live as concubines and expressed their refusal by committing suicide (the accepted and traditional form of protest allowed Chinese women), others agreed, provided they be given custody of a certain number of any children which might result from the union.[33] In some cases the woman agreed to give the man the first-born son, on condition that she could raise all the other children as Muslims; in another arrangement all the sons would go to the father, but the daughters to the mother. If the men did not agree to this arrangement, the woman threatened suicide, which was clearly not an idle threat. Upon the eventual death of the man, the woman was then allowed to leave the household with whichever children had been allocated as hers, in search of a Muslim community that had survived.

Because there were households in which the sons took their father's surname and the daughters retained their mother's, over time there were villages in which one family would have several different surnames. In other cases, no agreements or arrangements were made, and women were simply forced into concubinage. Even in these cases, though, I heard several stories in which sympathetic husbands chose to allow their secondary wives to retain their faith and religious customs. In some households the mothers secretly taught their children about their history and religion, and when the children were old enough to marry and move away they reclaimed their faith. There were also cases in which Bai, Han, and other non-Hui families who had adopted Hui children told the children they were

Muslim and allowed them to leave their homes when they became adults, in search of their relatives and other Hui.[34]

There were of course many Hui women who were not able to pass on their faith and identity to their children. In a small town in Eryuan county, north of Dali, I met an elderly Bai scholar. In addition to being the local historian, he also knew well the story of his own grandmother:

> My grandmother's father had served as an official in Du Wenxiu's administration. Following the defeat of the uprising, the whole family decided to commit suicide by drinking an opium potion, believing it was "better to be a shattered vessel of jade, than an unbroken piece of pottery." In the end, though, they could not bear to have my grandmother die, as she was the youngest. So they entrusted her to one of the family servants, giving him many of the family's valuables and asking him to take her to safety. Eventually they ended up in Bingyang, and later she was married off to a Bai man from Eryuan county.

Despite the knowledge of his own family background, this elderly gentleman identified himself as Bai, though he did have very close relations with the Hui in town.

In some instances individual women are credited with the survival and rebirth of entire villages. The following account was related to me by an elderly Hui teacher in Dali:

> There was a village called Xiawu in Yunlong, where more than ten thousand Hui used to live. This village was in fact recovered by two people, a mother and her daughter. After the defeat of Du Wenxiu there were very few survivors, and the town was left uninhabited. Among the survivors though there were a mother and her 7- or 8-year-old daughter who was taken away by force by a local military officer. The mother secretly followed her all the way to Yongping where the officer lived, and opened a small food stand close to his house in order to keep watch over her daughter. Eventually she was able to make contact with her and they began to plot her escape. A few years later when the daughter was 12 or 13, they managed to escape and returned to Xiawu, which had become a ghost town. They lived in the mountains above the village until the anti-Hui policies ceased to be enforced there.[35] They then returned home, set up house, married, and started families, and thus the village was able to gain a new lease on life.

According to the recollections of an elderly Hui woman in Dali (that were recorded in the 1950s), eighteen Hui families were spared during the massacres as the result of the efforts of a single young woman. Apparently during the occupation of Dali, the Qing military official Yang Yuke noticed a young woman of exceptional beauty and took her to be his concubine. She agreed to the arrangement under the condition that certain families be spared. According to one Hui historian, this kind of arrangement was not uncommon.[36] When the Hui spoke of their foremothers this way, it was always with great pride, and never in hushed tones of shame or dishonor.

Engendering Survival

That such arrangements existed, and apparently played a significant role in the rebuilding of a decimated community, raises a myriad of questions and calls to mind both the targeting of women and the extreme sacrifices forced upon them during periods of mass violence and genocide. That women should be the ones ultimately responsible for the survival of a community is not a fact lost on those determined to wipe out said community. In the introduction to their work, *Woman-Nation-State,* Floya Anthias and Nira Yuval-Davis identify five major (although not exclusive) ways in which women have tended to participate in ethnic and national processes and in relation to state practices. These are:

a) as biological reproducers of members of ethnic collectivities;
b) as reproducers of the boundaries of ethnic/national groups;
c) as participating centrally in the ideological reproduction of the collectivity and as transmitters of its culture;
d) as signifiers of ethnic/national differences;
e) as participants in national, economic, political and military struggles.[37]

The Muslim women of Yunnan provide a clear example of how these roles have been both forced upon women and actively taken up by them.

What is so striking about the case in China is that the women survived and were able to recreate Muslim communities by taking advantage of men's propensity in war to view women as "loot" to be plundered or victory trophies to be displayed. In addition, unlike the recent situation among Muslim communities in the Balkans, it appears that the Chinese Muslim women and their children were not stigmatized by surviving communities, but instead accepted back into the fold of communities when they finally had the chance to leave their positions of forced concubinage.

Societal use of shame and dishonor to further persecute women, who have already suffered grievous bodily and psychological abuse at the hands of men, represents just one of the ways in which women have not been viewed as individual human beings but as representatives of particular communities, cultures, and nations. In her work on the Holocaust, Judith Tydor Baumel writes of the "double jeopardy" faced by Jewish women during the Nazi period, who were persecuted by the Nazis in gender-specific ways, as well as because they were Jews.[38] However, many women in other periods of mass violence have faced what one could call a "triple jeopardy." Perhaps most egregious should women survive the violence perpetuated against them by the enemy was the subsequent wrath, scorn, and condemnation they had to endure from the men of their own communities. Such extremely vindictive traditions have led many men to simply kill the women in their families to avoid even the possibility of their being defiled, or to encourage the women to take their own lives. During the partition period both Hindu and Sikh women were particularly vulnerable to attacks from within their own communities. In their work on the partition period, Menon and Bhasin document numerous cases of men either killing the female members of their households or pressuring them into committing suicide by swallowing poison, drowning themselves, or throwing themselves upon huge fires set for that purpose.[39]

Wombs as Occupied Territory

In their book on women and the partition period in India, authors Ritu Menon and Kamla Bhasin have also incorporated recent analysis of events in Bosnia-Herzegovina to more clearly illuminate past periods of mass violence. With regard to the role of widespread rape during the partition period, they quote Stasa Zajovic's description of the mass rapes in Bosnia-Herzegovina during which "the female womb becomes occupied territory."[40] According to a wide range of sources, in Bosnia-Herzegovina Serbian men would often tell women as they raped them that they would now have to give birth to a Serb child.[41] In fact, although many of the mothers are reported to have rejected these babies upon their birth, the Muslim community did not consider them Serbs. In her ethnography of a Muslim Bosnian community, Tone Bringa notes:

> The fundamental difference between the perception of their collective identity by Bosnian Muslims and Serbs is clearly brought out in the horrific example of the mass rape of Muslim women by Serbs in northern and eastern Bosnia. While the Bosnian Serbs argued that the children who were born as a result of these rapes would be Serbs because they had "Serb blood," the head of the Bosnian Islamic community, *reisul-ulema* Mustafa Ceric, declared that the babies, if born to and brought up by these Muslim women, would be Muslims. His argument was based, however, not on "shared blood" but on the moral superiority and strength of the Muslim women in relation to their Serbian rapists. Reis Mustafa Ceric was supported in this by a fatwa issued by the Sunni Islamic scholars at Al-Azhar University in Cairo.[42]

That the Bosnian Muslim community should respond so quickly with a religiously based means by which to embrace these infants — the living evidence of brutal attacks — within the community, and pave the way for the acceptance of the women as well, initially led me to assume there was an historical precedent. But as yet, I have not been able to identify any other examples of the use of fatwas to defuse such potentially explosive situations as that found in Bosnia.

Although it is commonly held that in Islamic societies children inherit their religion from their father, in fact there is a *hadith* (collected accounts of the sayings and actions of the Prophet Mohammad) that deals specifically with the issue of children born to parents of whom one is Muslim and one is not. According to this hadith (Sahih al-Bukhari), the child is considered Muslim, because Islam "overcomes" other religions.[43] Moreover, as there is no concept of "purity of blood" within the Islamic tradition, these children, although clearly of mixed parentage, are not considered defiled or somehow tainted.

It is worth noting, as a point of comparison, that during the partition period in India, government agencies were established in both India and Pakistan to "recover" women left behind when their families fled. In many cases it took months, if not years, to find these women and return them to their families. According to Kamlaben Patel, a social worker who was stationed in Lahore between 1947 and 1952 and who was actively involved in the recovery operation, there were distinct differences in the degrees of willingness among Sikh, Hindu, and Muslim communities to accept women and children who had been "recovered." She writes, "It was not so important for the Muslims because they did not think of the woman as impure, but the Hindus did. With Muslims there was no problem about women's impurity and they hesitated much less when taking them back. This was my experience. A Hindu woman felt that she had been made impure, had become sullied, and was no longer *pativrata*. A Muslim woman did not feel like this. It was not in her blood, it is in our blood. We feel we have been polluted, we are no longer worthy of showing our faces in public... And Muslim women were not stigmatized by society."[43] These concepts of impurity and taintedness were passed on to the untold hundreds, if not thousands, of children born to women abducted during partition. The fate of these children was a fiercely debated topic, some insisting that the children remain with the fathers, while others that they be "recovered" with their mothers and returned to their communities. It soon became clear that babies born to Hindu mothers raped by non-Hindu men would not be accepted by their communities, whereas those born to Muslim women raped by non-Muslim men were much more likely to be accepted. Consequently the law was adapted to reflect these cultural concepts of identity: "the government passed an ordinance to say that those (Hindu) women whose babies were born in Pakistan after Partition would have to leave them behind, but those (Muslims) whose children were born in India, could keep them."[45]

In China, as in India/Pakistan, Muslim communities were able to accept and adopt as fully theirs the children born to Muslim women who had been raped by non-Muslim men. In both instances they were large Muslim communities who had lived among other communities for years, often intermarrying.

Fluid Concepts of Ethnicity

"It is the belief that counts, not the ethnic group."[46]

Although the Hui of China have always considered themselves to be a separate people, they are also fully aware that their ancestors intermarried with Han Chinese, and other ethnic groups for hundreds of years. In addition to intermarriage between Muslim men and non-Muslim women, over the centuries the Muslim communities throughout China acquired the custom of adopting abandoned Han children and purchasing children from parents selling them. Selling children in China, although not encouraged, was an acceptable practice during periods of famine or a family financial crisis. I do not know if the custom of adopting children is common in Muslim minority communities in other parts of the world, or is unique to China. However, given the special status accorded orphans within Islam, and the numerous Qur'anic injunctions and *hadith* enjoining Muslims to take care of orphans (as well as widows), and the lack of any concepts of purity of race in Islam, it should not be surprising that children adopted into the faith should be so readily accepted.

Another example of more flexible attitudes with regard to traditional familial practices is the long tradition among the Muslims of Yunnan of the adoption of sons-in-law into families without sons through marriage to a daughter. The children then take their mother's surname. Although this form of adoption/marriage exists in other parts of China, it is usually highly stigmatized, whereas in Yunnan it is relatively common and accepted.

Although ethnicity (*minzu*) is the category used by both the Chinese government and the different non-Han peoples of China to distinguish themselves, I frequently heard Muslims say their identity was based on faith, not ethnicity. One famous Hui historian tried to explain it to me in metaphysical terms: "When you combine ethnicity and religious belief, you are not simply putting two things together; rather, something new is created through the process of mixing these two things, something with its own unique characteristics." On the other hand, a Bai Muslim who was the head of an Islamic school, identified himself in the following way, "I'm a Bai who believes in Islam."

The fluidity of Hui identity can also be seen in the wide variety of Hui who live in Yunnan. There are for example, Bai-Hui, Zang (Tibetan) -Hui, Dai-Hui, Naxi-Hui, Yi-Hui, and even Wa-Hui.[47] Many of these communities date back to the early centuries of the arrival of Muslims in Yunnan, while others were created in the aftermath of the uprising, when Hui fled to remote areas and hid among other peoples in order to evade Qing forces which continued to kill Hui in the years following the defeat of Du Wenxiu. According to a resident of a Bai-Hui village north of Dali, "We Hui are more adaptable than the Han and more accepting of differences. Some of the Han have lived here as long as the Hui [more than 700 years] and yet unlike us, they have never learned to speak Bai."

There were also cases of individual Muslims who had completely lost their identity as Muslims and then later regained it.[48] While hiking up in the hills behind the city of Eryuan, I happened to meet a Hui peasant grazing his cow. We started to chat, and he told me of his own family's history:

> My great grandfather was from a Muslim family in Zhihua, and was the only member of his family to escape the killing. He was 7 or 8 years old when it took place and fled to Sanbeimen village where he was adopted by a Han family. He married a Han woman and had two sons; the older son — my grandfather — married a Han girl. None of the infants she gave birth to survived. He then consulted a fortuneteller who told him that he was originally Hui and he could bring his family back to prosperity if he married a Hui woman. He followed the advice and married a Hui woman. The advice proved effective, for subsequently all the children born to the Han wife survived, and the Hui wife also gave birth to many healthy children. The children of each wife followed their mother's ethnic identity, and the entire family lived harmoniously together. It is families like these which explain why there are so many extended families in this area with both Han and Hui parts.[49]

Hui after the Rebellion

In the aftermath of the rebellions, the first priority of the survivors was to pool their resources, rebuild their mosques, and open Islamic schools. Having lost most of their material possessions, they were clearly determined not to lose their religious legacy. This period saw renewed contact with other centers of learning in the Islamic world and the establishment of schools throughout the province.

In 1949, however, with the establishment of the People's Republic of China, all religious groups came under surveillance and suspicion. As Mao Zedong had needed the support of the Muslims in building his new socialist state, promises had been made guaranteeing their religious freedom. This promise, however, ended with the onset of the Cultural Revolution. Red Guards and other zealots targeted the Hui, their mosques, and religious leaders. The Muslims of Yunnan repeatedly sent delegates to Beijing asking for their protection, but to no avail. In the waning years of the Cultural Revolution, a second government massacre of Muslims took place in the town of Shadian, in southeastern Yunnan, a famous center of Islamic learning throughout China and Southeast Asia. The massacre took place in July, 1975, and consisted of several regiments of PLA soldiers occupying the village and systematically destroying it and killing the residents over a period of seven days. In addition to using heavy artillery and cannons, at one point Chinese MIG jet fighters were called in to use their rockets in a series of air strikes. By the end of the week, the entire village had been reduced to rubble; over 1,600 Muslim men, women, and children were killed and over 5,000 wounded. In 1979 the government officially apologized for the incident, rebuilt much of the village, including the mosques, and paid reparations to survivors, and the relatives of those killed.[50]

Muslims throughout Yunnan, as well as Muslims in other parts of China, are well acquainted with details of the massacre at Shadian. It was a topic mentioned to me in every region of Yunnan I visited; sometimes spoken about with rage and anger and at other times in hushed whispers (lest one be overheard), but mostly these stories were told with an almost fatalistic resignation about what happens when Muslims put too much trust in the state.

Throughout the Cultural Revolution, factional violence between different Red Guard groups was responsible for the death of many caught between them. What is now known as the "Shadian Incident" is one of the few cases in which a large number of civilians of one minority group were targeted and killed by the People's Liberation Army during the Cultural Revolution. One other such case involves the Mongols of Inner Mongolia, living in another frontier region. According to recent research by Uradyn Bulag, during the late 1950s and early 1960s the Mongols had been steadfastly working with the state to develop a policy in their autonomous region that supported both government goals and local Mongol cultural traditions. In 1966, however, the outbreak of the Cultural Revolution "provided a perfect pretext for the Chinese, long frustrated at the persistent criticism by and resistance of the Mongols, to crack down on the entire Mongol people. Over 16,222 people were killed by official Chinese count and hundreds of thousands more were tortured in perhaps the bloodiest episode of the Cultural Revolution."[51]

Commemorative Rituals

Today in Yunnan, Muslim communities throughout the province hold annual rites which incorporate local histories and collective memories into more traditional Islamic festivals. In Kunming for example, during the *'Id al-Fitr* celebrations marking the end of Ramadan, Muslims from different regions travel to the tomb of Sayyid 'Ajall where special prayers are held. First there are readings from the Qur'an, then the tomb is swept and cleaned (reminiscent of the traditional Chinese Qingming festival), and then the accomplishments of Sayyid 'Ajall are retold. In conclusion, a special service is held to honor the hundreds of thousands of Muslims killed during the Qing dynasty, and the hundreds slaughtered more recently in Shadian.

In Shadian itself, they have built a pillar commemorating those killed during the Cultural Revolution, and the ceremony focuses on the two massacres separated in time, but linked in memory.

In Dali the largest ceremony takes place just north of the city along the banks of a river at the site known as "The Pile of Ten-thousands." Every year services are held at that site, and prayers said to honor those who lost their lives there. The date of this ceremony is determined by the traditional Chinese calendar and is tied to the actual date of the event. This ceremony is attended by Muslims from throughout the region; government officials, leading imams, and local leaders are all invited. During these ceremonies the wealthier villagers provide food for everyone, and after the Qur'an is recited and the dead remembered, participants eat a meal together. Other communities have similar commemorations, usually at sites marking the worst atrocities, on a date calculated by either the traditional Chinese or Islamic calendar.[52] In his work on the Holocaust, Charles S. Maier comments on why such ceremonies tend to take place at sites most evocative of particularly graphic memories/images: "In its impulse to be retrieved and not to be explained, collective memory must claim some liturgical impulse... Since the objective is not causal sequencing but access to vivid and intense past experiences, collective memories tend to focus not on the long history of an ethnic people but on their most painful incidents of victimization... *Chacun a sa memoire* — the retrieval and reliving of a moment of transcendent victimhood is a people's choice."[53]

Throughout Yunnan, Muslim communities have chosen specific days on which to commemorate those killed during this period, usually the date of the fall of the village to Qing forces. Thus while some ceremonies have been tied to a religious date, others are tied to the date of an event.[54] The ceremonies themselves are all quite simple, and over the years attendance varies. In one village I was told that recently the women of the community had begun to take a more active role in the ceremonies. Given the very active role played by women during the recent revival of Islamic education in Yunnan, this development is not surprising.[55] In several different communities elder Muslims told me that in the years "after liberation" attendance at these ceremonies had fallen off; perhaps as the Hui came to believe that what had happened was history, and no longer as relevant to contemporary society. Events like Shadian, however, changed that, and I was told that afterwards the commemorative ceremonies took on another significance. Thus, the identity of the Muslims of Yunnan today is even more clearly linked to their fallen brethren.

Legacies: A Tale of Two Villages

At this point in time it would be difficult to document the range of ways in which the massacres of the late Qing period have influenced the social structures, outlooks, and collective memories of the different Muslim communities of Yunnan. There are however two distinct phenomena I noticed during my years of residence in Yunnan: the first is cross regional, while the other is region specific. In 1996, upon completing my early history of the Hui of Yunnan, I set about visiting different regions of Yunnan, and asking every Hui I met the following question: "What do you think is the most important challenge facing the Hui today?" As someone who had lived in China during the early 1980s when there was still an extraordinary level of state control over peoples' lives, but also a feeling of personal safety and political stability, I had assumed people would speak of the recent increase in crime, growing disparities of income, and general uncertainty about the state's future plans. Instead, what I heard about again and again throughout the province was the lack of education among the Hui, and the importance of improving their educational opportunities. I was rather taken aback by this answer, and at first would forget my supposedly objective "outsider" position, and immediately respond, "What do you mean?! The Hui have one of the highest average levels of education of any of the peoples of Yunnan, even higher than the Han." No one with whom I spoke, even the school leaders, were aware of this statistic, and perhaps it was irrelevant, for clearly, given the ubiquitousness of the response, education was seen as the key to the future.[56] It also became clear that when speaking of education they were speaking of both state-sponsored education and the religious education supported by individual communities. Perhaps like other groups who have lived through years of instability, and been the target of state-sponsored persecution, the Muslims of Yunnan have chosen to concentrate on the one resource which, once acquired, cannot be taken away from them.

The other phenomenon I noticed while visiting different regions of Yunnan were the striking disparities in living conditions and subtle differences in outlook among inhabitants. In some regions most individuals with whom I spoke exuded confidence in their future, and the future of Islam in their communities. In others, it seemed people had still not recovered from the aftermath of the Du Wenxiu uprising. In most cases, the present condition of a village or town could be directly related to the Qing government's policy in that particular region.[57] At one end of a spectrum lay the prosperous villages of Najiaying and Gucheng in south central Yunnan; they belonged to an established settlement of Muslims dating back to the Yuan dynasty with a very active religious community. At the other lay the villages of Tengchong county, where small numbers of Hui were scattered throughout a large area of Han Chinese villages, and where there was little, if any, religious activity in the villages with Muslim households.

Today Najiaying and Gucheng enjoy an exceptionally high standard of living. Small factories abound throughout the community, attracting migrant workers from as far away as Sichuan and Guizhou. According to local Muslim residents the Han and Hui in the area have always lived peacefully together and today the Hui assist those poorer Han Chinese living in their area, paving roads and installing electric lines for those who cannot afford the expenses and offering free training and instruction in how to open and operate small factories. Local Muslim leaders make a point of regularly inviting government officials and Han Chinese to all major religious events, as well as inviting representatives of the major government bureaucracies to give presentations on the responsibilities of their offices.

When asked to explain the long history of close relations with non-Muslim residents and neighboring villages, the elders of Najiaying and Gucheng talk about events surrounding the Du Wenxiu uprising and their survival. In the tense years leading up to the outbreaks of violence in Yunnan, the leaders of the Han and Hui villages in this area formulated a "mutual protection" agreement (*hubao*). At that particular point in time, relations between the Han and Hui were especially close because prominent men from both communities had recently returned from Beijing where they had sat for the imperial examinations.

The "mutual protection" agreement called on each community to guarantee the safety of the other community should it come under attack. During the course of the uprising, in fact, many areas of Yunnan were alternately under attack by either government forces or Du Wenxiu's followers. In Najiaying and Gucheng, if government soldiers arrived, the Han would come forward and claim there were no Hui there, and, when Du Wenxiu's forces arrived the Hui would come forward and claim there were no Han. It is said that during this period of massacres throughout the province, the only residents of these villages to be killed were those who panicked and fled the confines of the village. Someone noted that in another Hui village, only 15 kilometers away, 700 people were killed and that this village, which had had a much larger population than Najiaying and Gucheng, now had approximately only one fifth of its original population.

The situation in Tengchong was striking in its contrast. After arriving in the city and getting directions to the Hui communities scattered north over a wide plain, I set off. After a bus ride and a long walk I ended up in a small village that was the poorest I had ever encountered that was not located in the hills. After numerous inquiries I was finally able to locate the mosque. It was almost unrecognizable as such, save for the unique Arabic calligraphy inscribed over the entry to the courtyard.[58]

The mosque itself was a small wooden structure, with white-washed walls, and some calligraphy painted along the sides and on the *mihrab* (a niche in the front wall of a mosque indicating the direction of Mecca). A half curtain separated the men's from the women's prayer space. On the front of the mosque there were painted slogans dating from the Cultural Revolution declaring, "Long live Chairman Mao, our brightly shining red sun." The prayer hall looked out on to a small moss-covered courtyard. The courtyard was bare, except for two trees. I noticed large pieces of oddly shaped stones lying up against the base of the trees and went to investigate. They were the top halves of Muslim gravestones which had been vandalized during the Cultural Revolution, and later returned to the mosque by the Han villagers.

I spent the day wandering around the area and speaking to as many Muslims as I could find. They all spoke of the poverty of the region and their general lack of strong religious community. I later learned that this part of Yunnan had been the last holdout of Du Wenxiu's forces, lasting several months past the capture of the headquarters in Dali. Consequently, the Qing army instituted especially punitive policies in the aftermath of the uprising. The Hui who survived were forcibly resettled throughout the region in Han villages. By placing two or three Hui families in 16 different Han villages, and assigning three Han families to "supervise" (*guanli*) each Hui family, the Qing government had developed an effective means by which to hinder any effort on the part of the Hui to rebuild their community. I later learned that approximately 80 Hui from this area had managed to escape and fled to a remote border region inhabited by the Wa people. Not only did the Wa apparently agree to let the Hui settle in their territory, but eventually Hui were given tribal titles and responsibilities.[59]

In almost all areas of Yunnan, the Hui that survived the massacres suffered under policies established by Qing officials and implemented by local individuals. Many, in an effort to escape these restrictions became traders.[60] In some areas groups of ten to twenty Hui families organized themselves into "*gong*" or associations, which allowed them to more effectively defend themselves and pool their limited resources to carry out certain projects. The rebuilding of mosques and the establishment of Islamic schools were two of the most important projects.

Rebuilding Identities

Over the past century the Hui of Yunnan have gradually rebuilt their lives and communities, though their population today, estimated at 400,000, is still less than half of what it was a century ago. Recently there has been a major revival in Islamic education in the region; Islamic schools for all ages have been established, and a growing number of Muslim students have left China to study in centers of Islamic learning in the Middle East and Southeast Asia. When asked what explained this recent resurgence in Islamic education, community members cited two main factors: a desire on their part to rebuild that which was taken from them, and the hope that a strong religious faith would help protect Muslim communities from the myriad of social problems presently besetting China in this day and age of rapid economic development. Some of the main consequences of this economic restructuring include the dismantling of the state-sponsored social welfare system, widespread layoffs from state-owned enterprises, and a growing disparity in incomes.

As I traveled across China visiting Islamic schools and colleges I sensed a growing air of confidence among Muslims of all ages about their future, and the future of China. Older people, who have suffered through a lifetime of religious persecution and extreme poverty, finally see a time in which they can openly practice their religion, study in Islamic classes organized specifically for them, send their grandchildren to Muslim daycares, and have the rest of the family take part in evening or summer classes. Throughout the country Muslim communities are pooling their resources to build mosques (usually abandoning the traditional Chinese architecture and replacing it with a style which can best be described as "neo-pseudo Arabic"). Many communities have also built large multistoried classroom buildings, which are filled with students of all ages in the evenings. In the villages more and more young women are deciding to wear a veil. Although Muslim communities in different regions of China have always had their own traditional form of veil, they had usually only been worn by elderly women or women in rural areas. Today, however, "modern" veils made of synthetic fabrics are all the rage, and seen on even young girls.

As Islam flourishes throughout most of China, many Muslim communities are recreating and expanding their ties with the greater Islamic world. In March of 1999 I traveled to Cairo and Damascus to interview Chinese Muslim students studying at prominent centers of Islamic learning. Over the past ten years a rapidly growing number of Chinese Muslims have been allowed to travel overseas to further their Islamic studies.[61] This phenomenon is a continuation of practices that have existed for centuries — when Muslims from China made the pilgrimage to Mecca many stopped along the way for extended periods to study in different centers of Islamic learning. This new wave of Chinese Muslim students is especially important, for they are arriving at these centers of Islamic learning during a period of intensive reflection within Islamic communities on what it means to be a Muslim today. At these universities they meet local Muslim students, but also students like themselves, Muslims who are minorities in their homeland, and Muslims from countries in the midst of economic reform and the social unrest created by rapid economic development. With Arabic as their *lingua franca*, students from as wide a variety of places as Bosnia, Australia, Tajikistan, the Philippines, the United States, Kenya, Russia, and Thailand form communities; studying together in programs that usually last from two to six years. As these young people meet and exchange stories of their own communities, what will it mean to the Chinese Muslims to hear other Muslim minorities telling them of similar histories of persecution, perseverance, and survival? Will they start to remember their own history in a different light, and reanimate the stories that have been passed down to them with a different understanding?

Conclusion

Although women have always been targets of violence in times of war, the recent well-documented atrocities perpetuated against the women of Bosnia and Kosovo have allowed scholars to further their understanding of the relationship between men, war, and women and to re-examine earlier instances. In her excellent article, "The Second Front: The Logic of Sexual Violence in Wars," Ruth Seifert seeks to answer the question: "What function does rape fulfill in wartime and what strategic purpose is served by sexual violence against women?" She answers, in part, "Sexual violence against women is likely to destroy a nation's culture. In times of war, the women are those who hold the families and the community together. Their physical and emotional destruction aims at destroying social and cultural stability... The destruction of women and/or their integrity affects overall cultural cohesion... The rape of women of a community, culture, or nation can be regarded — and is so regarded — as a symbolic rape of the body of that community." [62]

She also touches on the concept of rape as a form of pollution: "This idea was present in Bangladesh as well as Berlin in 1945 (the idea of subverting the 'pure race' Aryan project) and is an outspoken strategy of the Serbs in Bosnia who claim to imprint their identity on the Bosnian population by producing 'little chetniks' or Serbs. Pollution is, thus, envisaged in two ways. First there is a racist idea of contaminating the other community's blood and genes. Second, pollution also refers to dissolving a group's spirit and identity."[63]

Unfortunately there is no known written record left by the Muslim women of Yunnan describing their lives as part of non-Muslim households. Among the many questions that come to mind are the following: How were women treated by other members of the household? Were they able to maintain contact with other women in similar positions? How did they deal with the devastation of their communities, and loss of their families? How many were actually allowed to leave, and were promises of custody of their children honored? What happened to the children (usually sons) that had become part of the father's household, and were any of them allowed to follow their mother? When finally given the opportunity to leave, what were the challenges these women faced?[64]

Nevertheless, despite the extraordinary losses Muslim women experienced, and the untold hardships many of them faced, these women were finally able to undermine the efforts of both the Qing officials and many of the immigrant Han to destroy the Hui people.

One final legacy of this period is the recent very active role played by Muslim women in the revival of Islamic education. During his rule as Sultan Sulaiman, Du Wenxiu decreed that all children, including girls, were to be educated. Down to this day women have played a very active role in all aspects of education. I interviewed dozens of women attending Islamic schools and colleges and was repeatedly struck by their commitment to their religion and to working as teachers themselves. Many had settled in remote areas to work in newly established Muslim community schools, while others helped establish schools just for girls. The long-term benefits of women's education were quite clear to them for, as one woman put it to me, "Educate a woman, educate a nation."

In many respects the Muslim women of Yunnan enjoy a unique position compared to Muslim women in other parts of China. When Muslims from other regions visit Yunnan, they are shocked by the relatively open-minded attitude regarding gender roles and expectations. On the other hand, Yunnan Muslims who visit Muslim communities in the northwest speak of being utterly appalled by the extremely chauvinistic attitudes (in Chinese, *"zhongnan — qingnu"*) prevalent in those areas. They attribute these values to the adoption of traditional Han Chinese social values concerning the role of women.

The relationship between the decision of the Muslims of Yunnan to honor the role played by their female ancestors in the preservation of their communities, and the present-day more equitable attitude regarding gender roles, is not known. Have women always been especially appreciated in these communities, which would explain why their sacrifices in the aftermath of the rebellion were positively acknowledged, or do women today enjoy a relatively privileged status as a consequence of their earlier actions? Regardless, it appears that communities can gather strength and develop positive collective identities by acknowledging the efforts made by women to ensure their survival and future.

After months of reading about ethnic- and religious-based mass violence and genocide, I find I am no closer to understanding exactly what preconditions allow for such outbreaks, or whether there are societies immune to such violence. In conclusion, I would simply like to reiterate the importance of studying the different ways in which women have survived these periods of mass violence, for these massacres are continuing, and women continue to be targeted for violence as symbols of a community's future, for they are the ones left to rebuild it. At this point in time there are approximately 14 million refugees in the world, most of them women and children, and approximately two-thirds of them Muslim. The case of the Muslim women of Yunnan is especially compelling, for it is a story of survival in which the violence perpetuated against the female population has not been made a source of shame, but rather a badge of honor.

Acknowledgments

I would like to thank Yukiko Hanawa for encouraging me to write this article for *Traces*, and Mara Thomas, Gail Hershatter, and Mark Selden for their thoughtful comments on earlier drafts. I would also like to thank my research assistants Li Bo and Ma Yu, and the many Hui of Yunnan for sharing their history with me.

Bibliography

Armijo-Hussein, Jacqueline. "The Recent Resurgence of Islamic Education in China." *International Institute for the Study of Islam in the Modern World Newsletter*, 4 (1999).

Armijo-Hussein, Jacqueline. "Sayyid 'Ajall Shams al-Din: A Muslim from Central Asia, Serving the Mongols in China, and Bringing 'Civilization' to Yunnan." Ph.D. Dissertation, Harvard University, 1997.

Atwill, David. "Islam in the World of Yunnan: Muslim Yunnanese Identity in Nineteenth Century Yunnan." *Journal/Institute Muslim Minority Affairs*, 17(1): (September 1997).

Atwill, David. "Rebellion South of the Clouds: Ethnic Insurgency, Muslim Yunnanese, and the Panthay Rebellion." Ph.D. Dissertation, University of Hawaii, 1999.

Baumel, Judith Tydor. *Double Jeopardy: Gender and the Holocaust.* London: Valentine Mitchell, 1998.

Boyle, John Andrew. *The Successors of Genghis Khan.* New York: Columbia University Press, 1971.

Bringa, Tone. *Being Muslim in the Bosnian Way: Identity and Community in a Central Bosnian Village.* Princeton: Princeton University Press, 1995.

Broomhall, Marshall. *Islam in China: A Neglected Problem.* London: China Inland Mission, 1910.

Bulag, Uradyn E. "Ethnic Resistance with Socialist Characteristics." In Elizabeth J. Perry and Mark Selden, eds. *Chinese Society: Change, Conflict and Resistance.* London and New York: Routledge, 2000.

Daniels, Christian. "Environmental Degradation, Forest Protection and Ethno-history in Yunnan: The Uprising by Swidden Agriculturalists in 1821." *Chinese Environmental History Newsletter* (November 1994).

Ekvall, Robert. *Cultural Relations on the Kansu-Tibetan Border.* Chicago: University of Chicago Press, 1939.

Forbes, Andrew D. W. "History of Panglong, 1875–1900: A Panthay (Chinese Muslim) settlement in the Burmese Wa States." *The Muslim World* 78 (1988): 38–50.

Forbes, Andrew D. W. "The 'Cin-Ho' (Yunnanese Chinese) Muslims of North Thailand." *Journal/Institute of Muslim Minority Affairs*, 21 (1986).

Giladi, Avner. "Saghir." *Encyclopaedia of Islam*, new edition. Leiden: Brill, 1995: VIII: 821–827.

Gladney, Dru. *Muslim Chinese: Ethnic Nationalism in the People's Republic of China.* Cambridge: Harvard University Press, 1991.

Gourevitch, Philip. *We wish to inform you that tomorrow we will be killed with our families: Stories from Rwanda.* New York: Farrar, Straus and Giroux, 1998.

Hansen, Mette Halskov. *Lessons in Being Chinese: Minority Education and Ethnic Identity in Southwest China.* Seattle: University of Washington Press, 1999.

Hill, Ann Maxwell. "Familiar Strangers: The Yunnanese Chinese in Northern Thailand." Ph.D. Dissertation, University of Illinois at Urbana-Champaign, 1982.

Jenks, Robert D. *Insurgency and Social Disorder in Guizhou: The "Miao" Rebellion, 1854–1873.* Honolulu: University of Hawaii Press, 1994.

Jing Dexin, ed. *Du Wenxiu Qiyi* [The Du Wenxiu Uprising]. Kunming: Yunnan Minzu Chubanshe, 1991.

Jing Dexin, ed. *Yunnan Huimin Qiyi Shiliao* [Historical Documents of the Yunnan Hui Uprising]. Kunming: Yunnan Minzu Chubanshe, 1986.

Lee, James. "Food Supply and Population Growth in Southwest China, 1250–1850." *Journal of Asian Studies*, 41(4): 711–746 (August 1982).

Levathes, Louise. *When China Ruled the Seas: The Treasure Fleet of the Dragon Throne 1405–1433.* New York: Simon and Shuster, 1994.

Lipman, Jonathan. *Familiar Strangers: A History of the Muslims in Northwest China.* Seattle: University of Washington Press, 1997.

Maier, Charles S."A Surfeit of Memory? Reflections on History, Melancholy and Denial." *History & Memory: Representation of the Past,* 5(2): 136–151 (Fall/Winter 1993).

Menon, Rita and Kamla Bhasin. *Borders & Boundaries: Women in India's Partition.* New Brunswick: Rutgers University Press, 1998.

Notar, Beth. "Wild Histories: Popular Culture, Place and the Past in Southwest China." Ph.D. Dissertation, University of Michigan, 1999.

Organization for Security and Cooperation in Europe. *The human rights findings of the OSCE Kosovo Verification Mission* <http://www.osce.org/kosovo/reports/hr/part1/p0cont/htm>.

Polo, Marco. *The Travels of Marco Polo: The Complete Yule Cordier Edition.* New York: Dover Publications, 1992.

Postiglione, Gerard, ed. *China's National Minority Education: Culture, Schooling, and Development.* New York and London: Falmer Press, 1999.

Rittner, Carol and John K. Roth, eds. *Different Voices: Women and the Holocaust.* New York: Paragon, 1993.

Schwarz, Henry. "Some Notes of the Mongols of Yunnan." *Central Asiatic Journal* 2(1–2):101–118.

Seifert, Ruth. "The Second Front: The Logic of Sexual Violence in Wars." *Women's Studies International Forum* 19(1–2): 35–43 (1996).

Sells, Michael A., *The Bridge Betrayed: Religion and Genocide in Bosnia*. Berkeley: University of California Press, 1996. 1998 edition.

Stiglmayer, Alexandra, ed. *Mass Rape: The War against Women in Bosnia-Herzegovina*. Lincoln: University of Nebraska Press, 1994.

Wang Jianping. *Concord and Conflict: The Hui Communities of Yunnan Society in a Historical Perspective*. Lund Studies in African and Asian Religions, vol. 11. Lund: Studentlitteratur, 1996.

Weine, Stevan and Dori Laub. "Narrative Constructions of Historical Realities in Testimony with Bosnian Survivors of 'Ethnic Cleansing'." *Psychiatry* 58: 246–260 (August 1995).

Weitzman, Lenore J. "Living on the Aryan Side in Poland: Gender, Passing, and the Nature of Resistance." In Dalia Ofer and Lenore J. Weitzman, eds. *Women in the Holocaust*. New Haven: Yale University Press, 1998.

Yang Zhaojun, ed. *Yunnan Huizu Shi* [History of the Hui of Yunnan]. Kunming: Yunnan Minzu Chubanshe, 1994.

Yunnansheng Bianjizu [Yunnan Provincial Editorial Committee]. *Yunnan Huizu Shehui Lishi Diaocha* [Investigations in the Social History of the Hui of Yunnan], Four volumes. Kunming: Yunnan Minzu Chubanshe, 1985–1988.

ENDNOTES

1 In his work *The Bridge Betrayed: Religion and Genocide in Bosnia* (Berkeley: University of California Press, 1996) Michael Sells provides an excellent account of the historical background leading up to the violence in Bosnia, and a clear analysis of the manipulation of history, culture and religion for political purposes. For an important contribution to the study of the events leading up to the rebellion in Yunnan, see David Atwill's "Rebellion South of the Clouds: Ethnic Insurgency, Muslim Yunnanese, and the Panthay Rebellion," (Ph.D. Dissertation, University of Hawaii, 1999). The first section of this work clearly documents how the Hui were repeatedly the victims of avaricious Han Chinese who had migrated to the region, and only resorted to violence to defend themselves after repeated appeals to local officials and petitions to the emperor in Beijing were ignored.

2 Yang Zhaojun, ed., *Yunnan Huizu Shi* [History of the Hui of Yunnan] (Kunming: Yunnan Minzu Chubanshe, 1994), 194.

3 In addition, this work does not incorporate the experiences of the Muslim communities of northwest China, which also experienced several periods of unrest and rebellion during the 18th and 19th centuries, resulting in the killing of hundreds of thousands of Muslims.

4 The Hui are not the only minority people in China who feel they have no control of their own history. In China there is a standard national curriculum for primary and secondary education used throughout the country. Individual schools, even those located in predominately minority areas serving students from one particular ethnic group, are not allowed to develop courses on their own history and identity. For an excellent study on the impact of state education on minority communities in this region of China

see Mette Halskov Hansen, *Lessons in Being Chinese: Minority Education and Ethnic Identity in Southwest China* (Seattle: University of Washington Press, 1999), and for a more general view of minority education in China see Gerard Postiglione, ed., *China's National Minority Education: Culture, Schooling, and Development* (New York and London: Falmer Press, 1999).

5 Throughout this article I have chosen not to identify informants.

6 Earlier work by Western scholars on Islam in China was dominated by Christian missionaries with the stated goal of facilitating proselytization efforts among the Muslim populations of China. The most significant of these works is Marshall Broomhall's *Islam in China: A Neglected Problem* (London: China Inland Mission, 1910). More recently several Sinologists have made important contributions to this field of study. Two of the more important works include: Dru Gladney, *Muslim Chinese: Ethnic Nationalism in the People's Republic of China* (Cambridge: Harvard University Press, 1991); and Jonathan Lipman, *Familiar Strangers: A History of the Muslims in Northwest China* (Seattle: University of Washington Press, 1997).

7 The other predominately Muslim ethnic groups are the Uighur, Kazak, Dongxiang, Kirghiz, Salar, Tadjik, Uzbek, Baoan, and Tatar. There are Hui living in all of China's provinces, prefectures and cities, and 93% of China's counties, making them by far the most widely dispersed of all of China's 55 minority groups.

8 For further information on his impact on the history of Yunnan, Islam in China, and China during the Yuan period, see my "Sayyid 'Ajall Shams al-Din: A Muslim from Central Asia, Serving the Mongols in China, and Bringing 'Civilization' to Yunnan," Ph.D. Dissertation, Harvard University, 1997.

9 At the turn of the 14th century, Marco Polo traveled through southwest China and noted the presence of large numbers of Saracens in Kunming. Marco Polo, *The Travels of Marco Polo: The Complete Yule Cordier Edition*, 2 vols (New York: Dover Publications, 1992), 2:65–66. For Rashid al-Din's descriptions of Sayyid 'Ajall see John Andrew Boyle, *The Successors of Genghis Khan* (New York: Columbia University Press, 1971).

10 Although most of the Mongol settlers either eventually returned to Mongolia, or were assimilated over the years, several Mongol villages in central Yunnan remain. In 1997 when I visited these villages, both their language and style of clothing were still recognizable as being related to traditional Mongolian patterns. In the 1970s a group of Mongolian scholars traveled to Yunnan to document surviving traditions. For a report on this trip, see Henry Schwarz, "Some Notes on the Mongols of Yunnan," *Central Asiatic Journal* 2(1–2):101–118.

11 As Sayyid 'Ajall is remembered in Muslim communities throughout China, the memory of Zheng He has been maintained by several Muslim communities among the islands of the Malay Archipelago. For more on Zheng He see, Louise Levathes, *When China Ruled the Seas: The Treasure Fleet of the Dragon Throne 1405–1433* (New York: Simon and Shuster, 1994).

12 In the Qing period this radical was removed, and in the Communist period, the offensive radicals were removed from most of the names given to the indigenous peoples of China.

[13] The most important of these crops were peanuts, sweet potatoes, and corn. These crops could be grown on land previously considered not arable and thus not used by Han Chinese, and left for non-Han peoples. Once these lands became more valuable, indigenous peoples were pushed even higher up into the hills, and further away towards the border regions.

[14] In 1685 the population of China was estimated to be 100 million; less than 200 years later, the number had risen to 430 million. In addition to the introduction of certain crops, some scholars believe that global weather conditions in the late 18th and early 19th centuries were also responsible for bumper harvests throughout much of the world, with concomitant population increases worldwide.

[15] James Lee, "Food Supply and Population Growth in Southwest China, 1250–1850," *Journal of Asian Studies* 41(3) (August 1982), 729.

[16] Neighboring Guizhou province was also the site of increasing clashes between indigenous peoples and Han Chinese, eventually resulting in what came to be known as the Miao Rebellion which lasted from 1854 to 1873, and during which as many as four million people lost their lives. As was the case in Yunnan, land alienation carried out by Han immigrants with the assistance of local Han officials was an important factor in the conflicts leading up to the rebellion. For a detailed discussion of the role played by immigrants and officials see, Robert Jenks, *Insurgency and Social Disorder: The "Miao" Rebellion, 1854–1873* (Honolulu: University of Hawaii Press, 1994).

[17] A succinct example of such a world view, that allows people to simply not see others, is found in the once popular Israeli Zionist claim, "A land without a people, for a people without a land."

[18] Christian Daniels, "Environmental Degradation, Forest Protection and Ethno-history in Yunnan: The Uprising by Swidden Agriculturalists in 1821," *Chinese Environmental History Newsletter* (November 1994), 7–14. Daniels' article was written in part to broaden the audience for an important, but not readily accessible, article written by Takeuchi Fusaji, "Shindai Unnan yakihatamin no hanran: 1820 nen Eihoku Risu zoku hoki o chushin ni" [Rebellions by Swidden Cultivators in Yunnan during the Qing: the Lisu Uprising in Yongbei in 1820], in *Kumatsu Shu* 7 (1992), 276–288.

[19] Yunnan once again has become a popular "land of opportunity" for Han Chinese from the heartland. In recent years as government restrictions controlling movements of people have been rescinded or no longer enforced, once again millions of Han Chinese have migrated to Yunnan, and once again indigenous peoples are complaining bitterly about these outsiders who take advantage of them, swindle them of their land and businesses, and most recently established networks through which they traffic women and children to other regions of China.

[20] Daniels, "Environmental Degradation," 7.

[21] According to David Atwill, during this same period, attempts by other indigenous peoples to resist misappropriation of their land and resources by the Han migrants from Central China gradually ended ("Rebellion South of the Clouds," 119). How many chose to accept the consequences of the influx of migrants, or simply migrated to places further away, is not known.

[22] In many respects the systematic persecution of Muslims followed by the confiscation of their homes and property is similar to the government-sponsored attacks on the Muslims of the former Yugoslavia.

[23] For an excellent summary of the local histories of Hui communities in Yunnan before the outbreak of the rebellion see, Wang Jianping, *Concord and Conflict: The Hui Communities of Yunnan Society* (Stockholm: Lund Studies in African and Asian Religions, 1996).

[24] Yang Zhaojun, ed., *Yunnan Huizu Sh*i [History of the Hui of Yunnan] (Kunming: Yunnan Minzu Chubanshe, 1994), 125.

[25] This region of Yunnan had long been dominated by the Bai people. And although Muslims first settled there in the 13th century, and their numbers have grown over the centuries, the Bai have maintained their dominant position there to this day. For a view of this region and its local history from the point of view of the Bai, see Beth E. Notar, "Wild Histories: Popular Culture, Place and the Past in Southwest China," Ph.D. dissertation, University of Michigan, 1999.

[26] Yunnan is by far the most ethnically heterogeneous province in China. Of China's 55 officially recognized minority groups, 25 are indigenous to Yunnan. There is a long history in China, dating back more than 2,000 years, of perceiving non-Han peoples as "barbarians." In extreme cases this policy has resulted in widespread massacres of indigenous peoples who refused to allow themselves to be "civilized" by the Chinese state. In some respects this prejudice has survived down to this day, but the discourse has been modified to be more patronizing than outwardly racist. The extent to which it has become part of a national ideology can be seen in the fact that minority peoples regularly describe themselves as "backward," and are well aware of their people's position in the hierarchy of "civilization." The Bai, who have been designated the least backward and most civilized of the minority peoples in Yunnan, are especially quick to proudly share this information, not seeming to realize that according to the structure of the hierarchy, they are still all below the Han Chinese.

[27] David Atwill, "Rebellion South of the Clouds," 324–328.

[28] For more on the Yunnanese Muslims who settled in Thailand see Andrew D. W. Forbes, "The 'Cin-Ho' (Yunnanese Chinese) Muslims of North Thailand," *Journal/Institute of Muslim Minority Affairs* (1986) 21, 1–47; Ann Maxwell Hill, "Familiar Strangers: The Yunnanese Chinese in Northern Thailand," Ph. D. dissertation, University of Illinois at Urbana-Champaign, 1982.

[29] Yang Zhaojun, ed., *Yunnan Huizu Shi,* 194.

[30] Ibid., 203.

[31] Ibid., 204.

[32] Marshall Broomhall, *Islam in China: A Neglected Problem* (London: China Inland Mission, 1910), 144.

[33] In the region of Dali, Lake Erhai (whose shores run along the entire plain) was the easiest and most convenient site at which to commit suicide. In other regions though, without access to a lake or river, wells were used. The determination of some women to kill themselves can be seen in the following account: "In Tianxin, some women

jumped into the well to kill themselves. When later the well became full of bodies, other women pulled out the bodies to make room for themselves."

34 Yang Zhaojun, ed. *Yunnan Huizu Shi* p. 199.

35 In the years following the massacres, various proclamations were made allowing the Hui to return to their homes and their land. Not surprisingly, however, local officials and gentry, together with soldiers and Han immigrants who had occupied the property of the Muslims, refused to return it.

36 Yang, *Yunnan Huizu Shi*, 199.

37 Floya Anthias and Nira Yuval-Davis, eds., *Woman-Nation-State* (London: Macmillan, 1989), 7.

38 Judith Tydor Baumel, *Double Jeopardy: Gender and the Holocaust* (London: Valentine Mitchell, 1998).

39 Rita Menon and Kamla Bhasin, "Honorably Dead: Permissible Violence against Women," in *Borders & Boundaries: Women in India's Partition* (New Brunswick: Rutgers University Press, 1998), 31–64.

40 Stasa Zajovic, "Women and Ethnic Cleansing," in *Women against Fundamentalism*, vol. 1, no. 5 (1994), 36. Quoted in Menon and Bhasin, *Borders & Boundaries*, 44. In a morbid twist on the need to control women as vessels of reproduction, in the refugee camps for Hutus set up by an international relief organization in neighboring Zaire, the interahamwe (those who had taken part in actively carrying out the genocide against the Tutsi) conceived of yet one more role for women: "The birth rate in the camps was close to the limit of human possibility; breeding more Hutus was Hutu Power policy, and the coerced impregnation of any female of reproductive age was regarded as a sort of ethnic public service among the resident *interahamwe*." Philip Gourevitch, *We wish to inform you that tomorrow we will be killed with our families: Stories from Rwanda* (New York: Farrar, Straus and Giroux, 1998), 269.

41 The Serbs even went so far as to keep women confined in rape camps until their pregnancies were so advanced that abortions would be dangerous. Women in these camps who did not become pregnant were beaten and accused of using some form of birth control to thwart the Serbs' objectives.

42 Tone Bringa, *Being Muslim in the Bosnian Way: Identity and Community in a Central Bosnian Village* (Princeton: Princeton University Press, 1995), 237, fn. 30.

43 I would like to thank Avner Giladi for this information. For a detailed article on the infant and child in Islamic history and culture, see his "Saghir," in *Encyclopaedia of Islam*, new edition (Leiden: Brill, 1995), VIII: 821–827.

44 Menon and Bhasin, *Borders & Boundaries, 77*. *Pativrata* is the Hindu concept of ideal wife: chaste, virtuous, and obedient.

45 Ibid., 100.

46 Middle-aged Hui official in a remote village north of Eryuan.

47 For several articles on different groups of Hui in Yunnan see Yunnansheng Bianjizu [Yunnan Provincial Editorial Committee], *Yunnan Huizu Shehui Lishi Diaocha* [Investigations in the Social History of the Hui of Yunnan], Volume 3 (Kunming: Yunnan Minzu Chubanshe, 1986).

[48] This process continues on down to this day. In many of the Islamic colleges and schools I visited I met converts, among whom were people who said that their ancestors were Hui who had been forced to renounce their religion in the aftermath of the massacres.

[49] Interview in Eryuan county, Yunnan.

[50] Dru Gladney, *Chinese Muslims*, 137–140; and Wang Jianping, *Concord and Conflict*, 15.

[51] Uradyn E. Bulag, "Ethnic resistance with socialist characteristics," in Elizabeth J. Perry and Mark Selden, eds., *Chinese Society: Change, Conflict and Resistance* (London and New York: Routledge, 2000), 188.

[52] This custom of using two different calendar systems simultaneously (and now three with the gradual introduction of the Gregorian based calendar system) is no doubt common among other minority Muslim populations. In China, the degree to which these systems of calculating important community-based religious events are essentially fluid can be seen in the annual celebrations of the Prophet Mohammad's birthday, known as *Mawlid*. Whereas in most of the Islamic world the date corresponds to the Islamic calendar (which is a truly lunar calendar, with no leap months or years, and thus dates slowly revolve around a solar calendar year), in Yunnan this festive ceremony always takes place in the fall, after the major harvests have been completed. Communities assign dates over several weeks in which each village takes a turn hosting a Mawlid celebration, thereby allowing the communities to attend each other's festivities.

[53] Charles S. Maier, "A Surfeit of Memory? Reflections on History, Melancholy and Denial," *History & Memory: Representation of the Past*, 5(2) (Fall/Winter 1993), 144.

[54] Deciding whether to use a date tied to a religious holy day, or the date of a specific event, was one of the dilemmas facing the Jewish population of Israel when determining how to commemorate those killed in the Holocaust. For Yom Ha'Shoah the Israeli state chose a date which although calculated using the Jewish calendar (Nisan 27), represented the anniversary of the Warsaw ghetto uprising in 1943. By choosing a date which represented active resistance, the state was able to emphasize those who fought their persecution. Many Orthodox Jews, however, question the choice of dates and put forth Tish B'Av (also known as Tishah b'Ab, or Ab 9) as a more appropriate day because it commemorates the destruction of the First and Second Temples.

[55] For more on the Islamic education in China, see my "The Recent Resurgence of Islamic Education in China," *International Institute for the Study of Islam in the Modern World Newsletter* 4, 1999, 12.

[56] For more on the educational level of the Hui compared to other minorities in Yunnan and the Han, see Hansen, *Lessons in Being Chinese*, 23, 54, and 75.

[57] The most notable exception to this pattern is the town of Shadian. Since the town had to be completely rebuilt, it stands in stark contrast to the more traditional villages surrounding it. In addition, many of the survivors chose to use the reparations to invest in small businesses which prospered during the period of economic reform which immediately followed.

[58] Throughout China different Muslim communities have developed their own unique Arabic calligraphic styles. The style in Tengchong was significantly different from that

in other parts of Yunnan, reflecting its proximity to Burma and to southeast Asian Islamic traditions.

59 Yang Zhaojun, 201; and Andrew D. W. Forbes, "History of Panglong, 1875–1900: A Panthay (Chinese Muslim) settlement in the Burmese Wa States," *The Muslim World* 78 (1988):38–50. I would like to thank Magnus Fiskesjo for bringing the latter source to my attention.

In another part of Yunnan I met a young woman from Tengchong who was just finishing up her first teaching contract after graduating from an Islamic college. After being away from home for so many years, she was anxious to return to Tengchong to put to use her training and experience to establish an Islamic school there. She said her first priority was to start classes for the elders in her village, most of whom she said had very little understanding of the teachings of Islam.

60 The traditional role of traders proved crucial to the reunion of families separated during the massacres. As traders traveled throughout the region they would gather information on missing children and relatives and pass it along. In this way many children who had been forcibly adopted by non-Hui families were able to learn the whereabouts of relatives or Muslim villages which had survived. One such case took place near Weishan: "There was a boy who was taken away from home and sent to be the servant of a military official in Laoyaguan village near Lufeng. He refused to eat pork and later when a Hui caravan passed through his village, he learned that his elder brother had survived and still lived in their hometown. When the caravan passed the news on to his older brother he went all the way to find his young brother and helped him escape and return to their hometown." In Shadian in southern Yunnan, I heard a similar account, "Some Hui girls managed to escape the killing only to be forced into marriage with Han. But they remembered they were Hui, and when they found the chance they would tell the Hui traders who passed through town who they were and where they were from, and the traders would arrange for them to be returned home." Another important use of the trading networks involved match-making services. Hui who lived in particularly remote areas, or in areas with a small Muslim population, came to depend on the traders for appropriate recommendations for their children. This method of locating spouses came to a halt in the early years of the socialist state and the implementation of strict travel controls and residency permits (*hukou*). During this period many Hui who lived in areas with small Hui populations, had no choice but to marry non-Hui. More recently with the lifting of travel restrictions, and the relaxing of hukou enforcement, Hui are once again able to use these networks to meet and marry Hui from other regions. The Islamic schools and colleges which attract students from throughout the province and the country, have also proved a popular way to meet potential spouses.

61 There are also students presently studying in Saudi Arabia, Libya, the Sudan, Turkey, Jordan, Malaysia, Pakistan, and Indonesia. Although most of the students are male, I would estimate between 20% and 25% are female. For more information on this recent phenomenon see my article, "The Recent Resurgence of Islamic Education in China," *International Institute for the Study of Islam in the Modern World Newsletter* 4 (1999), 12.

[62] Ruth Seifert, "The Second Front: The Logic of Sexual Violence in Wars," *Women's Studies International Forum* 19(1–2, 1996), 39–40.

[63] Ibid.

[64] Returning home after a long period of forced stay in a man's household is not necessarily as easy as one might assume. Over the past decade in China there has been a huge increase in the number of women trafficked and sold throughout the country. Many of these networks use Yunnan as a base from which to kidnap women, transport them to distant provinces, and sell them to peasants living in remote regions who can't afford or can't find wives. Over the past few years, as the extent of the problem became evident, the government assigned extra police officers and resources to work on tracking down and rescuing these women. To the surprise and consternation of many involved in these police operations, in many cases the women who had been living in the homes of these men for several years chose not to return home. To begin with, the women were not allowed to take any children they had had. Moreover, many of the women realized that if they returned home everyone in their village would soon learn what had happened to them, and marriage would have been difficult, if not impossible.

Part 4

Displacement and National Ground

Polluting Memories: Migration and Colonial Responsibility in Australia

Ghassan Hage*

Introduction

The question of the migrant's participation in the political processes of the host society is often an object of popular debate in host nations. In the public arguments generated around this issue, the portrayal of migrants fluctuates. They can be portrayed as the people who are too "home"-oriented[1] and thus not participating, enough or as the fantasmically imagined people who are participating too much (so much so that they are feared to be taking over).

In Australia, the recruitment of migrants into political parties is often pathologised in terms of a rhetoric of "branch stacking." "Branch stacking" takes place when a faction within a political party manages to make newly arrived migrants join its party branch to ensure the dominance of the faction's candidate in internal party elections. Here the dominant image is that of so many migrant sheep, with no political interest of their own, undermining the political process by introducing feudal-like patron-client relations into a modern political system that assumes personal autonomy and independence in the making of political

* The author would like to thank Oliver Marchant and Hal Wooten for their helpful reading of an earlier draft of this essay.

choices.[2] Generally, it can be said that the question of participation is used in these debates to demonstrate that migrants are at best instrumentally interested in the institutions of the host society, but are not affectively attached to them.

Despite often reproducing racist stereotypes of migrants, these views nevertheless contain a lucid everyday differentiation between participation as a formal/instrumental process and participation as an affective relation to society, an indicator of how much one "cares." Indeed some of the popular phobic fantasies that are animated by this differentiation is the idea that the nation is controlled by those who can technically participate too well but who do not "care," at the expense of those who care but who are technically unable to participate. Here, caring is perceived as an important emotional investment in the nation, and thus an intense form of participation, that is nonetheless not recognised as such. In the sense of it being primarily a mode of belonging to the nation, I will call this form of participation *participatory belonging*.

The academic works dealing with participation often fail to incorporate this public intuition. In these works the interest in issues of participation remains dominated by political scientists and sociologists working around the theme of "ethnic mobilisation" or through the formal categories of "rights" and "responsibilities" associated with the analysis of citizenship. Examined from this perspective are the way ethnic organisations function as political "lobby groups," or, at a more grassroot level, the way migrant groups organise to combat racism or to protect individuals against class and migrant-specific forms of disadvantage.

A major recent theme inspired by the analysis of citizenship has been the problem of "exclusion". Here, it is the institutions of society, and above all the state, that are perceived as erecting, or neglecting to deal with the existence of, barriers to the participation of migrants (e.g., the failure of the state to curb racism or to provide enough migrant-specific social services). Exclusion becomes linked to the kind of citizenship encouraged by the state and when it dispenses it (for example, how long migrants need to be in a host country before citizenship is granted). It is to be noted that most of these analyses are done in complete abstraction of the migrant's own wish to participate. The latter is perceived as merely awaiting the disappearance of the exclusionary mechanism for him or her to begin participating wholeheartedly.

Despite the unquestionable value of the insights produced by this body of work, its formal conception of participation remains at best an indicator of a technical capacity (to organise or to work within political institutions, for example) but tells us very little about the degree of identification of the migrant with what he or she is participating in. Thus, a rise in migrant participation detected by political scientists in the form of an increase in the number of individuals visiting their local Member of Parliament is far from being an indicator of a greater sense of national participatory belonging. The figures of such participation might indicate that the migrants visiting their MPs do so to raise issues linked with the migration of relatives, for example. That is, for all practical purposes, migrants who do not visit their MPs but who might be more concerned with local political issues, and would discuss them passionately in the evening or at work, are precluded from such an analysis of rates of participation. Here we can see how participation as "caring," as participatory belonging, is precluded from analysis while participation as a technical capacity is emphasised as an object of study.

In recent times in Australia, the idea of participation as including a moral dimension has made a strong emergence, albeit from a somewhat different perspective. The belated public recognition of the atrocities committed against Australia's indigenous people has led to political debates regarding how to act towards healing the wounds inflicted on indigenous Australians. The various calls to take responsibility for past acts in which today's citizens have not been directly involved invariably advocate forms of national participation and belonging that go beyond the more instrumental conceptions of citizenship usually made available in the public arena. This becomes fertile ground for consideration of the deeper meanings of citizenship, national identity, and belonging by political philosophers.

In this article, I review some of the issues concerning national memory and national responsibility that have arisen in this debate and examine the way notions of participation and national belonging implicitly or explicitly underlie them. I then move to examine the way post-war migrant participation and responsibility has been conceived within this debate, particularly the question of why and how migrants from non-English speaking backgrounds should shoulder some responsibility for what happened at a time when neither they nor their ancestors lived in Australia. I will critically examine the answers given to this question and the way they can help us reformulate our conceptions of the meaning and significance of participatory belonging.

A Brief Introduction to the History of a "Memory War"

In 1992 the High Court of Australia decided in favour of a group of indigenous people claiming to be the original owners of land formally under the control of the state of Queensland in the North East of Australia.[3] The group was led by a man called Eddie Mabo and the decision became popularly known as "the Mabo decision" or simply "Mabo."

The Mabo decision was the first Australian official/judicial acknowledgment of a lawful ownership of land by indigenous people pre-existing the British colonisation of Australia. In a historical precursor of the famous Zionist slogan that accompanied the settlement of Palestine ("A land without people for a people without a land"), the colonisation of Australia occurred under the legal aegis of what was known as *terra nullius*. This was the claim that, at the time of the early settlement of Australia, British eyes could not discern any traces of an appropriation of the land by Aboriginal people (for example, no recognisable housing or agricultural activities).[4] As such, the land was considered "up for grabs" and was made legally so — a "land without people for a people with plenty of land" on that particular occasion.[5]

In what remains a legally controversial finding, the High Court judges did not only rule that the land in the particular claim being considered was not *terra nullius*. They asserted that their ruling had more far reaching implications concerning the relationship of indigenous people to the land throughout the nation. Furthermore, some of the judges (Justices Deane and Gaudron), in later comments, moved into moral territory arguing that the practices of dispossession that emanated from the *terra nullius* principle "constitute the darkest aspect in the history of this nation." And, they added, "The nation as a whole must remain diminished unless and until there is an acknowledgment of, and a retreat from, those past injustices."[6]

In this sense, "Mabo" aimed at fostering a new sense of caring about the nation, of participatory belonging, grounded in the willingness of today's citizens and their national representatives to acknowledge and address injustices resulting from colonial episodes in Australian history now being remembered, in the present, as particularly shameful.

It must be stressed that these calls, and the creation of this "new" memory, were also, if not primarily, inspired by the growing political strength and the local and international activism of the indigenous people themselves. Of equal importance was some brilliant, straightforwardly empirical work by some Australian historians. Such works have helped to make common knowledge among the nonindigenous population what has so far been hidden and contested. It emphasised to a wider public that Australia's settlement was far from being the kind of settlement portrayed in the majority of the school history books produced in the 1950s and 1960s. The only significant hardships discussed in such texts were the hardships of the penal system and of confrontation with an undomesticated natural environment experienced by settlers. Instead, the newer critical historiography emphasised that settlement of Australia involved a violent appropriation of the land and a subjugation of a whole people. It also showed that those people whose land was being appropriated countered this violent colonisation process with an equally violent resistance, including forms of guerilla warfare (see in particular Reynolds 1981).[7]

Indigenous struggles, the diffusion of the new critical historiography, and "Mabo," all worked together to create an important cultural transformation within Australia. For the first time, talking about "the British invasion of Australia" no longer positioned the speaker on the radical fringe. The histories of this invasion were being slowly transformed from marginal, radical, or academic topics to a quasi-official discourse competing for the prized status of "public truth."

The newly acquired status of this version of colonial history reasonably encouraged by the then sympathetic Labour government of Paul Keating (1992–1996) led to a culturally conservative backlash against what was portrayed as a "black armband" view of history. This was a history, the conservative critics argued, that worked on denigrating the achievements of the early colonists. Yet it was those achievements that led to the building of the prosperous democratic nation that Australia has become. As such, these achievements of early colonists should not be downplayed in favor of a history of violence that has been, at best, marginal, if not highly exaggerated. Australia's history, according to conservative critics, should inspire pride in Australians rather than shame.

By the mid-nineties, Australia was witnessing a full-blown "memory war" over its violent colonial past. The election of a Liberal Party government in 1996, led by what (even by Liberal Party standards) was the unusually culturally conservative politician, John Howard, gave an important boost to the forces of cultural restoration.[8]

It was in such a climate that the Human Rights and Equal Opportunity Commission report, *Bringing Them Home: Report of the National Inquiry into the Separation of Aboriginal and Torres Strait Islander Children from Their Families,* appeared. The report specifically detailed one of the most inhumane practices that accompanied colonisation and which epitomised its racist/genocidal tendencies towards Aboriginal people and Aboriginal culture. This was the practice of taking Aboriginal children, particularly those categorised as "half-caste," away from their Aboriginal parents, often forcibly removing them from the arms of their mothers, and placing them under the foster care of white parents or white institutions in order to "assimilate" them.[9] The children became known as "the stolen generation." The report was based on testimonies made by members of this stolen generation.[10]

Like the discourse surrounding the Mabo High Court decision before it, the report did not only call for reparations for the particular indigenous individuals concerned. It saw the issue as something diminishing the nation as a whole. Thus, it called for more nationally encompassing symbolic measures such as a national "Sorry Day." It also recommended that state and federal parliaments, along with other institutions such as churches and the police forces, acknowledge the responsibility of their predecessors for the practices of forcible removal. It urged such institutions to consult with the Aboriginal and Torres Strait Islander Commission (the most official body representing indigenous people) on the best way to offer a formal apology for such practices.[11]

This led to a considerable shift in the significance and the intensity of the memory war that was now well under way. For if Mabo triggered a debate about historical responsibility for events that occurred more than two hundred years ago, here was a report that brought home the fact that colonial history was still being lived in the 1960s. For many Australians, this brutal colonial racism was a practice being carried out in their own lifetimes. And, while there were no indigenous people left to tell stories of how they felt when their land was directly taken away, there were still quite a few who could publicly remember what it was like to be taken away in a truck with your mother running and wailing after you, or what it was like to have "the man of the house" where you've been sent to work come and "visit" you in the middle of the night. Memories of lived events cannot but have a more serious moral intensity than those of a more distant past uncovered by historians.

Consequently, the *Bringing Them Home* report added a further dimension and a further intensity to the debate about the significance of colonial memory in Australia's history and its present. Of particular importance was the report's significance in defining the kind of citizenship and participatory belonging required from nonindigenous Australians if they were to address and rectify the injustices of the past. For, while the occurrence of colonial violence was no longer seriously contested, it was its significance, particularly the extent to which today's Australians ought to be considered responsible and accountable for it, that became the object of an important struggle.

The complexity of the debate on participatory belonging and responsibility for the past lies in the way it intimately links issues of national identity with the highly abstract issues of commitment to justice for deeds one does not necessarily feel personally responsible for. Different ways of thinking about the significance of the colonial past translate into different ways of conceiving one's own intimate national identity. Different ways of conceiving what constitutes justice in the present for Australia's indigenous people leads to different ways of conceiving who ought to be affectively and practically implicated in the delivery of such justice. The question of the migrant's relation to such processes could only complicate matters further. Is there a difference between the migrant saying that "these events do not concern me" and the established Australian citizen saying the same thing on different grounds? Can a migrant relate affectively to a past that is not his or her own? Can a migrant ever genuinely care for the nation without such an identification with the past? Can he or she ever experience an intense sense of participatory belonging the way people who are assumed to identify more fully with the past experience it?

Philosophy, National Memory, and National Responsibility

One of the interesting features of the Australian political scene has been the way the "memory war" described above has constituted fertile ground for the Australian chapter of the international revival of the debate on moral and political philosophy that began with the publication of John Rawls' *A Theory of Justice* and the critical responses it generated in the following decades.[12] Subsequently, in a specific attempt to untangle the complexities of the situation, Australia has recently witnessed the production of a relatively large body of philosophical writing asking questions such as: How do liberal conceptions of justice relate to issues of past injustices, cultural difference, and colonialism? What responsibilities do citizens have towards the past? What constitutes justice in relation to Australia's indigenous population?

Paul Patton has presented one of the clearest accounts of how the question of justice emerges in relation to the Mabo judgement from a philosophical standpoint. He argues that the popular reactions to the Mabo judgement are an expression of three competing intuitions about justice: equal treatment, reparation, and recognition of the other. He suggests that the tensions around the Mabo judgement are a reflection of a tension in these ideas of justice as they are present within it.[13]

Insofar as equal treatment is concerned, the liberal defenders of Mabo (including some of the judges who delivered the judgement) have argued that the recognition of Aboriginal land rights is merely a recognition that they have an equal right to property, something that has been previously denied to them. But the conservative interpretation of this law and the attack on Mabo's claim to provide justice in the form of equal treatment is not an ungrounded one. It is equally based on an intuition about justice. What conservatives argue is that Mabo clearly invites a situation where common law recognises a form of property right that is not available to all citizens since indigenous people alone among Australia's citizens can lay claim to native title. This, Patton points out, challenges Rawls' liberal notion of justice based on an identity of rights for all citizens.[14]

As to reparation, Patton points out that: "it is common place to assert that the past cannot be changed and that what is done is done. But there is still an important strand of thinking about justice which says that it should involve reparation for past injustices."[15] Agreeing with an article by Jeremy Waldron (1992),[16] Patton stresses that "the aim of such reparation is not to undo past wrongs but to go some way towards removing their consequences and re-establishing what would have been the case if those injustices had not been perpetrated."[17]

Finally, as far as the recognition of the other is concerned, Patton explains that :

> Here, the underlying intuition is that justice requires the recognition of the other as other, that it requires giving what is due to others in accordance with their conceptions of right and not simply in the terms of the one giving or in those of a supposedly neutral third party.[18]

These intuitions, as Patton shows and as we shall see later, were fraught with contradictions. Suffice it to say at this point that they form the implicit background for the most disputed issue of all, the issue of responsibility.

The differences around this issue are epitomised by the different positions taken by Paul Keating, the Prime Minister and leader of the Labour Party until 1996, and John Howard, the conservative leader of the Liberal Party who followed Keating as Prime Minister. Keating was a strong supporter of the Mabo decision and advocated a full acknowledgment of the current generations' responsibility for the past as part and parcel of a process of reconciliation with the indigenous people. For Keating:

> ...the starting point might be to recognise that the problem starts with us non-Aboriginal Australians. It begins, I think, with that act of recognition. Recognition that it was we who did the dispossessing. We took the traditional lands and smashed the traditional way of life. We brought the diseases. The alcohol. We committed the murders. We took the children from their mothers. We practised discrimination and exclusion.[19]

John Howard, on the other hand, sees that the best way to deal with such a past is to forget it and concentrate on present socioeconomic injustices. When asked to apologise in the name of the nation for the kind of actions that figured in the *Bringing Them Home* report, John Howard stated that he could not apologise in his capacity as prime minister. Instead, he offered his personal apology. As one of his ministers explained: "The government does not support an official national apology. Such an apology could imply that present generations are in some way responsible and accountable for the actions of earlier generations."[20]

Generally speaking, it would be fair to say that Paul Keating was far more inclined to help foster the climate of reconciliation advocated by the High Court Judges, and, later, the writers of the *Bringing Them Home* report. And, not surprisingly, given their general liberal disposition, philosophers and other academics have also tended to support the Keating position and see in John Howard's reluctance to apologise a regressive step, if not an outright continuation of colonial racism.

My moral position does not differ much from such academics on this question. I will, however, argue that the Keating position raises many more difficulties than have been acknowledged by the advocates of a "national apology." But these difficulties remain largely unnoticed and unexamined in the attempts at providing philosophical groundings for this position. In what follows, I look at two recent philosophical works that have tackled this question and see how they are weakened by their inability to notice, let alone deal with, this difficulty. I will then show that these difficulties are important enough to make it impossible to think through migrant participatory belonging without an attempt to confront them.

In a recent work, commendable for the clarity and thoroughness with which it tackles the issue of nationalism and identity in general and then brings it to bear on the issues arising from the Australian situation, the philosopher Ross Poole has strongly argued the case for linking national memory with national identity and national responsibility. This is how he formulates the question of responsibility:

> If in virtue of their history and current position, Aboriginal people have certain rights, it is important to ask: Who do they have rights against? The usual and I think the correct answer to this question is: non-Aboriginal Australians. But it is important to ask why this should be so. After all, most contemporary Australians will never themselves have acted with the intention of harming Aborigines, and most of the worst atrocities were committed in the past. By what line of inheritance do contemporary Australians inherit the sins of the predecessors? And which contemporary Australians? Is it only those of us of Anglo-Celtic stock whose ancestors came to Australia in the nineteenth century? Should we exclude those recent immigrants, especially those whose background is free from the taints of European colonialism and imperialism? And what of those Australians whose ancestors had no choice in the decision to migrate, but were brought over as convicts?[21]

Poole develops his argument through an interpretation of the relation between identity and memory based on the work of Locke and Nietzsche. He emphasises Locke's idea that responsibility for the past does not result from a mere remembering of the past but from an identification with the subject performing the remembered act. It is because of this identification through the appropriation of past actions that "present feelings of pride, shame, guilt, remorse, pleasure, obligation are usually present and appropriate" and that people can be held responsible for the past.[22]

Poole further develops the notion of an identity formed through the appropriation of the past through Nietzsche's well-known proposition that "to breed an animal with the right to make promises — is not this the paradoxical task that nature has set itself in the case of man?"[23] He argues that for Nietzsche (and in this he interprets him as very similar to Locke), "we learn to remember what we have done, not merely in the sense that certain acts remain present to consciousness, but because we identify ourselves with the self that performed those acts."[24]

But for Nietzsche memory is not somehow there to appropriate. A memory has to be made, as he put it. With Nietzsche a new dimension emerges when we learn to appropriate the past as our particular past. For it also means that we recognise our promises and develop what we come to call our conscience. As Poole explains, "We were that self which promised, its will is our will, and the suffering it would endure with the failure of its projects is our suffering."[25] Thus for Poole, "memory and anticipation are not merely modes of cognitive access to what we did in the past and will do in the future, but are the very forms through which our identity is constructed."[26]

It is with the help of this construct that he reaches his conception of how national identity, national memory, and responsibility relate. It is worth quoting from his argument at length:

> A national identity involves, not just a sense of place, but a sense of history. The history constitutes the national memory, and it provides a way of locating those who share that identity within a historical community. The history is not given, but subject to debate and reinterpretation. For example, Australians of earlier generations grew up with a history of British achievements, the European "discovery" and "exploration" of Australia, the trials and triumphs of the early settlers, and so on. It was a history in which Aboriginals were marginal or absent. But this history has been and is being rewritten. It is now recognised that Australia did not come into existence with European discovery; that Aboriginal cultures and ways of life had existed for millennia; that Aboriginal practices had formed the land which was to be appropriated and exploited by the European immigrants; and that Aborigines had with flair and courage resisted White advances into their country. Australian history is now coming to terms with the suffering, destruction and human tragedy consequent upon the European settlement of Australia. The details of this history may be debated, but it cannot be disavowed. Acquiring a national identity is a way of acquiring that history and the rights and the responsibilities which go with it. The responsibility to come to terms with the Australian past is a morally inescapable component of what it is to be Australian.[27]

The second philosophical work dealing with this question I want to consider here is Moira Gatens and Genevieve Lloyd's *Collective Imaginings: Spinoza, Past and Present.*[28] Despite Ross Poole's materialist disposition, his conceptualisation of appropriative memory makes remembering and responsibility appear as if they result from an act of free will by a subject who chooses to take responsibility for the past. Gatens and Lloyd's *Spinoza* allows for a somewhat more materialist analysis, where the communal imagining of the past is grounded as a necessity produced through the material interconnection between the past and the present.

Most important for them are the ramifications of Spinoza's conception of the individual as the product of social relations rather than an a priori starting point for them. As they put it:

> Our understanding of responsibility is restrained by thinking of individuals as bordered territories, firmly separated from others in such a way that the issue of where the responsibility lies is always in principle determinable. Spinoza's treatment of individuality — especially that aspect of it which Balibar terms "transindividuality" — gives us insight into the nexus between individual and collective identity... It can help us understand something which otherwise... can seem puzzling and inappropriate: that individuals can take responsibility for what they have not themselves done.[29]

This is a remarkable work in its capacity, like previous works by the two philosophers, to make Spinoza appear like a highly relevant avant-garde contemporary. More specifically, here, Spinoza's idea is convincingly presented as a complement to Hannah Arendt's version of collective responsibility. For Arendt, Gatens and Lloyd point out, "we are appropriately held responsible for things we have not ourselves done where the reason for our responsibility is our membership in a group which no voluntary act of ours can dissolve...."[30] In *The Human Condition,* Arendt conceptualises this involuntary membership with the help of the Augustinian concept of "natality."[31] Gatens and Lloyd observe that, in the case of Arendt, the "beginning of an individual self as a bearer of responsibility is here construed in terms of entry into a community rather than in terms of the physical fact of birth — an initiation into language and socially meaningful action."[32] It is here that Spinoza's work is most useful:

> Spinoza's treatment of individuality can offer here a way of thinking of individual selfhood which will complement the strength and clarify the limitations of Arendt's political version of collective responsibility.

> ... (For Spinoza) The modification of our own bodies by others is constitutive of our determinate individuality, as well as causally determining what we do in the here and now. The implication of memory and imagination in these determining processes means that our past is not a shadowy unreal being of thought which we can conjure up or away at will. It is here in our present — in the modifications which stay with us in the ongoing bodily awareness which makes us what we are.[33]

This bodily awareness is part of what Spinoza calls the imaginary and it is through it that "we" come to terms with ourselves as members of historical communities materially linked to a past for which we assume responsibility. This Spinozist conception of the imaginary informs Gatens' and Lloyd's commentary on the Mabo case.

> The Mabo judgement disturbed not only mining, farming and other financial interests of present-day non-indigenous Australians, it also severely disturbed the social imaginary which grounds the "we" of contemporary Australian identity. This imaginary is the site and cause of direct and indirect harms experienced by indigenous Australians. No amount of redistribution of goods, compensatory financial arrangements, or even the return to the land will cancel or alleviate the past and present effects of the European imaginary on indigenous peoples. This is not an argument against redistribution, compensation or the return of land. Rather, these measures, though necessary, are far from sufficient. It is here that the "we" of Keating's speech is crucial. Who — if not we — possesses the capacity to accept responsibility for the harmful effects on others of the social imaginaries which we inhabit and which have formed us as the types of persons we are? Responsibility for our social imaginary can only be a collective responsibility that "we" take up toward the past.[34]

The affinity between Spinoza and Nietzsche translates into an affinity between the position of Poole and the positions of Gatens and Lloyd. Both arguments provide excellent groundings for the idea that those who relate materially and imaginatively to the history of the appropriation of Australia from the indigenous population ought to feel responsible for the injustices caused by this appropriation. I would like to argue, however, that they both suffer, very directly in the case of Gatens and Lloyd, from what we can call the undeconstructed colonial effect of Keating's "we."

As I will now argue, both of their theorisations of national responsibility are considerably weakened where, despite their analytical awareness of national multiplicity, at the point of conceiving the "apologizing national subject" they implicitly assume the unproblematic possibility of a noncontradictory national imaginary from which "we" ought to relate to the past. It is that point which also weakens the position of all those who take Keating's "We took the lands...We committed the murders... We took the children" speech, quoted above, as the example of what a national apology should entail.

Australia's Impossible National Memory

Let us begin by noticing that when Keating makes his statement, it is not clear if he is using a national "we" and as such making a national apology. What he says very explicitly is "the problem starts with us non-Aboriginal Australians." But this phrase may be interpreted in two different ways. If Keating, and those who take him to be making a national apology, suppose the national "we" to exclude Aboriginal people, his "us non-Aboriginal Australians" is a national "we" which considers the Aboriginal people to be another national "we." Or, he sees a national "we" as including Aboriginal people and in this case a national apology is a very difficult acrobatic act indeed. It will have to involve the Aboriginal people as part of their new "Australian" communal selves apologising to their past "Aboriginal" communal selves: "We took the lands... we committed the murders"! Not even Nietzsche and Spinoza can make them do this!

Now it seems to me that this is the fissure from which conservative thought in Australia gains its moral legitimacy. When John Howard is saying that he cannot apologise in the name of the nation he is saying just that. In this sense, he is more truthfully reflecting the hegemonic wish of the state of Australia to represent all the people of the nation and to thwart any possibility of Aboriginal sovereignty. This is why an apology becomes perceived as "divisive." Unlike Keating, Howard does not want to use his role as a representative of the nation — one nation which includes indigenous people — to speak in the name of one part of the nation, be they Anglos, the Europeans, or the nonindigenous population. But John Howard here faces a contradiction of his own. If he is really consistent in only using the national we to include "everyone" and does not want to speak of national shame when only one part of Australia can relate to it, then he has to refrain from using it when expressing national pride and remembering rosier "national memories." Australia's national day itself, Australia Day, commemorates the British landing. It cannot be plausibly advocated as a genuinely national day on such grounds. Indeed, this is something that many indigenous people, who remember the day as a day of sorrow, have pointed out.

But, of course, John Howard is not interested in being consistent but in achieving his political goals. Nor is Paul Keating, for that matter. This is why neither Howard nor Keating can face the reality pointed to by the above: a national memory or a noncontradictory plurality of memories of colonisation in Australia is impossible. This is the all-important reality the ramifications of which are left out of the analyses by Poole, Gatens, and Lloyd.

Obvious as this may be when stated explicitly, this fact is often forgotten in the discussions concerning responsibility: Aboriginal people do not relate and cannot appropriate "Australian history," even in its morally and empirically corrected version, because what is posited as Australian history is simply not history from their perspective. In this sense, they have their own separate history, or more exactly, their own pool of separate histories with its own agreements and disagreements, to appropriate a memory from. This does not mean that they cannot share anything with other people living in Australia, but that what they share cannot be taken for granted at all.

Gatens and Lloyd's Spinoza appears at first sight all ready to encompass such a multiplicity of histories and imaginaries.

> Selves are born into a future in which they will make individual decisions, in which they will be held responsible, praised or blamed. But they are also born into the past of communal life which both precedes and awaits them — a communal life which, under modern conditions, is not the life of one culture alone, but, in Tully's terms "inter-cultural." Such selves have not just one but a multiplicity of pasts — pasts of collective memory and imagination which must be reckoned with in the present; and not just one "identity", but as many as can be constructed, and carried into the future, out of this inner multiplicity. Our responsibilities, no less than our freedom, come from understanding what in this rich profusion of "finite modes" we are — in all senses — determined to be.[35]

Unfortunately, in invoking Keating's "we" as a national imaginary in which we are all positioned, this Spinozist potential for dealing with a multiplicity of memories is left unexploited. Instead, Gatens and Lloyd end up reducing the multiplicity of pasts to a noncontradictory multiplicity in which all communities have the possibility to "strive to persevere in their own being." What they see as "conflicting imaginaries" are two White imaginaries of colonisation: a bad one (represented by the idea of *terra nullius*) and a good one (represented by the Mabo decision). The fundamental contradiction between the settlers' and aboriginals' imaginaries which makes the striving of one communal formation happen at the expense of the striving of the other is left out of the field.

The impossibility of a single Australian national memory or a smoothly plural set of national memories is not the result of a war between two sides, a winning and a losing side. National memories have been forged out of such wars, later constructed as "fratricidal." As Benedict Anderson argues in the second edition of *Imagined Communities,* there is such a thing as a nationally reassuring memory of fratricide.[36] But this is not possible in Australia today and this impossibility resides in the fact that the very sides which have fought this colonial war have not melded together into one. Despite the hegemonically inspired symbolic gymnastics of some, there remain two separate communal identities with two separate memories trying to live together in one state.

Reflecting on the preoccupation with the need for forgetting in *Qu'est ce qu'une nation?* by Renan, and in particular, Renan's statement that "tout citoyen français doit avoir oublié la Saint Barthélémy," Anderson comments "in effect, Renan's readers were being told to 'have already forgotten' what Renan's own words assumed that they naturally remembered!" And he asks, "How are we to make sense of this paradox?"[37]

In fact there is not much of a paradox to make sense of here. Any person who has ever used the exclamation "let's forget about it" will know very well what Renan means by this "forgetful remembering." "Let's forget about this argument," for instance, will often mean that since we cannot but remember this event let us do so without the passion that led us into it in the first place. It is an invitation to a remembering that is no longer one-sided and affective. Anderson himself points out, "It is instructive that Renan does not say that each French citizen is obliged to 'have already forgotten' the Paris Commune. In 1882 its memory was still real rather than mythic, and sufficiently painful to make it difficult to read under the sign of 'reassuring fratricide'."[38]

It is then a difference between a "neutral" and an affective remembering that Anderson is partly aiming for in differentiating between real and mythic memory. When two parties to a conflict remember it affectively, it means that each or at least one of them has still an investment in remembering the conflict as a two-sided affair, and in continuing to remember it from the particular side he or she belongs to. Thus, remembering affectively is not just about getting worked-up about a particular memory. More importantly it means that parties remember the conflict from "their own" perspective. Here, at least one of the two sides is refusing to share a neutralised memory of the event, and consequently, each side will have their particular memory of it. This is why when we speak of memory we need to analyse its relation to the imaginary gaze of the remembering subject as a way of understanding its social significance for that subject. "I remember fighting you" is a language that would more often emphasise a "lived memory," a memory of the event as experienced from the specific one-sided perspective of the one remembering. This is why Anderson is right in calling it "real" memory. Such a memory does not lend itself to a "we" language. A memory has to lose the investment of both parties in it as a real memory for this investment to change and become an investment in a distant mythic "event." Only then can a sentence such as "we remember our fight" become possible and credible.

This is why it is not an exaggeration to say that the possibility of a noncontradictory set of national memories of Australia's history today is very remote. We are far from reaching a stage where "we," Aboriginal and non-Aboriginal people, can remember the acts of dispossession and murder together without its partisan affective intensity.

This is the contemporary reality of Australia: two contradictorily located fields of memories and of identification. But this is not the end of the story. For these two sets of memories and identities also mean two communal subjects with two wills over one land; two sovereignties of unequal strength.[39] The first is a dominant one deriving its legitimacy from the force and the history of its occupation. This is not only the brute force of numbers and technological superiority, but also the moral force behind a history of inhabiting, transforming, and defending the land as it has grown to be. The second is a dominated will, deriving its legitimacy from its historical status as the resisting will of the original inhabitants. One can turn this whichever way one likes but this is as good a definition as any of a colonial situation; a colonial situation that is still with us today. If we are fishing for injustice and responsibility there is no need to appropriate the past here, there is still plenty to appropriate from in the present.

The Australian situation is not a postcolonisation situation (in the unlikely sense of a state where the process of colonisation has reached its goals of fully neutralising the colonised) because the will of the colonised has not been rendered completely inefficient by the will of the colonisers. But it is not Algeria or South Africa either, in that the will of the colonised is much too weak to challenge the coloniser for a recapturing of the land. It is not a postcolonial situation because the colonial project failed to eradicate any significant trace of the colonised will. But it is not a situation of colonial struggle for regaining a colonised land, either, because the colonial project eradicated enough of the strength of the colonised will to make this impossible.

This is what constitutes the objective difficulty of the Australian situation. For a long time to come, Australia is destined to become an unfinished Western colonial project as well as a land in a permanent state of decolonisation. A nation inhabited by both the will of the coloniser and the will of the colonised, each with their identity based on their specific take on, and memory of, the colonial encounter: what was before it and what is after it. Any national project of reconciliation that fails to reconcile itself with the existence of a distinct Aboriginal will, a distinct Aboriginal *conatus*, whose striving is bound to make the settlers experience "sadness," is destined to be a momentary coverup of the reality of the forces that made Australia into what it is.

It should be remembered that it is always the dominant who have an interest in the dominated forgetting that there ever were sides in a conflict. Consequently, to speak of an Australian memory is not politically innocent. It is part of a hegemonic disposition on the part of the coloniser to complete the integration of the colonised into the reality of the coloniser. One can call for justice and hold oneself responsible by identifying with the history of the coloniser. One can call for justice and put oneself in an accusatory position by identifying with the history of the colonised. The very idea of "recognising" injustice, and assuming responsibility for it, admirable as it is, is still a specific coloniser's take on Australia's history, even when it is, at best, a repentant coloniser's take. This is not to make such recognition less necessary but to clearly spell out its limits.

What I have tried to argue in this section is that, as far as its colonial history is concerned, Australia continues to have antagonistic histories with antagonistically positioned historical subjects produced by those histories. To recognise that the coloniser's history involves a history of land appropriation, massacre, and "stolen children," and to want to take some form of responsibility towards such acts, is of course ethically superior to trying to retreat from facing them. Nevertheless, responsibility for a shameful act is an answer to a coloniser's trauma — not the trauma of the colonised. The colonised has an equally Australian history and traumas specific to them as colonised. The shame of the colonised is the shame of defeat, and its relation to injustice is not one of "recognition" but of endurance and resistance. To take the traumas of the colonised as the only "Australian" history someone assuming an Australian identity ought to face is to continue the process of marginalising the history of the colonised; that is, the process of colonisation itself — even at the very moment of expressing shame for colonisation. This is what is of utmost importance when thinking of migrant participation in relation to Australia's colonial history.

Through his neglect to analyse the ramifications of this colonial antagonism, Ross Poole, though showing himself well aware of it throughout his book, ends up approaching the question of migration and responsibility from a coloniser's angle. Thus, he rightly argues that "Where the immigrant desires permanent settlement… they (*sic*) should be treated as potential citizens. They should be expected to participate in the public culture of their new country, and provided the means and the opportunity to do so."[40] And he, equally rightly, goes on to call for the importance of the migrant's "commitment to participate in the public culture of the nation which will be one's new home." Applying his Nietzschean/ Lockian perspective he argues that "Migration ... should also carry with it a commitment to participate in the public culture of the nation which will be one's new home, to acquire a new national identity, and also ... to accept the responsibilities which go with this."[41]

One can only agree with the above. But when it comes to specifying what these responsibilities are, we are left with no doubt as to whose history the migrant is being asked to relate to:

> The responsibility to come to terms with the Australian past is a morally inescapable component of what is to be Australian.
>
> It is in this context that we must understand one of the dangers of multiculturalism. In so far as it involves a diminished sense of Australian historical identity and a strengthened sense of the affiliations which migrant Australians have to the countries of their origins, it also carries with it a weakened sense of the responsibilities which are written into Australian history. Many recent migrants do not feel implicated in it. It is not just that

> they personally have not been involved with or had direct dealings with Aboriginal people; this is true of most Anglo-Celtic Australians. It is because their cultural identity implicates them in a different history and, perhaps, with a different set of responsibilities. It is only if they have a sense that coming to be an Australian involves coming to share the history that they will recognise that they have acquired the responsibilities which go with that history.[42]

I have argued elsewhere that migration is, in an important sense, a continuation of the colonisation process, so, in this sense I can see why Ross Poole can instinctively position the migrant "on the side" of the "Anglo-Celtic Australians." But migrants have shared some important realities with indigenous people, too. Through enduring the racist "White Australia Policy," for example.[43] To use a somewhat old but useful language, let us say that migrants are in a contradictory colonial location, and as such, they are also equally capable of relating to Australia's history from within the imaginary "we" of the colonised. Here, becoming responsible no longer means contributing to the coloniser's postcolonial trauma-therapy that oozes out of the "coming to terms with the Australian past" discourse, but by contributing in a struggle for Aboriginal sovereignty, for instance.

An important issue that emerges here is the very mechanism through which migrants come to care about Australian history — whomever's history it is they are relating to. How does one come to relate to the memory of another as if it is one's own? Ross Poole suggests that this is what "ought" to happen but he does not tell us either how or why it happens. Gatens and Lloyd's Spinoza as a refinement of Arendt's "natality" concept is more explanatory in this regard:

> Thinking through the implications of Spinoza's philosophy we can see that human bodies are not born into a single community, but into complex criss-crossing structures of reciprocal affinity — constantly formed and re-formed under the impact of rival conatus. It is a version of what Arendt calls 'natality' which lends itself better to the complexities of identity under contemporary conditions of cultural diversity than more unitary conceptions of contemporary community.[44]

But it remains to be seen how these criss-crossing structures of reciprocal affinity lead to the transmission of affect from the perspective of the body itself. It is to this issue of participatory belonging with which I began this essay that we now need to return to explain the process of "caring" for the memory of the other.

Polluting Memories: On the Transmission of Affect

Explaining the nature of the affect involved in the process of recognition, Raymond Gaita argues that it is mainly a variety of shame. As he put it:

> shame is as necessary for the lucid acknowledgment by Australians of the wrongs the Aborigines suffered at the hands of their political ancestors, and to the wrongs they continue to suffer, as pain is to mourning. It is not an optional emotional addition to the recognition of the meaning of their dispossession. It is, I believe, the form of that recognition.[45]

He further reiterates that:

> The attachment that makes shame appropriate and sometimes called for is inseparable from the desire to celebrate achievements which shape an historically deep sense of communal identity. The pained, humbled acknowledgment of the wrongs committed by the ancestors, of those who are rooted and nourished by their country, who feel as do Justices Deane and Gaudron, that those wrongs constitute a stain on their country, and whose joy in its achievements is thereby sometimes blighted — that acknowledgment I take to be one of the forms of shame. If it is not, then I do not know what to call it.[46]

Gaita's powerful and subtle moral analysis of what I have called above the relation to the coloniser's "we" is not accompanied by an equivalently powerful sociological analysis of the mode of transmission of affect. In the above, we somehow learn that to be afflicted by this "healthy" sense of shame, those who have committed the wrongs need to be our ancestors. However, he also sees that:

> There are borderline cases as, of course, there are with any concept. More importantly, there is a condition which is neither guilt nor shame and which is not a state borderline between them. Ron Castan, a QC who played a prominent part in securing native title legislation, alerted me to it in discussion when he described the response of Adolf Eichmann's son to the fact that he was the child of one of the architects of the genocide of the Jews and the gypsies. The oppressive and ineradicable gloom of that condition was neither shame nor guilt, but more like the condition the ancient Greeks described in their tragedies as "pollution."[47]

I understand the historical basis for Gaita's usage of such a restricted conception of "pollution." However, I would like to suggest that, at least for my own purposes, it is more suitable as a general category capable of encompassing all the affective states analysed by Gaita, be they shame, guilt, or that "other" state that is neither. To think of shame and guilt as specific forms of pollution helps us think of affect in a more materialist way, as circulating particles of guilt or shame.

More importantly for our analytical purposes in this section, it allows us to think of the modes of transmission better than the generally idealist categories of shame or guilt allow us to. We ask such questions as, how do such particles of affect circulate? How do people get "tainted"?

Memories of genocide are polluting memories. They taint those who relate to them. But how does one get polluted if one is not the originator of the polluting act? Gaita's source for the idea of pollution, Eichmann's son, sees it acquired through kinship. The son is polluted by the deeds of the father. But how does one get polluted through kinship? After all shame does not circulate in the blood. What does one receive from one's father or, more generally, one's parents, other than blood?

I would like to suggest that the answer to the above question is simply "family life" itself, one's first collective imaginary. The family, as Bourdieu, has pointed out, is not only the social space where the first "I" is formed but also the first "we," and it has an enduring effect on how later, more encompassing, "we"s are formed.[48] This is not an incidental subjectivity — one that I might or might not have. The "we" I manage to be "interpellated" to forms the core of what I am as much as any "I." In that sense, the family remains a good microcosm for the study of the circulation of affect within communally imagined subjects.

By living within a family (or whatever other communal form that helps us develop and grow), we receive from our parents (or whoever is positioned as such), the first sense of communal life. This is our first sense of that vital imaginary life where we see ourselves protected and cared for, and where we perceive ourselves as part of a historical subject that originates well before us. It is within this imaginary collectivity that we also learn that for what we have received we are expected to give back. We have responsibilities. Indeed, if what we have received is reasonably positive, we don't feel the weight of such an expectation, we see it as a natural moral obligation. We receive the gift of family life, and insofar as this gift is well given, insofar as we have internalised it well enough, we feel in return responsible for its maintenance: we care for it and for the people within it. That is what motivates and shapes our participation in such a family life and forms the basis of our family identification, or our identification with whatever we grow up to perceive as our "community/family" entourage. This is what I called in the introduction to this essay "participatory belonging."

This collective identity is as much my individual identity as it is an expression of my social viability. My parents offer me a gift of a communal family life that I cannot refuse, short of committing social suicide. As such I have to accept it whichever way it comes. It might carry with it stories of family greatness of which the family (and I) are and will be proud. It might carry stories of evil deeds (that I might learn about from others) of which the family (and I) are ashamed.

I cannot possibly relate to a social milieu to which I feel I owe nothing or only negativity. This seems to me the importance of Eichmann's story above. If Eichmann's son had only experienced evil and violence from his father, he could have easily imagined no affective ties with him at all. He could have experienced a sense of having received nothing but bare biological life from his father. Eichmann's son would not have had such an experience of "pollution" if this was the case, for pride and shame are not transmitted biologically. Paradoxically, but more probably, it is because he inherited his father's evil through the love and protection that the latter would have given him that he experienced such a form of oppressive pollution. It came with the gift of social life itself. The pollution defined one of the "we's" that constitutes his social viability despite him, and he is forced to relate to it.

What I am suggesting, then, is that like family life, all social communal life is communicated to us as a gift which, like all gifts, creates obligations when well given. Participating in, and "caring for," whatever community we belong to is the common, though not necessary, mode of returning such a gift.[49] It is through this process of gift-exchange that communal affects such as pride and shame circulate.

I believe that it is from such a perspective that we can analytically capture best the nature of migrant participatory belonging in the host society. This explains why, to begin with, migration is often a guilt-inducing process. To leave the communal setting that has given us the gift of social life is precisely to refrain from repaying the debt.[50] But migration also involves receiving a new gift of social life. Whether such a gift is well given is part of what determines whether or not it will create an obligation. Another important aspect, however, is whether the migrant is psychologically and socially equipped to receive a well-given gift. It is when (and if) migrants experience a sense of communal solidarity, of being cared for, and so forth, and when and if they become capable of appreciating such care, that they will begin to "care for" the host society themselves. And it is at this point that they will start identifying with all or some of its "we" or "we's" and all the affective luggage they carry with them.

I will now conclude by briefly narrating, in a somewhat more anthropological, but also more literary manner, through a condensation of subjectivities encountered in my research, the way such an approach can lead us into the complexity of the Australian situation whose philosophers I have critically interacted with above.

ON RECEIVING THE GIFT OF SOCIAL LIFE IN A LAND TAKEN WITHOUT BEING OFFERED ... BY SOMEONE I DON'T LIKE ... BECAUSE HE REMINDS ME OF MY GUILT

> It is the Australian Arabic Communities Council's annual dinner. I am having a drink, listening to a couple of Arab-Australian youth discussing Mabo when a piece of absolute wisdom is jokingly delivered by one of them in response to a long liberal tirade defending the Mabo decision:
>
> *What are you going on about anyway, if the Anglos didn't do the killing you wouldn't have been able to immigrate here. You owe 'em mate. They cleared the land... ESPECIALLY FOR YOU! (imitating a TV product promotion)*
>
> Is this a moment of Spinozist lucidity about those "complex criss-crossing structures" making us into what we are... The migrant "owes" the colonisers... No spears waiting at the harbour or the airport. Maybe there would have been no airport! All thanks to the coloniser.
>
> But doesn't everyone owe the coloniser (in some cases even the colonised — depending on what social inheritance they choose to value)? *The migrant's voice elucidates what the discourse of "recognition" does not want to recognise: colonial violence is but the condition of possibility of the attempt to transcend it through "recognition."* If my ancestor has not broken *their* spears and *their* will, *they* would be still spearing and I would have to be as much of an "ethnic cleanser" as my ancestor.
>
> But they've done a reasonably good job, my ancestors, and I can now say how sorry I am for them doing such a good job. I can comfortably engage in my post-colonial trauma therapy... Don't let guilt run you down.

Special treatment for first fleet descendants: modes of apology and recognition of injustice guaranteed to soothe. But doesn't the discourse of apology *produce* the very guilt it is supposed to soothe. A soothe-able guilt rather than that non-soothe-able colonial one.

They've done a good job, my ancestors, but they could have done a better job. They could have put me in a position where the indigenous people would have been grateful for my "recognition". The Prime Minister, John Howard, waited so long to offer his "personal apologies" he was clearly expecting its recipient to be grateful. He's come a long way. The postcolonial art of apology as gift: *thank you for expressing your regrets... we owe you mate!*

In the meantime the migrant is also grateful... *"We owe you mate". A beautiful gift to be allowed to live in Australia. We would be happy to reciprocate...if only you learn to give this gift a bit more gracefully!*

This is where we come to yet another complex criss-crossing structure determining us. A gift of social life will create an obligation to reciprocate if it is well offered...offered gracefully. Many migrants to Australia are offered the gift of a new social life: visa, work, social security. Not many are offered it gracefully.

"They finally gave us the visa. They made us feel like beggars," a Lebanese woman says. Australian Embassies are the last bastions of the White Australia Policy. The gracefulness with which you are offered the gift of an Australian life is strictly proportional to your Whiteness... or your capital. We are very instrumentalist in choosing our migrants but we don't want our migrants to relate instrumentally to us.

Nevertheless, I felt like saying, *Beggars? but isn't that what we are?* Begging on the international market for a more economically sustaining "we." I would have complicated the interview.

Come to think of it, it would have been easier than saying it here. Now I am complicating the analysis. More criss-crossing structures. A well-offered gift of social life will create an obligation if it is well received. But is the migrant always ready to receive well even what is most generously and ethically offered: the shame of belonging to a country that cannot give you a decent enough gift of social life to keep you in it and then the added shame of migration...*everyone has to know that I belong to a sick "we" animated by centrifugal forces!* The bad breast of my motherland exposed...[51] Excuse me, sir, my motherland's breast cannot feed me, can I have a suck of yours. Who would want to relate to his or her mother while envying someone else's?

And so the man is apparently treating the migrant like a beggar. He is a racist: a good object of transference of repressed centrifugally-induced shame if there ever was one. *It's all your fault if I don't feel at home in your country! I was all geared up to do it otherwise, of course! I CHOSE to stay here you know!*

Ressentiment: *I don't like my hosts to begin with. Everything about them reminds me of the person I should have been. The person who stayed put! The person whose mother(land) knew how to keep her. I envy your centripetal force...*

Even before that man in the shopping centre spat on me and said, "Why don't you go home where you belong, you son of a bitch," I hated him. Yes, I am hurting, of course I am. He called my mother bitch. How dare he lay bare what I am escaping from most: the thought of my mother as that bitch who did not manage to feed me and keep me. But at the same time: *Thank god he said it, I can hate him a little bit more comfortably. I hate him because he is a bloody racist. And He IS.*

Finding a rational reason to hate those we hate already for no good reason: how soothing!

And now I learn that they've killed all these Aboriginal people when their ancestors invaded Australia. So it wasn't your mother's breast after all: you stole it. You're worse than me!

Sophisticated psychoanalysts might call this: longitudinally maintained transference of repressed centrifugally-induced shame. We might recognise this little convenience by the name of "being onto a good thing." *Why should I be grateful to you anyway for letting me have a suck? It is not your mother's breast anyway. You haven't offered me anything. Stolen goods: that's what you have offered me. I don't owe you anything. You thought you DIDN'T offer me hospitality. In fact, you COULDN'T. It's not your land. I am liberated. NO OBLIGATIONS.*

I ought to thank the Aboriginal people for letting me in... Except they didn't give me a visa either... I ought to apologise... to each her therapy...

I might be onto another "good thing" here: the struggle for the equal right to apologise and recognise injustice! That must go far... Actually, maybe I can belong here. That guy Noel Pearson said that Australia is made out of indigenous and nonindigenous people. I like that. Finally a category that puts me and John Howard in the same position. Maybe I can belong here... Who says I don't care...

This is how the sea of subjectivity around Mabo can present itself on a stormy day. As Spinoza understood, "man's strivings, impulses, appetites, and volitions... are not infrequently so opposed to one another that the man is pulled in different directions and knows not where to turn".[52] No neat relation to Australian history here, and too many vacillating *conatus*... a very postcolonial *colonial* situation.

ENDNOTES

1 "Home," here, is, in a matter-of-fact manner, taken to mean homeland of origin.

2 As recent research by a number of political scientists has recently shown, while there is no doubt that branch stacking occurs, newly arrived migrants are far from being the blind followers they are supposed to be in this process. People who accept being "stacked" have often very clear goals and use this institutional mechanism to achieve them (see in particular Giovanni Zappala, *Four Weddings, a Funeral, and a Family Reunion: Ethnicity and Representation in Australian Politics* (Sydney: Australian Government Publications, Department of the Parliamentary Library, 1997.)

3 The land itself was not physically part of the state of Queensland, but an island in the Torres Strait.

4 Legally, *terra nullius* was proclaimed in Australia in the early 1800s some fifty years after the first settlements. There were clear indications of uncertainty within the British government as to whether the Australian Aboriginal people should be considered the rightful owners of Australia. These uncertainties disappeared as the squatters and pastoralists began forming as an Australian ruling class in their own right.

5 Of course, it was the British as a general national category who figuratively "owned a lot of land." The people actually sent to Australia were themselves largely landless peasantry.

6 Mabo v Qld, *The Mabo Decision* (Sydney: Butterworths 1992), 82.

7 Henry Reynolds, *The Other Side of the Frontier* (Townsville, Queensland: The History Department, James Cook University, 1981).

8 The Liberal Party in Australia is more an equivalent of the Conservative Party in Britain or the Republican Party in the U.S. It is the Labour Party which actually espouses liberal values, as such.

9 This practice began in the late nineteenth century, but was most intense and sporadic between the 1930s and the 1960s.

10 Human Rights and Equal Opportunity Commission, *Bringing Them Home: Report of the National Inquiry into the Separation of Aboriginal and Torres Strait Islander Children from Their Families* (Sydney: 1997).

11 Ibid., 284–293.

12 John Rawls, *A Theory of Justice* (Cambridge, Massachusetts: Harvard University Press, 1971.) For critical responses, see *Magazine litéraire, Le renouveau de la philosophie politique*, no. 380, Octobre 1999.

[13] Patton Paul, "Justice and Difference: The Mabo Case" in *Transformations in Australian Society*, ed. Paul Patton and Diane Austin-Broos (Sydney: University of Sydney, Research Institute for Humanities and Social Sciences, 1997), 83–98.
[14] Ibid., 87–88.
[15] Ibid., 88.
[16] Jeremy Waldron, "Superseding Historic Injustice," *Ethics* 103 (1992): 4–28.
[17] Patton, 88.
[18] ibid., 91.
[19] Moira Gatens and Genevieve Lloyd, *Collective Imaginings, Spinoza, Past and Present* (London and New York: Routledge, 1999), 142.
[20] Raimond Gaita, *A Common Humanity: thinking about love and truth and justice* (Melbourne : Text Publishing, 1999), 99.
[21] Ross Poole, *Nation and Identity* (London and New York: Routledge, 1999), 138.
[22] ibid., 50.
[23] ibid., 55.
[24] ibid., 56.
[25] ibid., 56.
[26] ibid., 64.
[27] ibid., 140–141.
[28] see note 13 above.
[29] Gatens and Lloyd, 74.
[30] ibid., 75.
[31] Hannah Arendt, *The Human Condition* (Chicago: University of Chicago Press, 1958).
[32] Gatens and Lloyd, 76.
[33] ibid., 76.
[34] ibid., 146.
[35] ibid., 83.
[36] Benedict Anderson, *Imagined Communities: Reflections on the Origin and Spread of Nationalism* (London and New York: Verso, 1991), postscript.
[37] Ibid., postscript.
[38] Ibid., 199–201.
[39] Paul Patton in his activation of Derrida to assess the nature of Mabo as an act of "recognition of the other" has been one of the few to hint towards this. As he points out:

> "In Derridean terms, the difference between European law and native law and custom is at once both a condition of the possibility of justice and a condition of its impossibility. This means that justice in the sense of a full and complete recognition of the other is impossible, since any such recognition of the other is impossible, since any such recognition will always be carried out in the language and on the terms of one party." (Patton 1997: 94–95)

Indeed, as Patton concludes his article by saying:

> "Aboriginal law is not fully recognised as a body of law grounded in the sovereignty of the Aboriginal peoples. The recognition of indigenous law is therefore both accomplished and deferred. This feature of the judgement ensures that it will always be open to criticism from the perspective of the very grounds which make it a substantial improvement in justice for indigenous peoples. It also ensures that the issue of sovereignty will remain with us for some time to come." (Patton 1997: 96)

40 Poole 1999: 125.

41 Ibid., 126.

42 Ibid., 141.

43 The White Australia Policy was one of the first acts of parliament that followed the formation of the Australian commonwealth in 1900. It was designed to stop the migration of non-white people to Australia. It rallied conservatives and radicals alike: the former because the idea of purity related to ideas of a strong unified nation; the later because they associated white Australia with strong democratic and union traditions which they felt were threatened by people from non-white "races." The White Australia Policy was officially abandoned in the late 1960s. It was considered as properly buried with the rise of Australian multiculturalism in the early 1970s.

44 Gatens and Lloyd 1999: 76–77.

45 Gaita 1999: 92.

46 Ibid., 101–102.

47 Ibid., 94.

48 Pierre Bourdieu, *La Domination Masculine* (Paris: Seuil 1998).

49 As Nietzsche has well perceived, the community can go after those who do not repay the debt. In the "Genealogy of Morals," he comments that:

> "the community, too, stands to its members in that same vital basic relation, that of the creditor to his debtors. One lives in a community, one enjoys the advantages of a communality (oh what advantages! We sometimes underrate them today), one dwells protected, cared for, in peace and trustfulness, without fear of certain injuries and hostile acts to which the man outside, the 'man without peace,' is exposed — a German will understand the original connotations of Elend — since one has bound and pledged oneself to the community precisely with a view to injuries and hostile acts. What will happen if this pledge is broken? The community, the disappointed creditor, will get what repayment it can, one may depend on that." (Friedrich Nietzsche, "Genealogy of Morals," in *Basic Writings of Nietzsche*, ed. Walter Kaufmann (New York: Modern Library, 1992), 507.)

50 It is important to stress that there is no necessary communal entity we feel indebted to. Not all migrants feel indebted to their nation, for example, but most will feel indebted to their family. This guilt inducing state of indebtedness is most apparent in times of crisis when your family, your village, or your nation is going through a hard time and

you (the subject organically related to the community through the original debt of social/communal life) are not there to help. When you do not share the fate of the collectivity which gave you social life you are guilty of letting others pay alone for a debt you are collectively responsible for.

51 It is true as Bourdieu argues that centrifugal orientations are to centripetal orientations what male is to female (Pierre Bourdieu, *The Logic of Practice* (Cambridge, UK: Polity, 1990). But this is only valid in so far as such orientations are orientations of the will. The gender of centripetal and centrifugal forces becomes more confusing, however, when one is perceived to be under the effect of centrifugal or centripetal forces, propelling her against her will. In this case, the subject becomes more often than not feminised, perceived and perceiving itself as lacking control of its orientation.

52 Benedict de Spinoza, *Ethics* (Ringwood, Victoria: Penguin Books Australia, 1996), 104.

Response to Ghassan Hage:
A Few Fragments

Sakiyama Masaki
— *translated from Japanese by Brett de Bary*

> "La trace est à la route comme la révolte à l'injunction et la jubilation au garrot."
>
> — Edouard Glissant, *Introduction à une Poétique du Divers*[1]

In offering some comments on Ghassan Hage's paper, I'll start with some thoughts provoked by the opening sections of the paper, in which he discusses the Mabo Decision (Eddie Mabo vs. Queensland, 1992), according to which the High Court of Australia recognized that indigenous residents of Australia had rights which preceded and in some cases survived European settlement. I'd like to relate this to legislation affecting the status of the Ainu people in Japan.

On March 2, 1899, during the thirteenth session of the Imperial Diet, a law entitled "Former Hokkaido Aboriginal Peoples Protection Act" was adopted; it took effect on April 1 of that year.[2] Let me summarize the aims of this legislation, which are made clear in the explanatory section of the bill introduced before the legislation was adopted.

This introduction to the bill stated that *Wajin* (a term used by Ainu prior to modernization to describe Japanese from the mainland) were monopolizing the natural resources ("riches of nature") upon which the Ainu had depended for their survival, and had reduced the Ainu to poverty. Such a situation should not be ignored. For this reason, it stated, it was necessary to establish laws according to which measures of assistance could be dispensed to the Ainu people, assuring their survival. These measures were presented as a "duty of our nation, in accordance with the desire of His Majesty, who fixes his compassionate gaze on all subjects equally."

We can see here an articulation of the assimilationist ideology according to which the modern Japanese state made people imperial subjects by incorporating them into the emperor system. We can also see a blunt expression of the racism and colonialism of the Japanese empire, which began to develop rapidly after the colonization of Taiwan in 1895. Nor do these passages merely record phenomena from the distant "past." The contents of this law, the crux of which was to declare that the lands of the Ainu people were "a gift to them from the Emperor" (and thus were not lands they had legal ownership of) was inserted into the "Social Welfare" sections of the Meiji government's laws and ordinances, under the designation "Protection of Livelihood." As a law whose real aim and origin were thus rendered hidden and invisible, it remained in effect until 1997.

That the Japanese government, which had repeatedly insisted that Japan had "no indigenous peoples," finally recognized the Ainu as such, effecting some minimal changes in their status, was one result of the transnational movement which designated 1993 the "International Year of Indigenous Peoples." One outcome of the movement was that the Japanese Diet adopted what has been called the "New Ainu Law," a law "concerned with the fostering of Ainu culture, education of the public, and dissemination of greater awareness of its traditions." The proposal for the "New Ainu Law" was introduced into the Lower House on April 4, 1997, and adopted by unanimous vote on May 7 — approximately the same amount of time as had elapsed between passage of the Former Aboriginal Peoples Protection Law and its promulgation as law. That is to say, the new law was adopted with surprising speed. This law abrogates the Former Hokkaido Aboriginal Peoples Protection Law. Despite its bourgeois, cultural relativist trappings as an expression of multi-ethnic, multi-racial ideology, however, the new law is merely a stand-in for its more than 100-year-old predecessor, one that lacks the flavor of old-fashioned racism.

The new law defines legally recognized Ainu lifeways as "culture" or "tradition", and presents a façade of recognizing the rights of Ainu to appeal for the "return" of what was defined as "common property of the former Hokkaido

Aboriginal Peoples" under the old law. Needless to say, it proposes to convert such common resources to a cash value: the law sets forth strict provisions for how long the "return" may take, using a "one-year from date of claim" rubric similar to the one applied to cash loans in civil law. The common properties of the Ainu have been assigned a cash value of 980,000 yen.

While the cash value of such compensation is not ultimately what is at stake here, the ruthlessness of this settlement, in financial terms, should not go unremarked. But more important is the fact that the new law does not even broach the issue of what the historical, cultural, and social basis for calculating compensation owed the Ainu might be, and thus it cannot provide a starting point for assessing the damage done through the Japanese state's annihilation of Ainu culture, a process in which the violence of its assimilationist ideology was consistently manifested. Under the new law the value of Ainu lands — their most concrete and visible "property," which has occasioned numerous conflicts between Ainu and Japanese or *"Wajin"* (the disposition of which at present devolves primarily around the dispute over lands deemed ownerless, but has also been affected by the collapse of the 1980s bubble economy) — and the value of Ainu "culture" (that intangible "property" which could not have come into existence without a shared "space" in which labor, including daily life and customs, were organized) are being decided in a vacuum, utterly divorced from history, from the facts of plunder and exploitation, and from every aspect of their "worldliness."

In all of this we can see that "culture" has been accommodated to a logic which sees the money form as being the essence of all forms, and one which exerts on them its "normalizing influence." Insofar as the law itself is concerned, we might say that that the "Ainu people" (*minzoku*) could only be named as such once something called their "culture" had been assembled and salvaged in the temporality of nationalist jurisdiction. The "Ainu people" is thus an existence that cannot be stipulated outside the force of the law, nor can the "Ainu people," in a sense, be an "outlaw" force.

This is something most clearly manifested in the debate over "indigenous rights" that took place within government circles leading up to the enactment of the New Ainu Law. For example, in 1996 the chief Cabinet secretary was being privately advised by a group of experts on so-called "*Utari* Policy." (The term "*Utari*" is a plural word [*Utar-i*] that originally meant "followers" or "subordinates" but has been adopted by Ainu and used with the same connotations as the word "*Ainu,*" which refers to "a human being" or "a man." The term was adopted to counter the discriminatory uses of the word "Ainu," which contains the Japanese word for dog, "*inu.*") This group issued a report on April 1, 1996, that tried to define "indigenous rights" as a kind of security measure that would protect the boundaries of the Japanese ethnos against infringement. In their writing, one might even detect a kind of fear of the potential influence of such "Southern" developments as the Mabo decision, the emergence of the Zapatista Liberation Army in Chiapas, Mexico, or the establishment of Carib autonomous zones on the coast of Nicaragua. Referring to the concept of "indigenous rights" that was being discussed in the United Nations and elsewhere, they wrote: "It will be important to continue to monitor discussion [on the issue of indigenous rights], but we also believe it is necessary to make decisions concerning new measures for dealing with Japan's Ainu people that take the actualities of Japanese society into account. In the Japanese case, the new policy should not be premised on the establishment of Ainu rights to self-determination, including the right to secede, to declare independence, or to demand compensation for the return of land and resources in Hokkaido."

Without concerning ourselves with a legalistic interpretation of the notion of "indigenous" (which assumes, as it does, a linear temporality) let us simply note here that through this law the Ainu people are completely deprived of their "constitutive power" (to use Antonio Negri's terminology), so that they cannot constitute themselves as autonomous subjects. Instead, they are reduced to being an object of judiciary control, and contained within the reified framework of nationalist jurisdiction.

But let me now offer some comments on a certain kind of discourse (or what Laclau and Mouffe, severing their ties with the base/superstructure model, would call a "hegemonic formation") emerging with real strength within the social movements we observe at present, and the political tendencies that accompany it. This is a discourse of political representation exemplified by the "we" in the speech of Australian Labor Party leader Paul Keating, which was cited so effectively and interestingly in Hage's essay. It is a discourse that is based on a process of comparison.

When one "compares" the words of Keating with the discourse of the Ainu "experts" I quoted above, one can almost feel something like envy. It is as if, by contrast to Japan, Australia were "advanced" in the degree of concern shown for the issues of indigenous rights (with the implication that Japan needs to "catch up.") But what makes such a comparison possible? It is the positing of a unit called the nation state or, in the case of a hegemonic formation in politics, the positing of some kind of uniform standard. But as Gayatri Spivak has pointed out in her essay "Ghostwriting," such processes entail an insertion of sub-altern subjects — who have no "national origin" but at the same time are not migrants — into the space of the nation.[3] Spivak calls this process "intra-national displacement" and correctly understands it as an exercise of power. Nevertheless, even such a critique of ontopological processes — by virtue of its very abstraction and apparent independent conceptual existence — can constitute a reproduction and tacit affirmation of the global movement of transnational capital. Let me again cite Spivak, who observes that, "The kind of ontopological and ontopologocentric understandings that are affixed to each and every movement of the 'South' prevent us from gathering news about sub-altern struggles against global movements of capital." Such struggles transcend national boundaries or often (in ways that we are unaware of) unfold in concert with each other. Although it is inevitable that in the process of breaking through boundaries there will be slippages and diversions of an "ontopological" nature, we nevertheless need to form movements that can bring about encounters between situations that are, in fact, linked.

Aware that the nature of "comparison" is deeply ambivalent (although it is surely also true that comparisons emerge in relief from the dynamic linkages among transnational movements), let me continue with my comments on the trajectory of Hage's argument. Hage takes up the problem of the political participation of migrants under the sign of an Australia that is constructing a new national body that is "sovereign." He points out the link between two processes: (1) the process through which the Aboriginal peoples are being inserted into the nation and (2) the process through which migrants to Australia are being incorporated as political subjects to be mobilized in the "host" society.

The politics of the nation state — the place or topos within which it is possible for these two processes to be linked — is not a level playing field. It is a multiply determined site, a layered space that, insofar as the hegemonic formation produced by diverse social relations extends to it, is a space of closure. It is this that makes it possible to speak of the Aboriginal subject and the sub-altern together. And it is only from within this hegemonic space (both "political" and "cultural") that it is possible to take up the perspective from which the temporal process of "receiving" migrants can be construed as one of offering them the "gift" of political participation in the "host" society.

Certainly, such a perspective opens up an important and distinctive arena: we could say it exists at the intersection of the national and the transnational. And certainly, within this hegemonic space, the suggestion that the activities of "migrants" be understood in terms of a "gift" represents a kind of interpretive liberation of Mauss' text, which has been canonized almost to death.

Yet, using as a point of reference Derrida's concept of "given time," I can't help wanting to ask what would happen if we thought of the "gift," not as the action of political participation, but as an event. In other words, is there a way of thinking about these problems, not from within hegemonic logic, but from a marginal position that might dare to challenge the "inside" and "outside" of hegemony itself? I am not talking about a margin articulated in a binary opposition to the center. I would like us to pay attention to the existence of that which can never be clearly reduced to a "margin" — regardless of whether we are considering the situation described in the past perfect tense as one of migrants' "having been incorporated," or one in which they "have not been incorporated."

If we take the concept of the gift that Hage proposes and look at it from the hegemonic perspective, we might understand it as being something like a cycle of interest. In the temporal delay after "receiving", one makes restitution; one pays back one's debt. Or, we might understand the cycle in terms of an economy in which currency represents the ultimate form of existence for all phenomena. On the other hand we could say that, even granting that something called "the gift" existed, the "event of the gift's impossibility" would also, surely, take place, and that this would cancel out or invalidate the possibility of reciprocating the gift.

Hegemonic logic always already demands that "what is possible" be maintained. Yet it can never completely repress the event of its own ceaseless dislocation by, for example, the movement of migrants with their marginal, improvised, fragmentary subjectivities. This kind of movement is not a matter of what we usually refer to as a person's "subjective perspective," intention, knowledge, or awareness. Rather, it is that which veers away from the endlessly repeating cycles of capital, that which negotiates the unknown, that which, even when caught up in the almost irresistible, self-aggrandizing momentum of power, continues to constitute itself, unexpectedly, as a subject of antagonism, dislodged from hegemonic regularity. It is the event of the Multitudes to come.

In the points above, I am asking Ghassan Hage to pluralize the centripetal force of his essay into many different forms of praxis. To undertake such a project would add yet greater depth to his work.

ENDNOTES

1 Edouard Glissant, *Introduction à une Poétique du Divers* (Montreal, Quebec: Presses de L'université de Montréal, 1995). The translator would like to thank Natalie Melas for locating the original French text of this poem.

2 Regrettably, in some cases this 1899 law (known in Japanese as *Hokkaidô Kyûdojin Hogo Hôan*) continues to be translated into English as the "Former Hokkaido Aborigine Protection Law". Trans.

3 Gayatri Spivak, "Ghostwriting," *Diacritics* 25.2 (Summer 1995).

Nibutani Project: A Sculpture Addressing the Issue of the Ainu People and the Nibutani Dam

Tomotari Mikako

— translated from Japanese by Brett de Bary

"Recollection — Nibutani Dam", Sculpture in Black Marble, 1999.

When I first confronted the Nibutani Dam, I was transfixed. I stood there unable to think. I had not even a fragment with which to recollect the life that had taken place on this site. It was as if I were performing a rite of memorial, but with the sadness of one who has nothing to forget.

The meanings and memories that criss-crossed this dam: how could they be enunciated? Through facts? Through words? Facing layers of sediment, that which had seeped away made itself known to me only in flickers. How could I give meaning to what had accumulated here, or interpret it? I would never be able to produce a work that did more than express my personal experience of it, a futile exercise in self-discovery. Rather than trying to make a thing visible, I let its fissures penetrate my body. For me, this is the process of sculpting.

Fully aware that any knowledge or action of mine could never come into contact with memories of this land, I was nevertheless led on by my awareness of the reality I saw in flickers. In my creative work I sought to fix on one solid point from which to release energy into those elusive gaps and rifts, but everything that seemed like a certainty would shatter and move. The sculpture people now see is just the after-image of the fragments that I assembled and reassembled, again and again.

Now the course of the Saru River has been transformed. But is there any way the thoughts and memories brought to this place could cease to flow? I wanted to make my creative work a process of making connections among those memories, even if they were only fragments. Perhaps it was because I harbored a fear that I myself had no connection with my past, that I had come from nowhere.

It was not my intention to make the "Nibutani Project" into some kind of art or political movement. If I were forced to state the purpose of my work, I would say it was simply to become a device for making each viewer look intently, and to provoke the viewer to keep thinking without being limited by a notion of fixed meaning. My work is neither revolutionary nor an act of struggle. Rather, it exists first and foremost to capture people's attention through their sensations of it. Whatever the thoughts or relationships I take up in my work, they represent just one small cross-section of reality.

Different Aspects of the "Nibutani Project"

I felt it was important to breathe the air of that land, to learn by glimpsing things, as it were, in the interstices of everyday life. I tried to bring many people to Nibutani to assist in constructing the base for my sculpture. I began my work in August, 1998, living in a shed on the Kaizawa family farm. I helped on the farm, while getting my project set up. From this site, I put up a home page on the Web, which I maintained daily: *http://www.kyushu-id.ac.jp/~tomotari/nibutaniwork.html*

"Long ago indigenous Ainu people lived on this rich land. This is a fact that can never be changed. Together with Kaizawa Kôichi, I offer this scupture to those who sought to protect the culture they inherited." (Inscription on base of sculpture.)

Kaizawa-san makes an offering of water from the Saru River.

Nibutani Dam, with the sculpture in front of it.

In 1997 I had invited members of the Kaizawa Family to visit the Kyushu Institute of design to teach wood-carving and embroidery at a workshop we held on Ainu culture. In October of the same year I invited Keira Mitsunori, author of the book *Modernization and Structures of Discrimination Against Ainu* (*Kindaika no naka no Ainu sabetsu no kôzô,* Akashi Shoten, 1998), and his wife, to join me for a panel discussion. We discussed issues such as tourism, discrimination, and the restoration of Ainu culture.

We stressed that the situation of the Ainu will not improve until the attitudes of Japanese, who create stereotypes about the Ainu, have been transformed and deepened. People make a show of having "correct" attitudes, without engaging the real problems. I also learned that good will and a sense of joy (so often undervalued) can generate the strength to follow through where difficult matters are concerned. We have to realize that the actions of actually meeting Ainu people and listening to what they have to say constitute a form of understanding. The sensations generated by interaction, and a sense of inevitability, are necessary if we are to keep our dialogue from beginning and ending on a superficial level. If we see people through pre-established categories, we may not be seeing them at all.

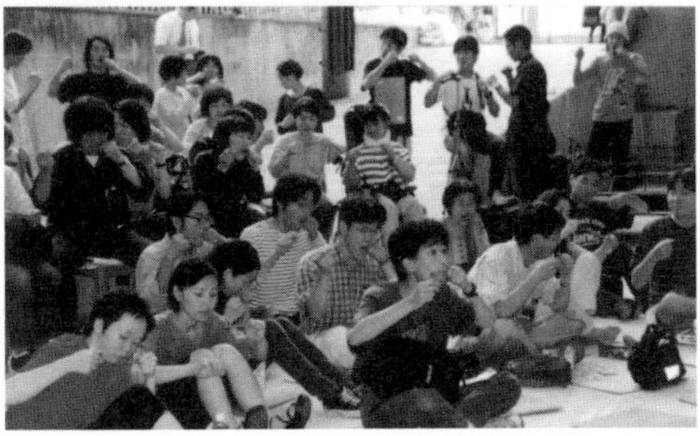

Our actions should not be a matter of "applying" theory from a book. In my own work I do not seek to attain any final conclusion — but simply to respond to things in a flexible way, by meeting people, making observations, and not fearing change. I recognize that to leave meanings and conclusions unresolved involves maintaining a kind of open-endedness that is difficult to sustain. Still, I have the sense that each person I become involved with requires a unique response…this is what I make my starting point. Perhaps I behave this way because my work is to make things.

For me, to think is to stand still. It takes time and effort to let the resistance I experience when standing still diffuse itself throughout my being. Although I have finished work on the Nibutani Project, I will continue to search for fragments, refining them and reworking them, spinning them into threads. By storing these things in my mind, I will go on trying to connect the different relationships that have criss-crossed my life. I am convinced something will emerge from the knots and joints I create.

I would also like to be able to convey to others the story of the Kaizawa family's struggle to halt the building of the Nibutani Dam. Yet I am hesitant about causing further upheaval in their lives. Their situation and desires are more important than my conception of the project. Only in the case that they need my support will I do my best to offer it.

Commentary on Nibutani Project

Môri Yoshitaka*
— *translated from Japanese by Brett de Bary*

Tomotari Mikako's artwork is deeply interesting to me as a practice which demonstrates how communal memory may be created, sustained, and transformed. At the same time, hers is not a practice in which the activity of calling forth memory simply means reproducing things from the past in their

---

* I have greatly relied on material the reader can find on Tomotari Mikako's home page: *http://www.kyushu-id.ac.jp/~tomotari/*. Some comment on the features of Tomotari Mikako's larger oeuvre also seems necessary here. She is a sculptor, and although in part her activities as a sculptor and her political activities overlap, the range of her political activities cannot be reduced simply to her artistic practice. The reverse is also true. It seems to me necessary to view her work, not in terms of whether art or politics (in an "either/or" sense) takes precedence in it, but rather from a "both/and" perspective. The written "traces" that she has produced, in addition to her sculpted pieces, have a certain directness of feeling in which, at first glance, it might be tempting to find a certain political naivete. I would prefer to think of this apparent naivete as the effects of a subtle positioning which cannot be reductively confined to the category of "art" or "politics."

I would also like to acknowledge my indebtedness to Kitahara Megumi's excellent introduction to Tomotari Mikako's activities in the journal *Inpakushion*, Volumes 114 and 116 (Tokyo: Inpakushion Publishers, 1999).

original form. Instead, she picks up the meager traces that have been left behind and, piecing together these shreds, creates new memory in the form of a creative work.

I do not mean to use the word "creative" here in a manner that unduly stresses concepts of "productivity" or "expression." Surely Tomotari Mikako creates, but through actions that are very restrained — so restrained, in fact, they are difficult to perceive. This subtlety is a hallmark of her work.

What she calls the "Nibutani Project" project grew out of an "emptiness" she experienced standing before the Nibutani Dam that had caused former homelands of the indigenous Ainu people of Hokkaido to become submerged under water. At that moment she tried to somehow think of what memories the Ainu people might have of this site. But as an outsider who was not descended from Ainu, she was, inevitably, unable to recall anything at all. Even the waters at the damsite — which should have had some tale to tell — offered no hint. What shocked the artist was the experience of being unable to think at all on that site.

The Nibutani Dam is an important site for all those concerned with the issues of minorities and indigenous rights in Japan. Planning to erect a dam in the Nibutani drainage basin of the Saru River, a river of immense importance for the livelihood and beliefs of the Ainu people, began thirty years ago. Many Ainu people who had been reduced to poverty by the Japanese government's coercive land policies, carried out in the name of modernization, had to give up their land, despite the importance attached to this specific site in Ainu memory.

Not all Ainu people were in agreement, however, about the building of the dam. Once the government's plans had been made public and while the acquisition of land was being carried out, Kayano Shigeru and Kaizawa Tadashi, two Ainu, filed a lawsuit to preserve Ainu culture from the damage that would be done by the dam. As they put it, "With the Nibutani Dam as our foil, we seek to establish the human rights of the Ainu people." Kaizawa Tadashi died in the course of the trial, and his son Aizawa Kôichi took his place. This trial thus became the first site at which the indigenous status of the Ainu people was ever publicly debated. In 1997, at the end of a lengthy struggle, the plaintiffs won a decision that the building of the dam was illegal, based on recognition of the status of the Ainu as indigenous residents of the land. However, in the end, regrettably, the plans for the building of the dam were implemented.

Tomotari Mikako first went to the Nibutani Dam after its completion. Her initial plan had been to make a sculpture and let it sink into the water at the dam. Each time water was released from the dam, the sculpture would come into view and the level of its deterioration would suggest the lapse of time since the trial. However, she abandoned this idea when she learned that — since the dam was a property of the state — submerging her sculpture there would constitute the crime of "illegal abandonment."

When she was on the verge of giving up her project, however, Tomotari Mikako met Kaizawa Kôichi, one of the plaintiffs at the trial, and he proposed to her that she erect her sculpture on land that he owned which bordered on the damsite. As he later explained it, Kaizawa thought that, "even though the dam had been built and the trial was over, the problem had not been solved — I thought of the stone image as something that could continue our appeal." The sculpture Tomotari Mikako completed and erected on this site is shown in her first photograph.

The work of production, however, did not proceed smoothly. Opinions about the dam among Ainu people were divergent, and, although some supported the Kaizawa's activities, others did not. There were some whose antagonism to the Kaizawas reflected their own very complex feelings about having sold their land to the government.

Tomotari Mikako, too, was criticized by some because she was not an Ainu herself. How could it be possible for someone who did not share the memory of the Ainu people to express that memory? Was she not simply making use of Ainu history as raw material for her art, as a means of making a statement in the art world? Despite this very hurtful criticism, Tomotari expanded the scope of her project. She invited people from Hokkaido to participate in a workshop she organized at the Kyushu Institute of Design, where she teaches. At the same time she brought people who were interested in her project to Nibutani to assist in its construction. This flow of people from north to south, and from the south to the north of Japan, was accompanied by a movement of material goods along the same trajectory. Tomotari Mikako felt that language alone was not a sufficient means for coming to understand something or for conveying it to others. The sounds and smells of an atmosphere, the physical nature of things and their feel — she attempted to mobilize all the senses. Her project tried to make use of daily activities to the fullest extent — activities in which people shared the same time and space or discussed things face to face.

It was through such activities that she sought to show how memory is formed.

Debates in the wake of post-structuralism have clarified that identity is neither biological nor essential, but that it is constructed amidst diverse historical and social relationships. They have revealed the historical specificity and socially constructed nature of concepts such as ethnic or racial identity, which were previously seen as fixed categories. The categories of "Japanese" and "Ainu" are neither universal nor immutable. They are simply products of the Japanese nation state as a modern institution. At the Kyushu Institute of Design workshop, for example, an Ainu writer who had left his homeland to live in the city addressed the participants, demonstrating how a new kind of Ainu identity could exist. Thus we could understand that what is usually thought of as "Ainu culture" was developed relatively recently, with the growth of tourism, and was interconnected with many other cultural phenomena. Also at the workshop, Keira Mitsunori — a "Wajin" or Japanese by birth — spoke about how he and his family had gradually become involved with Ainu issues, since his partner, Tomoko, was of Ainu ancestry. Such examples demonstrated how limiting it is to think of a people or an ethnicity as a biologically based category.

However artificial categories like ethnic identity may be, though, who can choose them freely? This was demonstrated by an interesting story told by Keira Mitsunori at the workshop. Before I introduce this story, however (and anticipating some points I will bring up later) I must offer an explanation. This is not a story I am reconstructing after hearing it directly from the people involved. I have created a small narrative about anonymous characters, rather roughly abstracting on the basis of what I picked up at the workshop. I realize that every concrete episode involves countless singularities that can be understood only by those directly involved, and that when one presumes to tell a story about another it always involves some arrogance and misunderstanding — one could even call it "cruelty." While I am fully aware of this, the possibility of my telling this story is, paradoxically, inseparable from this same arrogance and "cruelty."

The story involves a Japanese man and an Ainu woman who fell in love with each other. At first, the woman concealed from the man the fact that she was an Ainu. But as their marriage approached she grew more and more anxious about hiding this matter. (In Japan, marriage practices are still strongly linked to racial discrimination.) She decided to reveal the truth and plucked up her courage. "You've probably already figured this out, but I am Ainu."

The man's response, intended not to hurt her feelings was, "It doesn't matter."

But for her, the words were a shock. Certainly they were meant kindly, but to have what she had agonized about throughout her life dismissed with the phrase, "It doesn't matter," was painful. Who had the right to tell her that her suffering didn't matter? At the workshop, Keira Mitsunori used the word "cruel" to describe the man's phrase — for the woman involved, what appeared to be magnanimity on the surface was the cruel behavior of one who was unconditionally accepted as a "Japanese." However, this exchange was not only shocking for the woman but also for the man. He became distressed, realizing how deeply his words had hurt her. He was forced to reflect on the way what seemed to him a sincere gesture was unconsciously premised on his positionality as a member of the Japanese majority.

This story suggests the way ethnic identities are historically, geographically, and socially produced, rather than being biologically determined. But the experiences attached to these identities can never be understood as simply artificial, nor are we free to choose them as we will. They have their own specificity that entails their oppressive materiality, as well as bodily and psychological pain. Such experiential modalities of identity are thrust upon us in ways we cannot control.

It is nevertheless possible to communicate about such discrete experiences. In the incident above, we can see clearly that the man had not fully understood the woman's experiences. But it was truly at that moment — the moment of realizing he was unable to understand her — that he could begin to share her pain. In this moment he also must have discovered *inside himself* something that had been erased by his unconsciously maintained identity as a Japanese. Through such a painful experience, he could begin to make her experiences as an Ainu a part of his own memory.

I think that what Tomotari Mikako has attempted to do is to create collective memory out of the kind of interactions I have just described. Through the processes of sculpting, organizing the workshop, and so forth, she set up opportunities to engage herself in discussion with Ainu people, and thus to begin to make some of their memories her own memories. Although the process often left her with hurt feelings, it also opened her eyes to ways in which "differences" among Japanese people themselves (some of which were an aspect of her own identity) had been forcibly repressed and excluded.

Of course the transmission, sharing, and transformation of memory is not something that depends on text-based knowledge. It must be constructed amidst the practical social relations of those who share the memory. Face-to-face discussion, sharing the same time and space, breathing the same air, exchanging letters and telephone calls — all of these direct, embodied relationships constitute such sociality. Once again, I do not mean to imply that these activities lead to complete mutual understanding. Rather, they offer so many opportunities for recognizing that there is no such thing as rapid and easy communication — that the sharing of memory is, in fact, an impossibility. Yet it is in the moments when, in the midst of the intense effort of trying to transmit what can never be fully transmitted, one confronts that ultimate impasse, that a common memory may be forged, as if by some tiny miracle. This is the process that Tomotari Mikako's art attempts to suggest.

As cultural studies and post-colonial theory have been taken up by scholars around the world, questions surrounding the status of minority people who, like the Ainu, had rarely received serious scholarly attention, have become important issues. With the intensification of international scholarly exchange that has accompanied the development of information technologies such as the Internet and other new means of communication, it has become possible to undertake discussion of previously marginalized subjects on a global scale. This is a development to be welcomed. Still, we face the problem of how it will be possible to deconstruct essentialistic categories of ethnicity on the one hand, while, on the other, improvising new modes of political solidarity through the production, maintenance, and transformation of the shared memories of ever more diverse, multiple collectivities. Tomotari Mikako's project suggests what kind of time and care must be expended by those engaged in such a task. But it is in the "slowing down" that such time and care necessitate that the key to creating the means for such relationships, in all their materiality, must surely exist. Her work gives us a valuable, concrete instance of such an effort.

Words of the Other

Oka Mari
— translated from Japanese by Brett de Bary

What does it mean for people to come together in time and space and within that shared time and space to encounter language, indeed, the language of the Other?

We experienced something like this in Fukuoka, in Kyushu, over a two-day period this past December. "In Fukuoka, in Kyushu?" What could such words, almost too self-evident in a Japanese linguistic context, mean to someone existing apart from it? "Kyushu? What's Kyushu?" As I now address those living outside a Japanese-language context, those reading my writing in a *langue* which is not Japanese, perhaps I must rewrite those self-evident words. "In Kyushu," I might write, "a southwestern island in the Japanese archipelago, in a city called 'Fukuoka'..." But even then, is what I have written so clear?

This was, in fact, my first visit to the city of Fukuoka. In this, I imagine I was no different from the majority of people who had come, from Japan and elsewhere, to the TRACES Fukuoka Conference. To Fukuoka, which we think of as the westernmost city of Japan. But when I looked at an unusual map of the region, in which the Tsushima Straits occupied the dead center (I had discovered this map at an exhibit of East Asian art featured at the Fukuoka Museum of Fine Arts, where our conference was held), I could see how much closer to the Asian mainland, to the Korean peninsula, Fukuoka was than Tokyo, the national capital. On this map, Korea, China, and Kyushu constituted a world encircling a small ocean, while somewhere off to the east in the outskirts, at the edge of an island that looked like a crooked, narrow extension of a promontory off that ocean, was Tokyo. Looking at this map I felt as if my center of gravity had been shifted, center and periphery reversed, and, momentarily, the ground on which I stood seemed unsteady.

Living in Tokyo, as I have for the past ten years, I have always thought of Tokyo as the center of my world, the center of Japan. Often, for me, Tokyo and Japan seem interchangeable: to talk about Tokyo is to talk about Japan, and vice versa. But as my eyes traversed this map, on which my own existence had been peripheralized and relegated to the margins, my own world-view, centered on Tokyo as the capital city of Japan, seemed to go up in smoke, and I experienced some ever-so-slightly new sensation. My worldview, I realized, reflected nothing other than the hegemonic geopolitics of the Japanese modern nation state — indeed, by having internalized such a worldview I became a participant in it.

I was situated, then, not in Fukuoka, the regional city located on the margins, the western rim, of Japan but in a topos called Fukuoka, an East Asian city where I could temporarily dislocate the national identity I had come to embody. We spent two days in a museum in that city, in a windowless auditorium several floors above ground level, illuminated by spotlights with their characteristic, artificial glare. Despite the glare (even, perhaps, because of it), one could clearly sense the different shades in the particles of darkness that filled the air — particles of light and particles of darkness seemed to fuse in the space which was like a womb, like sea depths, like a prison cell, or like that medieval European monastery where layers of memory since classical times had been compressed, in Ecco's *Name of the Rose*.... We were in a space where memories, densely folded in upon one another, were evoked and testified to: imperial memory, national memory, group memory, and a kind of memory intricately bound up with national memory that we nevertheless think of as "personal."

And what does it mean — in an age where global sharing of information on the Internet is a matter of seconds — for people from different countries to commit themselves to assembling in a specific place at considerable expenditure of time and money? Indeed, to commit themselves to spending two days in that oppressive darkness, as if they were fetal existences or deep-sea fish? For one person to share time and space with another.... No doubt, it is this very coming together with others in time and space that makes the act of "testimony" possible. Or, perhaps one should say that this sharing of space with others is what makes a "telling" into a "testimony," an event. In the infinite expanse of our universe, and in the endless continuum of time into eternity, coming together in time and space constitutes a singular event — thus "testimony," too, must always be singular.

"Testimony" — language is summoned up so that we may share memories with others... Indeed, what linked those of differing backgrounds, nationalities, ethnicities, and linguistic orientations gathered together in that deep sea-like space, was precisely the unity of time and space, and language, the languages of others. For me, spending those two days in the sea depths, or in womb-like darkness, was an experience of being continuously exposed to the language of the Other.

To listen to testimony, to partake in the memory of the Other or the experience of the Other, is not to have language communicate meaning, as is commonly thought. Rather, it seems to me impossible to even talk about testimony except as an occasion for grasping language as that through which Otherness is exposed, as that which occludes the communication of meaning.

Within the context of Japanese society since 1990, the words "testimony" and "sharing the memory of the Other" inevitably have certain implications. But I need perhaps to reiterate the events to which they allude — indirectly but certainly — here. In 1990, beginning with Kim Hak Sun's announcement that she had been used as a "sex slave" by the Japanese Army during the Asia Pacific War, women in countries throughout Asia began to offer testimony about the unspeakable suffering they had experienced as former "comfort women." Provoked by these women's demands that the Japanese government punish those responsible for their mistreatment, and offer a formal apology and compensation, two groups emerged in Japan. One group sought to take this up as an issue of war responsibility — by taking part in the women's remembrance of the "events" they had experienced. Others sought to deny the events themselves, arguing that "comfort women" had not been coerced but were involved in a "commercial transaction." Indeed, beginning in 1990, Japan entered into a state that might be described as a civil war over memory. (This is a situation European societies had experienced 10 years earlier with the appearance of what was called "historical revisionism.") In this state we have had to ask ourselves very fundamental questions about "testimony" and "giving testimony" — what does it really mean to listen to the testimony of the Other, to take it seriously, to share memories with another?

In the East Asian city of Fukuoka, as I participated in the "events" of narrating and listening, for example, to the memories that had been erased from the history of the Japanese nation state (in Tomotari Mikako's presentation) or to the story of imperialist massacre of minority peoples in China (as in Jacqueline Armijo's presentation) I seemed simultaneously to hear, as in a basso continuo, reverberations of the processes of "testimony" and "sharing of memory" we had recently experienced in relation to the former "comfort women."

Against this background, let me offer some comments on Tomotari Mikako's "speech" — if indeed it can be called a "speech." Perhaps it might be better to describe Tomotari-san as engaging in a "process" of narrating personal memories, where what was at stake was her ability to share the remembrances of the Other. In other words, what she offered us was a "work" which attempted to suggest what the project of "testimony" means through its own multilayered performativity. Hers was a work of rare beauty which was also filled with pain and sadness. And this "work" was performed only once.

In trying to discuss this layered, polyphonic performance in words, then, I can only grope for a point of entry. "How can I ever describe this to my readers, who were not in that space at that time…it is utterly impossible," I found myself writing, only to be caught short by an observation. When someone has given testimony to a memory, the one who listens to it and tries to convey that "event" to another becomes, in turn, a new witness, a new bearer of testimony. Who was the philosopher who detected the word *le tiers* ("third party") in the word *témoin* (to "give testimony to")? Now I, too, found myself experiencing the difficulty inherent in the process of testimony. Suddenly I understood, in however small a way, the burdens Tomotari-san had taken upon herself when she tried to address an unknown audience. By building into her "speech" the impossibility of being summarized retrospectively, she ensured that this particular process of bearing testimony — for both narrator and listener — would be experienced as a singular "event."

Still I must try to offer some kind of summary here. I must attempt a clumsy translation of Tomotari-san's multilevel, polyphonic work into the essentially linear medium of language, reconstituting it as a fragmentary monody.

As an artist, Tomotari Mikako has spent time on Japan's northern island of Hokkaido living with the indigenous people who were forcibly assimilated into the project of building the modern Japanese nation state. At the very site where state violence is still being deployed against these people, she attempted to create a work of sculpture which would stand as a figure of memory — the memory of their community that now exists *only* in memory, the memory of how that community had been violently expropriated and destroyed, as well as the memory of the violence that had been visited upon Tomotari-san's own community. Memory, in all these cases, was synonymous with pain. From the perspective of the Ainu among whom she worked, however, Tomotari-san, as an ethnic Japanese, could only be seen as a member of the group of people who had colonized, invaded, and destroyed. Yet while appearing as an Other to the Ainu, she herself was descended from *yamabushi* people (itinerant shamans called "mountain priests" whose practices were banned by the modern Japanese state shortly after the Meiji Restoration of 1868). Just like the Ainu, the *yamabushi* had had their communities destroyed and had been forcibly assimilated into the modern Japanese nation state. (That the *yamabushi* had been the object of such state policies was something I learned for the first time hearing her speak.) The reason she could be especially sensitive to the sufferings of the Ainu was that she, too, had to live with the painful memories of such state violence whenever she reflected on her own identity. For Tomotari-san, I speculated, such painful memories must be constantly reawakened by daily, inescapable encounters with the ways in which the violence of forced assimilation — the violence of state formation itself — continues to be repeated in relation to Ainu, resident foreigners in Japan, and other groups who are discriminated against. What must prompt such a strong awareness of being a descendant of *yamabushi* in Tomotari-san is not so much *ressentiment* or *nostalgie* but the reality of the repeated violence of the Japanese nation state.

During her "speech," Tomotari-san noted that, insofar as communities of *yamabushi* were linked not by land or "blood" ties but by commonly shared life-ways, they were similar to the Ainu. In other words, for both groups it was shared life-ways that constituted the identity of the community. Ironically enough, however, it was because she was descended from people not related by "blood" to the Ainu, that Tomotari-san was rejected by them and treated as an "outsider" or an "other." In her presentation, the painfulness of remembering the past, and the loneliness of the present, were expressed through the overlapping of visual (computer-generated images) and aural (narration in her own voice) media. Yet her images themselves were further doubled: on the screen she projected both photographs and printed words. While the photographs were of Ainu people, and the lands and scenery they live among, they were accompanied by Tomotari-san's feelings expressed in English sentences that flickered on and off the screen — albeit in an English so broken one could hardly call it a *langue.* Furthermore, in a voice that seemed to envelope all these images, Tomotari-san narrated the memory of the *yamabushi,* her extremely personal narrative as a descendent of *yamabushi.*

Speech disassociated from vision.... What Tomotari-san's images conveyed to us was a quiet indictment of the succession of coercive policies that inflicted the violences of colonialism, of assimilation, and of an assault on their natural environment, upon the Ainu people. Hers was also a documentary about the way she had attempted to involve herself with these issues as an artist. At the same time, what her voice told us about was a thoroughly personal remembrance, that of an individual who lived with the pain of having had her ancestral community annihilated through processes of state-building and assimilation, and was thus forcibly assigned a "Japanese" identity. Tomotari-san's images, on the other hand, told the story of a self that had been othered as a Japanese or "*Yamato person*" by the Ainu, of the self who was an artist. Her voice told us of a self living in a present that repeated the violence of the past, of a self that — had Japanese modern history been otherwise — might have encountered the Ainu as a member of one, among many, collectivities premised on the holding of life-ways in common.

Were the multiple identities Tomotari-san superimposed on this fissure of image and sound, in the final analysis, linked in purely coincidental ways? We might begin to think about this question by considering her proper name. Surely not a single speaker of the Japanese language would read the three characters of her name with the pronunciation "*Tomotari*"! Tomotari-san's name itself is disloyal to the Japanese language, to the nation state. Although written with three characters that could be pronounced, respectively, *tomo, tari,* and *in,* this name that violates the rules of our *langue* is read as if the third character (*in*) were missing. According to Tomotari-san, this suffix was banned from use by all but aristocrats or those related to the imperial family by the Meiji government, and therefore removed from her family's name at that time. The memory of state violence is thus deeply inscribed in her name itself. It has only been recently that she has restored the suffix (and this in response to the suggestion of an Ainu person whose friendship she had gained). She has added simply the character-suffix, which she never pronounces when her name is read. In this way she hopes to etch the memory of her ancestors into her name, and to bear testimony to her own connection to the *yamabushi* community. She has done this so that each time her name is written or uttered, memory of the state violence inflicted upon the community she would have belonged to, had things been otherwise, is recalled. It is that memory that emerges out of the double structure of her name, out of the unbridgeable gulf between her name as written and her name as pronounced. Indeed, as I type this article and sound out, in my head, the name "Tomotari" each time I enter the phonetic syllables that might be converted into her three-character name[1], I cannot avoid being reminded of that violence — moreover, of the relationship between state violence and naming in general.[2] (But, I ask myself once again, however familiar those within a Japanese language context might be with that double structure, with the fracture between the character as visualized and the character as pronounced, would those who speak English, French, or Chinese understand what I am alluding to? And how might I convey this to them?)

Let us define the identity of *yamabushi* as a that "body" of people who lived in the mountains and had specific life-ways and values in common. If such is the case, regardless of whether or not Tomotari-san can use her name as descendant of such people (whose community has already been destroyed and who have come out of the mountains), she can never identify herself *as* a *yamabushi*. In her speech, she used the phrase "we *yamabushi*." But she also said, "In the eyes of the Ainu, I was a Japanese." Thus, as a *yamabushi*, she had to speak as "we," but as a Japanese, she was "I." For her to use the phrases, "I am a *yamabushi*" or "we, Japanese" was not possible. Confronted with the actuality of this person who could never speak of being Japanese except in the first person, I had the same vertiginous sensation I experienced looking at the map of Kyushu. It was the sensation — as Genet once said of his meeting with Palestinians — of having the rug swept out from under one's feet. Faced with Tomotari-san, I had to ask myself, what was I? All that was clear to me was that she and I did not constitute "we Japanese." Even if she was Japanese and I was also Japanese. By producing a gap, or discordance, in her modes of first person utterance (between "we *yamabushi*" and "I, as a Japanese…"), Tomotari-san was making "us" (that is, Tomotari-san and myself) ask what kind of "we" we could possibly be. I was reminded that for me to exist as a "Japanese" is an "event" that I can only and always experience in the first person singular. And at the same moment I was also reminded that I, too, was an embodied subject of the violence of the nation state, that I had been subjected to the violence of being made "Japanese." Tomotari-san's words, in which the phrase "we Japanese" never once occurred, summoned us to be mindful of that forgotten violence of "being made subjects" that is visited, not only on non-"ethnic" Japanese but, indeed, on "ethnic" Japanese themselves.

For me, then, Tomotari-san's "speech" was an occasion for a negotiation between her identity and mine, which opened up the possibility for a reconstruction, and rearticulation. But I can only imagine the perplexity she must have experienced in trying to address others in her audience for whom the word "*yamabushi*" was completely unfamiliar, who existed at a distance from Japan's modern history, and who regarded her "culture" and "langue" — so different from their own — with well-intentioned curiosity. More than the "meaning" she attempted to convey in her "speech," it was Tomotari-san's language itself — full of hesitation, delivered in a nervous voice, marked by stalls, advances, returns, and sudden shifts from English to Japanese and back again — that conveyed her anxiety, hesitancy, uncertainty, and confusion. The language of her "speech," in fact, functioned in a manner similar to the English statements she projected on the screen as a part of her "work" — statements in broken English which, while they failed to communicate her intended meaning, nevertheless communicated something else.

I like to think that it was through this specific *form* that Tomotari-san expressed something about what the project of bearing testimony is. The memory of an "event"...when we try to narrate our chaotic memories, like Tomotari-san, we do not know where to start, and we veer back and forth grasping at shreds of words. No, there is more to it than that. Is there not the constant fear that "you," you who are before my eyes, will not really understand, and that the "event" that is so important for me will not be received as such by you? Such waves of anxiety make one stammer, repeat oneself, and fall into silence. And while one seeks with almost embarrassing desperation for some sign of trustworthiness in the gaze of the listener, one is simultaneously fearful of meeting that gaze which may carry rejection and denial. Surely the language of the one bearing witness must at times run away with itself, far off from the witness' thoughts.

To offer testimony is to speak of pain. But pain, by definition, is that which cannot be put into words — it can only be spoken about figuratively. Following this logic, if to offer testimony is the kind of event taking place in time and space that I have just described, then to *listen* to testimony is also not simply to grasp the meaning of what can be conveyed in language, but to experience as bodily sensations the floating, incoherent, and fragmentary thoughts that fill that time and space. Wasn't it for this reason that, even in their confusing form, the sentences that vaguely approximated English, that Tomotari-san projected on the screen, managed to express something?

I must admit that on the day that I heard Tomotari-san speak, I was convinced that as a native speaker of Japanese (although what I was seeing performed painfully before me demonstrated that the existence of our common "mother tongue" could hardly be innocently taken for granted), I was in the privileged position of being better able to understand her words and the subtle nuances that evaded English translation than those in the room whose culture and *langue* were different from mine. In fact, I felt a kind of impatience with the interpreter's efforts to translate faithfully — or, to put it more accurately, to pick out from her speech those words that could be translated and that might produce a coherent meaning. I couldn't refrain from being a busybody, unceremoniously stepping in to call attention to the fact that Tomotari-san's Japanese was subtle and could not be translated, that it was precisely all those elements that could not be reduced to "meaning" that were the most important part of what she said. Yet when I reflect on it, it was I myself who, while insisting that the core of Tomotari-san's testimony lay in a realm other than that of "shared meaning," was fixated on being in the privileged position of "understanding" her *langue.* It was a conceit not dissimilar from that of the sighted, who believe they grasp the world better than the blind, or those who can hear and believe their reality is superior to that of the deaf. Just as the perceptions of the sighted are, in fact, greatly *limited* by the fact that they are sighted (and the same is true of those who can hear), my ability to pick up what was suggested by Tomotari-san's speech and images, the pitch and tone of her voice, and her silences, was no doubt limited by contrast to those who did not share the same *langue* with her, for whom her language did not necessarily convey meaning, and for whom her words were not inevitably laced with definitions. Who is to say that those whose *langues* differ, and for whom meaning is not readily accessible through language, understand each other less well than those whose *langue* is the same?

What you hear, and what I hear, situated in the same time and space, overlap, yet differ. This is because you and I are not the same. The process of listening to testimony becomes as many events as there are listeners, reflecting the multiple singularities that these listeners constitute. To say this, however, is not simply to advance a "relativized notion of truth." It is simply to say that the possibility of bearing testimony — the possibility of sharing memory with another — is an event that hinges on the unique relationship of one to one: the singularity that is my existence, listening to your words.

If it is shared life-patterns that make *yamabushi yamabushi*, those who do not share them are not *yamabushi*. When Tomotari-san used the words "we *yamabushi*," however, she was not referring to her family lineage as a daughter of *yamabushi*, but rather speaking as one who had made the memory of the state violence against the *yamabushi* community her own personal memory. In this instance, the identity of the *yamabushi* is not at all the same as the identity of a former ethnic community (with shared life-ways). It is the identity of those from whom the state wrested away existence as *yamabushi*, whose life-ways the state destroyed, and who were forced to assimilate. Insofar as *yamabushi* must now construct an identity out of the shared memory of state violence, their situation is comparable to that of the Jewish people dealing with the memory of the Holocaust.

For example, the privileged form of memory that sustains the state of Israel is that of the genocide waged against the Jewish race by Nazi Germany. This was experienced by European Jews, but can be shared by a "we" that includes, for example, even Jews in North Africa who have Arab–Islamic backgrounds. Experiences of persecution that took place in North Africa, as well as Europe, in differing historical contexts, are now being reconstructed into something that is remembered as a singular, yet universal, experience of "we Jews." A new "we," a new collective identity, is being born. (In Tunisia, Jewish followers of Tunisian descent remember their experiences of anti-Semitism at the time of Tunisian Independence as "another Holocaust," thus making it an example of a universal anti-Semitism historically experienced by "we Jews." At the same time, can we not see the experience of Tunisian Jews as an example of state violence, of the exclusion of others that always accompanies the formation of the nation state?) On the other hand, in Israel we can also see how memories of an Arab culture once shared by Jews with Arab Muslims and Arab Christians, is now being labeled "their" culture, the culture of the Other, in such a way that Palestinian Arabs who were once part of a "we" for Palestinian Jews have now been completely excluded from the nation state of Israel, and are discriminated against. We might say that in the moment when a new collective identity is created, based on the shared memory of experiencing violence in the past, the question of how to share that memory without privileging the community and excluding others comes to the fore.

What deeply interested me in Tomotari-san's presentation was her ability to talk about a *yamabushi* identity based on a shared memory of violence, without privileging the *yamabushi* experience as that of an ethnic group. Her words did not attempt to draw a definitive boundary between those ethnic Japanese who exercised violence against *yamabushi* (that is, those who were not *yamabushi*) and those against whom violence was exercised (those who were *yamabushi*), but rather incited ethnic Japanese toward (and even seemed like a prayer for) sharing of the *yamabushi* experience as "ours" rather than "theirs." At least, this is how I understood it.

Later, in Jacqueline Armijo's presentation, we learned that the memory of the massacre of a Muslim community by the Qing government is still being talked about in China, and a collective identity being reproduced. Armijo's testimony — necessarily, and meaningfully — evoked associations with the "event" of the recurring massacres of Muslims all over the world in places such as Lebanon, Bosnia, and Kosovo. But is it possible to make the memory of these "events," originally experienced by embodied Muslim subjects, "our" memory rather than "their" memory, in such a way that we do not establish a rigid boundary between "Muslims who are all victims" and "non-Muslims who are all persecutors and slaughterers"? Is there a way to make the event of the Holocaust — without relativizing it in any way — something that could be "our" memory, rather than only the privileged memory of the Jewish people? Could the Holocaust become a memory of all peoples (including Palestinians) who have been violently excluded from the nation state because they do not share the memory of the *ethnos*, and could it become "our" memory for all those who wish for the dismantling of the nation state as a mechanism inevitably producing others who must be expelled? Or, to put it the other way around, through constructing memories in such a form, might it be possible for us to produce a new "we"? In the same sense that Genet wrote, "The Palestinian revolution is my revolution...."

A possibility — to use the process of bearing testimony to share the memory of others and make them "our" memories, or to create a "we" that regards the memories of others as "ours." We may hope for such a possibility but, for example, we cannot forget about situations such as that of the East Asian nation partitioned into north and south, in which women from the south who go to the north, in an attempt to elicit narratives and fashion a common memory with their sisters, have been subject to arrest as spies or on other charges. In our last minutes of those days, in that space, in Fukuoka, we heard about this reality.

For us to dream of the path that leads to the sharing of the experience and memory of the Other, and by so doing to create a new "we" — even to dream of it is an important matter. Nor is it misguided for us to seek to make more sophisticated those well-intentioned gestures by which we attempt to decipher even the silence and inexpressible pain that is part of the memory of the Other. However, in a case like that of South Korean women who found that visiting their sisters and compatriots to hear their testimonies — indeed, that the very act of listening to those testimonies itself — constituted a severe crime against the state (and who therefore found their efforts physically impeded by an exercise of state violence) we are brought up short by a reality that rebuffs us. Indeed, in East Asia we inhabit a harsh world where coming together in time and space to share the memories of others and to build a new "we," as we have tried to do in this conference, can only be seen as a kind of privileged utopianism (in every sense of the word). Such a serene spot, where we could truly strain our ears as we listened to those who shared their memories, lest the slightest breath or trembling of the voice escaped our notice, has yet to exist in our world. And it was of this harsh reality that we learned, in the seemingly harsh form of words uttered by one participant to another: "You and I speak completely different languages." In their own way, these words, too, were a kind of testimony, the appeal of one living in East Asia and tenaciously seeking to share the memory of the Other — uttered with a kind of desperation, and just once. They were words of testimony that perhaps could only have been spoken in that space like ocean depths, in the East Asian city of Fukuoka.

"Completely different languages"? What was at issue in this exchange was not a matter of *langue*. It was not a matter of Japanese and English, French and Korean. Had it been a matter of *langue*, translation or interpretation would have been called for. But what, then, might it mean for two people's languages to differ if it was *not* on the level of *langue*. What kind of difference was at stake, and how might it be bridged? This leads me to a final consideration.

When we are able to decipher even the silences and hesitations of one who is telling of a memory difficult to reveal, is it not because from the start — prior even to the attempt to narrate the memory of the event — we share some kind of narrative in common? Is it not because the language of the testimony — no matter what it might be — can be accommodated within a narrative framework we can agree upon, and that we can understand? Isn't this why we can wait silently? Until the witness' mouth begins to open with great difficulty, narrating a memory that seems to be reeled out of the depths, as, quietly and gently, words begin to flow? Is it not because we already know what that silence is, because no matter what the nature of the words that follow upon the silence, we know their content and can anticipate it? Is this not why we wait, and why we strain our ears to hear? But, then, how could we know another's language even before the story is told? When we use the words "experience of the Other," is it really "the Other" we are talking about? Are we awaiting the arrival of that which is truly Other?

The testimony of the women of South Korea who had been former "sex slaves" of the Japanese army was offered after years of oppressive silence. The director Byon Young Joo's documentary film about the present-day lives of these women, *The House of Nanumu*, offers a visual commentary on their acts of narration in its final scene. In this concluding scene, Byon makes visible for us, for the first time, on screen, the ugly scars where the trace of the violence she had suffered was deeply etched on the abdomen of a former "sex slave." Byon shows her baring the scar in utter silence, as if to reveal her secret. The film seems to quietly ask, at the end, if we could ever really share these women's memories of unspeakable violence, experiences which they will never be able to fully capture in words.

At the same time, when I attended a symposium two years ago, a woman who had seen another video, documenting the experiences of former "sex slaves" now living in North Korea, described their very different approach to the process of testimony. These women began to talk about their former victimization without hesitation or silences and with what might almost be called "matter-of-factness." She asked members of the symposium how we might understand and account for this difference between the women of the north and the south, and between their different styles of narration.

This raises a final question. Perhaps what is truly beyond the limits of our mental vision, what really plunges us into incomprehension, is to confront the fact that for some women the narration of their memory of a violence unimaginable by us, and therefore of an experience extraordinarily difficult to verbalize (thus, we expect, one that requires us to listen with the utmost sensitivity and attention to silence and hesitation), can simply be talked about in a straightforward way. As if there were nothing secret, nothing that could not be talked about or translated into words....

In this instance, too, what eludes us is not a matter of *langue*. If it were a matter of *langue*, their testimony of sexual victimization by the Japanese Army would be 100% intelligible and translatable. No, it is the very apparent translatability of the experience that is problematic. It is the fact that their testimony makes it seem as if no differences in *langue*, no slippage between event and narration, no gap between the experience of violence and its telling, exist. We are left to wonder what constitutes the conditions of possibility for this narrative told by women of North Korea: how could they tell their stories in that manner — or rather, what *was* the story they told? Even if we posit that their narratives were implicated in some way or another with the very different arrangements of power in North Korean society, what exactly that implicatedness consists of would be extremely difficult for us to know. In a sense we could say that the very matter-of-factness of the narratives of North Korean women — their clarity and their presumption that they would be fully understood — presents us with something truly unfamiliar that plunges us into incomprehension. But is this not what it means to encounter the Other? Is this not truly the language of the Other?

Perhaps it is what we can just barely glimpse in the outlines of this event that constitutes "speaking different languages." *Langue* is that which can be translated without omission or residue. But a story may be narrated in a *langue* from which, for example, the words "I cannot understand you," can surely be accurately translated into any language, yet nevertheless what makes it possible for this to be a story can elude us. This is what is meant by the observation that, in offering their testimonies, the women of North Korea and South Korea "speak two different languages." This is, I repeat, not a matter of differing *langues*. Moreover, for women of the south to go to the north in an attempt to negotiate these differences is prohibited, in many different ways.

Our conference left us facing such questions. It was a conference committed to a principle of "multilingualism" which, despite the efforts which left the translators exhausted, brought us face to face with the problem of "speaking different languages" or "the language of the Other" in such a way that differences in *langue*, slippages in translation, and the like, seemed to pale into insignificance — to be, indeed, merely the "play of signifiers."

We were left ask what it really means to "speak different languages" or even to "speak the same language." And what it could mean to share the experiences of the Other.

ENDNOTES

1 The author refers to the practice of typing in the phonetic syllables on a Japanese word processor keyboard (which features both letters of the alphabet and Japanese *kana*), which the word processor then "converts" into the relevant Chinese characters. Each time the author types Tomotari-san's name, she needs to produce three characters, but she is also aware that the third character will not be read aloud as part of the name. Even in pronouncing the name in her mind, she must ignore the presence of the final suffix, and third character. This is the gap between writing, reading, and pronunciation she has referred to. (Translator's note.)

2 An example of such coercion would be the colonial policy of Japan in Korea, where Koreans were forcibly made to change their surnames and first names to Japanese names. Today, as well, because of both the manifest and latent systematic racism of Japanese society, it is a matter of expediency for the large numbers of resident Koreans in Japan to adopt Japanese surnames for daily use. In recent years the legal requirement for such changing of names has been abolished. But many resident Koreans (as well as other foreigners) continue to be "advised," when they present themselves at municipal offices, to use Japanese names and to eradicate the traces of their ethnic origins as much as possible, as a way of assimilating with ethnic Japanese.

Conclusion: Editing Journal

Brett de Bary

August 12, 2000

I am trying to fax author Huang Ping (should I address him as Professor Huang? But he has been signing his e-mail posts "Ping"...) who is in London. Repeated busy signals when I attempt to send the fax. I try to reach a long distance operator, but our new domestic company, Verizon (formerly GTE and Bell Atlantic) is experiencing a work slow-down and I'll be waiting for a long time. I abandon that route and dig out the phone bill, with contact number, from our (also new) long-distance carrier, Qwest (why on earth are we always switching phone companies?), and finally do get an operator, who quickly bamboozles me into letting her dial the number as an operator-assisted call. I'm miffed I wasn't quick enough to avoid this higher toll. But I finally get a fax signal — by now the whole process has taken about twenty precious minutes — and I fax Huang some questions about his citations. How can we include a reference to the Chinese translation of an American academic work he is citing in his endnotes? I fax him two pages of the English translation of his article with questions scribbled in the margins. Strangely enough, just last night I ran across a paperback edition of the book in question, Philip Huang's *Peasant Economy and Social Change in North China,* in a used bookstore on the chronically ailing Ithaca Commons. Proprietor says he can stay in business by selling a lot of his used stock to Amazon.com.

Didn't buy the book, of course; not my field. But one of the phrases Huang adopted from it, "too many people, not enough land," still resonates somehow. In Ithaca these days there seems to be too much land and not enough people left who want to farm it. Then what does the signified of Huang's "peasant" mean to me and *how* does it mean? I'm self-conscious about the highly mediated context within which I encounter Huang's analysis of migrant movement.

I casually used the words "broad, panoramic sweeps" when talking about the Huang and Boutang articles to Meaghan. Meaghan, in an e-mail, wondered if the interface between these articles might be problematic. Should we separate them, or group them together? If the latter, might we inadvertently create the impression that we regarded one as illustrating the other? How about letting the authors themselves comment on the order in which we juxtaposed their articles? There was an implicit politics that couldn't be avoided. We could not reach Boutang quickly enough, but we were able to contact Huang handily by e-mail. Huang read Boutang's article and said he felt comfortable with the relationship between the two, as he was departing for London. Does this mean, then, that Huang's article presents peasants, in the situation of "too many people, too little land," as virtual migrants? Boutang's article attacks the "classical prejudice" (it is a matter of epistemology, for him) that represents the interests of sedentary agrarian populations as pitted against those of mobile populations. Attempting to reconstruct a subjective dimension erased by states' administrative practices of memory, Boutang delineates the migrant, with his/her "freedom", as no longer passive, and thus, within the movement of history, as no longer the pure victim who is easily seen as an objective accomplice of exploitation, of industrializing capitalism. Huang, stressing, like Boutang, that the distinction between surplus and non-surplus labor forces is always extremely tenuous, warns of a similar prejudice against the mobile peasants of early twenty-first century China: "their seemingly aimless wanderings throughout the country would be viewed with suspicion." He counters by delineating a peasant migrant subjectivity — one calculating within constraints, whose actions may nevertheless provoke unintended consequences. Is this the political pay-off of deploying, as both articles do, the perspective of the *longue durée*? Well, Boutang's implied migrant is heroized and monolithic. And I'm romanticizing Huang's peasants, represented by those precise calculations of *jing* per *mu*, of taxes and fertilizer expenses (heartbreakingly, a family's own seeds and manual labor are not included as production costs). Who records these figures so confidently and meticulously? The peasants, the village–town–country administration, the ethnographer?

August 13, 2000

How can terms like "agency" and "subjectivity" be read as generalities in relation to the materiality (ah, but that's also a generality!) of signifiers in these pages? Of course I'm not talking about thetic splitting, which we can assume. A working assumption of the political efficaciousness of collective discussion of concepts ("agency", "subjectivity") is *also* evident in these pages. We act as if we believe in the possibility of that commonality and that efficacy. But if politics is always some form of coming-together (and not only that), Oka Mari suggests that such comings-together are singular and happen only once. There are also the different political registers of walking, talking, and writing. (Why stick with Derrida's neat *double* register of politics, anyway?) The discussions in Fukuoka are different from the collection of writings that make up this issue. The difference between the one-time-only-ness of talking and the foreverness of writing. Be that as it may, the walking is pretty much the missing dimension of both. Is the politics of this issue generated around that lack? We feel an ethical commitment to work (and it *is* a kind of labor) on the *concept*, even the conceptual "model." But we can not, will not, have not, are not, will never, or can never, walk the distance between "agency" and "subjectivity" and the person in Village 3 in Anhui responding (orally or in writing) to Huang's questionnaire. Or the women emigrants on the Korean peninsula that Lee Chonghwa, in Fukuoka, claimed could never simply stand in for the migrant subjectivity theorized by Boutang.

But, whoops, clearly I'm privileging certain instances here. I've asymmetrically assigned difference to China, North Korea, and the "peasant" apotheosized by socialisms and modern nationalisms: orientalized figures whose remoteness allures. The politics of walking is not the same thing as immediacy, and distance across time and space is not the same thing as disconnection (but it usually is).

It is *Traces* hubris to remark on the multi-layered processes of accretion of these signifiers through the media that enthrall us, through paper and electronic text, through the fingerskeyboardscreensminds and vice versas that manipulate words through shifts of linguistic register and among orthographic systems with their dynastic, tributary, colonial, national, neo-imperial, and what-have-you histories. Where are you who are our readers, and most of you who are not our readers, positioned in relation to these processes? Are we writing about you who are not our readers to you who are our readers? Can we call you who are not our readers "you", or do we want you to call us "you" (whether out of ethics, utopianism, or *méfiance*), or are we writing about you so that we can call ourselves we?

August 20, 2000

How does this collection of essays take up the theme of "panic" set forth in our title, which grammatically blurs the distinction between the subject and object of "panic"? Panic: fear of movement on many different levels; fear of invasion or of being overpowered. But who is afraid...colonizer or colonized, the "majority" or the "minority"? One fear mimics another. After some e-mail exchanges, we had settled on the phrase "race" panic for our title, rather than the "white" panic initially proposed for this issue, a problematic which Meaghan had developed in an earlier article on the Australian film series *Mad Max*. ("Why would our readers necessarily be interested in white panic?" Meaghan had asked.) In fact, the "white panic" she proposed was heuristic and deconstructive. It referred not to "white bodies in a state of panic" but to panic itself as a state of "whiteness" in which boundaries and distinctions were bleached out. "White panic" called attention to displacement, interchangeability, reversibility. A white mother's flight through the bush in *Mad Max* displaced and re-enacted the terror of Aboriginal children forcibly removed from their homes to foster-care under assimilationist policies in effect in Australia between the 1920s and the 1960s. (Barely) repressed historical memory becomes a premonition of suffering future injury; through a fantasized reversal, the violence visited on the colonized returns to the colonizers. The "majority" (often, though not always, bearers of the colonizer's legacy) fears becoming a "minority." Hoping for a magical, prophylactic effect, it discursively constitutes itself as a "minority," mimicking the minority's vulnerable, injured state. Thus the aggrieved words of Ishihara Shintaro cited by Jung Yeong-hae and Tessa Morris-Suzuki. The complex displacements described by Jung in the contemporary Japanese debate over immigration perhaps best exemplify the politics of a discourse of panic.

August 23, 2000

I've been re-reading articles over the past few days, listening for deep strains. Unexpectedly, and not by our design, certain striking patterns of chiasmic reversal can be traced across the articles. Jackie Armijo describes the "Pile of Ten-thousands," the site along a riverbed outside of Dali, in Yunnan, into which were thrown the bodies of Hui Muslim women and children massacred by the Qing imperial army in 1873. There was no nation state of "China" at this time, while among Muslims in Yunnan, as Armijo notes, Islam took precedence over "blood." But in 1975, soldiers now called "Chinese" again massacred Muslims in the Chinese village of Shadian. After the abortive anti-Suharto coup in Indonesia in 1965, however, it was "Chinese" victims of government-incited riots, many of whose families had lived in Indonesia for centuries, whose blood "dyed the river red." (Ien Ang's essay omits this image, for reasons her analysis may suggest, but it lingers in memory from her oral presentation in Fukuoka.) In their range across time and space, the two articles bring home the contrast between the ephemerality of historically produced notions of ethnicity and race and their often deadly weight in lived experience, as Môri Yoshitaka has noted.

They also caution against the urge to consolidate decontextualized notions of ethnicity and race. In a journal committed to translation, can we efface the histories through which words which are never the exact equivalents of *ethnos* or "ethnicity" have been produced in multiple languages? For example, the Chinese "*minzu*" first appeared as momentum for the revolution of 1911 grew in China, as the result of a circuitous process of orthographic and linguistic exchanges. Chinese intellectuals and activists translated the term from Meiji Japanese political texts which, in their turn , had recruited and conjoined two Chinese ideographs with separate and ancient semiotic histories to produce the hybrid "*minzoku*." The Japanese *minzoku*: translation for a range of English, French, and German words including, according to one Japanese dictionary, "People, ethnic group, ethnicity, nation [E], *Volk, Ethnos, Nation* [G], *peuple, ethnie, nation* [F]. Translation receding into translation. Another kind of distance.

Ang takes pains to evoke a historical panorama that links present-day, largely non-Chinese-speaking, Indonesian Chinese (including people who refuse to identify themselves in any way with "Chineseness" but whose "notional Chinese characteristics" still allow them to be labeled "Chinese"), through colonialism, to ancient traditions of Chinese trading and mercantile activity in Southeast Asia. Yet Indonesian Chinese entrepreneurs set against "natives" by the Dutch did not constitute "ethnics," in their own eyes or the eyes of others. In a complex, premodern agrarian society, Ang notes, they were "one among many" specialized minorities. It was with modern nationalism and the construction of a unified people that Indonesian Chinese were placed in the quandary of having to take on a formal, exclusive identity: "they had to become *either* Indonesian or Chinese." Victor Koschmann suggests that the quandary of modern national identity for those defined as "ethnics" may be paradoxically intensified as global capital both produces and reinforces virtual diasporic communities.

August 24, 2000

Historicizing ethnic or racial identities exposes their fictive dimension. But can we rest content with the description, as merely *catechretical*, of the distance between such fictions and so-called "lived reality"? Such a view itself reproduces a dichotomy between the conceptual and the empirical (or experiential), the abstract and the concrete. Luke Gibbons takes this a step further, tracing this dichotomy to Enlightenment thought (more properly to the British, French, and German Enlightenments), and then demonstrating the overlap between categories of knowing and social hierarchies in colonial discourses. The human casualties of imperialism's civilizing mission, Gibbons maintains, were consigned to confinement within the concrete, and, by extension, the somatic, the subjective, the narcissistic — everything that was the opposite of the enlightened modern citizen's abstract universalism and cosmopolitanism. Both Gibbons and Chow argue for reconceptualization and rewriting of the "ethnic," in ways that release it from the opposition between the universal, or cosmopolitan, and the particular.

More ambitiously, they move beyond routine invocations of splitting, doubling, catechresis, and so on (which might appear to banish or disavow the sociality of mediation itself), to designate the ethnic, less as a "fiction" than as a specific, transindividual mode of the social. With regard to the politics of writing, both call for more complex readings of the literatures of injury and wounding, which free them from exclusive (and dismissive) association with the personal and the private. Their arguments overlap when Chow asserts that "what the Asian-American cannot love is not just any part of her but precisely her 'Asian American-ness' —

a mark that is not reducible to a single individualized self," and Gibbons states that "it is not that which is distinctively human" (what is shared in common by all human beings), "not as an individual that one is shamed, but through one's membership in a despised group or culture." The transindividual is and can be a site of practical social relations. Gibbons, challenging the image of the Celt "sulking on his own rocks," asks us to reflect on how, precisely because of its social dimension, the individual's experience of discrimination may become the basis for solidarity with suffering others.

Yet, since both Chow and Gibbons would see the stigmatized difference of an ethnic group as *arbitrary* and historically produced, how does one precisely define the ethnic collectivity, as a mode of the social which nonetheless is not a positivity? Would it follow that the individual's belonging to an ethnic group is not a factual given, cannot be experienced immediately? Chow's essay offers an account of the ethnic subject's attainment of self-knowledge which, however implicitly, foregrounds its problematical status in a way that Gibbons does not. Although framed as individual life stories, Chow points out, Asian American autobiographies often make their point of departure an incident in group history, such as the wartime internment of Japanese Americans. Thus the wounding of narcissism is located at the "transindividual level of ethnicity." But, she asks, "how is the experience of an inaccessible narcissism to be 'represented'?...How can something that has not, as it were, been allowed to develop, and is therefore not empirically available, to be written about?" Am I pushing Chow's logic too far in suggesting that she implies, here, that ethnicity, as the subject's transindividual past, can only be produced through an active process of "self-composition," through a mediating practice such as writing?

While Gibbons omits an account of ethnic self-knowledge, however, he strikingly joins Chow in asserting that there is a specificity to the trauma of a minority subject's entrance into the symbolic. While he appears more optimistic than Chow about the possibility of "cultural cosmopolitanism" — a form of connectedness — based on specific histories of oppression, for both writers the prospects of healing for abjected subjects are fragile at best. For the descendants of defeated Scottish Highlanders among British imperial shock troops, no less than for John Yau's young men, humiliation ("confiscation of the image of the self," in Gibbons' terms) turns back on the subject, who can master it only through voluntary and repeated acts of self-abjection, even self-immolation.

September 29, 2000

In mid-August, Meaghan moved from Sydney to Hong Kong. In late August, I moved from Ithaca to Cambridge, Massachusetts. At this point, neither of us has been able to work on the issue for over a month. I'm finding it difficult to concentrate on writing these editing notes here; I had really hoped to write them from beginning to end in Ithaca. Tompkins County provided a frame I liked, in a bleak kind of way. In this metropolitan area I will go from one end of the semester to another without passing a dilapidated barn, or the herd of cows (admittedly, getting rarer) I see standing in the mud on dark days when I drive my dog to Varna. When would the city of Cambridge, Massachusetts, have had farms? I don't have time to find out. But from the perspective of their relation to a rural economy, the two cities seem at least half a century apart in time.

Oh, well, I'll write without a framework. To distract myself, I'm returning to editing details. The on-going project of checking the annotation for Huang Ping's essay turns out to be a point of continuity. At some point during the copy-editing, the translator made clear that books whose English titles appeared in Huang's bibliography (T. W. Schultz, *Transforming Agriculture*) were being cited, in Chinese translations, in the body of Huang's text. Given *Traces*' concern with economies and politics of translation, shouldn't the bibliography reflect these Chinese translations Huang actually used? I can't reach the translators to ask them to give me titles of the Chinese translations. Rather, I won't contact them because they feel overworked already. Huang is reachable by e-mail and very helpful, but he is now in Yunnan, without access to his books and journals. It turns out to be quicker to go to the library here, with its excellent Asian collection, learn how to search on-line, and look for the Chinese titles myself. The library, however, uses the pre-1949 Wades–Giles system of romanization for Chinese, not the *pinyin* used by Huang and his translators. I have a panic attack (it's always intimidating to use a new system). A librarian shows me that the computers here have software that will handily convert *pinyin* into Wade–Giles. But I need the reverse, to get the titles I've managed to locate back into *pinyin* from Wade–Giles, and he hasn't explained how to go the other way. It must be terribly obvious, as it always is retrospectively, but there've been too many obstacles. I give up for the day.

October 6, 2000

Over the past few weeks, and despite the disruption of the move, my sense of the matters being written about in the articles has become more focused than it was when I began to write, primarily preoccupied with the insurmountable distance between myself and many subjects dealt with by our contributors. In reading, I keep track of logical and conceptual trajectories, hear a cacophony of mental voices, and form images. Some images easily configure themselves into one or another topoi of the sublime which, however conventionalized, are startlingly powerful for me. (Armijo's image of the nineteenth century fortress city of Dali, with mountain passes on one side and a lake on the other, is one). And I often find myself trying to imagine writers imagining: what element of urgency is there, for the writer, in her or his subject matter, and what sensed vulnerability might this be linked to? (I'll take a break from narrators and author-functions today.) If *Traces* succeeds in building some sense of transnational solidarity or community, will it not, in practice, be based on such solitary acts of reading and envisioning? We haven't eluded the parameters of print capitalism and imagined communities yet.

October 9, 2000

Today the autumn has become cold, wet, and dark. Reading the *Times* I'm struck by the description of a Yom Kippur service: "If this day is about forgiveness, why do we remember people whose lives are over?" a rabbi asks his congregation. "Hasn't their chance for forgiveness passed?" Kim Seong-nae's and Tomotari Mikako's articles struggle with the problem of how to represent the asymmetricality of a relationship with those who are silent or dead.

Kim's article examines this process of remembrance as an aspect of nation-building which, for Korea, as for Indonesia, took place against the backdrop of global decolonization after World War II. Modern Korean nation-building, under the specific conditions of U.S.-imposed partition, is a striking reminder of the link between imperialism and nationalism, and of why not to construe such processes as evolving autonomously within presumably natural geopolitical boundaries. But more crucial for Kim is the interpretive work of recasting the narrative of the 1948 Cheju "Incident," subject of massive state-censorship until

1987, a task she would link to the retheorizing of Korean modernity. By creating slippages in the existing discourse about Cheju, that is, Kim seeks to unbalance the binary structure that has regulated its meanings and to call attention to the powerful, implicit hierarchies that structure reproduces. By renaming the Incident a "massacre," she transposes the story from a conventional one, affirming the use of violence in a struggle between state and opponents, to one which foregrounds the modern state's rationalization of life-taking for the purposes of making its own life (thanatopolitics in the name of biopolitics). Following a strategy somewhat similar to that of Spivak's work on the subaltern, Kim tries to find which voices have been absolutely occluded from the existing narrative. "In particular, there has been no direct testimony in any case involving the sexual assault of women who are still alive." Although Kim sets forth the issues of body, subjectivity, and pain in a different theoretical nexus from that of Gibbons or Chow, she, too, calls attention to the transindividual level — it is insofar as they are signifiers for the collectivity that women's bodies become the objects of assault and abjection. They are victimized as Cheju Islanders or "Reds," as well as as signifiers for the reproductive capacity of "Reds," and then subjected to a third violence, silencing, because they are made to bear the "taint" of sexual violation within local patriarchal structures. Kim's analysis is most powerful when she argues that such subaltern subjects are even dispossessed of their "own" pain. Bodily pain, always other to signification, is radically unknowable. Torture's legacy is the subject's devastating doubt of the reality of its own experience.

Like Gibbons, Kim is committed to the notion of solidarity in pain. She implies, however, that such solidarity comes into existence only in the process of testimony. Yet it seems to me such processes (through which solidarities come into being) do not themselves receive enough attention in this issue. We gesture towards the processes, even sliding, despite our best theoretical and political inclinations, into a language that invests them with the appealing potential for attaining stability. *Traces* is one such messy process. Are we disavowing the ennui that sets in, repeatedly, when we realize that solidarity, if it is not random, elusive, and momentary, so easily reverts back to institutionalized forms that have no novelty for us?

In her discussion of Tomotari Mikako's work, Oka Mari takes pains to explain why the relationship between testimony and representation must be one of dynamic instability, lest the incommensurability of pain to language be "betrayed."

Tomotari's open-ended "work" for this issue of *Traces* self-consciously plays, as Oka astutely shows, with the untranslatability that exists between diverse registers: aural, oral, verbal, visual, and also that of *langue* to *langue*. These gaps remind us of the irrevocable nature of the loss of the Saru River banks and the life ways that took place along them in Nibutani, but also of the paradoxical temporal reversibility entailed in all acts of remembrance ("Why do we pray for forgiveness for those whose time for forgiveness has passed?"), hence the creative dimension of memory. Our reviewer of Tomotari's article asked forthrightly if readers would find Tomotari's claim that her art was "not political" disingenuous, in the face of her description of her work with Ainu activists. Or, was it that *Traces* offered "protected status" to creative artists, who would not be held to the strict conventions of academic writing? I valued her frank query, since I could see how, in the lack of a more technical discourse on her medium, a certain sentimentality might seem *de rigeur* in responding to the Nibutani work. Yet it is also possible to read Tomotari's account as a more concrete and guarded discussion of the process of building "solidarity in pain" that other articles broach. More than they, she emphasizes the improvisatory and unfinished nature of her projects. Because her *yamabushi* forebears (what Ien Ang would call "one among many specialized minorities" in a premodern agrarian Japan) suffered persecution and loss of livelihood at the hands of the modernizing state, Tomotari deems herself a homeless subject compelled to create a sense of belonging rather than assume a natural one. Yet, as she describes, the fact that she and contemporary Ainu people share discrete histories of oppression does not guarantee mutual acceptance.

October 18, 2000

Like Tomotari, Ghassan Hage calls attention to the way responses to specific histories of discrimination may coexist in a disjunctive manner. Just for fun, he takes contemporary liberal discourses of multiculturalism literally and lets us watch them collapse under the weight of their own logical antinomies. (How could Aboriginal peoples be part of the "new" communal Australia and also be included literally in the "we" of former Prime Minister Paul Keating's confessional litany, "We took the lands...We brought the diseases. We committed the murders"?) Aware that binary oppositions often accompany the operations of a more hidden classificatory violence, Hage picks apart flimsy constructions of

Australian cultural pluralism which would reduce the late twentieth century conflicted Australian national imaginary into a divide between "bad" supporters of *terra nullius* and "good" supporters of the Mabo decision. Philosophers drawn into this debate have tried to set forth the steps of a moral reasoning that would make support for Mabo the moral responsibility of *all* Australians. But such influential post-modern philosophical perspectives, Hage maintains, while correctly affirming the intercultural rather than monocultural nature of life in modern conditions, too often assume that taking responsibility for a collective past involves empathy based on a *willed* identification with other cultures. The subject's relation to the collective imaginary, he objects, is never so simply *chosen*. And the divide between denial and recognition of the violence of the colonial past that preoccupies the debate over Australian "national apology" is uniquely the obsession of the colonist's imaginary. "It is always the dominant who have an interest in the dominated's forgetting there were sides to a conflict."

(While I want to bring out Hage's insistence on this unequal power relationship, however, let me not downplay my curiosity about the qualification he adds to this statement: this does not mean Aboriginal people "*cannot share anything with other peoples living in Australia,*" he writes, " *but what they share cannot be taken for granted at all.*") Why do such qualifications always remain so muted in our discussions of inoperable community?

Hage sets his writing about contemporary non-European recent migrants to Australia side-by-side with writing on Aboriginal–White relations within his own essay, although the two matters are often discussed separately. The "literary" coda to his essay, evoking the palimpsest-like layers and powerful oscillations of the migrants' imaginary (in its simultaneous relationship to an abandoned place of birth and to different parties in the conflictual history of colonialism in a new land) extends his effort to release discussions of national imaginaries from tired binaries. Interestingly, Hage, like others in this issue, explicitly identifies this "sea of subjectivity" as "transindividual" and would seek through concepts of affect and bodily awareness ("bodily modification by others" constitutes us as social beings and thus opens us to the collective) to respect the material constraints of history while at the same time asserting that individuals can take responsibility for what they themselves have not done.

Sakiyama Masaki asks for a reframing of this discussion at yet one more remove, at another level of self-reflexivity. He calls into question the processes of comparison that undergird Hage's essay, a matter that has implications for this issue, as well as for the *Traces* project itself. What are the gains and costs of creating a space where different things are brought together? (Is it not the case that the objective effects upon minorities of the policies analyzed by Jung Yeong-hae and those advocated by Paul Keating are different?) What is the uniform standard that enables comparison, and what are the conditions of possibility for the comparatist's gaze? Sakiyama's questions throw into relief organicist dimensions of Hage's argument that do not square with Hage's insistence on the disunity of the Australian national imaginary. For example, Hage interestingly turns to the family, site of the subject's initiation into the symbolic, to explain how the individual develops a sense of affective obligation to a past which is not simply the subject's own. Yet his simile, "like family life, all social communal life is communicated to us as a gift", suggests an unproblematic encompassing of small by large communities in a manner that is at least visually evocative of an organic space of national enclosure. Hage's moral economy of the gift opens up a way around liberal multiculturalism's assumption of freedom. But, Sakiyama asks, is the logic of the gift based on the same premise of equivalence through which the violence of social conflict under capitalism is routinely disavowed? And what if the gift, according to a post-structuralist temporal logic of delay and deferral, can never be repaid?

October 20, 2000

Today I am thinking about Komagome Takeshi's "Colonial Rule and Modernity: Successive Layers of Violence." It is the last essay for me to comment on, providing this "editing journal" with a formal, or at least formalistic, opportunity to conclude. Reading Komagome's essay after the others, I try to mentally articulate or conceptualize (because I can't really envision this) all the essays we've worked with in terms of layers or some kind of accumulation, although of course they follow no "succession" and cannot be summoned to mind all at once. Not all the arguments remain distinct. Yet, perhaps provoked by Sakiyama's comments, I find it is the moments in which one or another essay betrayed a hint of uncertainty, or engaged in some reflection on itself, however mannered or muted, that continue to interest me and stand in for the "whole." My own reading sympathies throughout have been mercurial: attracted alternately by stark assertions about inequality and incommensurability (the uncompromising nature of such positions has always seemed heroic, charismatic) but eager for the comfort of promised "connectedness," and acceptance. A sea of subjectivity, indeed. Yet this awareness, which will never congeal into a coherent a mental image, of the essays together with the traces of their authors' cautions, leaves me leery of bringing this issue to closure with an edifying gesture toward the context of the global.

Rather , I read Komagome Takeshi's essay with the same curiosity I felt towards other articles about the fitfulness of its efforts to locate itself. By now some writing concerns and strategies that traverse this issue have become familiar and I know Komagome's essay will inflect them in yet another way. Comparison and what enables it (the politics of comparison), writing and its relation to collective identities (diverse, historically determined, and never immediately knowable), the ethics of the twenty-first century subject who lives in an ever more intensely inter-cultural world, and among the material effects of violence whose origins may be remote in an epistemological, geographical, or temporal sense. Komagome articulates a view on the inevitability of comparison that is indeed intricate. Like Hage, he wants to place in the foreground *differences* of interest and perspective in a terrain of post-colonial academic discourse that may be in danger of neutralizing historical inequalities. The temporality of the "post-colonial", for him, properly represents the formerly colonized's perspective. Should not the former colonizer (those inheriting Japan's modern history, for example) speak from the more ethically responsible, if still mediated, perspective of "post-imperialism"? On the other hand, Komagome holds, the subsumption of difference under conceptions of discrete national cultures has been essential to the legitimization of imperialism and the reproduction and internalization of a Eurocentric notion of modernity. In other words, there has not been *enough* comparison, leading to the thorough naturalization of the view that each nation attains modernity through its own unique and lonely struggle. The powerful modern illusion of national autonomy, so hard to shake, erases the history of European imperialism's violent expansion and the inexorable pressure on premodern societies it exerted. The illusion of national autonomy is the flip side of the European enlightenment's confidence in its own universality, and its ability to bestow the blessings of civilization on others. There has not been *enough* comparative work, according to Komagome, to enable us to delineate the collusion of European imperial powers among themselves (and with their junior partner, Japan), and their ambivalent complicity with emerging local nationalisms. Thus postwar Japanese historians have rigidly separated the projects of writing diplomatic history (relations with the West) and histories of colonialism (relations with the Rest). Moreover, few, Komagome notes, have linked the well-known Japanese "amnesia" about colonialism in the late 1940s and early 1950s to the suppression of this issue in the Japanese War Crimes Trials, presided over by a U.S. that was re-establishing its colonial presence in the Philippines. The Japanese government's persistent refusal of requests for war indemnities perpetuates this view that modernization was ultimately "for the good" of colonized peoples.

Komagome's article allows us to return to the questions of ethnicity and its fictiveness that have been raised in many other essays through yet another route. His study of the micropolitics of a British missionary school in Taiwan in the early 1930s reveals it as a site of complex, overdetermined relations between British imperialism, Japanese colonialism, and emergent Chinese and Taiwanese nationalisms. Here he calls attention to the ways in which individual lives and their interests traversed and were traversed by a myriad of collective identities which overlapped and diverged in unpredictable ways. These complicated configurations give the lie to any notion of discrete ethnic or national identities.

Carrying this further, he asks us to consider whether or not the contradictions of an emerging and imperial Japanese nationalism, often the stuff of Japanese exceptionalism, were not rather familiar aspects of global processes of modernization. For modernization is a process in the course of which many who " 'converted' to modern civilization were themselves transformed into entities that exercise violence over subaltern others." Like Gibbons, Komagome cites the intolerant relation of Scots Highlanders to the Irish, after their subordination by the British, as one example of such a displacement. Like Ang, he, too, finds a concept of ambivalence helpful, to describe those who, in assuming positions of active promotion of modernization, had to confront the ambivalence of being simultaneously oppressed and oppressor. Analyzing the involvement of imperial "British," colonizing "Japanese", and colonized "Taiwanese" historical personalities in a local Taiwanese school, he finds the positionality of ambivalence hardly unique in the global vortex of modernization. "If the West is an imaginary identity," he thus asks provocatively, "can we not deconstruct it" by tracing such criss-crossing positionalities? The fictiveness of ethnic identities, that is, may offer us another tool for the deconstruction of Eurocentric histories.

Submission Guidelines

Traces is published in Chinese, English, German, Japanese, and Korean. Each article accepted for publication is translated into all the languages of the series. In addition to the languages of *Traces* publication, submissions in French, Italian and Spanish are particularly encouraged.

All manuscript contributors for publication consideration should be submitted in triplicate to: *Traces: A multilingual series of cultural theory & translation*, 388 Rockefeller Hall, Cornell University, Ithaca, New York, USA 14853–2502, A manuscript for submission should be prepared, in the first instance, with endnotes and not footnotes. The entire manuscript should be *double-spaced* throughout, including endnotes and block quotations. The author's name, address and email should appear only on a detachable cover page and not anywhere else on the manuscript. This applies to endnote matters where reference may identify the author. A disk version of the manuscript must be provided in the appropriate software format upon acceptance for publication.

English language submissions should conform to the reference system set out in the *14th edition of The Chicago Manual of Style*, following the guidelines for endnotes and not footnotes. Examples of the preferred style may be consulted throughout this issue of the journal.

Submissions in languages other than English, please provide the following references in the order listed:

Books: Author's full name/Complete title of the book/Editor, compiler, or translator, if any/Series, if any, and volume or number in the series/Edition, if not the original/Number of volumes/Facts of publication — city where published, publisher, date of publication/Volume number, if any/Page number(s) of the particular citation.

Chapter in a Book: Author's full name/title of the article/Title of the book/Full name of the editor(s)/Inclusive page numbers of the chapter in the book [follow the above guideline for Books, for the rest].

Article in a Periodical: Author's full name/Title of the article/Name of the periodical/Volume (and number) of the periodical/Date of the volume or of the issue/Page number(s) of the particular citation.

Unpublished Material: Title of the document, if any, and date/Folio number or other identifying number/Name of collection/Depository, and city where it is located.

Public Documents: Country, state, city, county, or other government division issuing the document/Legislative body, executive department, court, bureau, board, commission, or committee; Subsidiary divisions, regional offices, etc./ Title, if any, of the document or collection/Individual author (editor, compiler) if given/Report number or any other identification necessary or useful in finding the specific document/Publisher, if different from the issuing body/Date.

For all subsequent references to already cited reference: Author's last name/ short-title form/Page number.

Submission of an article implies that it has not been simultaneously submitted or previously published elsewhere. Authors are responsible for obtaining permission to publish any material under copyright. Contributors will be asked to assign their own copyright, on certain conditions, to *Traces*. For further guidelines, please contact the *Traces* office: <Traces@cornell.edu>.

Acknowledgment: Traces is receiving support from Hitotsubashi University, Japan Foundation, New York University, and the Dean of the College of Arts and Sciences, Asian Studies Department, and the East Asia Program at Cornell University.

TRACES PUBLISHERS

Chinese
Sanlien Shudian
SDX Joint Publishing Company
Meishuguang Dongjie 22
HaoBeijing 100010
China
Tel: +010.64002713
Fax: +010.64002729

Japanese
Iwanami Shoten Publishers
2–5–5 Hitotsubashi
Chiyoda-ku, Tokyo
Japan
Tel: +81.3.5210.4000
Fax: +82.3.5210.4039

Korean
Moonhwa Kwahaksa
#704 Namdo Bldg.
198–16 Kwanhun-dong
Chongro-ku, Seoul
Korea
Tel: +82.2.335.0461
Fax: +82.2.335.1239
E-mail: <transics@chollian.net>

English
Hong Kong University Press
14/F Hing Wai Centre
7 Tin Wan Praya Road
Aberdeen, Tin Wan
Hong Kong
China
Tel: +852.25502703
Fax: +852.28750734
E-mail: hkupress@hkucc.hku.hk
Website: http//www.hkupress.org

***Traces* Editorial Office**
388 Rockefeller Hall
Cornell University
Ithaca, NY 14853–2502
USA
Fax: +1.607.255.1345
E-mail: <traces@cornell.edu>